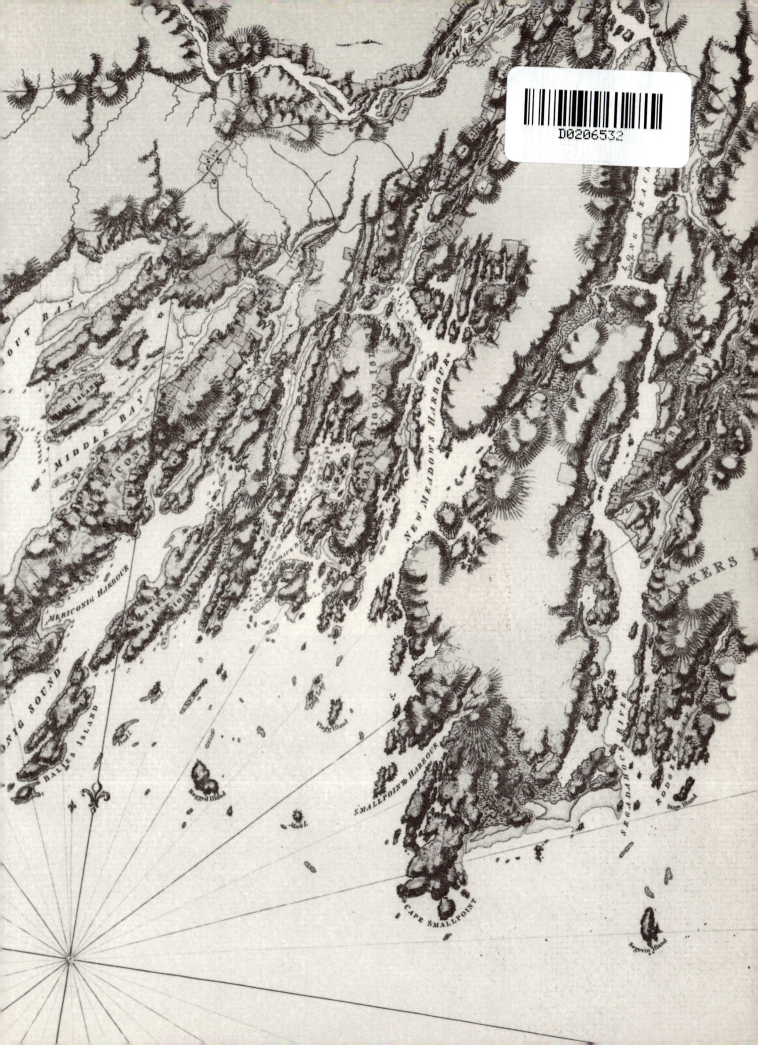

A
SMALL COLLEGE
IN MAINE

TWO HUNDRED YEARS OF BOWDOIN

A
SMALL COLLEGE
IN MAINE

TWO HUNDRED YEARS OF BOWDOIN

CHARLES C. CALHOUN

BOWDOIN COLLEGE
Brunswick, Maine
1993

A Small College in Maine: Two Hundred Years of Bowdoin
is published by Bowdoin College on the occasion of its
Bicentennial. The Editorial Review Committee in
charge of the project was chaired by Merton G. Henry
'50 h '84, Trustee Emeritus, and included Katharine
B. Bunge, director of the Bicentennial; Professor of
Psychology Alfred H. Fuchs; Associate Professor of
History Sarah F. McMahon; Elizabeth J. Miller, direc-
tor of the Maine Historical Society; and Susan L.
Ransom, publications editor. Overseer Emeritus Neal
W. Allen, Jr. '40 died in February 1992 and was
replaced on the committee by Peter C. Barnard '50,
secretary emeritus, President and Trustees, and
Overseer Emeritus.

Design by Michael Mahan Graphics, Bath, Maine
Printed by Penmor Lithographers, Lewiston, Maine
Cover: Ann Akimi Lofquist (American, b. 1964),
    Bowdoin College, December, 1992, oil on birch panel,
    5 1/2 x 18 1/2 inches. Bowdoin College Museum
    of Art. Gift of the Bicentennial Committee.
    1993.13
Cover photo by Melville D. McLean, Fine Art
    Photography
Endleaves:
front: British Admiralty chart of Casco Bay from
    Joseph F. W. Des Barres, *The Atlantic Neptune,*
    London, 1777. Courtesy of the Maine Historical
    Society, Portland, Maine.
back: A Plan of Brunswick Village, Surveyed and
    Drawn by C. J. Noyes, September 1846. Courtesy of
    the Pejepscot Historical Society, Brunswick, Maine.
    Photography by Erik C. Jorgensen '87
All Bowdoin College copy photography by
    Dennis Griggs, except p. 168, bottom, which is by
    Erik C. Jorgensen '87, and pp. 150, top, and 177,
    which are by Annalisa M. Ravin '92.

To Ruth Peck

When Anaxagoras of Clazomene was asked by the Senate of Lampsacus
how they should commemorate his services, he replied, "By ordaining that the day of
my death be annually kept as a holiday in all the schools of Lampsacus."
And, certainly, if any man may be said to have taken a bond against oblivion, it is he
whose name is worthily associated with a great institution of education. Who shall
undertake to assign limits to the duration of memories of Harvard, and Yale, and
Bowdoin, and the rest, as long as another, and still another generation of young men
shall continue to come up to the seats of learning which they have founded,
and to go forth again into the world with a grateful sense of their inestimable
advantages? The hero, the statesman, the martyr, may be forgotten; but the
name of the Founder of a College is written where it shall be remembered and
repeated to the last syllable of recorded time.
Semper—Semper honos, nomenque tuum, laudesque manebunt!

Robert C. Winthrop, speaking to the Maine Historical Society meeting
at Bowdoin College, 5 September 1849.

CONTENTS

KEY

CLASS YEARS

Holders of baccalaureate degrees from Bowdoin College are distinguished in the text with their class years after their names. Twentieth-century graduates always have the familiar apostophe and two digits (Elizabeth K. Glaser '81, for instance), while nineteenth-century graduates may have all four digits (Robert E. Peary 1877), the more formal "Class of" designation (Alpheus Spring Packard, Class of 1816), or, in obviously nineteenth-century contexts, the same designation given those of the twentieth century (Franklin Pierce '24).

Holders of honorary degrees have an h between their names and the year the degree was awarded (Kate Douglas Wiggin Riggs h 1904), and holders of degrees from the Medical School of Maine have a corresponding m (Henri Byron Haskell m 1855).

Holders of two or more degrees from Bowdoin have a string of numbers and letters after their names (Robert M. Cross '45 h '89).

THE BOWDOINS

Neither James Bowdoin II nor James Bowdoin III used roman numerals in referring to themselves. This designation is used as a convenience at the College and by historians.

ACKNOWLEDGMENTS

One of the great pleasures in preparing this book was the opportunity to visit so many libraries and historical societies in New England and beyond and to learn at first hand what a large role the thoughtfulness and skill of librarians and archivists play in any large-scale historical research. I am grateful for the kind assistance of the staffs of the following institutions: the American Antiquarian Society (Worcester, Mass.), the Massachusetts Historical Society (Boston), the Maine Historical Society (Portland), the Maine State Archives and Maine State Library (Augusta), the Pejepscot Historical Society and the Curtis Memorial Library (Brunswick), the Boston Atheneum, the Bostonian Society, the New England Historical and Geneological Society (Boston), the Houghton Library and the Harvard University Archives, the Schlesinger Library at Radcliffe, the Berkshire Atheneum (Pittsfield, Mass.), the Boston Public Library, the Society for the Preservation of New England Antiquities (Boston), the Dartmouth College Archives, the Middlebury College Archives, the Colby College Archives, the Bates College Library (Lewiston), the Sterling Memorial Library at Yale, the Stowe-Day Foundation (Hartford, Conn.), the University of Maine Library (Orono), the Forbes Library (Northampton, Mass.), the New York Public Library, the New-York Historical Society, the Avery Architectural Library of Columbia University, the Massachusetts State Archives (Dorchester), the Massachusetts State House Library, the Dyer Library and York Institute (Saco, Me.), the New Hampshire Historical Society (Concord), the Congregational Library (Boston), the Newberry Library (Chicago), the Library of Congress, and the Library of Christ Church, Oxford. I want to offer special thanks to Middlebury College, for allowing me to read in manuscript the second volume of David Stameshkin's history of that college, and to single out for praise one of the more underappreciated institutions in Maine: the Portland Room of the Portland Public Library, especially for its invaluable "Jordan Index" of early Portland newspapers.

In addition to those people mentioned in the introduction, there are many other individuals who have contributed in various ways, some of them quite substantial, to this project over four years. I wish to thank (in alphabetical order) the following friends, colleagues, and advisers for their help: Artine Artinian '31, Philip C. Beam, David P. Becker '70, H. Jay Burns, Jr. '85, Franklin Burroughs, Louis B. Briasco '69, Richard Candee, Kenneth E. Carpenter '58, Mrs. Hodding Carter, Jr., Patrick Chassé, Edwin Churchill, James S. Coles, Mrs. Robert P. T. Coffin, Jr., Paul D'Alessandro, George Daniell, Linda J. Docherty, Alison M. Dodson, Robert H. Edwards, Dennis Griggs, Neil and Sarah Van Sickel Gallagher, Mrs. A. LeRoy Greason, Martin Green, Andrew Hall, Stephen A. Hall, Heather Kenvin Hietala '83, Thomas C. Hochstettler, Dennis J. Hutchinson '69, Betty Hyde, R. Wells Johnson, Erik C. Jorgensen '87, Polly W. Kaufman, Donovan D. Lancaster '27, Theodora Penny Martin, A. Laura McCourt, John McKee, Arthur Monke, Judy Montgomery, Jason M. Moore '93, Nicholas Noyes, Paul L. Nyhus, Julia Oehmig, Clifton C. Olds, William C. Pierce '28 h '73, Mrs. John R. Rand, Glenn K. Richards '60, the late Francis Russell '33, Guy W. Saldanha, Candace and D. Neel Smith, Richard F. Seaman, Stephen T. Seames, Earle Shettleworth, Jr., Geoffrey R. Stanwood '38, Lucie G. Teegarden, Hervé Tessier, William A. Torrey III, John H. Turner, Ann Waldron, William C. Watterson, Kenneth Weisbrode '91, Susan E. Wegner, and David T. Wilkinson '67.

Finally, anyone writing about Bowdoin's history owes a special debt to those who have marked the way—in our own time, William D. Shipman, Gerard J. Brault, Marvin S. Sadik, Ernst C. Helmreich, and Patricia M. Anderson; in an earlier age, Alpheus Spring Packard, Nehemiah Cleaveland, George T. Little, Louis C. Hatch, and Herbert Ross Brown.

INTRODUCTION

College histories are an odd genre. At their worst, they resemble the old-fashioned kind of local history writing into which is crammed every scrap of information to have come down, and with any one scrap accorded about as much importance as the next. At their best, when they have been entrusted to writers with some sense of organization as well as scholarly scruple, they nevertheless rarely capture a sense of the place being chronicled. As a result, they sit in genteel neglect on institutional shelves, pulled down and dusted off as an occasional source of reference or as an act of piety on the part of a loyal and not very busy alumnus.

It is true that in the hands of an able professional historian the genre can be made to sing. Samuel Eliot Morison's books on Harvard will probably be read when his work on seventeenth- and eighteenth-century New England is forgotten. Quite recently, books on Middlebury College by David Stameshkin and on Wesleyan University by David Potts—in each instance, the first of a two-volume treatment—have demonstrated how institutional chronicles can be enlivened if you ask the questions of a college that a first-rate historian would ask of any institution. Similarly, David C. Smith's centennial history of the University of Maine is notable for its scholarly detachment and candor. But these are exceptions. In general, college histories are as dull and filiopietistic as the collegians they purport to write about were colorful and exasperating.

This book tries a slightly different approach. It is not a conventional institutional history in several respects. For one thing, the necessity of trying to cover the whole span of Bowdoin College's history in one volume has meant condensing or passing over portions of the story that would have been treated in more meticulous detail in a broader format. You will not learn as much as you might wish, for example, about the

Medical School of Maine (which was a part of Bowdoin for a century) or about the history of specific disciplines within the curriculum, and you will not find a very sophisticated treatment of the institution's often troubled financial affairs. At some point early in the next century, someone ought to write a far more detailed administrative history of post-1952 Bowdoin than has been possible here. On the other hand, in this book you will find out what Bowdoin students ate and drank and how they amused themselves, 150 years ago, and what several Bowdoin professors thought of their neighbors. You will also find a good number of illustrations—not to win a place for this volume on the coffee table, but because the power of many of these images is very much a part of the College's story.

In short, this is a book I hope Bowdoin people will read from cover to cover *as a story*, not simply set aside as a reference. (I also hope it will be of some interest to students of Maine history and of the New England college as a cultural phenomenon.) It is being published as part of a bicentennial celebration—an occasion that promises to be both a family gathering of sorts in honor of a college that has inspired exceptionally intense loyalties and, in a more Calvinist spirit, an opportunity to scrutinize that college's purpose and its future direction. In that latter spirit of self-examination, let me try to explain how this book evolved.

Bowdoin is a college with an unusually keen sense of the passage of time. By no means among the oldest American colleges and universities—there were at least 27 institutions that preceded it—it is nonetheless a place whose identity for each succeeding generation of students has been very much shaped by the thought of those who had walked there before them. As early as the 1820s, the College was being referred to as "old Bowdoin," perhaps ironically at first, but by the 1840s with considerable feeling of respect. Much of this sense of the past was anecdotal or familial—and later architectural as well—but as early as 1835 the *Quarterly Register* printed Alpheus Spring Packard's "Historical Sketch of Bowdoin College," the distant ancestor of the present volume. Nehemiah Cleaveland joined the same Professor Packard half a century later in a more ambitious work, their 1882 *History of Bowdoin College with Biographical Sketches of its Graduates from 1806 to 1879*, a treatment that affirmed the community's sense that the history of the College consisted of the accumulated histories of everyone who had matriculated there. George T. Little's more tightly focused "Historical Sketch" in the *General Catalogue of Bowdoin College and the Medical School of Maine, 1794-1894* helped mark the centennial of the chartering, but it was not until 1927 that a full-length history of Bowdoin was written. This book, by Louis C. Hatch, has remained the standard source on the institution for more than sixty years. (There have been modern scholarly studies of the architectural and religious history of the College but no attempt at a comprehensive treatment until now.)

Hatch was a very loyal alumnus, the sort of man who missed only one Commencement between his own in 1895 and his death in 1931. A scholar of independent means, with a Ph.D. from Harvard, he had published in 1919 a five-volume history of Maine—the last such comprehensive history of the state of any real value—and was to devote his last years to a never-completed history of the American vice-presidency. Late in life, though crippled by illness, he would hobble around campus each June, Commencement badge in his lapel, whacking trees and posts with his cane, on his way to the Deke House in search of someone patient enough to talk with him. Walter R. Whitney '23, however, remembered him more warmly from his own high school days in Bangor. He was one of the boys the elderly Hatch paid to read to him. As Whitney recalled in the *Bowdoin Alumnus* in 1935, his employer would occasionally and inexplicably shout out in his raspy voice "Phi Chi's in her ancient glory!"—the refrain of a mid-nineteenth-century hazing song. Rather

than read, however, the boys would walk arm in arm with Hatch from room to room in the cavernous house in Bangor, as if on shipboard, listening to his stories of Marie Antoinette or Charles I:

Of real friends he had very few; most of his contemporaries understood him no better than we did. And so he would walk among his teakwood chairs and inlaid cabinets and marble mantels, through the study, across the gloomy hall into the parlor where a hissing gasjet lit up the green wallpaper and the heavy, rich furnishings brought back from the corners of the earth. Followed by shadows, he walked about the murky rooms, swaying on the boy's arm, talking, talking, talking, sometimes about Hamlin's vice-presidency, sometimes about the licentiousness of the Restoration. . . . In those evenings men and women of the ages walked about the shadowy rooms with us—with Louis Hatch, to whom they were old, familiar friends, and with a boy who was being paid seventy-five cents to keep an eccentric, lonely man company.

This vignette is worth relating, possibly as a warning of what can happen to college historians, certainly as a reminder of what history was to Hatch and his generation: a tale of kings and queens, of battles and elections. College history, accordingly, was the tale of each great, or at least imposing, man who sat in the president's chair and of his relations with the important trustees and politicians of the day. A few colorful details of student life could be added, and a list of courses taught. This approach was attuned to nineteenth-century notions of the great man theory of history, as well as to a Whiggish belief that each development in the past led as if by plan to some present-day perfection. It had two great advantages: most of the documentary evidence easily accessible did concern the administration of the College, and college presidents typically used to serve terms so long, they became identified with their institutions in a way few of their late twentieth-century successors could pull off. William DeWitt Hyde's thirty-two years in office, Kenneth C. M. Sills's thirty-four—each represented a generation of the College's history. The average length of a college president's term in the United States today is said to be seven years.

When I studied history as an undergraduate at the University of Virginia in the late 1960s, this notion of history as the biographies of important men was still very much the dominant mode. Yet new ideas were seeping into even so conservative a place. The attempt to tell the truth about the nature of slavery in the American South—an attempt being made by scholars who themselves (at some risk to their careers) were sometimes in the front lines of the civil rights movement of the day—was for me the first indication that the United States was a far more complicated, and infinitely more tragic, place than we had been led to believe. In the quarter-century since then, the whole discipline of American history has been in a state of creative confusion as feminists, blacks, gays and lesbians, students of working-class culture and labor relations, cliometricians, academic Marxists, students of ethnicity, anthropologists, practitioners of the "history of the book," and scholars influenced by the notion of deep-rooted *mentalité* have, to some degree, pushed aside more traditional historians who still wish to chronicle the past politics of the elite.

Except for studies by feminists, little of this new history has been applied to the field of higher education. Admittedly, it is difficult to imagine that someone who wishes to practice "history from below" would spend time studying institutions that in antebellum America served perhaps one percent of the population. Likewise, in an age of increasing academic specialization, there are fewer people willing to take on a subject so diffuse and cross-disciplinary as the life of a 200-year-old college. (It is not surprising that when Harvard celebrated its 350th anniversary in 1986, it produced no new comprehensive history; instead a group of famous Harvard historians published a collection of essays in their fields of special interest.)

Yet one senses an opportunity missed. New England colleges are elite institutions, to be sure, but their histories are not only the stories of who attended, but of who was *not* allowed inside the college fence. Their relations (often quite strained) with the rural or working-class communities in which they existed are, in a sense, every bit as decisive as the deliberations of their governing bodies. And, to cite an even more contemporary concern, there are few subjects quite so "hot" in academia in the 1990s as the study of the social construction of masculinity in nineteenth- and twentieth-century America (i.e., the study of the ways of being that are perceived as "manly" and their shifts from decade to decade). What better arena to study this phenomenon than a tightly-knit, formerly all-male college where changing notions of "manliness" have been a controlling factor in institutional ideology for much of the past two centuries?

Similarly, little of the new history has reached Maine. There is still no comprehensive modern scholarly history of the state; in some respects, the best history of the place remains William D. Williamson's two volumes, published in 1832. No Maine community (not even Portland) has been studied with the scholarly thoroughness that has been applied in the last twenty years to, say, Newburyport or Lowell or Dedham or Andover in Massachusetts; there are entire fields, such as the economic history of Maine between the Civil War and World War II (save for the lumbering industry), that are virtually unexplored. Happily, there are signs of progress: Laurel Thatcher Ulrich's studies of women's lives in early Maine, Alan Taylor's account of class conflict between backcountry settlers and absentee landowners (such as the Bowdoins), James Mundy's work on the Irish community in Portland, James Leamon's forthcoming book on the Revolutionary era, and the recent collection of essays, *Maine in the Early Republic*—all these are promising steps (even if that last book mentioned had surprisingly little to say about education in pre-statehood times). I must, of course, confess that for a Bowdoin-connected writer to complain of this state of affairs is a bit ungracious; despite the College's strong identification with its geographical setting, no historian on the Bowdoin faculty has published anything of note on the history of the state.

Such, then, was the historiographical setting in which the people planning Bowdoin's Bicentennial for the academic year 1993-1994 found themselves and the institution.

The notion of writing this particular book occurred to me one day in Ruth Peck's house on Green Street in Topsham—the same house from whose windows Marsden Hartley had been inspired to write his poem "Androscoggin." I had recently read James McPherson's *Battle Cry of Freedom* and Simon Schama's *Citizens* and was deeply impressed by their authors' skill in being able to write for a general audience while maintaining a high level of historiographical sophistication—in Schama's case, by bringing the reader into the historians' quarrels. While it occurred to me that perhaps the history of Bowdoin did not have quite the drama of the Civil War or the French Revolution, I wondered if it could not be told in a way that had both narrative flow and human interest. For one thing, Ronald Banks's work on the campaign for statehood in 1790-1820 had revealed how closely the early history of the College was linked to the tumultuous political and religious life of the District of Maine. And I had come across another volume—totally unrelated, it would seem—that provided a clue as to how to proceed.

It was Rhys Isaac's 1982 book *The Transformation of Virginia 1740-1790*. Now it would be hard to imagine an American historical subject more thoroughly squeezed, as it were, for all it was worth. Yet Isaac revealed an entirely new way of looking at the life of eighteenth-century Virginia. It was one of those intellectual feats that, once it had been accomplished, seemed so obvious—all the pieces had been there for years—yet no one had thought to do it before. Much influenced by the cultural anthropology of Clifford Geertz and his theory of "thick description," Isaac studied the patterns of everyday thought and behavior of two somewhat antagonistic groups of Virginians: the Anglican slave-owning elite and the mostly Baptist evangelical smallholders. The history of a people was to be discovered in what one read or how one behaved in church or dressed one's family, not in the comparatively superficial acts of royal governors or militia commanders. History was ideology: not in the narrow sense of overt political beliefs, but in the anthropologist's sense of

unspoken habits of thinking and behaving that shape every aspect of life. History was also hegemony, the efforts of one group to impose its values on another (preferably without anyone's noticing it). Historical events took place in a cultural web, and the only way to perceive the true significance of those events was to study the patterns of the web which the culture had adopted or inherited.

The history of a college like Bowdoin does not fit neatly into such a scheme; Issac's approach works best for a well-defined society at one specific time and place. But the thought that the way to move beyond the usual tactics of institutional history-writing would be to view a college community as a cultural force, an ideological construct, is a very intriguing one. The college becomes no longer simply a corporate entity run by one set of individuals for the benefit of another, but a series of relationships between social groups, some of them on campus, others elsewhere in the state or beyond. The story of the College, then, is to be found not only in trustee records or student newspapers but in every cultural artifact the institution produces or absorbs—be it a style of architecture or the wearing of a necktie, an academic ceremonial or some other "tradition" invented to assert the College's cultural authority over the community. While operating within a chronological framework based on institutional archives, the historian could venture forth into any number of other modes of historical inquiry.

Meanwhile, it was clear to the Bicentennial's planners that any effort would be ephemeral without an attempt to produce a new—and more usable—general history of the College. Hatch had not aged well; for one thing, he had the irritating habit of quoting without footnotes from documents that no one has been able to locate again. His account, published in the early Sills years, had ended a decade earlier, with Hyde's death in 1917. There was a need, in other words, not simply to update Hatch but to reexamine the entire historical record. The plan that emerged was for two bicentennial volumes: a lavishly illustrated book with long captions chronicling the 200 years, and a more scholarly collection of essays concentrating on important topics in Bowdoin history. By 1989, however, it was clear that there was not much agreement on what those topics should be and that the time was too short to find the specialists required, bring them to campus, and allow them to explore the archives. The result was this book, which attempts both to present the chronological overview the first volume would have offered and to study some aspects of the Bowdoin community in more detail. It is very much a book of the 1990s, and sixty years hence—if not sooner—some of its concerns may seem as quaint and antiquarian as Hatch's long lists of the scores of Bowdoin-University of Maine football games. But it will have fulfilled its purpose if it encourages others to take up some of the themes it touches upon.

There is certainly more Bowdoin history to write. As this book was about to go to press, for example, I discovered Professor Marshall Cram's 1918-1919 diary—the historical equivalent of striking oil—as a result of a reference to it in a cardboard box of unsorted typescripts of the late Professor Herbert Ross Brown's occasional speeches. This book ends with the inauguration of President Robert H. Edwards in 1990, with only an occasional reference to developments after that date where continuity required it. Some of the best material has been put in the footnotes, in order not to interrupt a narrative that already may seem too episodic; the footnotes have been placed at the ends of chapters to encourage easier reference. Two other caveats: I am a journalist, not an academic historian, as I expect will be only too obvious, but I have tried at least to pose the types of questions a scholar today would be likely to ask. And, given the fact that the College itself is publishing the book, this is something of an authorized biography. But the "family" in question has been helpful and generous when asked, and unobtrusive when not; no one has told me what to write or to leave out.

A book of this nature is possible only through the help of so many people and institutions, that

I have had to acknowledge them elsewhere in this volume. But there are a number of people whose involvement was so central to the enterprise, I want to single them out here for very special thanks.

Some long outstanding debts, first. To four remarkable teachers in Charlottesville to whom I owe anything I know about the craft of writing history: Willie Lee Rose, Paul Gaston, Thomas Hammond, and David Underdown. And, even further back, to the best teacher I ever had, Carole Johnson, who in a Florida classroom amid the excitements of the Kennedy years revealed the power of history to illumine current events.

In Maine, the list is much longer. Above all, to Mark W. Cutler, who after many weeks in their papers surely knows Edith and Casey Sills better than anyone now alive and who did the computer-aided drawings in this book. And to the members of the Bicentennial Committee's Editorial Review Board: most especially, its chair, Merton G. Henry '50 h '84, and members Elizabeth J. Miller, Sarah F. McMahon, Katharine B. Bunge, Alfred H. Fuchs, Peter C. Barnard '50, and the book's editor, Susan L. Ransom (who, among other things, deserves the Nobel Prize for Patience). Thanks to their good nature and expertise, what could have been nit-picking sessions turned instead into far-ranging, occasionally hilarious seminars on Maine history. A. LeRoy Greason, president of Bowdoin from 1981-1989, played an especially supportive role in making the project a reality. I deeply regret the untimely deaths of two Bowdoin historians, Overseer Neal W. Allen, Jr. '40, whose early encouragement convinced me that I could actually write such a book, and Professor Roger Howell, Jr. '58, former president of the College, whose transAtlantic perspective, among other things, would have greatly enriched the final text. Let me single out, too, the important roles played by William B. Whiteside, Frank Munsey Professor of History Emeritus, and Paul V. Hazelton '42, professor of education emeritus, in creating the groundwork for this project. And without the thoughtfulness and skill of Dianne M. Gutscher and Susan B. Ravdin '80, curator and assistant respectively, at Special Collections in Hawthorne-Longfellow Library, such a book would never have been possible.

It was also an honor to work again with the talented staff of Mahan Graphics in Bath, especially William Fall, and with photographer Dennis Griggs of Topsham. The staff of the College's Office of Communications at Getchell House proved helpful, as always, and it was a special pleasure to discover how well Ann Lofquist's cover painting complemented the text. And, once again, Joseph Fillion and his staff have demonstrated that Penmor Lithographers of Lewiston is among the best printing houses in the country.

There is a sentimental debt I also want to acknowledge: to those people who, in 1984-1985, first welcomed me to Bowdoin and helped persuade me that, of all possible venues, a small college town might be the best place to live: Helen Pelletier '81, whom I succeeded as editor of *Bowdoin* magazine, and who is now director of Upward Bound; Martha J. Adams, assistant director of alumni relations; Mary Jo McGuire, secretary in Alumni Relations; Michael W. Mahan '73, who designed this book; Ruth and Campbell Cary '46; Katharine J. Watson, director of the Bowdoin College Museum of Art; Mary Chittim and the late Professor Richard L. Chittim '41; Anne W. Springer '81, assistant dean of admissions; Associate Professor Barbara Weiden Boyd; Professor John Ambrose; Associate Professor Steven R. Cerf; and—most especially—Robert M. Cross '45 h '89, secretary of the College emeritus, who demonstrated that devoting one's life to a single institution could be not a confining, but an enriching, experience.

Finally, I am grateful beyond the power of words to the family of the late Donald Colton Esty, Jr., amid whose hospitality and unfailing kindness much of this book was written.

Greening Island
Southwest Harbor
September 1992

PROLOGUE

If you had traveled down the coast of Maine in the summer of 1794, if you had ventured beyond the line of settlement and approached the great forest, you might have met a middle-aged Frenchman, lame of foot and sly of manner. His conversation most likely would have entranced you. Having once ensnared you with his charm, he would soon be asking you the questions. What had you seen on your travels? Where were the deepest harbors, the richest valleys, the most prosperous mills? What was the real worth of those dark woods that seemed to stretch northward over the curve of the globe?

And the people! There were of course some gentlemen to be found—General Henry Knox, at his great house on the St. George River at Thomaston, the enlightened Benjamin Vaughan at Hallowell on the Kennebec—but the farmers one met were, by the standards of a European agriculturalist, neither industrious nor wise. Why (the Frenchman would ask) did they persist in growing Indian corn, which so quickly depleted their soil, rather than winter wheat? Did they not see that the country was perfectly suitable for grazing livestock, rather than for scratching a living in the empty spaces between the stumps of felled pines? If most of the farmers lacked industry, the lumbermen upriver were even worse (as the Frenchman would later write): the beauty of the woods meant nothing to them, their ideal was mere destruction, measured by how many blows of the axe it took to cut down a tree. If the woodsman had no attachment to the land, the fisherman was even more rootless, a few codfish "his homeland." He plied a safe and lazy trade, rarely venturing far from shore or exerting himself other than to hang his arm over the side of his boat. To live on an infertile island and be a fisherman was one thing; to exist near millions of acres of excellent land and still fish for a living—that, the Frenchman would tell you, was "a natural vice of spirit and character" that the government should take steps to correct.

For all the natural splendors of the District of Maine, the population was a grave impediment to its progress.[1] "Indolent and grasping, poor but without needs," they had hardly advanced, it seemed to the visitor, beyond the natives they had replaced. Their economy was as primitive as their dwellings. Lacking specie, the inhabitants bartered to fulfill their needs: a cow for 6,000 feet of boards, a gallon of rum for a week's labor, even a prostitute for a few pins, "the small coin of the country." The low morals of the people betrayed a deeper failing: a lack of any sense of permanence, of well-rooted civilization. In most villages, the traveler could meet the original inhabitant, a man who thirty years earlier had cleared some land, happened to have built a mill at the falls of a river, and now was content to proclaim himself first citizen of the valley, lending out money to later arrivals and living by laws younger than himself. Worst still, farmers would offer their homesteads for sale upon the slightest encouragement. Why? So they could move elsewhere, perhaps to escape their creditors, perhaps simply because they felt no affection for the locale, having invested so little of themselves in the farm.

All this was perplexing to a visitor, especially one who had recently escaped from chaos in what had once seemed the timeless calm of his native countryside. What was clearly needed, he concluded, was European capital, enough of it to transform the district into a stable agricultural society of the kind he had seen in Massachusetts and Connecticut. Such, he would report back to his patrons, a group of British bankers eager to invest in post-Revolutionary North America, were the conditions he had experienced in a society "at the hour of its beginning."[2]

Talleyrand would not be the last visitor to regard Maine as an enchanting place filled with people who somehow failed to appreciate it. Throughout the early years of the Republic, that same note of condescension, even that touch of male swagger, would be directed by those who were told they owned the land toward those who actually lived on it. Talleyrand himself would soon return to France, his months in Maine a rustic interlude in a rather more eventful career. But others were already retracing his steps, seeking to build those institutions whose absence he had so keenly noted.[3]

Osgood Carleton's 1794 map of Maine. The location of Bowdoin College represented a political compromise between its friends in Portland and the landowners in the Kennebec Valley and points farther east.

CHAPTER ONE

*In the decade after the Revolution, the District of Maine rapidly increased in population
as newcomers pushed the line of settlement beyond the coastline and into the densely
wooded interior. In the eyes of "the great and the good"—the propertied and the pious—
such a frontier region needed civilizing institutions, notably a college.
Rivalry among Maine towns for such an institution helped delay passage of the
necessary legislation, but in 1794 a college was chartered by the General Court in Boston
and named for the statesman-scientist James Bowdoin II. Among the many
"friends of piety and learning" who fostered this new "seminary" was the Portland clergyman
Samuel Deane, who sought to transplant to his New World hillside the learning of the Old.*

VIRTUE AND PIETY

The story of Bowdoin College begins in the 1780s and extends, for our purposes, through the 1980s, two decades that have something in common: they were both periods of extraordinary growth, changing Maine's character forever. Between 1784 and 1790, the population of the district grew from 56,321 to 96,540—and jumped to 151,719 by 1800. This rapid growth in the decades following the Revolution pulled its people in two opposing directions: the increase in prosperity made many wish to recreate on the shores of Casco Bay or in the valley of the Kennebec the metropolitan culture of Boston and Salem and Portsmouth, while the increase in independence this new wealth gave to some of them made them question their traditional bond to the distant Commonwealth of Massachusetts. The campaign to establish a college in the district must be seen, among other things, as an attempt to resolve this tension, to make a gesture that was both rebellious and affirming.

Whatever hope there had been in pre-Revolutionary Maine for a local college was premature: Dartmouth and Harvard colleges satisfied the small demand on the part of those rich or ambitious enough to educate their sons as gentlemen.[4] But the late 1780s brought a new sense that Maine was not destined to be an appendage of Massachusetts forever. There were several ways this was expressed, a brief separationist movement the most obvious of them. The campaign for a college was less dramatic, though for six years similarly frustrating.

The first public notice of this campaign in the district appeared in the *Cumberland Gazette* of 7 February 1788, which published an act proposed the previous year "for erecting a College in the County of Lincoln" to be named in honor of the distinguished Winthrop family of Massachusetts. Whoever drafted the 1787 bill struck an egalitarian note that was not to appear in later proposals. In addition to the usual appeal for diffusing "virtue and knowledge," the proposal said collegiate education should be made "easily attainable, especially by the poorer classes in the community." This could best be achieved by "seminaries for literature being erected. . . upon the broadest basis of liberal principles, and equally open to people of every class and denomination." The exact location was left to be determined (Hallowell would have been a likely contender); the institution would be endowed with a tract of state-owned land between the Kennebec and the Penobscot. A convention of clergy or their delegates "from every town and plantation in said county" would meet with the justices of the peace to determine a site convenient not merely for the present generation but "most central for their posterity, when the said county shall be settled." Buildings would be funded by a public lottery, and the college governed on the Harvard model—viz., by a Corporation which included professors and tutors, and a Board of Overseers, among whose members would be the governor and Council of the Commonwealth and the ministers of the seven next adjoining towns.

This is an interesting document, given the subsequent character of the College, which was chartered in 1794. There was to be no institution in the district so popular in tone until the opening of the Gardiner Lyceum in 1825—perhaps not until the Morrill Act made the University of Maine possible after 1862. The heritage of the Revolution had been conceived by the merchants and lawyers of Federalist Boston as an affirmation of their hegemony, but it appeared in another light to some on the Kennebec frontier. The proposed act concluded with a flourish: "And the liberal man, the lovers of science, the friends of religion and the equal liberty of the whole human race, with patriots of every class and description, are called upon by the duty they owe their country and their regard for posterity, and are invited to give substantial proofs of such sentiments and feelings, by such donations. . . as may enable the Trustees soon to proceed upon the business of instruction. . . ."[5]

But the business of instruction had to take second place to the business of politics. One key to the process by which Bowdoin College emerged is the separationist mood of much of the district's elite in the late 1780s. As Ronald Banks points out, the curious thing about this mood is that it arose not on the part of radicalized debtors and disgruntled farmers but among the "substantial"—lawyers, doctors, clergymen, large landowners—including several people, such as the lawyer and gentleman farmer Stephen Longfellow, Sr., who were later to play a large role in running Bowdoin.[6] The first newspaper in the district, Titcomb and Wait's *Falmouth Gazette*, publicized the cause in 1785, and in October of that year about thirty gentlemen from York, Cumberland, and Lincoln counties met in convention to discuss separation at the meeting house of the Reverend Dr. Samuel Deane in Falmouth (present-day Portland).

Their motives were immediately questioned—some feared they were Tories, eager to deliver Maine to the British Canadians, others (such as the conservative Governor James Bowdoin II in Boston) feared social disorder of the sort that already bedeviled western Massachusetts. Somewhat tempered by the criticism, the separationists continued to meet through the late 1780s, still convinced that Maine's attachment to Massachusetts worked to the disadvantage of those who wished to see the district prosper. But the impact of Shays's Rebellion in the western part of Massachusetts in 1786 frightened the propertied throughout the commonwealth and turned many against the notion of further "disintegration." Meanwhile, the General Court (the state Legislature) passed a few measures designed to mollify the district. Since one grievance had been the cost and inconvenience of pursuing legal business in Boston, new courts and longer sessions were established for Maine. Steps were taken to reduce taxation on wild lands and to quiet the claims of squatters. There was even some interest expressed in establishing a college.[7] Writing a generation later, William Williamson saw this as one of the "measures calculated to cool and abate the high Separation-fever." Patronage of a college, he added, was "treated with marks of Legislative respect and attention. . . [b]y which conciliatory measures, the subject of Separation was rocked into a slumber, from which it was not aroused for several years."[8]

As Banks explains, a second wave of separationist sentiment did follow in the 1790s, again more Whiggish than populist in tone. And, once again, improving the "melancholy state of religion and learning" in the district was advanced as one of the arguments for local control. Without that improvement, Daniel Davis wrote in his 1791 tract urging separation, "mankind would soon degenerate into savage ferocity; and society, instead of presenting us with the scenes of delightful enjoyment, would exhibit the sad, uncomely picture of vicious and capricious folly." Only "the abandoned & profligate," he said, would deny "that the benefits of a good government greatly depend upon the instruc-

4

tions and examples of a learned and liberal clergy."[9] In the settled parts of Massachusetts, one could take schools and churches for granted, he added, but in Maine too many towns neglected with impunity the requirements of the law. Well into the 1790s the separationists persisted in the face of repeated rebuffs, but the changing demography of the district was not in their favor: Maine, once firmly in the hands of its Federalist elite, by 1800 had a majority of Jeffersonian Democratic-Republicans, citizens unwilling to defer to their "betters." By 1800, the separationists of 1785 had come to see the advantages of maintaining the union with Federalist Massachusetts.

The connection between all this and the efforts being made in the General Court between 1788 and 1794 for a college is not altogether clear from the record. To some, such a college would have been a symbol of Maine's independence; to others, a stabilizing institution promoting the republican virtues of the Founding Fathers. Within time, it was argued, a college could provide the cadre of talented and educated men whose absence in the district had been one argument against separation. But would such men seek to break the parental tie? The question eluded a clear solution but did not really need one. The immediate task was to fund such an institution, after which its allegiances would be up for grabs. What is clear is that the *nature* of the new college was conceived in an atmosphere of consensus. There was to be no single powerful founder; no attempt to boost the status of an existing academy; not even an obvious sense of religious zeal—none of the factors, in other words, that contributed so decisively to the foundation of other colleges in the young republic.

But the legislative path held many obstacles. If colleges were seen as stabilizing influences, there was far more urgent demand for one in turbulent western Massachusetts—one reason, perhaps, why Williams College, in the Berkshires, was chartered a year ahead of Bowdoin. And even the friends of education in the district could not agree among themselves as to the best location for such an institution. Should it be in

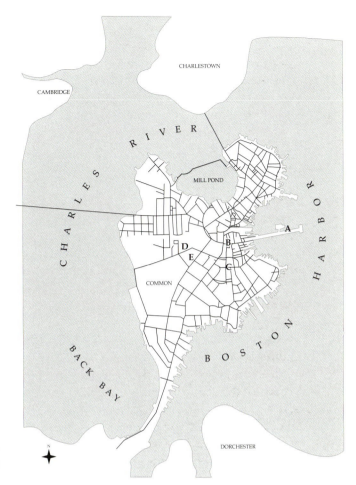

Eighteenth-century Boston, a peninsula joined to the mainland by a narrow neck of land, was more of a seaport than it appears today, after two centuries of landfills. Long Wharf (A)—on the site of modern State Street—linked the Bowdoin family's shipping interests with the ports of Europe and the West Indies. Leading merchants like James Bowdoin I and Governor James Bowdoin II conducted much of their business on the ground floor of the Old State House (B). Prosperity brought the family a large house in Milk Street (C), where James Bowdoin III lived in his early adult years, and a grander "mansion-house" (D) on Beacon Hill, at the corner of modern Beacon and Bowdoin streets. The family plot is in the Granary Burial Ground (E) on Tremont Street.

some prosperous port, open to the influences of the world? Or in the purity of some rural retreat? Should it be in well-settled southern Maine, or in the rapidly developing Kennebec Valley?

On 5 November 1788 a petition was sent to the General Court from Falmouth by "the Associated Congregational Ministers in the County of Cumberland." The petitioners, "being

James Bowdoin II served two one-year terms as governor of Massachusetts in 1785 and 1786. As governor, Bowdoin is best remembered for his role in putting down Shays's Rebellion. The Old State House, which still stands in downtown Boston, was the scene, after Bowdoin's death in 1790, of the legislative maneuvers that led to the chartering of Bowdoin College.

mostly sons of Harvard," expressed concern about the cost and inconvenience of sending students to Cambridge and sought the grant of a charter "for a College in this County, to a corporation of fit persons to promote the interests of learning." It would be endowed "with some considerable portions of the unlocated lands of the Commonwealth" and would afford both parts of the state "equal advantage of erudition." Soon the justices of the Court of General Sessions of the Peace for Cumberland County followed this appeal with a petition of their own. Since the 1780 constitution of the commonwealth encouraged "Arts and Sciences and all good Literature," and since "Wisdom and Knowledge as well as Virtue diffused generally among the People is necessary for the preservation of their Rights and Liberties," they argued, it was a duty of legislators and magistrates to promote education—and extend it to the eastern part of the

state. In both petitions, the expectation was for a publicly funded college, endowed by the sale of lands, and one that would teach the classical republican virtues. Neither petition made an overt appeal to religion (other than a perfunctory quote in the latter from the state constitution), perhaps because the interests of the Congregational churches were so closely identified in the minds of the petitioners with those of wise government, that no appeal was necessary.

The justices of the peace were prosperous landowners and lawyers to whom the notion of a settled commonwealth had great appeal, but we do not know exactly what persuaded them to petition the legislature.[10] The ministerial association, on the other hand, did keep minutes of its quarterly meetings. Despite their brevity, a picture emerges of a group of eight or ten colleagues who exchanged books, discussed each other's writings, encouraged missionary activity in the backcountry, talked politics, and generally deplored the presence of itinerant and unlicensed preachers on the district's frontier. These clergymen were, for the most part, men educated in the metropolitan world of Boston and Cambridge who had been called to live and work in more primitive surroundings. There was a convivial tone to their gatherings—they were of a clerical generation still allowed to smoke and drink—and they already had some sense of educational mission, for one of the purposes of such associations was to help train and support the younger of their members. It was quite in character, then, that within six months of their first meeting, they petitioned the legislature for a college in Maine.[11]

The two petitions were not ignored in the capital, but exact details of their legislative history over the next three years are rather obscure. Judge Josiah Thacher of Gorham, the senator for Cumberland County, was entrusted to guide the cause through the Legislature. His own career was emblematic for this undertaking. A native of Connecticut and graduate of Princeton, he had been settled as a minister in Gorham in 1767. In the early 1770s, his town and parish had been convulsed by the activities of the New Lights, or "Come Outers," as they called themselves: religious enthusiasts who refused to pay ministerial taxes to the drier sort of Old Light pastors like Thacher. A campaign to oust him proved powerful—at one point, the dissidents boarded up the church (Thacher and his supporters had to enter through the roof)— but not quite powerful enough to preclude a compromise, by which he left the ministry on his own terms in 1781. He immediately entered public life—to the applause of his townspeople, whom he represented in the General Court from 1783 to 1798 and whom he served as judge of the Court of Common Pleas from 1784 to his death in 1799. Judge Thacher was famous in Gorham for his cloak, which was blue with a lining of bright red. As the town's chronicler notes, "it was said that when on business, the blue side was always out, then it was the Hon. Mr. Thacher, dignified, always courteous, and polite to all, but when the red came out, a good story

A lawyer from York, Maine, David Sewall was a U. S. District Court judge for Maine (1789-1818) and first president of the College's Board of Overseers. In 1795, he established the College's first undergraduate prize, the David Sewall Premium, awarded to a member of the first-year class for excellence in English composition. John Johnston (American, ca. 1753-1818), Portrait of Judge David Sewall. Oil on canvas, 35 3/8 x 28 7/8 inches. Bowdoin College Museum of Art, 1870.8.

or a joke at some one's expense was sure to follow." Thacher was also locally renowned as a pomologist, and it is pleasant to think that Bowdoin's origins were in the hands of a man so useful, so versatile, and—once he had found his proper calling—so generally admired.[12]

But it would have taken a politician of even greater skill to hurry the district's cause through the General Court. For one thing, few could agree on a site for the college. The element of local pride, even of boosterism, which David Potts has traced in the foundation of so many colleges of the early republic was not absent in easternmost Massachusetts.[13] Thacher had understandably hoped the college would be in Gorham. In January of 1791 he presented a bill to that effect, which the Senate passed but the House postponed until its summer session.

Falmouth, now Portland, in Casco Bay, in North America, 1786. To the left is Bramhall's Hill, which was one of the sites considered for Bowdoin College.

When word of this spread back in the district, several other towns immediately began pledging funds in hopes they would be chosen instead. It was no surprise that when a bill to charter a college finally reached the floor of the House of Representatives on 15 June 1791, the exact location was not mentioned. The bill called for a college to be "established in the County of Cumberland for the instruction of youth in the learned Languages, the liberal Arts and Sciences, the principles of piety, religion and morality." It was to go "under the name of the Colledge of Maine which name the corporation shall have power to alter in honour of the greatest Benefactor." This corporation, or governing body, was to consist of seventeen persons, a majority of them laymen, and a president. Five townships, each six miles square, were to be granted from the commonwealth's public lands in York, Cumberland, or Lincoln counties, with proceeds from their sale going to endow the institution.[14]

In the view of many, Portland would have been the most logical site. The arguments in its favor were summarized in a long letter of 17 December 1791 from the Reverend Samuel Deane to the Hon. Daniel Cony, who represented Hallowell and Augusta in the General Court and who also happened to be James Bowdoin III's land agent in the Kennebec Valley. The people of his prosperous home town, Deane pointed out, were "better able to do something towards building and endowing a College than those in any other part of the County, or of the whole District of Maine." Portland was more central and convenient in the county than Freeport or Gorham, easily accessible from the rest of the settled district by water, and sufficiently distant from Harvard and Dartmouth to attract students. Should the two counties farther east become populous in time, "there will be plenty of room for another College, 150 miles eastward of this." But Portland's advantages were more than geographic: those seeking a public education find it best in a well-populated place, Deane said, "because it is a matter of importance that students should be in the way of getting some knowledge of men and manners, while their geniuses have a juvenile flexibility, and before their rustick habits become fixed and unalterable; that so they may be more fit to mix with mankind, and to fill publick stations with comfort, and a prospect of usefulness." The great universities of Europe and most of those of America were in populous places, Deane added, and ever would be, because their very presence attracted more people. As a practical consideration, Portland was considerable enough a market town to be able to provision a collegiate population, at a cost "at least one fourth part cheaper than [provisions] could be got in any other town in the county." The citizens already had a specific site in mind, "a plain on the top of a height called Bramhalls hill, about 3/4 of a mile from the central part of the compact settlement" (approximately where Maine Medical Center now sits).[15]

Deane argued that the more people a student encountered, the more good examples he would see and the more his ambition would be excited "to gain useful knowledge." This cheerful, rationalistic view of human nature was not universally shared in late eighteenth-century New England. When the citizens of North Yarmouth, for example, pressed their claim, the committee (consisting of the Reverend Tristan Gilman, John Lewis, and David Mitchell) pointed out that the town had a harbor but that a college could be sited some distance from it, "and yet stand upon some good Road in the Vicinity of a Number of Husbandmen, not so much exposed to many Temptations to Dissipation Extravagance Vanity and various Vices as great sea-port-Towns frequently are."[16]

From the start, it was assumed that a grant of unsettled public lands would only partially fund a college, and various towns began to compete for the honor of winning it with promises of further money and services.

Freeport was among the most enterprising. In 1835, Judge Alfred Johnson, Jr., of Belfast recorded for the College the reminiscences of his father, who at the time of Thacher's 1791 bill had recently been settled as minister at Freeport. Since it was clear the Legislature would not approve it, he "felt deeply the catastrophe of the Bill," his son reported, "& being young and ardent was stimulated to make an effort to rescue the project from destruction. To show the feeling existing among the people, he started a subscription in Freeport; and soon after an[other] was set on foot by Dr. Deane of Portland; by Judge Mitchell of N. Yarmouth—& Capt Dunlap of Brunswick. Little was raised in N. Yarmouth and Brunswick, but several thousand doll[ar]s were subscribed in Freeport &

Portland on the condition that the Institution be located in the respective towns."

Freeport's petition "to the Committee of the College of Maine," delivered by the Reverend Alfred Johnson, Sr., as the town's representative to the General Court in 1792, also advanced a geographic argument. "According to the census taken by the Marshall of the district, this town is in the centre of the inhabitants, the same number being East as West of it," it read. Moreover, "this town is also at equal distance from the two principal places in the district, viz, Portland and Kennabeck, and on the way between them." Being "at the bottom of Casco Bay, the fartherest up the County of any town on it, at the junction of five roads," it was easily reached by land or sea; and it offered in the middle of town "a gently rising hill which commands an extensive view of the water, islands and the adjacent Country, which has been thought a pleasant locality for the Buildings." Attached was a list of Freeport's eighty-three subscribers, whose pledges ranged from Josiah Little's $300 to a number of farmers' 50 cents each (with Johnson himself pledging $30, a substantial sum for a young minister). The total was reckoned to be 1,300 £ (or, approximately $3,900).[17]

Two other subscription lists that survive in the Massachusetts State Archives offer a glimpse into the district's economy. In writing Cony, Deane admitted that Portland's pledges had totaled only about 1,200 £ ($3,600) by the end of 1791 but said the subscribers were "both able and willing" to live up to their promises. ("This is not believed to be the case with the subscribers in and about Freeport," he tartly noted.) The Portland list of 12 January 1792 begins with Joseph Noyes's pledge of ten acres of his land on Bramhall's Hill (value: 60 £) and included Samuel Freeman's five acres on the hill plus 600 acres more (70 £), Peleg Wadsworth's 200 acres in Hiram (60 £) plus 15 £ of labor and materials, Benjamin Titcomb's 100 acres in Standish (60 £), Deane's own 100 acres (60 £) plus 10 £ in labor, and the like. But just as typical among the forty-seven subscriptions are Nathaniel Coffin's pledge of "Six pounds in labour," John Trasher's "12 pounds in material for building," and

9

Ebenezer Davis' "Nine pounds in Carpenters and joiners work." However fruitless, the list is a remarkable tribute to the corporate spirit of a Maine town in the 1790s.[18]

North Yarmouth's list has only a dozen names, ranging from Hannah Russell, who pledged 45 £, to Samuel Stubbs, who promised "one Month['s] Worth of a good Joiner." There was proportionately less cash, and more labor and materials, available than in Portland, but the degree of popular enthusiasm for a college in this rural, almost frontier, community is noteworthy.[19]

With people like Thacher, Deane, Johnson, and Gilman campaigning for their respective towns—and similar efforts being made on behalf of New Gloucester, Winthrop, and Turner (whose absentee proprietor, William Little of Newbury, was expected to make a large donation)—how did Brunswick, an unremarkable town of 1,387 in the 1790 Census, emerge as victor? Again, geography proved persuasive. A clue is found in a letter John Lewis, representing North Yarmouth in the General Court, wrote home on 20 February 1792 to his son Asa.

The Coledge bill had the first reading in the house last week. . . & it appears that the locality of it is all the difficulty, Mr. Thomson & the other eastern members Appear obstinately Set for Brunswick. Freeport Appears to have but few Advocates, tho' I should prefer it to Brunswick if they should come in competition. North Yarmouth has been mentioned as being a central Town in the County, but there is an objection Against placing it in Any Sea coast Town, how that will operate I know not, Portland & Gorham will be strongly Advocated for, if the Seacoast Towns Are All Struck out I suppose it will lay wholy between Gorham & Gloucester.

As late as 30 May 1794, Lewis again told his son, among other news of the Legislature, that as far as the college was concerned, "none can tel where it will be. Genl. Thomson is here & will do what he can for Brunswick. . ."[20]

The general did a great deal. As Judge Johnson explains, again based on his father's recollection of events in Boston, "Brunswick was selected as the classic spot, because a majority of the members from Maine who met to decide upon the location, were from parts east of the

Androscoggin, & of course wished to get it as near their constituents as possible. But as the petition originated from Cumberland it was thought right not to carry it out of that county. Winthrop was thought of by many eastern members. Portland had many strong friends, & had not the future growth of the country been taken into consideration, to have been a powerful, & perhaps a successful one."

In other words, the six-year delay had changed the political picture of the district: the "boom" of the 1790s, which had brought many new settlers from Massachusetts into the Kennebec Valley and the backcountry, had diluted the power of the southern coastal towns. In truth, Brunswick had no great advantages, other than its position between the falls of the Androscoggin and the landing at Maquoit Bay. It was a coastal town of sorts, but its tone was largely agricultural—in other words, it did provide the degree of rural retreat, of isolation from urban temptations, that Americans were beginning to expect of colleges and academies. It was as far east as a college could reasonably go and still be in Cumberland County.

Given the dignity and reputation for learning of Judge Thacher and Dr. Deane and their brethren, it is worth noting the role played in the establishment of Bowdoin College by Brigadier Samuel Thompson, of Brunswick and Topsham—the politician mentioned in Lewis's letters above. Thacher and Deane are Federalist New England at its most attractive—dabbling in science, dipping into the classics, practicing a calm and courteous religion, exchanging cuttings of their favorite apple and pear trees. General Thompson bursts on the scene, reeking of gunpowder and the stables, blustering at everyone. He represents a manic strain that was surely more characteristic of life on the district's frontier than Deane's horticultural concerns—a strain that was to appear again, from time to time, in Bowdoin's history. "In regard to his character," the historians of Brunswick drily note, "it is hardly possible to render Brigadier Thompson exact justice. . . . [O]wing to his outspoken and vehement manner, he made so many enemies that it is difficult to know the truth of some statements made in regard to him."[21]

He is best remembered by students of Maine history for "Thompson's War," the exploit in May of 1775 in which he led a band of adventurers, sprigs of spruce in their hats, who briefly captured Captain Henry Mowatt when he came ashore from the British war-ship *Canceau* for a stroll in the woods on Falmouth Neck. The local people were horrified, some because they feared British reprisals, some because they were less than enthusiastic about the Revolution to start with. When the acting commander of the *Canceau* demanded the captain's return, Thompson, who had a slight stutter, is said to have replied: "F-f-fire away! F-f-fire away! Every gun you fire, I will cut off a joint!"[22] Cooler heads prevailed. The burning of Portland the following October, under Mowatt's command, was widely regarded as retaliation for Thompson's rash act.[23]

In the post-Revolutionary world, the general relieved his aggressions at the General Court, in which he represented Brunswick and, after 1784, Topsham (where his house still overlooks the Androscoggin) and in which he developed a reputation as a fierce and skilled debater. The new federal Constitution outraged him, and in 1788 he and William Widgery of New Gloucester led a noisy but unsuccessful attack on it in the state's ratifying convention at Boston.[24] At the time of Shays's Rebellion, Thompson threatened to march through western Massachusetts and New Hampshire fomenting more trouble, should the grievances of the inland farmers not be taken seriously by the coastal merchants and financiers.[25] Yet he was himself a rich (though self-made) entrepreneur, a land speculator, a devout Universalist, a serious man. As one admirer of Thompson has written, "Once he overheard a person say, what a pity it was he had no better education, and turning, he replied, 'If I have no education perhaps I can furnish some ideas to those who have.'"[26] For all the enemies he made by his bluster and swagger, he was well-respected by his neighbors, who repeatedly elected him to office. Although he was to be one of the original Overseers of the new college, his

death in 1797 deprived the infant institution of his counsel. Yet his role in securing the prize for Brunswick ought not to be underestimated.[27]

But what was the new college to be called? Here again Judge Johnson offers the most detailed account:

It occurred to my father & probably to others that the late learned Governor Bowdoin had left both a name & an estate that might be honorable and useful to the College. He thereupon procured an introduction, made the suggestion to his son & heir, the late James Bowdoin [III], observing that Literature was poor & custom had connected patronage with the name. The thought took with him & he soon made proposals, but added that such were the vissicitudes of fortune, that he might never be able to do so much as might be anticipated from him.

The younger Bowdoin had other doubts, too. He "shrewdly cautioned my father not to let his father's name be given to the College in the Act which he said might be left to be given by the Boards afterwards; as he thought such was Gov. Hancock's antipathy to his father, that he would never approve of an act for a college with his father's name given to it; and related some curious anecdotes to confirm his suspicion."[28]

THE BOWDOIN FAMILY

In a famous letter from Paris in 1780, John Adams explained to his wife, Abigail, why he could not send her as complete an account of the marvels of France as he would have wished: more urgent business was at hand. "I must study politics and war," he wrote home, "that my sons may have the liberty to study mathematics and philosophy, geography, natural history and naval architecture, navigation, commerce and agriculture, in order to give their children a right to study painting, poetry, music, architecture, statuary, tapestry, and porcelain." Could he have been thinking of the Bowdoins?[29]

The first James Bowdoin had been a warrior statesman only in the sense that he was an aggressive entrepreneur (although in the volatile world of eighteenth-century international politics, a man might find himself a merchant one day, a privateer the next). As the son of an emigré, and himself French-born, Bowdoin had

11

Retained by members of the Bowdoin family until 1894, long after the other family portraits had come to the College, this portrait of James Bowdoin II, thought to be a good likeness but painted after his death, shows him surrounded by attributes of the arts and sciences. Christian Gullager (American, 1759-1826), Portrait of Governor James Bowdoin II, *ca. 1791. Oil on panel, 10 3/4 x 8 5/8 inches. Bowdoin College Museum of Art. Bequest of Sarah Bowdoin Dearborn, 1894.2.*

The bookplate that marks James Bowdoin III's books includes the family crest with the motto Ut aquila versus coelum, *"Soaring like an eagle toward the sky." The sun, which has since become an insignia of the College, is an ancient symbol for divinity and the light of learning.*

When Governor Bowdoin bequeathed his library to the American Academy of Arts and Sciences, this bookplate was designed to incorporate the academy's seal. It depicts Minerva, symbol of wisdom, and the rising sun of knowledge. On one side is the wilderness of the New World, and on the other are symbols representing the arts, trade, agriculture, and the sciences. His books have been housed with his son's in the Bowdoin College Library on permanent loan from the academy since 1947.

12

shown considerable skill in securing a place for his family in the top rank of Boston's mercantile elite, not least through a series of astute marriage alliances. The career of his remarkable son, James Bowdoin II, does fit Adams's pattern neatly: while never abandoning the world of commerce and affairs, he was recognized as one of the leading gentleman-scientists of mid-eighteenth-century America.[30] And his son, as we shall see, became one of the few Americans of his generation to whom the term connoisseur might be applied.

The Bowdoin family fancied a rather glamorous past for itself, as Huguenot nobles forced to flee La Rochelle after Louis XIV had revoked the Edict of Nantes, but what can be discovered of the truth is more prosaic.[31] Pierre Baudouin, a French Protestant merchant of unknown origins, had settled briefly in Ireland before emigrating to America with his family in 1686. He successfully petitioned Governor Andros of Massachusetts for a grant of 100 acres "in the town of Casco in the county of Mayne," today South Portland and at that time a frontier whose only European settlers were a few fishermen and farmers. Trouble with the French and the Indians soon forced him to flee with his family from Casco Bay, but over the next sixteen years he recouped his fortunes as a merchant, dying in 1706 a respected member of Boston's prosperous Huguenot community.

There were several Huguenot families who did very well in colonial America—the Jays and Delanceys in New York, the Legares and Manigaults in South Carolina, the Fanueils and Molineux in Boston, among others—but none who surpassed the Bowdoins in combining, over four generations, vast wealth with exceptional political and cultural achievement.[32] Pierre's son James I turned a prosperous family enterprise into what, at the time of his death in 1747, was reckoned the largest fortune in Massachusetts. But land, not money from commerce, was what made one a gentleman; both James I and his son invested heavily in speculative real estate as well as in houses and farms. The father began the *cursus honorum* too late in life to achieve political renown, but his selection to the Council (the

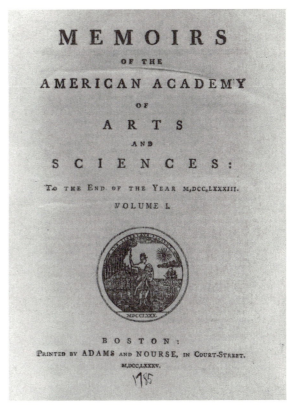

A merchant, politician, and real estate speculator, James Bowdoin II was also a serious student of the sciences. He owned scientific instruments, corresponded with Benjamin Franklin, wrote at least one scientific paper (on optics), donated a geological collection and an orrery (a mechanical device that demonstrates the movement of the solar system) to Harvard College, and was a founding member and first president of the American Academy of Arts and Sciences. The first volume of the Memoirs of the academy includes his inaugural address as president.

twenty-eight-member upper house of the colonial Legislature) marked the beginnings of an alliance with the royal governors which, until the eve of revolution, was to serve the Bowdoins well. James I's three marriages also helped. By the third generation, the Bowdoins were linked with the influential Pitts and Erving families in Boston and, through a son-in-law, with the powerful Grenville-Temple clan in Britain.

James Bowdoin II was too dignified a man to inspire many anecdotes, but there is an endearing story about a party at his house in the years before the Revolution. Bowdoin kept a famous table and an enviable cellar. His distinguished guests, having sampled liberally of both, found upon leaving that the long flight of stone steps from the front door down to the street had

The Pope Orrery was made in 1787 in Boston by local "mechanical genius" Joseph Pope and bought by Harvard College with money raised by a public lottery. The case is decorated with statuettes (said to have been cast in bronze by Paul Revere) of Benjamin Franklin, Isaac Newton, and James Bowdoin II, who had donated a smaller orrery, made to his order in London, to his alma mater in 1764. The Pope Orrery can be seen in a downstairs corridor of the Houghton Library.

Believed to be the air pump left to the College by James Bowdoin III, this instrument probably belonged to his father. The pump and its elaborate Chippendale case are on loan to the Smithsonian. Much early nineteenth-century science was devoted to exploring the properties of matter, in this case, the operation of a vacuum.

become glazed with ice. Their host's madeira had not befuddled their judgment, however, for they had the good sense to descend, one step at a time, on their rumps.[33] So Hogarthian a spectacle would have embarrassed their proper nineteenth-century progeny, but eighteenth-century Boston had a different sense of decorum, one in which the grand manner and a rather down-to-earth practicality existed side by side.

That James Bowdoin II lived in the grand manner is beyond doubt. In 1756 he had purchased the Erving mansion, at the corner of what is now Bowdoin and Beacon streets (a site occupied in our time by the former Hotel Bellevue, across the street from the Athenaeum). Beacon Hill, taller then, still had a rural air, and Bowdoin's garden and orchard stretched back to what is now Ashburton Place. He furnished the house in a princely fashion. General Burgoyne, who could have had any house in town, chose to live in Bowdoin's when his troops occupied Boston in 1775. (Bowdoin prudently had an inventory made of his extensive library upon leaving town.)[34]

That he was also a practical man is one clue to his politics. Any notion that Bowdoin set aside his business interests to devote himself to the common good would misrepresent eighteenth-century public life. In his mind—in the minds of all those New England gentlemen who served as magistrates or legislators or officers of militia—life appeared a seamless garment, in which the prosperity of the commonwealth was the most certain guarantee of its civic health. This seems particularly true in Bowdoin's case, for his first public criticisms of colonial policy in the 1760s grew out of his conviction that the Crown was foolishly harming the Massachusetts economy—*his* economy. That he soon became more radicalized—to the point where he could write as reckless a piece of propaganda as his *Short Narrative of the Horrid Massacre*—was a result of the economic stupidity of George III's ministers, Bowdoin's own reading in Whig political theory, and a purely personal hatred of the royal governor, Francis Bernard, who had offended Bowdoin's new son-in-law, John Temple.[35]

Even his reputation as a savant needs to be considered in light of his business activities. Bowdoin sat at the hub of a vast maritime enterprise. His complex business dealings stretched from Boston to London and Amsterdam and Madeira, to the Chesapeake, and as far south as Grenada and Dominica in the West Indies. He also speculated in property throughout the state, from the Housatonic Valley to the Elizabeth Islands to the "wild" lands of the Kennebec.[36] History, geography, navigation, meteorology, political economy, military science, husbandry—these were not subjects to be sampled at leisure in his study, they were the essence of his everyday life. What carried Bowdoin far beyond his equally shrewd colleagues, however, was an intense intellectual curiosity. Not a particularly original thinker, he nonetheless had an uncommon thirst for knowledge—and for the company of the knowledgeable. There were scores of amateur scientists in colonial North America, but few able to keep up a correspondence on optics and electricity with Benjamin Franklin or to become a fellow of the Royal Academy. An exceptionally genial man toward those whom he respected, Bowdoin saw science as a collegial venture among like-minded gentlemen on both sides of the Atlantic.

By helping to found the American Academy of Arts and Sciences in 1780, he sought to enrich the new republic with the sort of learned society the rulers of Europe had long patronized. But it was to be a peculiarly American academy, devoted not only to the natural sciences but to inquiries, as he reminded the charter members in his presidential address, on "the antiquities of America"—which included both the "aboriginal natives" and the first Europeans—and, taking up a subject Montesquieu had treated, on the influence of the northern climate on the American character.[37] And, like the men who were first to teach natural science at the college that would bear his name, Bowdoin saw the pursuit of such knowledge as a profoundly conservative, even pious, endeavor. God, in his words, had been "the first and the supremely great naturalist." To know was not to invent hypotheses and to test them by experiment; it was to *reveal* what was

The Bowdoin gravestone is in the Granary Burial Ground in downtown Boston, not far from the site of Governor Bowdoin's mansion. The tombstone represents the Bowdoin family coat of arms, which was later incorporated as a symbol of the College's library.

of the officers commanding forces in Boston just before the war—led his enemies to question his patriotism. But his position was solid enough for him to be elected in 1785 and 1786 governor of the Commonwealth, an office that was to associate his name and reputation with one of the most turbulent events in the first years of the rather shaky new nation.

When Shays's Rebellion—the popular name for a series of agrarian uprisings throughout western Massachusetts and beyond—broke out in the fall of 1786, the state legislature dithered, and the national government under the Confederation proved powerless to act. Governor Bowdoin and his fellow conservatives quickly raised enough of their own money to provide General Benjamin Lincoln with enough troops in the winter of 1787 to suppress the rebels (most of whom were yeoman farmers and Revolutionary veterans who claimed, with considerable justification, that they were being oppressed by high taxes, ruthless creditors, hostile courts, and a lack of money in circulation). However self-serving his motives, Bowdoin's decisive action probably minimized the bloodshed. Yet the patriot of 1770 had proven himself the defender of property and order and State Street banking when the spirit of protest threatened his own class. Bowdoin was decisively defeated by the populist Hancock in the 1787 election. Bowdoin College, by its name alone, was to enter the world with a certain amount of ideological baggage.[40]

Bowdoin "gave" that name to a street, a square, and a subway stop in Boston, two towns in Maine, a hill in Dorchester, a Harvard composition prize, and even a baseball team of the 1860s. Yet for all practical purposes he would now be forgotten, save by a few historians, had his son not endowed a college and had the College not survived into the twentieth century. (A rather small college at that, and one whose name even some New Englanders still have trouble pronouncing.) Bowdoin's failure to leave more of a mark on the history of his time is at first puzzling. He was certainly the equal in influence and probably the superior in intellect of John Hancock and Samuel Adams and James Otis.

already there, to look at things so closely that the secrets of creation would be unveiled, to be marveled at—and then catalogued in the traditional Baconian way.[38] And there was another goal for an *American* academy: the improvement of agriculture, manufactures, navigation, and commerce—"every art and science, which might tend to advance the interest and honour of their country, the dignity and happiness of a free, independent, and virtuous people."[39]

Bowdoin's chronic ill health—he was consumptive—prevented his playing as dramatic a role in the later stages of the Revolution as he had in the 1760s, and his unbroken friendship with a number of Englishmen—including some

Yet they are heroes of the Revolution in a sense that Bowdoin is not. Partly this was a matter of bad luck: Bowdoin should have led the Massachusetts delegation to Philadelphia in 1774 but was unable to travel because of the severe illness of his wife. Hancock got the glory instead. Partly it was a matter of politics: Bowdoin lacked the common touch and never caught the common imagination.[41] Scrupulously honest in his business dealings, most at home with his family and his books, torn emotionally between attachment to England and loyalty to Boston, he was among the first in a long line of New England patricians who thought politics their natural business—but who were never quite able to persuade the electorate of it.[42]

THE COLLEGE CHARTERED

While there was no public opposition recorded to having a college in Maine, by 1791 there was still no agreement on a site or on a name, and Thacher's bill of that year called for governance by a single board of trustees.[43] A good deal went on behind the scenes, we can safely assume: for one thing, the final version that emerged early in 1794 had a provision for a board of overseers. This was very much on the Harvard model and accorded with the theory of bicameralism familiar to every well-read republican through Harrington's *The Commonwealth of Oceana*, a seventeenth-century utopian tract much studied by American Whigs. By greatly expanding the number of governors of the college, bicameralism had the further advantage of linking a wider selection of the district's elite with the institution. It was nonetheless a drawback in the nineteenth century, when strong-willed Overseers frequently clashed with equally stubborn Trustees, often to the detriment of the institution. (In the twentieth, it was to have some fundraising advantages.) But the College learned to live with a system that few other institutions chose to emulate.[44]

There is an interesting piece of evidence that the debate in the General Court concerned details, not essentials: in the petition signed by the trustees of the Williamstown Free School on 22 May 1792 seeking to have their academy rechartered as "Williams Hall," they assume Bowdoin already exists: "There being already two colleges within the Commonwealth [Harvard and the college in Maine] cannot . . . be a reasonable objection against the addition of a third, especially as the interest of the last, from its local situation, cannot interfere with either of the former. The interests of the whole will perfectly coincide, and like a threefold cord, mutually conform and strengthen each other."[45] Whether Harvard was that complaisant is another unanswered question. An attempt to establish a college in western Massachusetts in 1763 (Queen's College, at Hatfield, Hampshire County) was denounced by the Harvard overseers as a step that would "make learning contemptible" and was thrown out by the General Court.[46] Whether a more brotherly spirit prevailed in the early 1790s is unclear, but surely Harvard had reason to be concerned about diminished subsidies from the Legislature and loss of students from the district.

The friends of what, on 22 June 1793, became Williams College had an advantage the Maine delegation lacked: an existing academy, with a building, trustees, some funds, and a preceptor who became the president. In addition to the major question of locale, these other details were doubtless the occasion for much negotiating and delay on the part of the Maine legislators. In seeking the reasons for the six-year wait, we ought to look also at the nature of the General Court itself: a cumbersome, inefficient body in which committees were formed for each bill (and reformed each session), and one so dominated by the Massachusetts seaboard towns (whose representatives could reach the State House with much less difficulty than their distant colleagues), that the affairs of the district were frequently neglected (as the Maine separationists liked to point out).[47] James Bowdoin III—who represented Dorchester in the Senate at this time—was right about Hancock's dislike for the elder Bowdoin; a personal enmity going back to Hancock's mismanagement of Harvard funds when he was treasurer and Bowdoin a member of the Corporation had gradually taken

This page from the official record of the General Court of Massachusetts for 1794 shows Chapter XV, "An Act to Establish a College in the Town of Brunswick, in the District of Maine, within this Commonwealth." Maine was a part of Massachusetts until 1820, and any change in the College's charter must still be approved by the legislatures of both states.

a more ideological tone in the 1780s, becoming extremely bitter in the gubernatorial elections of the Shays period. But whether this delayed the bill is unproved; Samuel Adams, who had been on much better terms personally if not politically with Bowdoin, also delayed signing at an earlier session in 1794. Allowing for all these complications, the most plausible explanation for the delay is that, session after session, the district's legislators simply could not agree upon a location for the college or the composition of its boards.

The long-awaited day arrived: on 24 June 1794, the bill passed both houses and was signed by Governor Adams. The General Court had enacted that "there be Erected and Established in the Town of Brunswick in the District of Maine, a College for the Purpose of educating Youth, to be called BOWDOIN COLLEGE." Its purpose was to promote "Virtue and Piety and the Knowledge of such of the Languages and of the Useful and Liberal Arts and Sciences as shall hereafter be Directed from Time to Time by the said Corporation." Eleven worthy gentlemen residing in the district were named as Trustees; forty-two others were appointed Overseers.[48] From its public lands in the district, the Commonwealth of Massachusetts granted the college five townships, each six miles square. Three days later, the governor's son, James Bowdoin III, wrote to the new Boards from Boston to make official the support he had already promised behind the scenes. "You'll permit me," he said, "to suggest that the honourable testimonial of respect paid in the establishment to the name, the character, the talents, and virtues of my late father, must attach me in a peculiar degree to an institution in the success of which I feel myself deeply interested." As a first step, he offered $1,000 in specie and 1,000 acres of land in the town of Bowdoin, which was at that time part of Lincoln County.[49]

In December, on behalf of the Board of Overseers, Daniel Davis, Samuel Freeman, and the Reverend Elijah Kellogg accepted the donation, with a courtly flourish. "We anticipate," they wrote from Portland, "with a high degree of confidence that under a government which depends upon the spread of knowledge for its support, the learned and wealthy part of the community will bestow upon it *their* smiles & patronage, so that it may soon and lastingly flourish under a name which has been so justly dear and valuable to the friends of humanity & science. . . . [I]t affords us additional pleasure to reflect that its patron is cloathed with the mantle of his father's virtues. We devoutly wish him every earthly felicity and an immortality in that happy place where charity will receive its complete reward."[50]

CONGRESS, ST. IN 1800.

Congress Street, Portland, in 1800. This early drawing shows a house built by Daniel Davis in 1794, left; the Reverend Samuel Deane's house, built in 1765, center; and First Parish Meetinghouse, 1740-1825.

VIRGIL ON THE PRESUMPSCOT

Bowdoin College is not the lengthened shadow of one man; its founder was not an individual but a group, one might even say a social class. The most famous of the Bowdoins had been dead four years at the time of its charter; his son was to take a friendly but distant interest in its affairs. The College was the corporate expression of the hopes and fears of a small but locally powerful group of men—in the language of the day, the friends of piety and learning in the District of Maine.

Yet one of these men does seem more central than the rest. Among the charter members of the Boards, he was not politically the most influential—that distinction probably belongs to Judge David Sewall, of York, the first president of the Overseers. Nor was he the most learned—his eccentric colleague, the Reverend Dr. Moses Hemmenway, of Wells, had earned that reputation (for being, in the words of a later admirer, a scholar on easy terms with "the faithful Justin Martyr, the admired Polycarp, the grave Irenaeus, the severe Tertullian, the holy and eminent Cyprian, the scholastic and fanciful Origen," and so forth, through the Church Fathers).[51] He was not even a man whose name would have been easily recognized outside his own county—such notoriety belonged to the rambunctious Brigadier Thompson and to Peleg Wadsworth, the Revolutionary war hero from Portland.

He was Samuel Deane, the scholarly clergy-

19

John Brewster, Jr., Portrait of the Reverend Samuel Deane.
*An agricultural reformer and man of the Enlightenment, Deane
played a crucial role in the establishment of Bowdoin College.*

THE

NEW-ENGLAND FARMER;

OR, GEORGICAL

DICTIONARY:

CONTAINING

A COMPENDIOUS ACCOUNT

OF THE

WAYS AND METHODS

In which the moſt Important

ART OF HUSBANDRY,

IN ALL ITS VARIOUS BRANCHES,

IS, OR MAY BE,

PRACTISED TO THE GREATEST ADVANTAGE

IN THIS COUNTRY.

BY SAMUEL DEANE, A. M.
FELLOW *of the* AMERICAN ACADEMY *of* ARTS *and* SCIENCES.

" FRIGORIBUS PARTO AGRICOLÆ PLERUMQUE FRUUNTUR,
MUTUAQUE INTER SE LÆTI CONVIVIA CURANT.
INVITAT GENIALIS HYEMS, CURASQUE RESOLVIT."—*VIRGIL.*

PRINTED AT *WORCESTER*, MASSACHUSETTS,
BY ISAIAH THOMAS,
Sold at his Bookſtore in WORCESTER, and by him and COMPANY in BOSTON.
MDCCXC.

TO THE HONOURABLE

JAMES BOWDOIN, ESQUIRE, L. L. D.

PRESIDENT

OF

THE AMERICAN ACADEMY

OF ARTS AND SCIENCES,

&c. &c. &c.

THE FOLLOWING WORK

IS INSCRIBED,

BY HIS MUCH OBLIGED,

AND MOST OBEDIENT

HUMBLE SERVANT,

THE AUTHOR.

Portland, Maſſachuſetts, 1790.

The Reverend Samuel Deane's The New England Farmer; or,
Georgical Dictionary, *was the first American dictionary of
agriculture. In it he attempted to apply the ideas of English
agrarian reformers to New England's climate and soil.*

Deane dedicated his New England Farmer, *1790, to Governor
Bowdoin, a fellow member of the American Academy of Arts and
Sciences and a major landowner in the District of Maine.*

man and agricultural reformer who had campaigned so ardently for placing the College in Portland, where he was minister of the First Parish Church. A former tutor and librarian at Harvard, he was one of the few people in the district who knew how a college actually worked.[52] And as author of a lexicon called *The New England Farmer* and member of the American Academy of Arts and Sciences, he was the northernmost representative of a cosmopolitan circle of moderate, enlightened clerics who saw Boston (or, more precisely, Cambridge) as their intellectual home. The first meeting of the College's trustees adjourned to Deane's parsonage (which was next to First Parish, with a garden extending from present-day Congress Street down to Back Cove), and he rarely missed a meeting in his nineteen years on the Board. (His only rival in such faithful attendance was the Board's secretary, John Frothingham, a Portland attorney.)

To his contemporaries, Deane was best known for his "georgical dictionary" (as the subtitle of *The New England Farmer* reads), a work dedicated to James Bowdoin II as president of the academy and printed in 1790 in Worcester by Isaiah Thomas, who was to be an early donor to the College Library.[53] Deane covered the subject from *Ants* ("an insect which sometimes annoys fields") to *Zephyr* ("the west wind"). In the words of its title page, the dictionary was intended to be "a compendious account of the ways and methods in which the most important art of husbandry, in all its various branches, is, or may be, practical to the greatest advantage in this country." The book had a message: that American farmers lacked ambition, that they clung too stubbornly to their ancestral ways and ignored the eighteenth century's advances in husbandry and estate management. Contrary to the belief expressed by Talleyrand and other European travelers, it was not the unlettered yeomen who were at fault; it was the better sort, "persons of a liberal or polite education," who treated agriculture with contempt. Deane looked ahead, to a day he thought at hand, "when the rich, the polite, and the ambitious, shall glory in paying a closer attention to their farms. . . and when,

instead of being ashamed of their employment, our laborious farmers shall, as a great writer says, 'toss their dung with an air of majesty.'" He was right; the next generation of the New England elite—James Bowdoin III's generation—was to make a cult of country life.[54]

But for the moment he had a more immediate goal: to Americanize his subject. European texts written for a more temperate climate had proved ruinous if followed too literally. What Deane provided was a compendium of his own experience on his farm in Gorham, judiciously augmented with extracts from "some of the best authors." His motive was patriotic—he feared his country depended too much on imported food and clothing—and his method was practical and experimental, based on an exchange of information between fellow republicans, each of them "monarchs over our farms." Great good would follow, he said. A self-sustaining agricultural nation would be a manufacturing nation as well:

As a good system of national government is now established, I see no reason to doubt but that a spirited attention to husbandry and manufactures, accompanied with a more general practice of frugality and economy, would do it effectually; so that such a foundation would be laid for the increasing wealth that we should be able, in a short time, to cancel our publick debts; and might reasonably hope ere long to become an opulent, respectable and very powerful nation.[55]

In calling his dictionary "georgical"—a synonym among the classically educated in the eighteenth century for agricultural—Deane was making more than a casual reference to Virgil and his *Georgics*, the most widely read Latin poem on husbandry.[56] The tastes and smells of the Roman poet's world—bees, wine, honey, dung—fill Deane's pages. Like another learned agronomist 400 miles to the south at Monticello, Deane was convinced, for example, that "there is not the least reason to doubt of the practicality of cultivating the [grape] vine to advantage in the North American states," New England being situated at much the same latitude as France.

Though he was wrong about that, Deane achieved some local reclame for another conscious effort to make "classic" his native hillsides—one hillside in Gorham in particular. Too modest to promote his own work, Deane at least did not prohibit a newspaper from publishing his topographical poem *Pitchwood Hill* in 1785:

Friendly Muse ascend thy car,
Moving high in liquid air:
Teach thy vot'ry how to soar
Heights he never reach'd before.
PITCH-WOOD HILL demands a song:
Let my flight be bold and strong:
May the landscape, bright and gay,
Raise to fame my rural lay.
(lines 1-8)

The Virgilian note of loss is struck—"Pine, alas! are no more seen" (the peasants had cut them for fuel, hence the name of the hill)—but Deane as good husbandman goes on to celebrate the crops that have succeeded the "tow'ring" trees. Yet traces of forest remain, and the poet and his "sweaty swains" repair to them to refresh their spirits—no Puritan hatred of the woods for him. Ascending the height, he succumbs to "Fancy":

Down the eastern slope below,
See the grand PRESUMSCUT flow!
Noble river, broad and deep,
Majestick, slow his waters creep!
Winding his serpentine way,
From SEBACOOK to the sea.
Fancy, on the verdant banks,
Views the Fairies' midnight pranks.
Naiads, Tritons, here may seem
To wanton o'er the limpid stream.
(lines 83-92)

Like Virgil, the poet has known war and loss of home—Deane and his wife had fled to their Gorham farm after the British shelled and burned Portland in 1775—and he offers an invocation to peace.

Sacred height! may army vile
Ne'er gain possession of thy soil;
Nor batt'ries dire deform thy front,
To break the Muses fav'rite haunt.
(lines 129-132)

He ends on a note both pagan and Christian: a longing for *otium*, for quiet repose away from the "courts, and crowds of busy men," but in the hope that his contemplative retreat will "fit me for a happier Hill."[57]

We are a long way from the world of the seventeenth-century Puritan divines or the more extreme of their Edwardian successors, and with Deane we catch hardly a glimpse of the earnest reformers, the benevolent empire-builders, of nineteenth-century Congregationalism. As Stephen Marini has pointed out, Deane is an example of the "metropolitan" style of Federalist clergyman, undemanding in his theology, conciliatory in his manner.[58] His proto-Unitarian views would have caused trouble among the orthodox of the next generation at Bowdoin, but much of his long career coincided with a state of mind, at least on the part of the non-evangelical coastal elite, in which Christianity could tolerate a large dose of classical humanism, even Naiads prancing on the parson's hillside. The point is worth pausing over, because the religious nature of the college Deane played so large a role in establishing has been so often misinterpreted.[59]

In both the Reverend Dr. Samuel Deane and the Honorable James Bowdoin III we glimpse something else at work. The notion of *translatio studii*, of transfer of knowledge, of the progress of learning, from the Old World to the New was a powerful trope in the minds of educated Americans in the new republic. But experience had long ago proved, and national pride demanded, that literal transfer was not enough: *translatio* had to be joined to *renovatio*, to renewal.[60] What Deane borrowed from British agricultural reformers he filtered through what he and his neighbors had learned in the harshness of New England's climate. As we shall see, when the younger Bowdoin sought to improve the native flocks on Naushon Island with his prize merino rams from Spain, he likewise was engaged in more than oneupsmanship with his rich friends. He was playing the role of patriot, of friend of his people. A work like *The New England Farmer*—the first of its kind in this country—was neither entirely European nor peculiarly American, but an amalgam of the two. So also was to be the college which the one man inspirited and the other endowed.

NOTES

BCSC is Special Collections, Hawthorne-Longfellow Library, Bowdoin College.

1. Until Maine became a state in 1820, it was a noncontiguous part of Massachusetts and was customarily distinguished from it by being called the District of Maine (it had been a separate admiralty district during the Revolution).

2. Charles Maurice de Talleyrand-Périgord, "Letter on the Eastern Part of America," pp. 69-86, in Hans Huth and Wilma J. Pugh, eds., *Talleyrand in America as a Financial Promoter 1794-96*, vol. 2 of the Annual Report of the American Historical Association for the Year 1941 (Washington, 1942). According to local tradition, Talleyrand visited Brunswick on his tour, staying in the public house owned by Captain John Dunlap.

3. Talleyrand plays one more small, indirect role in Bowdoin College's history: in part, it was his unaccommodating behavior (as Napoleon's foreign minister in 1806) that helped make James Bowdoin III's diplomatic life in Paris so miserable (see p. 109 below).

4. The Reverend Alfred Johnson, Jr., said his father had told him there already was agitation for a college in Maine before the Revolution. But there is no contemporary evidence to support this, and Johnson may have confused his dates in thinking of a later bill. Johnson to A. S. Packard, 19 January 1835, "College History: Founding," BCSC.

5. *Cumberland Gazette,* 7 February 1788, copy in "College History: Founding," BCSC.

6. Ronald F. Banks, *Maine Becomes a State: The Movement to Separate Maine from Massachusetts, 1785-1820* (Middletown, Conn., 1970), p. 12.

7. Banks, p. 24.

8. William D. Williamson, *The History of the State of Maine* (Hallowell, 1832), vol. 1, pp. 532-533.

9. [Daniel Davis], *An Address to the Inhabitants of the District of Maine. . .* (Portland, 1791), p. 14.

10. The justices of the peace in the 1780s performed administrative as well as judicial duties: they laid out roads, granted retail licenses, recommended the county tax rate to the General Court, etc. Each county had a large number of them—there were twenty-five in Cumberland in 1788—and they sat together as the County Court of General Sessions of the Peace to hear criminal cases and serve as the county's governing body. Van Beck Hall, *Politics Without Parties: Massachusetts, 1780-1791* (Pittsburgh, 1972), p. 48.

11. Reverend Issac Weston, "History of the Association of Ministers of Cumberland County, Maine, from 1788 to 1867," *Congregational Quarterly,* 9 (October 1867), pp. 334-347.

12. Hugh D. McLellan, *History of Gorham, Me.* (Portland, 1903), p. 188; James McLachlan, *Princetonians, 1748-1768* (Princeton, 1976), pp. 328-329.

13. David B. Potts, "American Colleges in the Nineteenth Century: From Localism to Denominationalism," *History of Education Quarterly* (Winter 1971), pp. 363-380; on the "booster" college, see also Daniel Boorstin, *The Americans: The National Experience* (New York, 1965), pp. 152-161.

14. Copy in "College History: Founding," BCSC.

15. Deane's letter to Cony is printed in James W. North, "The Establishment of a College in the District of Maine," *Maine Genealogist and Biographer,* 1, no. 4 (June 1876), pp. 113-116.

16. Copy in "College History: Founding," BCSC.

17. Johnson to A. Packard, 19 January 1835, "College History: Founding," BCSC; Freeport's petition is in the Massachusetts State Archives, Boston, among papers related to the college in Maine, 1792. For about a generation after the Revolution, pounds sterling and dollars were both used in New England.

18. *Loc. cit.*

19. *Loc. cit.*

20. John Lewis to Asa Lewis, 20 February 1792 and 30 May 1794, Maine Historical Society, Lewis Family Papers, Coll. 36, Box 1/5.

21. George A. Wheeler and Henry W. Wheeler, *History of Brunswick, Topsham, and Harpswell, Maine* (Boston, 1878; repr., 1989), vol. 2, p. 812.

22. Nathan Goold, "General Samuel Thompson of Brunswick and Topsham, Maine," *Collections of the Maine Historical Society,* series III, vol. I, p. 439.

23. For details on Thompson's involvement, see Donald A. Yerxa, "The Burning of Falmouth, 1775: A Case Study in British Imperial Pacification," *Maine Historical Society Quarterly*, 14, no. 3 (Winter 1975), 119-160, esp. pp. 129-134.

24. Thompson's shrewd and pungent comments in the ratification debate make good reading. He was called to order, for example, for insulting former Governor Bowdoin when he said, "I think, Sir, that had the last administration continued one year longer, our liberties would have been lost, and the county involved in blood: not so much, Sir, from their bad conduct, but from the suspicions of the people of them." *Debates and Proceedings of the Convention. . .* (Boston, 1856), p. 112.

25. James S. Leamon, "Revolution and Separation," *Maine in the Early Republic* (Hanover, N. H., 1988), p. 94.

26. Goold, p. 427.

27. "Once walking with some gentlemen in Brunswick, he pointed to a lot of land saying that it was intended by the God of nature for an institution of learning. That is now the location of Bowdoin College," Goold, p. 428. Why so outspoken an Antifederalist should support the college effort is in some ways puzzling, except that Thompson may have seen it as a step toward separation and, as a local landowner and merchant, surely hoped it would prove an economic windfall. The College's political tone would not have been as evident in 1794 as it would be by 1802. For another vivid account of Thompson's personality, see Wheeler, vol. 2, pp. 811-816. The best account of his political career as the district's most outspoken Antifederalist is James S. Leamon, "In Shays's Shadow: Separation and Ratification of the Constitution in Maine," in Robert A. Gross, ed., *In Debt to Shays: The Bicentennial of an Agrarian Revolution* (Charlottesville, 1993), pp. 281-296.

28. Johnson, see note 17.

29. Charles Francis Adams, ed., *Letters of John Adams, Addressed to His Wife* (Boston, 1841), vol. 2, letter 78 [1780], p. 68. The pattern Adams describes is a familiar one over three generations, but it is interesting to note that shortly before sailing for France in 1779 he had served with James Bowdoin II on the drafting committee of the Massachusetts Constitutional Convention (over which Bowdoin presided) and had been a leading force in founding that same year the American Academy of Arts and Sciences (of which Bowdoin was the first president). And, as a young lawyer, Adams had represented the Kennebec Proprietors in Maine land cases. For their role in the convention, see Gregg L. Lint *et al.*, eds., *Papers of John Adams,* (Cambridge, Mass., 1989), vol. 8, p. 230.

30. Gordon E. Kershaw, *James Bowdoin II: Patriot and Man of the Enlightenment* (Lanham, Md., 1991) is helpful in sorting out some archival puzzles, such as the disposition of property under James Bowdoin I's will. Among topics one would like to know more about are Bowdoin's rivalry with John Hancock, the influence on Bowdoin of Whig and classical republican thought, and Bowdoin's relationship with his only son, the College's patron. The best introduction to Governor Bowdoin remains Clifford K. Shipton's delightful essay in *Sibley's Harvard Graduates*, vol. 11; see also R. L. Volz, *Governor Bowdoin and His Family* (Brunswick, 1969) and Gordon E. Kershaw and R. Peter Mooz, *James Bowdoin: Patriot and Man of the Enlightenment* (Brunswick, 1976).

31. Gerard J. Brault's scrutiny of the Bowdoin family tree is the sort of essay that gives genealogy a good name. ("Pierre Baudouin and the Bowdoin Coat of Arms," *New England Historical and Genealogical Register*, October 1960, pp. 243-268). His conclusion, supported by the research of Robert C. Winthrop, Jr., is that no reliable evidence survives concerning the family until Pierre Baudouin turns up in Dublin in 1684.

32. On the Huguenot phenomenon in general, see Roger Howell, Jr., "'The Vocation of the Lord': Aspects of the Huguenot Contribution to the English-Speaking World," *Anglican and Episcopal History*, vol. 56, no. 2 (June 1987), pp. 131-151, and on their assimilation, Jon Butler, *The Huguenots in America: A Refugee People in New World Society* (Cambridge, Mass., 1983), esp. the chapter "If All the World Were Boston," pp. 71-90.

33. Justin Winsor, *Memorial History of Boston* (Boston, 1881), vol. 2, p. 522.

34. The inventory is printed in *Proceedings of the Massachusetts Historical Society*, 51 (June 1918), pp. 362-368. The imposing house was set well back from the street, as were its neighbors, the Bromfield house to the east and the Molineux house to the west (and, just beyond the latter, John Hancock's house, a marker for which on the State House grounds is the only

memorial of that era of large estates on Beacon Street). Considering what a landmark the Bowdoin house was in eighteenth-century Boston, it is curious that no pictures of it survive. What Kershaw identifies as "the only surviving representation"—a distant view in a painting of the Park Street Church—is more likely the Molineux house (*James Bowdoin*, p. 86). The original three-story Erving house was considerably improved by Bowdoin, with various neoclassical touches. The clapboards in front, for example, were replaced with wide, close-fitting boards, shipped from Bowdoinham, to simulate stone (Kershaw, *James Bowdoin*, p. 100). The house was torn down in the 1840s, a little too soon to be photographed; much of the garden had already disappeared when Asher Benjamin built townhouses early in the nineteenth century along Bowdoin (originally, Middlecott) Street. For more details, see Robert M. Lawrence, *Old Park Street and Its Vicinity* (Boston, 1922), pp. 139-142. It is still something of a Bowdoin neighborhood: the governor and others of the family rest in the Old Granary Burial Ground around the corner, and not far away is Milk Street, where James Bowdoin I and, later, James Bowdoin III lived.

35. Some further insight into Bowdoin's character comes in the memoirs of his enemy Thomas Hutchinson, the loyalist governor whose career Bowdoin helped wreck: "Mr. Bowdoin's father, from a very low condition in life, raised himself, by industry and economy, to a degree of wealth beyond that of any other person in the province, and, having always maintained a fair character, the attention of the people was more easily drawn to the son, and he was chosen, when very young, a member for Boston, and, after a few years, was removed to the council. He found more satisfaction in the improvement of his mind by study, and of his estate by ecomony, than in the common business of the general assembly. . . In general he was, in those times, considered rather as a favourer of the [royal] prerogative. . . But Mr. Temple, the surveyor-general of the customs, having married Mr. Bowdoin's daughter, and having differed with governor Bernard, and connected himself with Mr. Otis, and others in opposition, Mr. Bowdoin, from that time, entered into the like connexions. The name of a friend to liberty was enough to make him popular. Being reserved in his temper, he would not have acquired popularity in any other way. His talents for political controversy, ecpecial-

ly when engaged in opposition, soon became conspicuous. He had been used to metaphysical distinctions, and his genius was better adapted to entangle and darken, than to unfold and elucidate." *History of the Colony and Province of Massachusetts-Bay* (Cambridge, Mass., 1936), vol. 3, p. 211.

36. On Bowdoin's role as a major absentee landowner in Maine, see Gordon E. Kershaw, *The Kennebeck Proprietors 1749-1775* (Portland, 1975). After the Revolution, he also invested in Ohio lands.

37. James Bowdoin II, *A Philosophical Discourse, addressed to the American Academy of Arts and Sciences* (Boston, 1780), pp. 10-20.

38. Following Bacon's method, Bowdoin explained, meant that scientists "proceeded on fact and observation, and did not admit of any reasonings or deductions, but such as clearly resulted from them." *Discourse*, p. 28.

39. *Discourse*, p. 29.

40. For an account of Bowdoin's behavior during the crisis, see David P. Szatmary, *Shays' Rebellion: The Making of an Agrarian Insurrection* (Amherst, 1980), pp. 70-90. Bowdoin's post-Revolutionary political career has had its admirers; W. A. Robinson, for example calls him "'the great governor' of that long interval between the departure of Gen. Gage and the inauguration of John A. Andrew." "James Bowdoin," *Dictionary of American Biography* (New York, 1929), vol. 2, p. 499. Several conflicting revisionist accounts of the political and economic situation in Massachusetts in the 1780s can be found in Gross, *In Debt to Shays*.

41. A French visitor quickly noticed this: "Mr. Hancock is not as highly educated as his rival, Mr. Bowdoin, and seems even to scorn learning. Bowdoin is more esteemed by men of education; Hancock is more loved by the people." J. P. Brissot de Warville, *New Travels in the United States of America 1788* (Cambridge, Mass., 1964), p. 105.

42. The fact that James Bowdoin III produced no heir also tended to diminish the family's historical clout; although a nephew took the name in order to claim the inheritance, the direct James Bowdoin family line ended in 1811. The closest the defunct Bowdoins had to a champion was a collateral relation, Robert Winthrop, Sr., who collected many of the family papers now in the Massachusetts Historical Society and at Bowdoin College. Other lines of the family have survived and carry the name Bowdoin.

43. For details of the legislative history, see "College History: Founding," BCSC, which includes copies of extracts from the journals of the House and Senate, 1788-94. While the parliamentary steps can be traced, little survives in the official record that would convey the nature of the debate.

44. In New England, only Harvard (1636), Brown (1764) and Bates College (1855) have bicameral governing bodies. In the case of Harvard, for example, the seven-member Corporation is so small, it is more analogous in operation to the executive committee which in recent times at Bowdoin has conducted much of the Governing Boards' business.

45. Quoted in Arthur Latham Perry, *Williamstown and Williams College* (Norwood, Mass., 1899), pp. 210-211. Some of the arguments echoed those being made in Maine—e.g., "Williamstown, being an enclosed place, will not be exposed to those temptations and allurements which are peculiarly incident to seaport towns," p. 211.

46. Leverett Wilson Spring, *A History of Williams College* (Boston, 1917), pp. 42-44. The campaign by orthodox Congregationalists to charter Amherst College in the 1820s was also opposed by Harvard, this time on religious grounds.

47. On the nature of the legislative process in Massachusetts, see Jackson Turner Main, *Political Parties before the Constitution* (Chapel Hill, 1961), pp. 83-119, and Robert Zemsky, *Merchants, Farmers and River Gods: An Essay on Eighteenth-Century American Politics* (Boston, 1971), which deals with the pre-Revolutionary period but has some relevance for the early Republic as well.

48. The charter Trustees were Reverend Thomas Brown, Reverend Samuel Deane, John Frothingham, Reverend Daniel Little, Reverend Thomas Lancaster, Hon. Josiah Thacher, David Mitchel, Reverend Tristram Gilman, Reverend Alden Bradford, Thomas Rice, and William Martin, in addition to an as-yet unnamed president and treasurer.

The charter Overseers were Edward Cutts, Thomas Cutts, Simon Frye, David Sewall, Nathaniel Wells, Reverend Moses Hemmenway, Reverend Silas Moody, Reverend John Thompson, Reverend Nathaniel Webster, Reverend Paul Coffin, Reverend Benjamin Chadwick, Reverend Samuel Eaton, Reverend Samuel Foxcroft, Reverend Caleb Jewett, Reverend Alfred Johnson, Reverend Elijah Kellogg, Reverend Ebenezer Williams, Reverend Charles Turner, Daniel Davis, Samuel Freeman, Joshua Fabyan, William Gorham, Stephen Longfellow, Sr., Joseph Noyes, Isaac Parsons, Robert Southgate, John Wait, Peleg Wadsworth, William Widgery, Reverend Ezekiel Emerson, Jonathan Ellis, Jonathan Bowman, Edmund Bridge, Daniel Cony, Henry Dearborn, Dummer Sewall, Samuel Thompson, John Dunlap, Francis Winter, Nathaniel Thing, Alexander Campbell, and Paul Dudley Sargent, plus the president and a secretary of the corporation.

49. James Bowdoin III to the Overseers of Bowdoin College, *Collections of the Maine Historical Society*, 7th ser., vol. VI, Part II, pp. 210-211.

50. Committee of the Overseers to James Bowdoin, 27 December 1794, *MHSC*, 7th Ser., vol. 6, Part 2, pp. 211-212.

51. William D. Williamson, "Sketches of the Lives of Early Maine Ministers," *Collections of the Maine Historical Society*, 2nd ser., vol. 6 (1891), p. 187.

52. A member of the Harvard class of 1760, Deane was appointed butler and keeper of the library after graduation and in 1763 was appointed to a three-year term as tutor. According to Shipton, "the one thing which the College never forgot about his tutorship was the occasion when a stranger whom he was showing through the museum asked the history of a rusty sword. 'I believe,' said Tutor Deane, 'it is the sword with which Balaam threatened to kill his ass.' 'No,' protested the visitor, 'Balaam had no sword, but only wished for one.' 'True,' said the Tutor, 'but that must be the one he wished for.'" *Sibley's Harvard Graduates*, vol. 14, pp. 591-592.

53. To historians of Maine, Deane is best known for his diary, edited and published (with biographical essays) by William Willis in 1849 as *Journals of the Reverend Thomas Smith and the Reverend Samuel Deane, Pastors of the First Church in Portland.* (Smith had been minister almost forty years when Deane joined him as associate in 1764; Smith died in 1795, leaving Deane as sole minister until 1809, when he was joined by Ichabod Nichols.) Deane's entries, interleaved in his almanac, are a major source for early Portland history but unfortunately convey little information about the new college, other than to note meetings of the Trustees.

54. On the cult of country life, especially its moral character, see Tamara Plakins Thornton, *Cultivating Gentlemen: The Meaning of Country Life among the Boston Elite, 1785-1860* (New Haven, 1989).

55. Reverend Samuel Deane, D. D., *The New England Farmer, or Georgical Dictionary* (Worcester, Mass., 1790), pp. 1-8. There was a second edition in 1797 and a much expanded version, long after Deane's death, in 1844.

56. James Bowdoin II also cited the *Georgics,* which he saw as a didactic poem echoing the same quest for useful knowledge as had inspired the new American Academy. *Discourse,* p. 8. Being able to translate the poem was an entrance requirement at Bowdoin and many other colleges through much of the nineteenth century. Although some writers have been skeptical about the usefulness of the *Georgics* to a real farmer, Virgil did know something about agriculture; see M. S. Spurr, "Agriculture and the *Georgics,*" in Ian McAuslan and Peter Walcot, eds., *Virgil* (New York, 1990), pp. 69-93.

57. Reverend Samuel Deane, D. D. *Pitchwood Hill. A Poem. Written in the Year 1780. . .* (Portland, 1806). For a context for this sort of poetry, see Lawrence Buell, *New England Literary Culture* (Cambridge, 1986), p. 476.

58. Stephen A. Marini, "Religious Revolution in the District of Maine, 1780-1820," *Maine in the Early Republic,* pp. 121-125.

59. However liberal his theology, Deane's politics were conventionally Federalist. His 1794 Election Sermon urged Governor Adams and the General Court to educate "intelligent republican rulers; as on [them] depend the peace, prosperity, and perpetuity of the state." The alternative was "an ignorant people. . . excited by an eloquent demagogue to rebel. . . and introduce anarchy, confusion and ruin." *A Sermon, Preached Before His Honour Samuel Adams, Esq. . . May 28th, 1794* (Boston, 1794), p. 17. The copy in Special Collections is from James Bowdoin III's library.

60. *Translatio*—literally, "translation"—was the first step in the Renaissance concept of *imitatio,* the process by which artists and poets tried to reproduce in their own idiom the masterworks of the classical world. See, e. g., Thomas M. Greene, *The Light in Troy: Imitation and Discovery in Renaissance Poetry* (New Haven, 1982), especially on the notion of "historic solitude" in a post-classical age. *Translatio studii* was a concept that reappeared in the eighteenth-century and—if recent writers on republicanism are correct—had considerable influence on eighteenth-century American political theory. As Kenneth Silverman explains, "When a town widened its lanes, when a new college opened its doors, when an extra wharf suddenly became needed, British Americans understood the event as the result of Translation. . . Their language naturally magnified such events, since in their minds each improvement evidenced a larger process that at last would civilize and refine the continent." *A Cultural History of the American Revolution* (New York, 1987), pp. 9-10.

The College's first Commencement was held in the First Parish Meeting House while it was still under construction. Built in 1806 to replace a church that stood farther south on Maquoit Road, the church was the site of Bowdoin's Commencements until it was pulled down in 1845 to make way for the present First Parish Church.

Joseph McKeen (1757-1807), Bowdoin's first president, was a Dartmouth graduate who came to the College from Beverly, Massachusetts, where he had been a popular and well-respected Congregational minister.

Chandler's Band (at left) has been playing at Bowdoin Commencements for more than a century. This photograph from about 1900 shows the graduating class forming a double line for the president, faculty, and visiting dignitaries to walk through on their way into the First Parish Church.

CHAPTER TWO

The opening of Bowdoin College in 1802 linked two symbols: the pine woods of Maine,
against which stood the first academic building, Massachusetts Hall, and
the ancient rites of the Republic of Letters. Republicanism of another sort—the civic spirit
of the Revolution—inspired the leaders of the infant institution, among them the
Reverend Joseph McKeen and the diplomat and dilettante James Bowdoin III.
The early years of the new century saw a widening gap between the elite who patronized
the College and the majority of Maine's population, between the established Congregationalists
and the backcountry dissenters, even between young women of the Republic and
their collegiate brothers and cousins, as the letters of Eliza Southgate reveal.

A STAGE IN THE FOREST

Late in the morning of 2 September 1802, the people of Brunswick were treated to a sight no one had ever before seen in the District of Maine. At half past eleven, a solemn procession of dignitaries came out of the south door of the three-story brick "College"—a building that still smelled of fresh paint and new plaster—and symbolically wrapped themselves in the academic garment of the ages. "The interest excited in the public mind, by so novel and important a transaction, in a country so recently inhabited only by the savages of the wilderness, drew together the greatest concourse of spectators ever witnessed in the District of Maine," reported the Portland *Gazette* four days later. "The meetinghouse not being large enough to contain one fourth part of the people assembled, a stage was erected, under a grove of pines upon the plains, on which the several ceremonies took place. Notwithstanding the concourse was so great, the utmost decency, order and attention was shewn; and the solemnities were performed without any interruption."[1]

First in line was the Committee of Arrangement, followed by the secretaries of the two Boards, one bearing the charter and seal and the other the Laws of the College. The treasurer carrying the keys was next, then Samuel Deane as vice president, the Trustees two by two,

the president and the professor-elect, the president and vice president of the Overseers, the other Overseers two by two, and, at the rear, the local clergy and various "gentlemen of distinction invited to dine at the Hall." Once the dignitaries had taken their places on "a stage in the forest," as the Trustees' minutes describe it, Deane told the audience that the president of the Board of Overseers, Daniel Davis, would announce the name of the College's first building. In the words of the *Gazette*, Davis "declared that in honor of the State which had so generously founded and endowed the institution, the name of the building was ever to be, *Massachusets Hall.*" The Reverend Elijah Kellogg "then addressed the throne of grace with an animated and appropriate prayer," followed by a speech in English by Davis. The new president responded in Latin and was invested in office by the delivery of the seal, charter, and keys. He gave his inaugural address in English, to which Deane replied, followed by a prayer by the Reverend Thomas Lancaster. The singing of "an appropriate Psalm" brought that portion of the ceremony to a stately close. Next it was the turn of John Abbot to be inducted as the College's first professor of languages. He gave his inaugural in Latin, and the historic event ended with more singing.

Returning to Massachusetts Hall, the company dined—it would have been early afternoon by then—and afterwards (as the *Gazette* reported) fired volley upon volley of toasts. To the governor of the Commonwealth! To our forefathers, whose enterprise, perils, and perseverance laid the foundations of our inheritance! To the enlightened legislature of Massachusetts, which founded and generously endowed this seminary! To the memory of the late Governor Bowdoin, the philosopher, statesman, and Christian! To the Hon. James Bowdoin, Esq., the patron and benefactor of this institution—may his noble example provoke others to love and goodness! To the Town of Brunswick—may its inhabitants and the students of this College dwell together in unity and happiness! To our sister colleges in America and throughout the world—may they be sureties of sound doctrine, legitimate science, and pure virtue! And finally (the Reverend Dr. David Tappan, the Hollis Professor of Divinity at Harvard, having been called upon to round off the salute) to the District of Maine—may it be as distinguished for its knowledge, piety, and virtue as it is for its local and temporal advantages![2]

This ritual of induction for president and professor had roots in the medieval university, as interpreted for New England by 166 years of Harvard ceremonial. But other links with the cosmopolitan world of maritime Massachusetts were also evident that day. The new college building may have seemed plain, even austere, but a three-story structure of brick in the new Federal style was a novelty on the plains of Brunswick, and it would have at least suggested to those who traveled not only the "colleges" at Harvard but also the domestic architecture of the merchant-princes of Boston and Salem and Newburyport.[3] The new president himself—the Reverend Joseph McKeen, of the Dartmouth class of 1774—had been persuaded to leave the large and prosperous parish of Lower Beverly, another rich Federalist seaport, north of Salem, to take up the supervision of the new College's eight students and enjoy the company of its single professor.[4]

McKeen's inaugural address—which was to become one of the canonical texts in Bowdoin's understanding of itself—reflects an awareness of how momentous a step the friends of learning and good order had taken for the District. The organization of "a literary institution" in Maine was an important epoch in its history, he reminded his audience. For more than a century, "the sword of the wilderness was a terror" to the scattered and defenseless inhabitants, who were plagued by the Indians and the French and whose remote coastal settlements were far from the civilizing influence of education. Moreover, "deep and strong prejudices" against the district's soil and climate had retarded immigration. "These mistakes have yielded to the correcting hand of time," he noted, "and Maine is rapidly advancing to that state of maturity, in which, without being forcibly plucked, she will drop from her parent stock"—a statement that must have gratified the separationists in the crowd.

Alluding to a well-known passage in Isaiah that had echoed throughout New England since the seventeenth century, McKeen said: "While the wilderness is literally blossoming like the rose, and the late howling desert by the patient hand of industry is becoming a fruitful field, it is pleasing to the friends of science, religion, and good order, to observe a growing disposition in the inhabitants to promote education; without which, the prospect of the future state of society must be painful to the reflecting and feeling mind."[5] Attempting to find some middle ground between disorderly enthusiasts of religion and the rationalists who thought human wisdom sufficient for happiness, McKeen outlined a view of education which promoted the moral health of both the individual and the body politic. Without knowledge of "the duties of his station in life," a man cannot act his part honorably, he explained; without an informed sense of how to spend his time, "he will be strongly tempted to abandon himself to sensual gratifications." An education in fixed principles was also what saved a man from falling "prey to the delusive arts of any pretender to superior knowledge, especially in medicine and theology." Anxious as all the established clergy were over the success of Methodists, Baptists, Universalists, and other unorthodox sects in the district, McKeen warned his listeners of the danger of seeking "instruction on the subject of his eternal interests as he can obtain from the most illiterate vagrants, who understand neither what they say, nor whereof they affirm." Whatever may have been the case in an earlier age of direct revelation, McKeen insisted that "only by reading, study, and meditation" could a minister today prepare himself for his calling.

"That the inhabitants of this district may have of their own sons to fill the liberal professions among them, and particularly to instruct them in the principles and practice of our holy religion, is doubtless the object of this institution; and an object it is, worthy of the liberal patronage of the enlightened and patriotic legislature, which laid its foundation, and of the aid its funds have received from several gentlemen, especially that friend of science"—a word whose usage at that time embraced all knowledge, not just the natural sciences—"whose name it bears."

There followed the most memorable statement any Bowdoin president has made to date:

It ought always to be remembered, that literary institutions are founded and endowed for the common good, and not for the private advantage of those who resort to them for education. It is not that they may be enabled to pass through life in an easy or reputable manner, but that their mental powers may be cultivated and improved for the benefit of society. If it be true, that no man should live to himself, we may safely assert, that every man who has been aided by a public institution to acquire an education and to qualify himself for usefulness, is under peculiar obligations to exert his talents for the public good.[6]

McKeen went on to express the conventional views of his time on disciplining young men and on instilling in them the habits of industry and application—indeed, even his use of the phrase "the common good" was something of a commonplace by his day.[7] But what is important in understanding his inaugural is not to search for any originality in it—most other Congregational ministers would have said something similar, given the formulae, the fund of metaphors and Biblical allusions, that were the stock of every educated writer of sermons—but to see how, taking advantage of the novelty of the occasion, McKeen lays claim to a certain spiritual and intellectual ground. The ceremony itself had served to sacralize a literal piece of ground, to declare to the world, or at least to the inhabitants of the district, that what had been a hillside on the edge of Brunswick now was fraught with new significance.[8] Urbane and convivial, the festivities in the new hall after McKeen had spoken were a means of affirming that the College had allied itself with the values of the coastal elite. In essence, the new president's own remarks proclaimed three principles: that the College would serve to foster order and stability in the district, that producing a supply of learned clergymen would be its other chief mission, and that in order to sustain these two purposes the College would honor the republican ideology of the young nation's founders.[9]

On all three points, there was to be lively debate for at least a century. From our own perspective, it is the third point that is likely to be the most perplexing—but, then, the notion of what it meant to be a good republican was not entirely clear to McKeen's contemporaries, either. To older Federalists of, say, Samuel Deane's generation, the ideological heritage of the Revolution was so evident, it required little elucidation. A handful of words—"virtue" and "liberty" on the one hand, "luxury" and "corruption" on the other —were enough to evoke this legacy in any educated mind.[10] Drawing upon the anti-monarchical writings of seventeenth-century English commonwealthmen and, more remotely, upon notions of civic humanism produced in the Italian city-states of the Renaissance, the American patriots of the Revolutionary generation had adopted a vocabulary of republicanism that helped to turn a quarrel over mismanaged government into a full-scale war for independence.[11] This Whig ideology did not vanish after Yorktown; on the contrary, some elements of it were intensified, once Americans realized their own nation was to be assailed by all the evils that had threatened the old republics of Europe—or at the very least would be subject to the cycles of history in which "civilization" was only one step short of decay.

There had long been an overwrought quality to this rhetoric of republicanism—British government had rarely been as tyrannical or as conspiratorial as pamphleteers and orators on this side of the Atlantic had pictured it—and, in a post-revolutionary age, this anxiety had to find other outlets. In the case of the New England elite of the 1790s, the enemies of all things decent were no longer the Tory ministers in London but the French and their Jacobin sympathizers in America. As a result of Jefferson's victory in the presidential election of 1800, Federalist hostility turned to frenzy, especially as the results of the president's embargo of all European trade in 1807 began to ruin the commerce of New England.

In the ideal world of Massachusetts Federalists like McKeen, society would exist in equilibrium. There would be a large class of trustworthy yeomen, plowing their ancestral soil and sending some of their sons to crew the ships on which New England's prosperity depended. There would be a somewhat smaller group of "middling" folk, providing the services and trades that linked the seaboard towns and the countryside. And there would be an even smaller elite of "the great and the good"—the prosperous and the civic-minded—who would apply the advantages that wealth and education had given them to assure the civic health of the entire commonwealth. This would be a society almost as hierarchical as its eighteenth-century models, although with enough "bend" to it so that the most talented (say, a particularly intelligent clergyman) could rise above modest origins. Above all, it would be a deferential society, in which each citizen would find the meaning of his civic life in perfectly performing his duty and in meeting the obligations he owed others, below and above him. (All men might vote, but a few leading men would be best equipped to help them determine how to vote.) And it would be a stable society, in which no one would seek to undermine the

Thought to be the only adult portrait of James Bowdoin III taken from life, this miniature belongs to the Bowdoin College Museum of Art. Edward Green Malbone (American, 1777-1807), James Bowdoin III, 1804. Watercolor on ivory, 3 3/16 x 2 1/4 inches. Gift of Mrs. Dorothy Hupper in honor of Kenneth C. M. Sills '01 and Mrs. Sills h '52. Bowdoin College Museum of Art, 1951.7.

essential order of things by striving to gain too much wealth and power and thereby courting the ever-present dangers of licentiousness and corruption.[12]

Something more than bad behavior was meant by those terms; they were concepts of political as much as personal morality. Similarly, when McKeen used the word "virtue"—certainly the key term in understanding his inaugural address—he was suggesting something far beyond individual goodness (though he was suggesting that, too). "Virtue" encoded that entire body of republican political philosophy, as most of his listeners would have recognized. So, too, his exhortation to serve the "common good." In later years, the phrase came to be taken to mean a vague charitable benevolence or perhaps a willingness to sacrifice a more lucrative career for one of more obvious public benefit. But to McKeen and his friends and patrons, the common good was a *political* ideal that reached to the very heart of their society. It was the *res publica*, the "public thing," a concept representing something more than the sum of each individual's contributions to the commonwealth. It was a corporate and communal good, one to which every selfish desire had to be sacrificed. The enemies of this good were those who threatened the time-honored bonds of that classic republican ideal—be they Jeffersonians, religious dissidents, or ambitious, striving men who did not know their place. Friends of this good sought to preserve it through institutions like the new college in Maine.

In view of what came later, there is something to admire in this version of Federalism—its frugality, its civic-mindedness, its respect for learning, its hatred of ostentation and waste. But there were at least two problems with it: it simply didn't work in a burgeoning commercial economy, and the Jeffersonians were republicans, too. These problems were to confound the men who led Bowdoin College in the early republic.

JAMES BOWDOIN III

One dignitary who was not present that day, who in fact never visited the campus as far as the records indicate, was the College's leading donor. It is one of many unanswered questions about James Bowdoin III's life exactly why he decided to endow the institution and then kept his distance from most of its affairs. He was, of course, available to the Boards members who visited Boston. But aside from an occasional complaint about the slowness of the College's establishment or suggestions for modeling the new buildings after Hollis Hall at Harvard, Bowdoin seems to have been occupied with his own affairs. He served on the Harvard Corporation from 1792 to 1799, he was becoming more involved with his horticultural and agricultural pursuits on Naushon Island and elsewhere, and—while not as vigorous a businessman as his father—he had a small empire of undeveloped land to look after in the district. (Much of his time seems to have been devoted to trying to keep his agents diligent in evicting squatters from his Maine property and recovering damages for timber cut by trespassers). And ill health continued to plague him until his early death at age fifty-nine.[13]

Despite the survival of his letterbooks and his engagement in a well-documented public life that brought him into contact with many of the notable figures of his day, James Bowdoin III remains difficult to bring into focus. A comparison of the portrait of his father by Robert Feke in 1748 and that of Bowdoin by Gilbert Stuart about half a century later is especially revealing.[14] The smooth self-satisfaction and commanding air of the father and the sense of vulnerability, of self-doubt, in the son have a good deal to do with changing conventions of portraiture. But it is the manner in which these two family portraits work as cultural artifacts that is worth noting: the elder Bowdoin—whose silk waistcoat has more life than his face—is presented as a cool and lordly figure, painted on an aristocratic scale. The younger Bowdoin is a private citizen, a well-to-do one, to be sure, but someone living in a society in which grandiloquent pictorial gestures are becoming somewhat suspect. The relationship beneath the surface of these two men is barely known to us. The younger seems to have wanted to honor the elder's memory while attempting to create a selfhood of his own. Despite his undoubted sense of *pietas*, the younger Bowdoin did not share his father's politics. The only son of one of the most conservative leaders of the mercantile and banking circles of post-Revolutionary Boston became a Jeffersonian Republican, a member of a party bitterly opposed to much of what his father's friends represented.

There are several reasons James Bowdoin III might have decided to endow a college in Maine, any one of them sufficient, but none of them documented. Sometime in the early 1790s, he seems to have become disenchanted with Harvard, possibly as a result of its increasingly Federalist tone.[15] Moreover, as a man of Jeffersonian sentiments, he appreciated the urgency of establishing educational institutions on the rapidly developing frontier. As a major landowner in Lincoln County, he knew that the existence of such an institution in the district would sooner or later enhance the attractiveness of his properties. As the pious son of a worthy father vilified by the Hancock faction and the Shaysites, he could anticipate that the future fame of the institution would keep the family name bright. And as an only son in a childless union of his own—he had married his first cousin Sarah Bowdoin in 1780—he may have felt that he had a dynastic obligation to keep the family name alive. Some combination of these factors could have prompted him to act; there may have been some other stimulus—perhaps a feeling that he had not yet done anything to equal his father's accomplishments—but to date his inner life has escaped a biographer's scrutiny.

If we can only guess at his motivation, we do know of his schooling and of some of his views on the subject. He had had the usual education of a young man of good family, at Boston Latin School and then, as a member of the Class of 1771, at Harvard, where he managed to avoid too direct a role in the student disorders of the pre-Revolutionary era. He received his degree *in absentia*, however, because his father had sent him on the first of two voyages to Europe in hopes that the sea air would improve his health.[16] Given the rigors of eighteenth-century travel, this seems an improbable rationale, but there was a well-established belief that sea travel was a restorative, and the opportunity both to escape his father's kind but ever-watchful eye and to encounter a society less earnest than that of mercantile Boston surely raised the young man's spirits.

Bowdoin senior was a solicitous father. The notion of arranging an advantageous match for young "Jemmy" had long been a concern, for example. Sugar was the petroleum of the eighteenth century, in terms of the huge profits it brought through international trade, and the prospect of an alliance between the Boston Bowdoins and a West Indian nabob, for example, must have been an attractive one in a family known for its skill at marrying well. "The proposal you make about connecting honest Jemmy with the daughter of your brother at Jamaica is very agreeable," James Bowdoin II wrote in 1767 to George Scott, husband of his wife's sister and governor of Grenada and Dominica. "He is fourteen; not ugly; will have the best education this Country affords; bids fair to be a clever fellow. . . To be short, the boy is at your disposal."[17]

Nothing came of that scheme, and four years later, when James Bowdoin III sailed for England, his father provided him with letters of introduction to Benjamin Franklin and other distinguished men and entrusted him to the care of another well-connected uncle, Duncan Stewart. The elder Bowdoin at this point believed his son's "inclinations lead him to merchandize," as at least three generations of Bowdoins had been inclined before him, and he asked his English business associates to show the young man how the great shipping houses operated. He hoped he would learn bookkeeping

and perfect his commercial French. Writing from Boston, he urged upon his son the virtues of temperance and recommended that he "unite the *utile dulci*, the useful with the agreeable: in which case improvement & entertainment will go together."[18] Young Bowdoin's grandfather John Erving sent even more good advice, again urging upon him moderation in drink and diet and reminding him that he would be expected to move in the company of gentleman who would closely judge his manners. Speak evil of no man nor of any country, Erving wrote, "especially the place of your Nativity which has been so notoriously practiced by many of the Youth of this Country[;] when abroad they have joined in Ridiculing the place of their birth to their great shame & dishonour."[19]

When Bowdoin senior learned of Jemmy's interest in reading law at Oxford, he acquiesced, thinking that such study might be useful to a future merchant.[20] He also urged him to read "An Essay on a Course of Liberal Education for Civil and Active Life," by the progressive Joseph Priestley, an early attempt to make the classical curriculum more "useful" by introducing into it what we would now call social studies—history, political economy, and political theory.[21] Priestley shared an interest in optics with the elder Bowdoin, who saw him as a fellow scientist rather than as a political radical and religious dissenter, and who thought his son would profit from a term at Dr. Priestley's academy at Warrington. "If you mean to be distinguished in your profession, or as a man of sense among gentlemen, now is the time for you to exert yourself: in which case you will not suffer the amusements and dissipations of England to divert you from your purpose."[22]

Probably on the advice of his well-connected English relations, Jemmy was entered instead as a gentleman-commoner at Christ Church, the most aristocratic of the eighteenth-century Oxford colleges. However unruly the Harvard of the 1760s had been, Bowdoin was now exposed to a new level of personal freedom and adolescent hedonism: it was said of Christ Church at this period that the only volumes an undergraduate needed to open were the stud book and the racing calendar. He had only a taste of it, for by autumn he was back in London, causing his father to wonder why he quit Oxford so precipitously and to hope that at least he was improving his French.[23] The presence in London of the only son of one of the richest men in North America had surely not escaped polite notice, and there is more than a hint in the family correspondence that Jemmy—who had taken up the study of riding, fencing, dancing, and a French that doubtless was anything but commercial—sampled the pleasures of the *jeunesse d'orée* of the time. Surely his father thought so, for he complained that Jemmy had overspent his ample allowance. This was not the year abroad his family had envisioned. They were glad to see him safely home that spring.

Despite the parental frugality, young Bowdoin—again seeking relief for his chronic ill health—set out in 1774, like a young English milord, with his friend Nicholas Ward Boylston on the Grand Tour. They sailed to Naples and then traveled north and by way of Rome, Florence, Lyons, and Amsterdam reached London in the autumn. His artistic interests, perhaps awakened on his previous sojourn, now had the opportunity to flourish, and he may have begun accumulating the rooms of paintings and objets d'art that were to enable him to introduce to New England the world of the *dilettanti*. At any rate, he was spending the money on something, for his father's letters are full of alarm. The worsening political situation in Massachusetts not only made it more difficult for his father to pay the son's bills—Bowdoin was having trouble collecting money owed him because debtors were hoarding their cash—but finally made it impera-

James Bowdoin III's sister, Elizabeth (1750-1809), married John (later Sir John) Temple, a Boston native employed there by the British customs service until he was appointed surveyor general of customs in England, and then British consul to the United States. Edward Green Malbone (American, 1777-1807), Elizabeth Bowdoin, Lady Temple, 1804. Watercolor on ivory, 3 3/16 x 2 7/16 inches. Bowdoin College Museum of Art. Gift of Mrs. Dorothy Hupper in honor of Kenneth C. M. Sills '01 and Mrs. Sills h '52. 1951.8.

tive, in April of 1775, for the father to insist that the son return home without delay.

Although he rode with General Washington into Boston in December of 1776 and took him to dine at his grandfather Erving's—according to family tradition, on a piece of salt beef, the only meat Boston could offer that day—Bowdoin spent most of the war out of gunshot tending to the family's mercantile interests. The Revolution put an end to his father's hopes that Jemmy would go to Grenada to collect a large debt owed the Bowdoins by the Scott estate and set himself up as a planter there.[24] Instead, the young man pursued the family business, traveling at least as far as Virginia, where he disposed of cargoes of West Indian sugar and reinvested in hogsheads of tobacco for the Boston market. There is some evidence that he helped provision the Continental Army as well.[25]

In these commercial ventures, he had to draw on that wide range of practical knowledge that had carried his forebears to prosperity, but he had learned to appreciate the more formal varieties of learning as well. Writing to his sister, Lady Temple, in 1793 about her own son's education for the Bar, Bowdoin advised her that "there is such a connexion between all the learned professions that success in any of them very much depends upon a well directed collegiate education in which the rudiments of science are to be deeply laid. . . . Young men who go to college should have before them the expectation of a learned profession, and not be suffered to justify their inattention to study by thinking they will take to other pursuits. For in such cases the mind is left without an object, and is thereby deprived of a necessary stimulus to exertion. . . . My own negligence for the first two

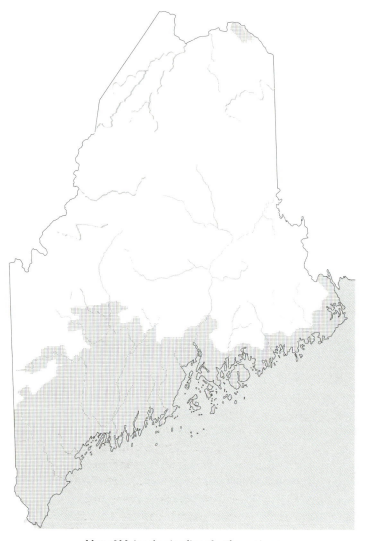

Map of Maine showing line of settlement in 1790.

embassy, which Rufus King was about to leave, but in 1805 had to settle instead for serving his country as minister to Spain, at a time when quarrels over West Florida and Spanish depredations on American shipping had brought relations to a low point. Amid his cultural and political pursuits, Bowdoin often had to turn his attention to Maine—not to the new college so much as to affairs of the Kennebec Proprietors, who were trying to sell their vast holdings before squatters and timber thieves devalued their patrimony.

THE CLASSICAL GROUND

The rude and grasping seemed to have their way; it was the gentlemen who were moving too slowly. "It is high time that measures more spirited were taken to carry into Execution the proposed College," Bowdoin had written to his land agent, Daniel Cony, just over a year after the charter had been granted. "Must the Institution give way to its Administrators or its Administrators to the Institution?"[27] The post-Revolutionary economic slump was a memory by the late 1790s, when a combination of maritime prosperity (due in large part to the Napoleonic wars in Europe) and a rush of new settlers into the district created a society badly in need of collegiate authority.[28] When the Trustees met for the first time—at the courthouse in Portland, on 3 December 1794—they knew they had three tasks to perform if the college described in the charter was ever to welcome students: they had to convert some of its real estate holdings into cash, they had to commission and pay for a building, and they had to select a president. Among much other business—designing a seal, soliciting further donations, squabbling with the other Board—these three tasks occupied much of their semi-annual meetings for the years between the chartering in 1794 and McKeen's inauguration in 1802.[29]

The land was in two parcels: an undefined tract to be carved out of the state's unappropriated public lands and the 1,000 acres in the Town of Bowdoin given by James Bowdoin III.[30] One of the Trustees' first votes was to appoint William Martin, Stephen Longfellow, and John

years I was at college has occasioned me more uneasiness than all the other circumstances of my life."[26]

Such was the education, and what little we know of the educational philosophy, of the patron of the new seminary in the District of Maine. The decade between his father's death in 1790 and Jefferson's election as president saw James Bowdoin move away from the politics of most of his friends and relations and become more identified with what was being called the Democratic-Republican party. He admired its leader, to whom he sent the neo-classical statue of a reclining woman—thought to be Cleopatra, but in fact Ariadne—which can still be seen at Monticello. Bowdoin aspired to the London

Dunlap as a committee "to lay out, under the direction of the committee for the sale of eastern lands, the five Townships granted by the General Court. . . obtaining the best information they can where the most valuable lands are to be found, and to cause the same to be run out and bounded and plans of these to be taken."[31] Five townships in the seventh range north of the Waldo Patent were chosen—four of them, today, are the towns of Sebec, Guilford, and Abbot and the southern, Foxcroft, half of Dover-Foxcroft; the fifth was exchanged for one in the first range which became the town of Dixmont. Unlike the medieval English colleges, which lived off the rents from their agricultural tenants, Bowdoin College wished to sell its property quickly, either to individual settlers or to a speculator. This was common practice on the part of the numerous schools and other institutions that had been endowed with wilderness lands.[32] But it was not to be easy. As the Reverend Alfred Johnson's father remembered, by arguing for so long over rival locations, its sponsors had already lost a valuable opportunity. "During the two years the College lay asleep (from '92 to '94) the best State lands had been selected by other grantees; & the 5 townships given by the Commonwealth of Mass. were of course taken from the less eligible residuum," the younger Johnson recorded. "Timber townships were then not appreciated. My father thinks from the general estimation made at that period, that the true value of the Legislative endowment was diminished one half by the numerous intermediate selections made by others, from what the Gen. Court intended to give it . . . ."[33]

Bowdoin had also given the College $1,000 in specie, deposited in the Union Bank of Boston. At their second meeting, on 4 February 1795 in Portland, the Trustees decided to invest $900 of this "in such securities, as [the treasurer] may think, upon the best information he may obtain, will be most productive."[34] Another gift from Bowdoin that year—a note for a loan to Brigadier Thompson of 823 pounds, four shillings ($2,744), secured by a mortgage of land in Bowdoin and intended to endow a professorship—proved more troublesome;

Thompson had to be reminded to pay the interest. The donor asked that the proceeds be applied to the support of a professor of mathematics and of "natural & experimental Philosophy" (i. e., of science) at the College, the interest being added to the principal until such time as such a professor could be found.[35] Since little could be done with so modest a treasury, the Boards began to search for other friends. Two obvious candidates—William Bingham of Philadelphia and General Henry Knox of Thomaston—failed to perform as wished. Bingham, who owned 2 million acres in Maine, was more interested in Dickinson College in his own state. General Knox, who had started out as a bookseller before achieving fame in the Revolution and fortune in the property boom that followed, sent good wishes—and a book. (Contemporaries, impressed by his house, Montpelier, did not realize how badly he had overextended himself and how close he was to financial ruin.)

From its meager resources, the College paid $40 to one of the Overseers, the Reverend Charles Turner, for expenses he incurred in seeking funds. He had even turned to the federal government for help—not from public funds, but from the legislators' own pockets. Appealing in 1797 in the name of "the interest of Literature, and for the advantage of our District," he asked George Thatcher, who represented Maine in the House, to present a subscription paper "to the Senators and Members of Congress generally." He also wanted the president and vice president of the United States to be solicited for donations.[36] The idea did not get very far. As the years passed, and the Overseers fretted over whether the Trustees were trying to sell the lands vigorously enough, the College found a number of benefactors willing to give books, but few ready to part with cash.

The many delays may explain the testiness that began to appear on the part of the two Boards. News of their disagreement soon reached the Legislature. On 9 November 1797, Daniel Davis petitioned the General Court on behalf of the Board of Overseers to increase the number of Trustees from thirteen to twenty-one, in hopes

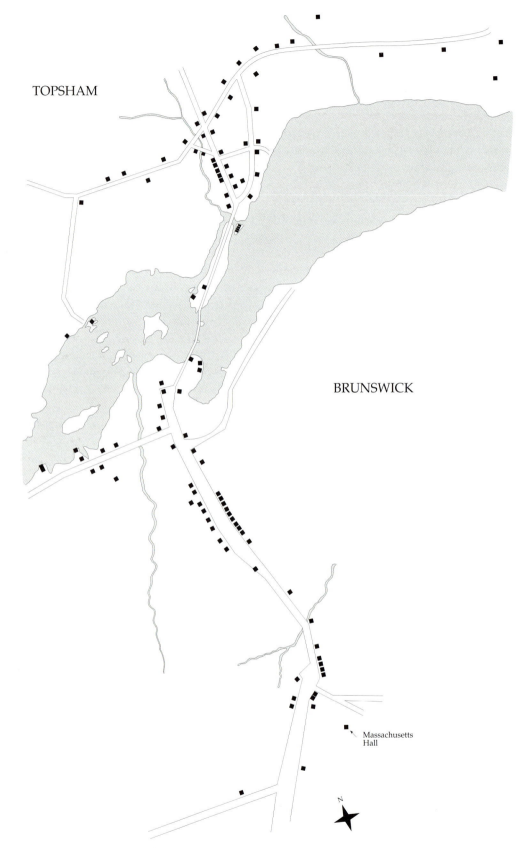

TOPSHAM

BRUNSWICK

Massachusetts
Hall

N

Map of Brunswick and Topsham villages in 1802.

of improving the smaller Board's ability to do business. "It is with a mixture of anxiety and regret," he wrote, "that your petitioners find, after a lapse of three years and a half, and after seven meetings of the Board of Overseers, nothing effectual has been done." The reason, he said, was the difficulty of assembling a quorum because of the distances involved—eighty miles in one Trustee's case. Moreover, "many of the honorable and reverend members of that Board are aged and infirm," suggesting that perhaps the College's affairs were being neglected for reasons that went beyond the condition of the roads. The Overseers had done their best, "constantly and (hitherto) cheerfully," but feared that "one year after another, so precious to the rising generation, is passing away, and the opportunity of furnishing them with the means of useful knowledge."

The Trustees were incensed. In their counter-petition of 18 May 1798, they begged leave "humbly to suggest that as our Corporation is not expressly charged with any particular misconduct, or omission of duty," they were under no obligation to defend themselves. Nonetheless, they wished to point out they had done everything practicable to bring the new College into operation. "We have, by an able surveyor, explored the Townships of land, with which the Honble. Legislature have so generously endowed the College. One of the Townships, being that judged most saleable, we have ordered to be run into lots, that it might meet with more speedy sale, and be more productive; three thousand acres of which are sold; but we must wait one, two and three years, for the payments." A committee to solicit donations had been formed and several of the principal towns of the commonwealth visited, resulting in almost $800 in gifts ("mostly in books"). William Bingham of Philadelphia, the largest landowner in the district, had been approached. The Bowdoin money was drawing interest in the bank; the Bowdoin lands were being surveyed and prepared for sale. The Trustees themselves had given liberally of their own time and money in order to attend to college business. "We hope these things will serve to shew our care and zeal

for the advancement of the Institution, tho' they have not yet proved effectual to enable us [to] support the necessary instruction of Pupils, nor to effect any buildings for their accomodations."

One charge that particularly rankled was that the Trustees were too old for the job. Only one member was "aged and infirm," not "many," the petition declared, and in one instance only had a quorum not assembled. The Overseers' problem, it seemed to the Trustees, was that by meeting at the same time as they did, the larger of the two boards lacked any real business to do, other than indulging its members' whim to contest whatever course of action the Trustees had approved. Moreover, the Overseers lacked any full understanding of the College's finances. "We know of no radical evils under which the Institution labours but the want of money to enable us to put the wise and beneficent design of the Hon'ble. Legislature into effect," said the petition, which was signed by Deane and Frothingham. "We are not at this time able to command more than about fifteen hundred Dollars, nor even this without selling our securities." Rather than increase the number of Trustees, the petition concluded, better halve the size of the Board of Overseers and "assemble them only when Trustees need their consideration of something."[37]

Part of the problem may have been that Bowdoin College still existed only in the minds of its friends. Brunswick had been selected as the place, but after three years no specific site had been chosen. On 19 July 1796, however, the Trustees had met in Brunswick at John Dunning's inn and examined the most obvious site, a slight hill toward the southern side of the settlement. Nehemiah Cleaveland's highly colored reconstruction of the moment deserves to be quoted:

Let us, in imagination, go back to that hour. Brunswick has witnessed many academical processions, but this was the precursor and predestinator of them all. No ordinary promenaders, these who move down the narrow lane from John Dunning's, spread out over the twelve-rod road [today, Maine Street], wind up the little hill, and then wander in groups over the open plain and beneath its bordering pines. What dignity, what picturesqueness, in their very costume,—the cocked hat, the white wig, the broad skirted coat, the tight knee-breeches, and the large bright buckles! Well may they look grave, for a grave question is before them. They are to determine, for all time, where a great seat of learning is to have its home. With them it rests to say whether that tame, uninteresting plain shall become classic ground, enriched thenceforth and hallowed by all delightful associations.[38]

However they were dressed—the description may be accurate for the clergymen at least—their minds were more on property than on posterity. The thirty-acre hillside tract offered as a gift by William Stanwood had a complicated (and, as it later turned out, clouded) title but would do. An adjoining tract of 300 acres was also required, the Trustees argued, but the town agreed to give only 200 of them. The site was about a mile from the falls of the Androscoggin, already a busy—and, at logging time, boisterous—locale with its mills and boatyards, and some three miles from the town's Maquoit Bay landing, to and from which vessels of shallow draft plied the coastal trade. Brunswick, which like many New England towns had been a scattered, semi-rural settlement for the previous forty years, was forming into a more centralized village in the final years of the eighteenth century; a more commercial society began to replace an almost wholly agricultural one.[39] The new College property "anchored" one end of the central street and soon drew into its orbit a new meeting-house that in 1806 replaced the earlier and more isolated structure on the Maquoit road. There is no adequate contemporary description of the original college grounds, but they seem to have included part of a woodlot (later to be known as the Bowdoin Pines) adjoining the open blueberry fields that, until the arrival of the naval air station in the 1940s, stretched as common land down to Middle Bay.

The next step was to design a building—a "college," in the language of the day—to house the new institution. Harvard provided the obvious model, not in its original Georgian buildings, but in the somewhat more stylish Hollis Hall of 1763. The Trustees voted to copy its dimensions and erect a four-story brick structure, 100 feet long and 40 feet wide. They also approved building a house for the College's president, a three-story wooden structure 48 feet by 38, to be "used and occupied for the instruction of such students as may be admitted into the college until the building above mentioned shall be prepared for their reception." But the sale of land moved too slowly to provide the necessary funds, and in 1798 the Trustees had to scale down the brick building to a less ambitious 50 by 40 structure of three stories. The talented Melcher family of housewrights was hired to do the work, which progressed by fits and starts as money trickled in. As late as 1799, the Boards had to replace the lead that had been stolen from the chimneys during a long halt in construction. Captain John Dunlap, Brunswick's leading citizen, was appointed agent to oversee completion of the structure "in a plain manner according to the finishing of Hollis Hall, & that he make all his contracts both for labour & materials, for payment in cash only, in order that the building may be finished in the cheapest manner."[40] A slightly smaller house was constructed for the new president, to the southwest of the academic hall and facing the main road, on a site now occupied by the southern end of the Searles Science Building.

As one might expect, the choice of a first president was not uncontested—there were at least six candidates—but McKeen had strong support. He had presided for sixteen years over the church in Beverly, on the North Shore—so successfully that, once word spread of the College's offer, his parish tried hard to persuade him to stay. (Their previous minister, Joseph Willard, had left to become president of Harvard.) McKeen's parishioners had included some of the richest and most powerful men in eastern Massachusetts—including several Federalist politicians of the "Essex Junto"—and his connections in nearby Salem promised further possibilities for the College's fundraising effort. He moved easily among the gentlemen-scholars of his day and had published several papers as a member of the American Academy of Arts and Sciences. There is an anecdote about him that perfectly captures the notion that a man could be both a Christian and a savant. "On one occa-

40

sion, long remembered in Essex County," writes Nehemiah Cleaveland, "a man was on trial for house-breaking. On the question whether it occurred by night or by day, his life depended. A nice calculation by Dr. McKeen in regard to the precise moment of dawn saved the culprit from the gallows."[41] In terms of the religious factions of the day, McKeen was a fairly moderate Congregationalist, sharing many of the same Arminian (i.e., non-Calvinist) views as Samuel Deane; in 1802 the battle lines between orthodox and liberal had not yet been clearly drawn. (One of the many interesting "what if's" in Bowdoin's history is the question of whether the College might have turned Unitarian had the popular and well-respected McKeen lived longer.)[42]

Above all, McKeen was not a controversialist, a quality that made him admirably suited to an institution struggling to survive in a time of increasing political and sectarian bitterness. He was on good, if not intimate, terms, for example, with his Salem colleague, the diarist William Bentley, one of the very few established New England clergymen to belong to Jefferson's party. One of McKeen's best known efforts was his Fast Sermon of 1801 entitled "A discourse against speaking evil of rulers." At a time when Jefferson was being denounced from many a New England pulpit, McKeen called for restraint. A civil ruler, he pointed out, stood in a fatherly relation to the citizens of the state. Hence the commandment to honor one's father "is considered by all commentators as extending to other relations, civil, as well as natural, and as enjoining servants to obey their masters, and subjects their lawful rulers"—and all the more so, since "civil government is a divine institution." McKeen deplored the way the nation's rulers "have been more vilified and abused than those of any other country" despite the twelve years of peace which the Americans, unlike the Europeans, had enjoyed. But McKeen, a staunch Federalist, was not distressed simply because the nation's first magistrate was under attack. He saw something more menacing at work. "When many people freely and publicly censure and condemn their rulers, the factions, the discon-

tented, and the unprincipled are encouraged to transgress the laws. . . . When licentious tongues and licentious presses are constantly calumimating the rulers, . . . those who wish to be freed from the restraints of law will lose their fear of the government," he said. "Hence arise tumults, riots, opposition to the execution of the laws, insurrections, rebellions and civil wars." Better to tolerate rulers we dislike, he concluded, than loosen "the most wholesome and necessary restraints." Like his fellow devotees of civic virtue, McKeen found himself asking: "Is it impossible for a people to be free without suffering their liberty to degenerate into licentiousness? We are making the experiment. The issue will be highly interesting to ourselves, and to the human race."[43]

The call he answered to leave the comforts of Beverly for the near-wilderness of Maine surely provided a test of this republicanism. McKeen had skillfully negotiated a better arrangement than the Boards had originally offered—not only his salary of $1,000 a year, but the gift of 1,000 acres of college land (as a sort of annuity for his family), and an assurance that he held the job "for good behavior," rather than a fixed term of years—and he was allowed to tour the other colleges and universities of New England before drafting laws for Bowdoin and fixing its curriculum. James Bowdoin III gave him $100 to pay for the move. He had been consulted in advance about the arrangement of rooms in the president's house, and possibly as a result the building was still not ready for occupancy when he arrived in Brunswick. The McKeen family moved temporarily into the "College house" (Massachusetts Hall), where in improvised quarters they set up housekeeping, with the eight undergraduates as fellow lodgers. Only two floors had been finished. The eastern half of the building housed the McKeens (chambers above, parlor in the southeast corner, kitchen in the northeast, pantry in the projection on the side); the western half, the hall and chapel (on the ground floor, where two rooms had been thrown together) and the students' chambers (two rooms upstairs); and a hallway ran through the building, with exterior doors to the north and

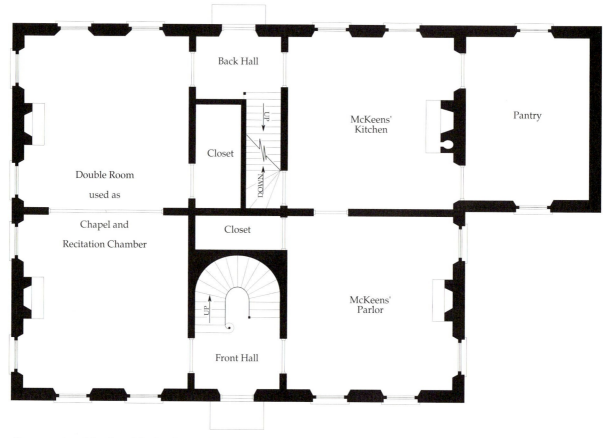

Reconstruction of the plan of the first floor of Massachusetts Hall, ca. 1802. (The arrangement of rooms is based on contemporary descriptions, although details of the central hallways are conjectural.) President and Mrs. McKeen lived in the house with the students until 1805, when they moved to the original President's House, a wooden frame structure on the site of the Searles Science Building. The interior of Massachusetts Hall has been completely rebuilt at least twice, but the McKeens' kitchen fireplace still stands in the room used by President Sills (and President Coles after him) as his office, now the McKeen Study.

south. When McKeen wished to summon the students to prayer, all he had to do was rap on the stairway with his cane. Order had arrived in the District of Maine.[44]

WERE I A MAN

Mrs. McKeen's impressions of her new home, alas, do not survive. There is no reason, however, to doubt that she accepted her responsibilities as a republican wife and mother. As any number of gentlemen could have told her, the new nation needed reliable sons, and it was a mother's duty to instill in these youths the notions of virtue and self-sacrifice which had won the Revolution. (It was the father's duty, too, but the presumption was that he would be so active in the public forum, there would be less opportunity for him to form his sons' character in their earliest years other than by example.) Alice Anderson McKeen produced three sons—Joseph, John,

and James—and two daughters, Alice and Nancy, and outlived her husband by twenty-seven years. Two of the sons went to Bowdoin—John in the Class of 1811, James in 1817—and the daughters married well, Alice to a Thomaston lawyer, William J. Farley 1820, and Nancy to David Dunlap, a leading citizen of Brunswick. As in almost every family of property, the males were allowed to pursue a collegiate and professional education if they wished—though it was by no means expected of them—and the females were either taught at home or sent, for a few years, to one of the many new academies that had appeared throughout New England in the 1790s. Neither daughter could have aspired to anything higher, in terms of formal education, other than what they might have read in their brothers' college texts.[45]

Whether even an academy education was appropriate for a young woman was a subject of much debate in the early republic. Earlier

Though the College was established on a "sandy plain," it was transformed by trees planted along the paths and perimeter in the mid-nineteenth century. This bucolic view of Massachusetts Hall from about 1900 shows what is now the Class of 1916 Path.

notions that females must be either productive or ornamental persisted, alongside a widespread conviction that any education beyond being able to read and write would only serve to "unsex" a woman.[46] But a few more progressive voices were heard. Some were bold, such as Judith Sargent Murray's in Gloucester in the 1790s; she declared women the intellectual equal of men and capable of being taught to earn their own living. Most voices were cautious, however, such as Dr. Benjamin Rush's in Philadelphia; he thought knowledge ought to be diffused more widely among all Americans, women included, for "there have been few great or good men who have not been blessed with wise and prudent mothers."[47] On occasion, one especially compelling voice could be heard, at least within her circle of family and friends, from a house just across the river from Brunswick in Topsham.

In the first years of the nineteenth century, a young woman named Eliza Southgate wrote some of the best letters to have survived from the early republic.[48] To be sure, the district did not lack intelligent and literate women—there was, for example, the novelist Sally Sayward Barrell Keating Wood in York and, among good letter writers, Zilpah Wadsworth Longfellow (the poet's mother) in Portland. But Eliza Southgate's letters are on a different level of accomplishment: upon starting to read the more than 200 pages of them published long after her lifetime, one feels Jane Austen has just come into the room. Southgate is better humored than Austen but has the same eye for social detail as well as the same strain of irony—at age eighteen—that enabled a young woman to survive in a society generally suspicious of female intelligence. And she shared with Jane Austen one of the most valuable gifts anyone living in a provincial society can possess: the ability to find comedy in the minutiae of everyday life.

Eliza Southgate was the daughter of Robert Southgate, a Scarborough doctor turned lawyer turned judge (and a charter Overseer of Bowdoin College), and granddaughter on her mother's side of Richard King, Scarborough's leading citizen. Rufus King, the New York Federalist politician and diplomat, was her uncle; Frederic Southgate, of the Bowdoin Class of 1810, her youngest brother; Longfellow, a distant cousin. After several years at an academy at Medford, Eliza Southgate passed a few more years in a genteel round of visits to her relatives in Portland, Topsham, Bath, Wiscasset, Boston, and New York. In 1801 she found the perfect companion, though they rarely met: her young cousin Moses Porter, of Biddeford, a graduate of the Harvard class of 1799 who, amid preparing himself for the Bar, found the time to answer her long letters. He offered her something of great value—he took her opinions seriously. In return, she poured forth letter after letter, Mozartian in their gaiety and, occasionally, in their depth of feeling.

A niece of both William King and Benjamin Porter (see chapter 3), Eliza Southgate described her visits with their families in Bath and Topsham in her letters. Daughter of Overseer Robert Southgate and sister of Frederic Southgate 1810, Eliza lived before collegiate education was open to women. She was nonetheless a sharp-eyed and witty observer of her life and times.

What Eliza and Moses really felt toward each other is never made clear—one of the fascinations of the correspondence is in trying to read beneath the badinage—and, despite her beauty and charm, he may have been frightened off by the incipient bluestocking in her. "You unaccountable wretch! You obstinate fellow! you malicious, you vain, you . . . provoking creature!" she writes in mock outrage from her uncle's house in Topsham in October of 1801. Moses Porter's long overdue letter has just arrived and she has hidden it in her pocket and the very thought of it upsets her concentration at the card table. "I played wrong, discarded the wrong card, knocked over the candlestick, split my wine." Yet when dinner is announced, she forgets the letter entirely and doesn't think to read it (she tells him) until she retires to bed.[49] Moses Porter's letters to her do not survive, but some of their content can be guessed at, for Eliza Southgate and her cousin soon launched a lively debate on the subject of the education of women.

"I have often thought what profession I should choose were I a man," Eliza Southgate writes from Portland in May of 1802. "I have always thought if I felt conscious of possessing brilliant talents, the *law* would be my choice. Then I might hope to arrive at an eminence which would be gratifying to my feelings. I should then hope to be a public character, respected and admired,—but unless I was convinced I possessed the talents which would distinguish me as a speaker I would be anything rather than a lawyer;—from the dry sameness of such employments as the business of an office all my feelings would revolt, but to be an eloquent speaker would be the delight of my heart. I thank Heaven I was *born* a woman. I have now only patiently to wait till some clever fellow shall take a fancy to me and place me in a situation. I am determined to make the best of it, let it be what it will. We ladies, you know, possess that 'sweet pliability of temper' that disposes us to enjoy any situation, and we must have no choice in these things till we find what is to be our destiny, then we must consider it the best in the world."[50]

The sarcasm was not lost on Moses, for he evidently reminded his cousin that any scheme of female improvement which (in her paraphrase of his words) did not "render one a more dutiful child, a more affectionate wife, &., &."—even Eliza's "&s" carried small barbs—was unworthy of her sex. But virtue must grow out of principle, not momentary impulse, she reminded him, and an educated woman would have a stability of character not commonly found among females. "From having no fixed guide for our conduct we have acquired a reputation for caprice, which we justly deserve," she admitted. "You undoubtedly think I am acting out of my sphere in attempting to discuss this subject, and my presumption probably gave rise to that idea, which you expressed in your last, that however unqualified a woman might be she was always equipt for the discussion of any subject and overwhelmed her hearers with her 'clack'. On what subjects shall I write you? I shall either fatigue and disgust you with female trifles, or shock you by stepping beyond the limits you have prescribed."[51]

The correspondence comes to an abrupt end. Moses Porter caught yellow fever while visiting a ship just arrived from the West Indies and died within a few days, in July of 1802. Eliza Southgate continued to write amusing letters to her relations, married a New York businessman named Walter Bowne in 1803, had two children, and died in the winter of 1809, aged twenty-five, in Charleston, South Carolina, where she had been sent in the hope that a milder climate would strengthen her consumptive body.

In her brief life, Eliza Southgate had followed one of the three paths open to a woman of intelligence—she had married, and married well. The second choice would have been to teach in one of the new female academies, such as Mrs. Rowson's, which she had attended in Medford, or in one of the male academies which, in summer, allowed females to attend. The third choice, at least for a woman of Eliza's connections, would have been a genteel spinsterhood, in which she would have lived with married relatives or perhaps started a school of her own. As Mary Beth Norton has noted, "an educated woman in 1800 had only a modicum more control over her destiny than her uneducated grandmother had had in 1750" and "could not, realistically, aspire to leave the feminine sphere altogether."[52] Women had a well-respected role to play in the new republic, but not one that required a collegiate education; they were expected instead to sustain a supportive home for republican husbands and engage in virtuous childrearing of republican boys. It was not a menial role—"the model republican woman was competent and confident. . . . rational, benevolent, independent, self-reliant."[53] Yet there were a few women bold enough to suggest that some-

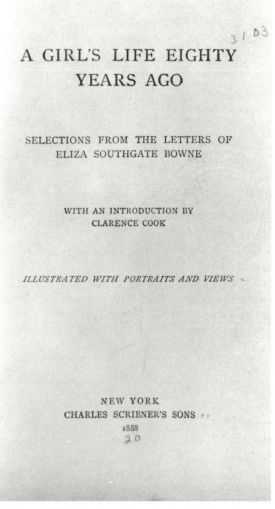

The letters of Eliza Southgate Bowne (1783-1809) contain lively observations about life on the coast of Maine and in New York in the earliest years of the College.

thing was lacking. "Do you suppose the mind of woman the only work of God that was 'made in vain'?" Eliza Southgate asked her cousin.[54]

Such women probably could be found at nineteenth-century Bowdoin—on the edge of the crowd as the academic processions passed or seated amid the flock of genteel ladies who endured hour after hour of the young men's "exhibition" speeches and recitations in the learned languages. It was not until one hundred years after Eliza Southgate exchanged letters with her cousin that the College even welcomed a female into its ranks of honorands—another writer with Bowdoin family ties, Sarah Orne Jewett (Hon. D. Litt., 1901). And it was to be sev-

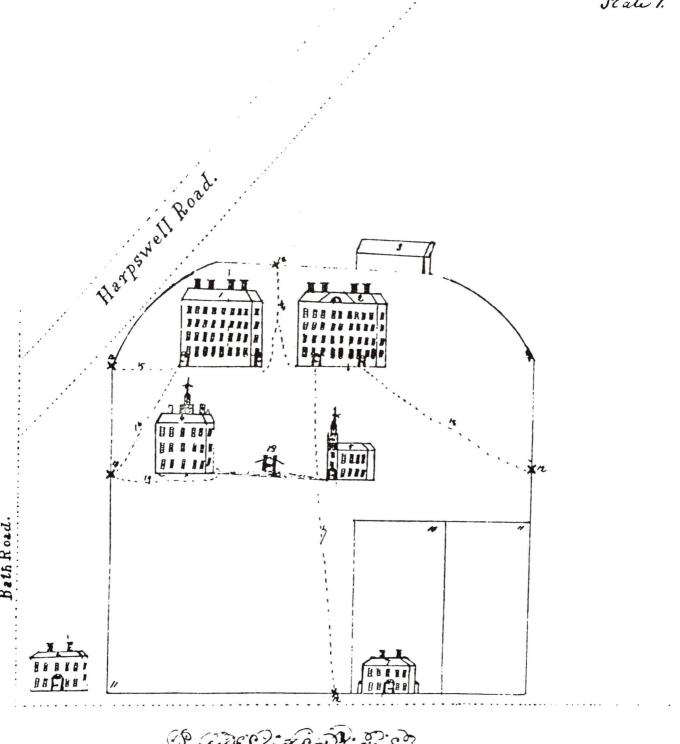

Luther D. Sawyer, Class of 1828, included this hand-drawn map of the Bowdoin campus in his scrapbook, which is dated 1826. The five main buildings are Massachusetts Hall, with its early cupola, since removed; Maine and Winthrop Halls, at the top; the first Chapel, topped by a weathervane; and, below the Chapel, the President's House in its yard. The building in the lower left corner is Moorhead's tavern, and the stick figure in the center is the college pump. The outline at the top is the woodshed. Sawyer calls Maine Street '"Portland Road" and includes the houses of two of the College's neighbors, Col. Pierce (left bottom) and Col. Estabrook (right bottom). The turnstiles in the center of each side of the fence imply wandering livestock.

46

enty years more before the likes of Eliza and Moses could match their wits in a Bowdoin classroom.

TO CIVILIZE THE COUNTRY ABOUT THEM

In August of 1806, Leverett Saltonstall, a young lawyer in Salem, traveled by mail stage to the Penobscot valley in order to settle some family business involving Maine lands. His only regret, he told a friend, was having to miss his own *alma mater*'s Commencement, an event he

Leverett Saltonstall attended Bowdoin's first Commencement, in September of 1806, and reported that "the College is very respectable in its infancy" in spite of pouring rain and muddy streets.

made a point to attend each of the nine years since he graduated. But if he could not be at Harvard, he would look in at Brunswick, he decided, and request a Bowdoin degree *ad eundum*.[55] Marveling at the speed of the mail stage—it took only thirty-one hours, with brief stops for meals, to travel from Salem to Wiscasset—he attended to his business (pausing to admire Camden and Castine) and made his way back to Portland. "I found a number of my acquaintances from Boston, pleasant fellows, on the way to Brunswick Commencement, to which novel celebration I determined to tarry." He saw the sights and attended Dr. Deane's church in the morning and Elijah Kellogg's in the afternoon and by September 1 noticed that Portland was filling up with "a great many respectable people. . . on their way to Brunswick. . . so many that they found accomodations with difficulty." Brunswick was even more crowded the next day, its streets muddied after an all-night storm, but his friend George Thorndike had saved part of a bed for him. "A great many people came into town from Boston, Salem, Portland, etc and many very respectable," he noted. Sharing the Portland stage with him had been one of the more rough-hewn of the College's Overseers, William Widgery, a former privateer turned lawyer; the genteel Saltonstall disliked him instantly ("it is a disgrace to the Commonwealth

that such a man should be one of its Councillors," he sniffed).

The next day proved inauspicious: "it blew a gale in Brunswick and the rain poured down in torrents." The Boards moved the ceremonies to the following day, when the rains let up slightly. "The performances were held in a new meeting [house], which is yet but little more than a shell," Saltonstall wrote. "President McKeen presided with ease and dignity. Seven took degrees and a number of others from other Colleges particularly Cambridge were admitted *ad eundum*. I took a degree of A. M. . . . Col. Thorndike and Mr. Cobb of Portland had made provision for a large and elegant entertainment in a grove, but were obliged to have it in a hall." The party was a success—"I almost imagined myself at Cambridge"—but the ball that evening was "crowded and confused."

He regretted the bad weather. "Had it been pleasant other circumstances were very favorable to have made this first commencement brilliant. Several of the graduates were men of property and large and respectable connexions. Many respectable people from a distance assembled from their invitations, and had it been fair weather we should all have been much pleased and have done much by our representations to have made Brunswick Commencement a place of fashionable resort. But as it was, people were disappointed, and will not again go a three day journey to a celebration which a storm may spoil." On a more positive note, Saltonstall found that the "College is very respectable in its infancy and I hope it will grow in advantages and become a very important seminary. All their efforts are necessary to civilize the country about them."[56]

McKeen was not the only person to leave his mark on the College in those years between his inaugural and that memorable first Commencement. Saltonstall's friend George

The Thorndike Oak, with Burnett House (1858) in the background. Class Day, an important event on the senior-year calendar, was often held under the tree. When it was built in 1894, Searles Science Building obscured much of this view.

Thorndike also had a role to play. One morning about four weeks after McKeen's induction as president, his eight students were standing on the steps of Massachusetts Hall after chapel, remarking on the scene about them. The youngest of their number, thirteen-year-old Thorndike, of Beverly, spied a fresh acorn on the ground and picked it up. Since there were only pines, not oaks, in the vicinity, he was puzzled. Someone later surmised that it had fallen from one of the festoons of oak leaves that had decorated the hall for the inaugural dinner.

Thorndike buried the acorn next to the steps. When McKeen invited the students to cultivate a small plot by way of recreation the following spring, Thorndike remembered his acorn and found that it had sprouted. He tenderly transplanted the seedling to the McKeens' garden, where it was looked after by two succeeding presidents and where it long survived the house in whose yard it had flourished. In 1811 Thorndike died, aged twenty-one, at St. Petersburg, presumably while on business in the Baltic for his father, Colonel Isaac Thorndike, who in addition to being one of the richest merchants in Essex County had extensive landholdings in Maine. The elder Thorndike is said to have visited the tree whenever he passed through town, and perhaps as a result of this and other attention the Thorndike Oak became a landmark of the College. It was the custom, through much of the nineteenth and early twentieth centuries, for the graduating seniors to meet under its branches in order to take their leave of each other as a class. Long after most of McKeen's words had vanished from memory and the Bowdoin family had slipped out of the history books, that tree remained a symbolic link with the earliest days of the College.[57] The New York newspaper editor Edward Page Mitchell tells of venturing over to the Thorndike Oak as a freshman in 1867 and discovering there "five gentlemen of patriarchal aspect but hilarious demeanor in the act of dancing around the tree like children in the game of 'round-the-ring-rosy.'" They were the Class of 1817, back for their fiftieth reunion. "There was a Bowdoin Cummings, a Bowdoin McKeen, youngest son of President's Sills's earliest predecessor, a Bowdoin Moody, a Bowdoin Packard, and a Bowdoin Widgery in that saltatory group—five out of the eight" who had graduated, Mitchell wrote in 1921. "It seems but yesterday; and yet those alumni whose elderly skippings and loyal shoutings these eyes of mine and these ears of mine actually beheld and heard in 1867 had been sophomores in Massachusetts Hall when Waterloo was being fought."[58] The oak lived into the 1970s and survived another decade as a concrete-filled trunk before finally being hauled away.

48

NOTES

BCSC is Special Collections, Hawthorne-Longfellow Library, Bowdoin College.

1. Portland *Gazette*, 6 September 1802.

2. The toasts are taken, almost verbatim, from the *Gazette's* account, as is the order of the ceremony.

3. For an analysis of the meaning of high-style Federal architecture in the district, see Richard M. Candee, "Maine Towns, Maine People: Architecture and the Community, 1783-1820," in Charles E. Clark, James S. Leamon, and Karen Bowden, eds., *Maine in the Early Republic: From Revolution to Statehood* (Hanover, N. H., 1988), pp. 26-61.

4. That the Boards did not choose a president from among their own members is worth noting. Deane would have been the most likely candidate on his merits, but his age—sixty-nine in 1802—may have been seen as a drawback (college presidents were expected to serve lifetime terms), and he was not imposing in public performance. The young John Quincy Adams, who heard him preach at Harvard in 1786, complained that "a whining sort of Tone was employ'd by Mr. Deane, which would have injured the Sermons if they had been good." D. G. Allen *et al.*, eds., *Diary of John Quincy Adams*, vol. 2 (Cambridge, Mass., 1981).

5. "The wilderness and the solitary place shall be glad for them;/And the desert shall rejoice, and blossom as the rose," *Isaiah* 35: 1-2.

6. McKeen's inaugural address is reprinted in full in *Bowdoin* 62, no. 3 (Summer 1989), pp. 3-5. It was originally published as a pamphlet, at the Boards' request, by Joseph Griffin in Brunswick in 1802.

7. "No phrase except 'liberty' was invoked more often by the Revolutionaries than 'the public good,'" writes Gordon S. Wood. "It expressed the colonists' deepest hatreds of the old order and their most visionary hopes for the new day." *The Creation of the American Republic 1776-1787* (Chapel Hill, 1969), p. 55. For other eighteenth-century variations on this theme, see his chapter "The Public Good," pp. 53-65. There was another source for the concept that predated the spread of classical republicanism in New England: Puritan notions of communitarianism, as expressed in John Winthrop's "A Modell of Christian Charity," written aboard the *Arbella* in 1630 ("the care of the publique must oversway all private respects").

8. On the notion of "sacralization" of the New England landscape in general, see John R. Stilgoe, *Common Landscape of America, 1580 to 1845* (New Haven, 1982), pp. 56-57.

9. Whether the College's *primary* mission was to turn out Congregationalist ministers is by no means as well-established as some nineteenth-century sectarians claimed, especially in light of the secular interests of many of those involved in the founding. But it was certainly a major concern for the orthodox: by 1790, only one-fifth of mid-Maine's sixty communities had organized a Congregational church. Congregationalism remained the religion of the prosperous coastal and valley towns; only one out of twenty-four backcountry communities supported such a church. Alan Taylor, *Liberty Men and Great Proprietors* (Chapel Hill, 1990), p. 132.

10. "Luxury" was a moral concept, not a strictly economic one, in eighteenth-century usage. While it could be a good thing, the word implied (according to one dictionary) "all superfluity and excess in carnal Pleasure; sumptuous Fare, Riot." See Susie I. Tucker, *Protean Shape: A Study in Eighteenth-Century Vocabulary and Usage* (London, 1967), pp. 146-147.

11. In addition to Gordon Wood's book above, the essential texts for understanding eighteenth-century republicanism are Bernard Bailyn, *The Ideological Origins of the American Revolution* (Cambridge, Mass., 1967) and J. G. A. Pocock, *The Machiavellian Moment: Florentine Political Thought and the Atlantic Republican Tradition* (Princeton, 1975), which is especially good in explaining the importance of the language used by republicans. For a useful summary of their views and of the criticism of them, see Robert E. Shalhope, "Republicanism and Early American Historiography," *William and Mary Quarterly* 39 (1982), pp. 334-356. For a different point of view, see Joyce Appleby, *Capitalism and a New Social Order: The Republican Vision of the 1790s* (New York, 1984) and Isaac Kramnick, *Republicanism and Bourgeois Radicalism: Political Ideology in Late Eighteenth-Century England and America* (Ithaca, 1990), both of which challenge the theory of the dominance of classical republicanism over American Whigs.

12. To a degree almost impossible to imagine today, many late eighteenth-century Americans were troubled by the notion of "economic man"—a detached entity, free of any communal values, who pursued his own interests in the expanding market economy. According to this view, each citizen had legitimate interests, to be sure, but they were based on irrational and selfish motives and, contrary to Mandeville, the mere sum of all these individual interests could not be a *common* good. As J. E. Crowley writes, "It was assumed that each society had a proper order, but in fact people knew only about the sources of that order—virtue and reason—and were confused about the nature of the order itself. Thus the public good was often negatively defined as the absence of selfishness. It was impossible to give legitimacy to gain which came at the expense of others. . . ." *This Sheba, Self: The Conceptualization of Economic Life in Eighteenth-Century America* (Baltimore, 1974), p. 155.

13. The most complete account of Bowdoin's life to date appears in Clifford K. Shipton, *Sibley's Harvard Graduates* 17 (Boston, 1975), pp. 487-500. The most recent account, now in press, is Richard H. Saunders, "James Bowdoin III (1752-1811)" in *The Legacy of James Bowdoin III* (Brunswick, Me.: Bowdoin College, 1993).

14. On the difficulties of dating the Stuart portrait, see Marvin S. Sadik, *Colonial and Federal Portraits at Bowdoin College* (Brunswick, 1966), pp. 135-151. It is likely to have been painted between 1793 and 1805.

For more on all the Bowdoin portraits, see Linda J. Docherty, "Preserving Our Ancestors: The Bowdoin Portrait Collection," in *The Legacy of James Bowdoin III* (Brunswick, Me.: Bowdoin College, 1993).

15. A search of the Corporation minutes during Bowdoin's tenure reveals no overt reason for his becoming estranged from Harvard; in fact, he continued to attend meetings through the period. But Shipton's speculation that there were political differences is a plausible explanation (p. 491).

16. Bowdoin senior owned a copy of Dr. Ebenezer Gilchrist's *The Use of Sea Voyages in Medicine* (London, 1757), now in BCSC. The author cites many cases of dramatic improvements in health once one had embarked; ". . . there is something in the air at sea highly vivifying and restoring," he writes, while admitting he doesn't know what it is (p. 149). Being at sea was especially recommended for consumptives, "a disease scarcely more frequent than it is fatal; and especially to those of 'the finest spirit, and the finest make' who, from this their frame, seem to be destined early victims to the insidious cruelty of a slow but sure-killing distemper" (p. 147).

17. James Bowdoin II to George Scott, Boston, 8 May 1767, Winthrop-Temple Papers, Massachusetts Historical Society, Boston.

18. James Bowdoin II to James Bowdoin III, Boston, 17 January 1771, Winthrop-Temple Papers.

19. John Erving to James Bowdoin III, Boston, 28 February 1771, Winthrop-Temple Papers.

20. Between 1654 and the Revolution, 98 Americans (more than half of them from Virginia and South Carolina) are known to have attended Oxford or Cambridge, and at least 181 Americans had read law at one of the Inns of Court in London. Christ Church, Oxford, (with 9 Americans) and Trinity, Cambridge (with 13) were the leading choices for a university education. Willard Connely, "Colonial Americans in Oxford and Cambridge," *American Oxonian* 29 (1942), pp. 6-17, 75-77.

21. Reprinted in Ira V. Brown, ed., *Joseph Priestley: Selections from His Writings* (University Park, Pa., 1962), pp. 78-100.

22. James Bowdoin II to James Bowdoin III, Boston, 7 November 1771, Winthrop-Temple Papers.

23. James Bowdoin II to James Bowdoin III, Boston, 28 January 1772, Winthrop-Temple Papers.

24. James Bowdoin II to James Bowdoin III, Boston, 15 February 1775, Winthrop-Temple Papers.

25. The evidence is in a letter Martha Washington wrote from Valley Forge to Mercy Warren, 7 March 1778: "I left Mr. Bowdoin in Alexandria. He was a good deal distressed on account of Mr. Pliarne [Emanuel de Pliarne, a Frenchman who provided arms and munitions to the Continental Congress], a french gentleman, his partener who was by accident drowned crossing the Potomack river. . . ." *Warren-Adams Letters,* vol. 2, in *Collections of the Massachusetts Historical Society,* vol. 73, p. 6. "Mr. Bowdoin" is identified in the index as the father but it was the son who was in Virginia at that time.

26. James Bowdoin III to his sister Elizabeth, Lady Temple, 31 October 1793, *Collections of the Massachusetts Historical Society,* 7th Series, vol. 6 (The Bowdoin and Temple Papers), Part 2 (Boston, 1907), pp. 207-208.

27. James Bowdoin Letterbook, 17 August 1795, BCSC.

28. For social conditions in the district in the 1790s, see Alan Taylor, and see Stephen A. Marini, "Religious Revolution in the District of Maine, 1780-1820," in *Maine in the Early Republic,* pp. 118-145.

29. The courthouse stood on the site of the present Portland City Hall, very close to Samuel Deane's parsonage.

30. James Bowdoin II's real property had been divided equally, in thirds, among his son, daughter (Lady Temple), and wife. James Bowdoin III received 12,130 acres, for example, in Kennebec Purchase lands in Lincoln County, in addition to land elsewhere in Maine and in Massachusetts proper, Connecticut, New Hampshire, Vermont, and the Ohio territory. Gordon E. Kershaw, *James Bowdoin II: Patriot and Man of the Enlightenment* (Lanham, Md.: University Press of America, 1991), p. 291. Bowdoin, in other words, was generous to the new college, but cautious.

31. Trustees Minutes, December 1794, p. 2, BCSC.

32. Public land was the chief form of public wealth, as the General Court had recognized in paying off Revolutionary veterans with land grants. Similarly, disposing of "wild" lands in the district was the handiest way of endowing new schools and colleges throughout the commonwealth. In the three years before Bowdoin's charter, for example, such grants helped found Washington (Machias), Berwick, Hallowell, Fryeburg, and Portland academies. Typically, the grant was made at the time of chartering or by subsequent resolve, and the trustees negotiated with the Legislature's Committee on the Sale of Eastern Lands to determine the site. To sell often proved difficult, however, for many of the grants were far inland or along the disputed New Brunswick boundary. Between 1780 and 1824, Massachusetts granted public land in both parts of the state to 38 academies (17 of them in Maine) as well as to Harvard, Williams, and Bowdoin. Further grants were made to various civic associations, such as the state's medical and agricul-

tural societies. For details and a map, see Harriet Webster Marr, "Grants of Land to Academies in Masachusetts and Maine," *Essex Institute Historical Collections*, vol. 88 (1952), pp. 28-47, and her *Old New England Academies* (New York, 1959), pp. 19-33, 55-67.

33. Alfred Johnson, Jr., to A. S. Packard, 19 January 1835, "College History: Founding," BCSC.

34. Trustees' Minutes 1795, p. 4, BCSC.

35. James Bowdoin to David Mitchell, Boston, 6 January 1795, James Bowdoin Letterbook, BCSC.

36. Charles Turner to Hon. George Thatcher, Boston, 19 June 1797; photocopy in BCSC.

37. The two petitions are in the Massachusetts State Archives, Boston, among papers related to the college in Maine, 1797.

38. Nehemiah Cleaveland and Alpheus Spring Packard, *History of Bowdoin College* (Boston: James Ripley Osgood and Company, 1882), p. 6.

39. For an explanation of growth patterns in Federal towns, including Brunswick and Topsham, see Joseph S. Wood, "The Origins of the New England Village" (Ph.D. dissertation, Pennsylvania State University, 1978). The "classic" New England setting of village green, high-steepled church, and neatly fenced houses was a phenomenon of the early republic, not the pre-Revolutionary period.

40. Trustees' Minutes, 1800, p. 31, BCSC.

41. Cleaveland and Packard, p. 112.

42. In simplest terms, Unitarianism was a more rationalistic form of Christianity which had abandoned such supernatural aspects of traditional belief as the divinity of Christ and the existence of the Trinity. In the first decade of the nineteenth century, Unitarianism captured the allegiance of most of the educated elite in Boston and eastern Massachusetts.

43. Joseph McKeen, "A discourse against speaking evil of rulers: delivered on the Anniversary Fast in Massachusetts, April 9th, 1801" (Salem, 1801).

44. For an early description of Massachusetts Hall, see the undated memorandum by A. S. Packard "relating to College matters in early days," College Records: History, Jan 1795-Sept 1833, BCSC.

45. The academies for young ladies taught the eighteenth-century's ornamental accomplishments (needlework, dancing, music) but were serious about also teaching composition, history, geography, and occasionally French. Like many of the new colleges of the period, they were usually in small towns, though often attracting a regional, even national, enrollment. Mary Beth Norton, *Liberty's Daughters: The Revolutionary Experience of American Women, 1750-1800* (Boston, 1980), p. 273.

46. On eighteenth-century fears that intellectual accomplishments made women "masculine" and inca-
pable of running a household, see Linda Kerber, "Daughters of Columbia: Educating Women for the Republic, 1787-1805," in Stanley Elkins and Eric McKitrick, eds., *The Hofstadter Aegis: A Memorial* (New York, 1974), pp. 49-56.

47. Benjamin Rush, "On Women's Education," in Wilson Smith, ed., *Theories of Education in Early America 1655-1819* (Indianapolis, 1973), p. 264.

48. Clarence Cook, ed., *A Girl's Life Eighty Years Ago: Selections from the Letters of Eliza Southgate Bowne* (London, 1888). For an insightful account of Southgate's letter-writing, see Laurel Thatcher Ulrich, "'From the Fair to the Brave': Spheres of Womanhood in Federal Maine," in Laura Fecych Sprague, ed., *Agreeable Situations: Society, Commerce, and Art in Southern Maine, 1780-1830* (Kennebunk, Me., 1987), pp. 215-225.

49. Cook, pp. 78-80.

50. Cook, p. 102.

51. Cook, pp. 104-105.

52. Norton, p. 295.

53. Linda K. Kerber, *Women of the Republic: Intellect and Ideology in Revolutionary America* (Chapel Hill, 1980), p. 206.

54. Cook, pp. 60-61.

55. Leverett Saltonstall to William Minot, Salem, 6 August 1806. Robert E. Moody, ed., *The Saltonstall Papers, 1607-1815* (Boston, 1974), vol. 2, pp. 325-326. "In American colleges, a Bachelor or Master of one institution was formerly allowed to take *the same* degree at another, on payment of a certain fee [at Bowdoin, $5]. By this he was admitted to all the privileges of a graduate of his adopted Alma Mater." B. H. Hall, *A Collection of College Words and Customs* (Cambridge, Mass., 1856), p. 3.

56. "Leverett Saltonstall: Travel Journal, August-September 1806," ibid., pp. 326-343. Alpheus Spring Packard, in his "College Reminiscences," gives other vivid details of this first Commencement: e.g., McKeen's presiding in the pulpit of the unfinished church with an umbrella over his head and General Knox's carriage full of passengers overturning down a muddy bank. Nehemiah Cleaveland and A. S. Packard, *History of Bowdoin College* (Boston, 1882), pp. 83-85.

57. The definitive version of the Thorndike Oak story was told by President McKeen's son John, who said he saw Thorndike plant the acorn, and published in Leonard Woods, Jr., *Address on the Opening of the New Hall of the Medical School of Maine* (Brunswick, 1862), p. 11.

58. Edward P. Mitchell, "Alumni Dinner Speech," *Bowdoin College Bulletin* 116 (January 1922), pp. 8-9.

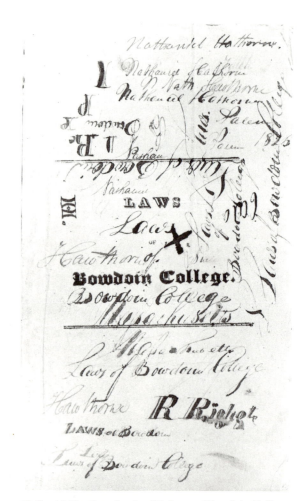

This early silver Phi Beta Kappa key (possibly made in Portland, Maine, ca. 1825) belonged to Henry Wadsworth Longfellow and bears the society's insignia of a finger pointing toward the stars. On the reverse are the initials S P, which stand for Societas Philosophiae, or Society of Philosophers, and the inscription "Alpha of Maine" and "Feb.y 22.d 1825." For most of the nineteenth century, Bowdoin's chapter of Phi Beta Kappa was an honorary society for graduates, with no undergraduate members.

Students at antebellum Bowdoin had the choice of joining one of two rival literary and debating societies, the Peucinian and the Athenaean. This is Longfellow's silver Peucinian Society medal (probably Portland, Maine, 1823). On the reverse are two pine trees and an abbreviation of the neo-Latin motto "Pinos Loquentes Semper Habemus" ("We always have the whispering pines.").

Nathaniel Hawthorne's copy of the Laws of Bowdoin College, 1824, on which he has practiced his penmanship. Although some scholars have concluded that he changed the spelling of his name after he left Bowdoin, these inscriptions show him experimenting with the change that led from Hathorne to Hawthorne. On the back of the pamphlet is further graffiti in Hawthorne's hand, including the repeated phrase, "A Truant Boy."

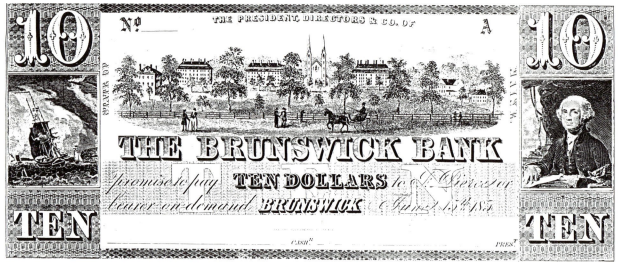

In the early nineteenth century, in the absence of a paper currency, banks issued their own notes and often illustrated them with a scene of local significance. The Brunswick Bank chose an early view of Bowdoin College for this $10.00 bill in the 1850s.

This painting shows the campus in the age when Hawthorne and Longfellow were students: l to r, Massachusetts Hall, 1802, showing the cupola that was later removed for structural reasons; Winthrop Hall, 1822; the original wooden chapel, which also served as the library; Maine Hall, 1808 (the facades of Maine and Winthrop were simplified in later renovations). The figure in the foreground is "Old Tench," a local character who sold root beer and gingerbread to students.

John G. Brown (active 1821-1858), Bowdoin Campus, ca. 1822. Oil on canvas. Bowdoin College Museum of Art. Gift of Mr. Harold L. Berry '01, 1961.82.

Son of the Huguenot emigré Pierre Baudouin, James Bowdoin I, of Boston, made his fortune in merchant shipping, invested heavily in land in Maine, and died perhaps the richest man in New England.

Joseph Badger (1708-1765), Portrait of James Bowdoin I. *Oil on canvas. Bowdoin College Museum of Art. Bequest of Mrs. Sarah Bowdoin Dearborn, 1826.6.*

James Bowdoin II's fortune enabled him to play a leading role in the politics of Boston on the eve of the Revolution as well as to pursue his personal interests in science and the arts. A merchant like his father, he served after the Revolution as governor of the Commonwealth of Massachusetts during the difficult time of Shays's Rebellion. Bowdoin College was named in his honor.

Robert Feke (1707-1752), Portrait of James Bowdoin II, *1748. Oil on canvas. Bowdoin College Museum of Art. Bequest of Mrs. Sarah Bowdoin Dearborn, 1826.8.*

These are the children, aged about ten and eight, respectively, of James Bowdoin II and his wife, Elizabeth Erving. Their daughter, Elizabeth Bowdoin, married John Temple, who became the eighth baronet of Stowe in 1786 and served as British consul-general in New York after the Revolution. After his death in 1798, Lady Temple returned to Boston.

Joseph Blackburn (active in America 1754-1763), Portrait of Elizabeth and James Bowdoin III as Children, ca. 1760. Oil on canvas. Bowdoin College Museum of Art. Gift of Mrs. Sarah Bowdoin Dearborn, 1826.11.

Like many rich young Anglo-Americans in the late eighteenth century, James Bowdoin III traveled abroad to further his education—and in his case, to improve his precarious health. This portrait may have been painted by an English artist in Italy when Bowdoin made his grand tour of the Continent in 1774.

Unknown artist, Portrait of James Bowdoin III *(as a young man). Oil on canvas. Bowdoin College Museum of Art. Bequest of Mrs. Sarah Bowdoin Dearborn, 1826.1.*

Now believed to be based on an 1804 miniature by Edward Greene Malbone (see p. 32), this portrait depicts Bowdoin about the time of his appointment by President Jefferson as U. S. minister to Spain. Although not as skilled at politics or business as his forebears, James Bowdoin III was one of the first serious collectors of art in the United States and perhaps the first to understand the role that the fine arts could play in a liberal education.

Gilbert Stuart (1755-1828), Portrait of James Bowdoin III. *Oil on canvas. Bowdoin College Museum of Art. Bequest of Mrs. Sarah Bowdoin Dearborn, 1870.6.*

Painted by Gilbert Stuart as a companion piece to the plainer one of her husband, this portrait depicts Sarah Bowdoin wearing a mantilla, a possible allusion to her husband's diplomatic appointment to Madrid. Sarah Bowdoin was the daughter of William Bowdoin and Phebe Murdock, and hence was James Bowdoin III's first cousin. Two years after her husband's death in 1811, she married their old friend Major General Henry Dearborn. Most of the Bowdoin family portraits came to the College after her death in 1826.

Gilbert Stuart (1755-1828). Portrait of Mrs. James Bowdoin III. *Oil on canvas. Bowdoin College Museum of Art. Bequest of Mrs. Sarah Bowdoin Dearborn, 1870.7.*

Marie Malleville Wheelock was the daughter of John Wheelock, president of Dartmouth College. In 1813 she married William Allen, who succeeded her father as president of the short-lived Dartmouth University (1817-1819). Accompanying the family to Brunswick in 1820 was an African-American servant, Phebe Jacobs, who, after Mrs. Allen's early death in 1828, became a local religious figure and a possible inspiration for Harriet Beecher Stowe's Uncle Tom.

Rembrandt Peale (1778-1860), Portrait of Mrs. William Allen. *Oil on canvas. Bowdoin College Museum of Art. Gift of Mrs. Malleville McC. Howard, 1950.14.*

The son of a famous Revolutionary War "fighting parson" from the Berkshires, William Allen inherited his father's religious zeal and aggressive manner. In the early 1820s he played an important role in the College's adjustment to the political realities of statehood and was largely responsible for establishing the Medical School of Maine at Bowdoin. By the 1830s, however, his overbearing personality had made him many enemies. He was removed from office by the Legislature, only to be restored in the 1833 case of Allen v. McKeen. *He left Bowdoin amid general bad feeling in 1839 and returned to western Massachusetts.*

Rembrandt Peale (1778-1860), Portrait of William Allen. *Oil on canvas. Bowdoin College Museum of Art. Gift of Mrs. Malleville McC. Howard, 1950.13.*

As her cashmere shawl suggests, Phebe Lord was a young woman of fashion; her father, Nathaniel Lord, was one of the richest men in York County. In 1825 she married a young Bowdoin professor, Thomas Cogswell Upham. The author of seven devotional tracts, Mrs. Upham helped her husband in his own writings and in welcoming the Stowe family to Brunswick in 1850. Though extremely pious, she made a nuisance of herself in the eyes of the minister of the First Parish Church by championing the right of women to speak in church meetings.

Gilbert Stuart (1755-1828), Portrait of Mrs. Thomas C. Upham. *Oil on canvas. Bowdoin College Museum of Art. Gift of Mr. Edward D. Jameson, 1919.1.*

Richard Upjohn's watercolor rendition of the Bowdoin College Chapel shows the building in a pastoral setting that gives no hint of the other buildings on the campus. The Chapel is one of the earliest examples in the United States of the German Romanesque Revival style. It also provided space for a library, an art gallery, and meeting rooms, as well as the space for the College's daily assemblies.

As a poet and man of letters, Henry Wadsworth Longfellow 1825 was the most popular literary figure in nineteenth-century America (and, after Tennyson, the best-known poet in the English-speaking world). His career as a writer began when he was a young professor of modern languages at Bowdoin (1829-1835). He celebrated the College in his poem "Morituri Salutamus," delivered at the fiftieth reunion of his famous class in 1875.

Thomas Buchanan Read (American, 1822-1872), Portrait of Henry Wadsworth Longfellow, 1859. Oil on canvas. Bowdoin College Museum of Art, 1985.50.

Though not as well known as Longfellow during his lifetime, Nathaniel Hawthorne has eclipsed his classmate in the twentieth century and is today perhaps Bowdoin's most celebrated graduate. His first novel, Fanshawe *(1828), was set at a college somewhat resembling Bowdoin. Some of the friends he made during his undergraduate days, such as Franklin Pierce 1824, remained close associates throughout his life.*

Charles Osgood (American, 1809-1890). Portrait of Nathaniel Hawthorne, *1840. Oil on canvas.*

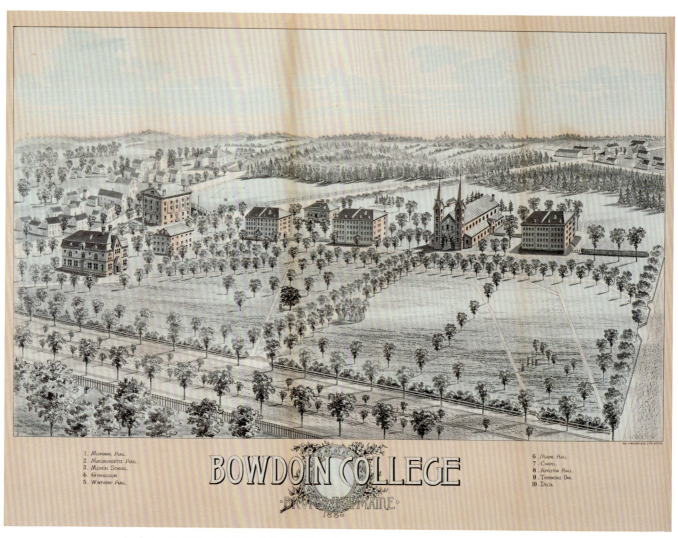

1. Memorial Hall.
2. Massachusetts Hall.
3. Medical School.
4. Gymnasium.
5. Winthrop Hall.

6. Maine Hall.
7. Chapel.
8. Appleton Hall.
9. Thorndike Oak.
10. Delta.

BOWDOIN COLLEGE

BRUNSWICK MAINE
1886

In the pre-Civil War period, the College buildings formed a row facing Maine Street, but by the time this view was made in 1886, with the addition of Memorial Hall (1867-1882), a quadrangle was beginning to form. In the background, to the left, is Adams Hall (1861), half of which housed the Medical School of Maine until its demise in 1921. Beyond Adams is the playing field known as the Delta. In the center rear are the Bowdoin pines. Earlier attempts to landscape the campus had been thwarted by the sandy soil, but by the 1880s avenues of trees had taken root.

For much of the nineteenth century, Commencement took on the air of a public festival, for which even people unconnected with the College came from some distance. This hand-colored slide, ca. 1890s, shows gowned graduates and guests sitting out under the trees in the Quad preparing for what may be a Commencement or Class Day celebration.

American Impressionist William Gilchrist and his family retreated from their East Harpswell farmhouse to rented houses in Brunswick in the winter. Dean of the College Kenneth Sills and the painter struck up a friendship, and Sills made a habit of stopping by in the evening. One result was this portrait, now in the possession of the artist's son. Sills was president of the College from 1918 to 1952.

William W. Gilchrist (American, 1879-1926), Portrait of Kenneth C. M. Sills, 1916. Oil on canvas.

"A May training at Bowdoin in the olden time," an illustration accompanying an article on Bowdoin College in Scribner's Magazine in 1876. It depicts the annual procession of students through town in the 1830s in costume. The parade was intended as a burlesque of the military drill required of college students at that time.

"The Rope-Pull between the freshmen and sophomores." The Rope-Pull was a contest in which members of the rival classes tried to drag the opposing side across the campus. According to Scribner's, "The field of battle wears a grim look for days afterward, and is furrowed as though it had been upturned by that delicate instrument of the husbandman, the 'subsoil plow.'"

The Hold-In was another form of interclass competition. When the freshmen tried to leave the Chapel, "sophomore skirmishers would seize the oncoming freshman, and the melee was suffered to continue long enough to give the upperclassmen their needed recreation, and then the battered battalions would retire from the room in light marching order. It is remarkable that no fatal injury ever followed this rough encounter, and that the wounds of the combatants required the tailor's, and not the doctor's, needle."

69

John Abbot, a Harvard graduate of 1784, was cashier in a Portland bank when he was appointed the College's first professor in 1802. While not remembered as a strong scholar, he nonetheless showed great enterprise in exploring the College's wild lands after becoming treasurer of the College in 1816.

The presidency (1820-1839) of the Reverend William Allen (1784-1868) was marked by controversy over the political and legal status of the College. Was it a public institution answerable to the Legislature (which provided a subsidy) or a private one under the sole direction of its Governing Boards?

The Reverend Jesse Appleton (1772-1819), a moderate Congregationalist and Bowdoin's second president, saw himself as the students' minister as much as their teacher. He died after twelve years in office, apparently of tuberculosis.

70

CHAPTER THREE

*From its earliest days, Bowdoin's future had been inextricably linked
with the land of Maine—land as a source of revenue, as a stage on which to act out
the College's cultural mission, as an inviting retreat from the world.
But not everyone agreed with the College's cultural mission, and in the first four decades
of the nineteenth century a host of other forces—religious, social, political, legal—arose
to contest the College's claims to authority over the life of the new state.*

A FOREST LIFE

John Abbot was an unlikely woodsman—
"he always seems like a frightened bird,"
Eliza Southgate once said of him, "so hurried in his manner and conversation"[1]—
but in the fall of 1812 he spent ten weeks exploring the Piscataquis country north and west of
Bangor. His errand into this particular wilderness had a practical goal: to supervise the work
of the surveyor who was laying out two of the
College's townships in the Seventh Range, in
anticipation of their sale to settlers. Yet the
enthusiasm found in the long letter he wrote
upon his return to his brother, who was preceptor of Dummer Academy in Massachusetts, suggests another source of energy. Possibly the professor had been touched by the first wave of literary Romanticism coming from Europe; possibly
he had been exposed to the first wave of medical
fads that would soon wash over the Republic.
Whatever the influence, being out of doors
made him *feel* good. His account of the trip—
covering much of the same territory near
Moosehead Lake that Thoreau was to visit a generation later—pays tribute to the restorative
powers of Nature in ways that Abbot's successors
at Bowdoin a century and a half later would
unconsciously emulate.[2]

As if to symbolize his transfigured state, Abbot
had exchanged his professorial coat, "surtout"
(an overcoat), and boots for a pair of mooseskin
moccasins, a woolen "frock," a knapsack, and a
blanket. In the preceding months he had fretted
over his health—to the point of spending two
months on "a milk diet entirely"—and as late as

Commencement wondered if "my health &
strength were such as would justify my encountering the fatigues & privations of a forest life."
The surveyor had gone ahead some three weeks
earlier and was to meet him on the tenth of
September at Number 7 Township in the
Seventh Range, the uppermost settlement by
that date on the Piscataquis River, about fifty
miles from Bangor. Abbot found his way there
by following marked trees. He stopped to dine
on "some bread & cheese which I procured at
the house where I slept the night before, &
drank nature's beverage" (i. e., water) and feeling "so braced by the journey, that I ventured to
sally out into the [unmarked] forest, to explore
a place to make the [township] location."

His party included the surveyor, a hunter
hired as a guide, and a bearer; they carried
enough pork, bread, tea, sugar, and ginger for a
march of ten or twelve days. "My object was
Moose head Lake, beyond the ninth range,
north of the Waldo patent," he explained in his
letter. On the fifth day, they reached an arm of
the lake, built a raft, coasted along the shore for
a mile, then crossed over, leaving the raft:

We ascended a mountain which commanded a very
extensive view of the Lake & the country. The
prospect was very fine, & generally fine settling land.
We then explored eastward two or three days, to see if
we could find materials for three & a half townships—
two for Bowd. Colledge, one for the medical Society
[of Massachusetts], & a half township for Saco
Academy. . .

On the last day of the eleven-day trip, he fell
and "lamed" one leg and "great toe very badly,
which rendered travelling very painful to me."
He had found the march more tiring than

expected—"so much so, that I frequently sweat my clothes through to my pack"—but despite sleeping "without any covering than the heavens," he caught no colds. "A very outrageous appetite" helped him to eat even raw pork "with a fine relish." As he told his brother, "Let your difficult folks who piddle with the victuals march in the woods a few days. . . ."

Determining to locate the townships that year, Abbot sent the surveyor, two chainmen, and an axeman with ten days' supplies back into the woods. Temporarily crippled, he traveled by horse downriver about thirty miles to Sebec to obtain more provisions. Traveling as far as Brownville in search of flour, he managed to get back to Sebec Lake with so many supplies it took three men to carry them. They made their difficult way by paddling "a large log canoe" and by portaging several miles, then building another raft, and so on until they met up, as planned, with the surveying team. When he was certain that the College's two townships—Numbers 7 and 8, in the Tenth Range—had been "run" by the surveyor, Abbot paid the crew and headed for Brownville, where the east and west branches of the Pleasant (or Ebeeme) River meet. Recalling the terrain in his letter to his brother, Abbot described the passage of the west branch of the Ebeeme through Township 7. "For about 1 1/2 miles in the township this stream makes its way through the bowels of a mountain, in a track which Nature seems to have made for it in a frolick, or by some great convulsion. You may in some places look down from the banks 150 feet to the bed of the stream." Wishing to see the falls and the "gulph" they formed, he and his companion:

climbed the wild, rugged cliffs till we got in sight of the falls, when the young man who attended me, chilled by the rain & cold, refused to follow me. After

Silhouette of Harrison Allen, Class of 1824. Allen died in 1831 on a mission to the Choctaw Indian tribe in Elliot, Mississippi. In the days before photography, traveling artists cut silhouettes that could be inexpensively reproduced as mementoes of one's classmates.

some very sublime views from these craggy cliffs, we descended 3/4 of a mile to our packs. We then had a very steep & rugged mountain, more difficult than any we had seen, to climb, & then to descend to the intervale at the foot of the gulph.

Abbot had been removed from the world until he rode back on the rain-soaked roads to Bangor. "Hardly anything of news reached me in the forest. I slept in the woods in the whole about one month. Sometimes without any shelter, & sometimes, when we could get it under a shed made of rift cedar. When in the forest a very fine appetite. Bread & pork, roasted or raw, trouts and pattridges, beaver's meat & muskrat—all about equally acceptable."

As far as his letter to his brother reveals, Abbot did not feel that psychological unease in the face of untamed nature that Thoreau was to experience in the North Woods, but his longing for the primitive went far beyond the conventions of the eighteenth-century "sublime." (Augustan experience of nature had not included eating raw pork.) Abbot never "lost" himself or his goal—every new fall of a river was a potential mill site to him—but there is evidence in his account of a new mode of feeling about what the land of Maine could mean for those who set out to experience it. Perhaps a state of nature could be a state of grace, despite the deeply engrained fears which most people of European descent still felt when confronted with untamed wilderness.[3]

What Abbot does not mention is the presence of squatters on the land, for he was traveling beyond the line of settlement in 1812. But the officers of the College were quite familiar by that time with such hindrances on College-owned lands at nearby Bowdoin and Lisbon. The dispute between owners with title and squatters in possession raised troubling questions about one's right to the fruits of one's labor.

WHOSE LAND IS IT?

If history is a series of stories we construct from the past, how we tell those stories becomes part of that history. The condition of the District of Maine in the years in which its economy was formed and its identity took root—an age when many men were venturing into its wilderness as Abbot had done—is a case in point. Working with many of the same documents, historians in this century have "read" the district in strikingly different ways.

For example, in 1938, when Frederick S. Allis, Jr., a historian at Phillips Academy, Andover, first saw a portion of the William Bingham archive, he had been commissioned to edit only those papers related to General David Cobb, a physician who had become the agent managing Bingham's land speculations in eastern Maine. It soon became clear that a remarkably detailed record survived of all of Bingham's activities as the absentee owner of some two million acres of land in the district. Allis was commissioned by the Colonial Society of Massachusetts to edit and annotate this mass of business letters and accounts, the results of which—though delayed by the war—appeared in 1954 in two handsome volumes, bound in light blue and gold, and carrying as a frontispiece Gilbert Stuart's viceregal portrait *William Bingham of Philadelphia, Proprietor of the Maine Lands*. The years of painstaking work by Allis, a distinguished man in his own right, involved at one time or another the lawyers for the Bingham Estate, such luminaries of late Brahmin culture in New England as the historians Walter Muir Whitehill and Samuel Eliot Morison, and even a peer, Lord Ashburton, into whose family, the Barings, one of Bingham's daughters had married. The editing was skillful, unobtrusive, well-informed; the printing was of the usual standard of austere beauty achieved by the now lamented Anthoensen Press of Portland, Maine. Merely as a physical object, this was an impressive performance, a monument to a heroic age of venture capitalism, produced at a time and place in which few Americans questioned the values it commemorated.[4]

From the 1,315 pages of *William Bingham's Maine Lands 1790-1820*, a picture of the district emerges. It is not too different from Talleyrand's. "Eastern Maine had been populated by a pioneer stock which compared unfavorably with frontier folk in other sections of New England," Allis writes. A "squatter class" discouraged potential buyers of the land, and this "disrespect for private property and for law and order generally. . . [acted] as a deterrent to the more law-abiding settler who might develop Maine economically and socially." The lumbermen in particular—slothful, wasteful, drunken, irresponsible—not only despoiled the land that belonged to others but precluded the establishment of "a more civilized way of life." The whole region Down East was filled with "a backwash of Yankee migration."[5] Whatever one thinks of William Bingham as an individual—he was a Philadelphia banker and politician who rarely visited Maine and whose speculations there, perhaps as a result, proved disappointing—the importance that Allis gives to his affairs is designed to leave no doubt that Bingham and his fellow proprietors were engaged in a civilizing mission.[6]

By 1990—the year in which a university press published an inexpensive paperback edition of Alan S. Taylor's *Liberty Men and Great Proprietors: The Revolutionary Settlement on the Maine Frontier, 1760-1820*—the District of Maine of the 1790s could be pictured in a very different light by a younger generation of scholars. Taylor shares Allis's encyclopedic spirit—and pays tribute to him in an essay on sources—but displays none of his respect for "the great and the good." Painting a much broader picture of life in the district, especially in its central backcountry, Taylor celebrates the yeoman farmers—many of them Revolutionary veterans squatting on absentee owners' land—as the true heirs of republican virtue: men who lived off their own labor, who cleared the forests and tended crops, who fiercely defended their independence, who experienced religion as enthusiasm rather than as an exercise in good citizenship, and who often found themselves caught in a web of debt and clouded title not entirely of their own making.

This campus view from about 1839 shows the original wooden chapel (on the right), built in 1805 and torn down in the late 1840s to make way for the present granite chapel.

Taylor chronicles the low-key, though occasionally violent, resistance on the part of these settlers to efforts by proprietors to evict them from their land, efforts often based on dubious and poorly surveyed claims going back to seventeenth-century royal grants. Disguised as "savages" or "white Indians," the settlers took matters into their own hands: they harassed the proprietors' surveyors and bailiffs, burned deeds and eviction notices, and tore down boundary posts. The more patient of them prevailed, not as rural insurgents, but as supporters of the new Democratic-Republican Party and, after 1815, as champions of statehood. Taylor's account is full of vivid details of frontier life, illumined by a different sense of the heroic. *Liberty Men and Great Proprietors* is a truer account of life in the district than Bingham's archive can yield. Its emphasis on rural insurgency is not simply a reaction to the consensus history of the not-too-distant past, but a portrayal of the Maine frontier as one further example of the political and social instability of the Early Republic.[7]

What all this has to do with Bowdoin College is twofold. The College took shape in the same years as the struggle which Taylor describes—a struggle between an educated elite seeking to establish its hegemony over the district and an uneducated population quite good at finding ways to resist it. And the College found itself at times a participant in this ideological wrestling match.

Taylor reports, for example, on three days in the fall of 1804:

25 September. Bowdoin, Lincoln County. Settlers steal and mutilate a horse belonging to John Merrill, a surveyor working for Bowdoin College.

26 September. Bowdoin, Lincoln County. Armed settlers fire shots and issue threats to frighten surveyors working for Bowdoin College.

27 September. Bowdoin, Lincoln County. Armed settlers obstruct surveyors working for Bowdoin College; they give up the attempt.[8]

These are the only Bowdoin-related entries in Taylor's sixteen-page list of "Incidents of Extralegal Violence" arising from disputed land claims in Maine; the College was not a proprietor on a large scale. Yet with his gifts of land James Bowdoin had also given the College several decades of friction with the people already living on that land. When the College's representatives went to inspect the 1,000 acres given in 1794, for example, they reported back that "there were five or six Families on said land, who with others, we are informed, are destroying the little remaining timber on the land. . . We are also informed that there is one saw mill erected on the premises."[9] Eventually settlements were reached by which squatters, more often than not, paid for the College land they occupied, at its unimproved price. But the disputes were one further cause of estrangement between the friends of order and a majority of the district's settlers.

There were other fissures that seemed each year to widen. The day was passing when the representatives of traditional New England Congregationalism could assume that they enjoyed the leadership of the community—the day when, in Henry Adams's words, "the minister put his three-cornered hat on his head, took his silver-topped cane in his hand, and walked down the village street, knocking at one door and another of his best parishioners, to warn them that a spirit of license and of French infidelity was abroad."[10] To one side, the Standing Order of orthodox clergy saw their authority being undermined by the well-placed Unitarians of the rich seaboard towns, heirs to the moderate Enlightenment's project of reconciling Christianity and rationalism. On their other flank, these same orthodox Calvinists faced the challenge of evangelicals and other dissenters, the unlettered enthusiasts who filled the backcountry and "seduced" the unwary. The Reverend Paul Coffin, a liberal Congregationalist and charter Overseer of the College, encountered on his missionary tours in the district many such self-appointed preachers. "I think our new settlements are much to be pitied," he concluded after such a trip in 1796, "as they are over run with Methodist teachers. How truly lamentable is it, that New England should despise a learned ministry, or, through covetousness, go destitute of it, till, by their ignorance and God's righteous judgment, they become fit for every wind of doctrine, and every ruinous error of delusion!"[11]

Yet it would be a mistake to assume that Bowdoin College bolted its door to the forces of change. Troubles with squatters and despoilers continued through the 1820s, but in other ways the College adapted itself, to a degree which its adherents may not have realized at the time. Consider, for example, the difference between the College's first president and its second. McKeen's untimely death in 1807 deprived him of much opportunity to shape the growth of the new institution, but as far as the record indicates, he seems to have been an undogmatic and undemanding Congregationalist, liberal enough to have been mentioned as a future president of Harvard College.[12]

But his successor, the Reverend Jesse Appleton, introduces a new intensity.[13] Piety is in the air. Appleton is not a controversialist—he had had enough bickering in his previous parish, in Hampton, New Hampshire, where the town had angrily divided into Congregationalists and Presbyterians—but he sees his duties as pastoral as much as academic.[14] For Appleton, in the words of his biographer, the students "constitute a society, in many respects resembling. . . a parish," and requiring from their president "much of that solicitude and attention which none but a devoted pastor knows, or is wont to bestow."[15] It is difficult to know how many students were touched by this pastoral care, but at least one of them remarked afterwards that "it is impossible to go through Bowdoin College without receiving serious impressions," and by 1816 it was estimated that almost one-third of the undergraduates were "pious."[16] Appleton, like McKeen, died prematurely—at age forty-seven, of what seems to have been tuberculosis, possibly brought on by overwork—but he introduced the College to the so-called Second Great Awakening, the evangelical revival movement that was to reshape Congregationalism—indeed, all of American Protestantism—in the first half of the nineteenth century.[17] From his deathbed, Appleton is said to have looked out his window and across his garden at the small cluster of buildings and proclaimed, "God has taken care of the college, and God will take care of it."[18]

The extent to which the challenge from Baptists, Methodists, Universalists, and others pushed mainstream Congregationalists in an evangelical direction is not entirely clear; the process did not lessen denominational quarrels, as the career of Appleton's successor, the Reverend William Allen, was to demonstrate. Religious difference was only one of the conflicts to strain the social fabric of the district in these years of rapid growth, a period that had begun in Maine at the end of the Revolution and that was to extend, with only a few interruptions, into the Age of Jackson. But, meanwhile, a more immediate problem was literally on the horizon.

THE BRITISH ARE COMING

On 20 June 1814, as part of the British blockade of all Atlantic ports, the seventy-four-gun frigate *Bulwark* anchored off Seguin Island and sent scouting parties up the Sheepscot River. The news quickly spread to Bath, where anxious citizens petitioned Major General William King for militia to guard the mouth of the Kennebec at Phippsburg. King sent Captain John Wilson from Topsham with a detachment of infantry and artillery to man an existing fort there; a few soldiers also guarded the entrance of the New Meadows River in Harpswell.[19] Memories of the burning of Falmouth by Captain Mowat were still fresh in many minds. Some coastal dwellers sent their children to take refuge farther inland, and banks in Bath and Wiscasset concealed their specie in safe hiding places. "We feel fearful that to-night will be more hazardous than the day has been," wrote the Reverend William Jenks, a sometime Bowdoin professor, from Bath on 20 June to President Appleton. "Mrs. Jenks is therefore very desirous that the children should tarry at Brunswick till the morning." He went on:

We have near 700 men in arms—but the barges & launch, which have been manned & sent up the Sheepscot, are furnished with rockets, & can do execution beyond the reach of musquetry. The fort at the mouth of the river remained at the last account uninjured—& the powder has *at last* been sent down. The utmost supineness & negligence have indeed heretofore been manifest. . .

[I]t is thought expedient by several to send out a flag of truce, should it appear necessary from regard to superior force, & they wish me to go in it.

May the "Watchman of Israel" be our safeguard![20]

War had come to Maine, and in more decisive fashion than the relatively minor skirmishing of the Revolutionary era. For the first year of hostilities, the district was untouched, other than by a disruption of trade on the high seas.[21] September of 1813 had seen the duel between the U. S. brig *Enterprise* and the British brig *Boxer* off Portland; the captains of both vessels were killed in the battle and buried with honors by the victorious Americans. The year 1814 brought a more serious threat from the British fleet at Halifax, Nova Scotia, which had been ordered to secure a direct route overland to Quebec by seizing the easternmost third of Maine. This was easily done. Eastport fell to the British—leaped might be the better word—without a struggle, Castine was occupied and garrisoned, Belfast was taken, and in September a small expedition sailed up the Penobscot to defeat the local militia at Hampden and plunder Bangor. Anxious citizens between the Penobscot and the Kennebec prepared for the worst.[22]

Except for a few minor raids, it never came. This has been something of a mystery, given the strength of the British garrison at Castine. Moreover, the British knew that the war was unpopular in much of New England and that the national government had decided to require Federalist Massachusetts to defend itself, probably at the sacrifice of the District of Maine. For whatever reason, though, Maine towns were spared the fate of Washington, D. C. On the contrary, for many residents of Maine the war brought a prosperity unknown since Jefferson's hated Embargo of 1807. In addition to the usual smuggling, many people Down East happily traded with the British, who needed provisions for their forces.[23]

The degree to which so many respectable citizens of the district consorted with the enemy helps to explain William King's charge, in the post-war statehood debate, that President Appleton had visited the British commander at Castine, presumably on some clandestine mission.[24] Possibly this was King's way of countering well-founded rumors that he had continued shipping after his own party's embargo had been proclaimed in 1807; possibly it was one more expression of the nationalism that had surged after Jackson's victory at New Orleans and that had cast New England Federalists in the role of traitors to their country.[25] There is no evidence that Appleton made such a visit, or even had reason to contemplate one. But the charge itself is further evidence of the bitterness of the political life of the day.[26]

Spared an invasion into Merrymeeting Bay or raids on the Harpswells, the College nonetheless was marked by the War of 1812 in less direct ways. For example, the war did much to discredit the Federalist party with which Bowdoin's leadership was linked. Angry at Madison to start with, the Federalists of New England had grown apprehensive as well, as they began to see power flowing toward the central government during the war, threatening the republican values they were determined to protect. The anger, especially among younger, second-generation Federalists, led to the ill-timed Hartford Convention of 1814-15, a regional protest meeting which its organizers saw as a legitimate exercise of their right of dissent but which their enemies denounced as a secessionist plot against "the people." Among the dozen delegates from

Stephen Longfellow, Jr., father of the poet, was a leading Portland lawyer and Federalist politician who represented the College in McKeen v. Allen *in 1833.*

Massachusetts were the Portland lawyer (and Bowdoin Overseer) Stephen Longfellow, Jr., and the Kennebec Valley lawyer Samuel Wilde, a member of the Gardiner-Hallowell-Vaughan circle that had many ties with the College.[27] Above all, the vulnerability felt throughout the district as a result of Boston's inability to defend Maine's coast proved a major factor in reviving the separationist campaign. Statehood, from Bowdoin College's point of view, was to be far more dangerous than the British fleet.

A RIVAL IN WATERVILLE

The idea of a Baptist college in Maine had evolved in the same sort of conversations that, twenty years earlier, had helped create Bowdoin, only this time the ministers conferring were Calvinists who had dissented from the established church. There had been Baptists in Maine as early as 1682, but they were a small, though

William King sustained heavy losses when local sawmills and the bridge over the Androscoggin River between Brunswick and Topsham were damaged in the spring floods of 1814. This early nineteenth-century engraving shows one of the sawmills that lined both banks of the river near the site of the present Frank J. Wood Bridge.

annoying, sect in the eyes of "the Standing Order" of Congregationalist clergy until the last decade of the eighteenth century, when, as we have seen, many of the new settlers in the district found the independent spirit and evangelical fervor of the Baptist ministers more attractive than the cool, correct religion of their orthodox rivals. These backcountry evangelicals had been indifferent at first to the tradition of a learned ministry—learning being associated with what they saw as aristocratic pretension—but by the first decade of the new century, the Baptists in Maine had achieved a degree of respectability.

The first record of a campaign for a Baptist college appears in the minutes of the Bowdoinham Association (a conference of all the Baptist churches in the district outside of York County), meeting in Livermore in 1810. Among the five clergymen appointed to a committee to advance the proposal was Benjamin Titcomb, one of the founders of the state's first newspaper, the *Falmouth Gazette* (1794), and pastor of the Brunswick church. The Reverend Daniel Merrill of Sedgwick was leader of the group, which in 1812 petitioned the General Court for "a tract of good land. . . in the center of the district." Since they, too, paid taxes, the petitioners argued that their educational needs should be treated on an equal basis with those of the Congregationalists. As they reminded the legislators, "the Baptists are, undoubtedly, more numerous in the district than any other denomination, if not than all others." These numbers were growing daily, "yet we have no seminary over which we have any control. It is our judgment that it would be for the furtherance of the gospel and the general good that a seminary should be founded in which some of our religious young men might be educated under the particular inspection of able men of the same sentiments." Senator William King promised his support. But the bill did not get very far, in part because Bowdoin's friends did not think the district (whose population in 1810 was 228,000) was large enough to support a second college, in part because others did not want to see degree-granting colleges established by dissenting denominations.[28]

Had the Baptists only sought a charter for a seminary to train their own ministers, there would have been little or no opposition. They tried a different tack, and in 1813 they succeeded. A "literary and theological institution"—more than a seminary, but less than a degree-granting college—was chartered and given a township of what proved not very good land on the upper Penobscot. Although not a Baptist, King took an active interest in an institution supported by so many Baptist voters and agreed to serve as a trustee, just as he had agreed to serve at Bowdoin.

William King looms larger than life over the district in the second decade of the nineteenth century. As John Adams once predicted, "I can tell you how it will be when there arises in Maine a bold, daring, ardent genius, with talents capable of inspiring the people with his own enthusiasm and ambition. He will tear off Maine from Massachusetts and leave her in a state of mediocrity in the Union."[29] General King—so called from his militia days in the War of 1812—rose to fulfill at least the first part of Adams's prophecy. According to the political myth that he invented for himself, he had arrived barefoot, driving a team of oxen, at Topsham in 1790 and had

William King, the "Sultan of Bath" and a major general in the War of 1812, who later served as a state senator and governor, pledged $6,000 toward the construction of the Chapel. In his later life, however, his merchant shipping, lumber, and real estate empire crumbled, leaving his estate unable to pay the pledge.

amassed a fortune by sheer genius—a tale of self-improvement that appealed greatly to the new settlers in the district who hoped to emulate his success. In truth, in the early 1790s King was a well-connected young man whose half-brother Rufus was U. S. minister to England and whose Topsham ventures with his brother-in-law, Benjamin Jones Porter, were merely a prelude to a remarkable career in business and politics. Building ships and sawing lumber on the banks of the Androscoggin, the firm of Porter & King traded between Maine, the West Indies, and Europe. On a typical voyage of one of their vessels to Montserrat in 1800, for example, they shipped square timber, planks, square-edged boards, shingles, red oak shooks, "scantling," codfish, salmon, pork, herring, mackerel, red oak staves, and spermaceti candles, and presumably brought sugar and molasses back home.[30] King soon moved his business to the better-situated port of Bath, where he built a shipyard on the Kennebec near the present Carleton Bridge and a mansion on what was later the site of the Customs House. "I believe there is not a window in the house that does not command a view of the water," wrote his niece, Eliza Southgate, during a visit in 1801.[31] As Henry Owen, a historian of Bath, notes, for the first thirty years of the century King dominated local affairs through his involvement in politics, commerce, shipbuilding, farming, real estate speculation, religion, education, banking, and insurance. To his contemporaries, he was "the Sultan of Bath."

Yet there was something insubstantial about it all. King is an enigmatic figure, awaiting a good biographer who might be able to explain why he quickly left the governorship of the new state he had done so much to create or why he seems to have lost his business sense in later life (as Bowdoin College was to discover when he died in 1852).[32] But, in 1814, the disaster that struck was not of his making. An unusually violent spring flood on the Androscoggin damaged the bridge between Topsham and Brunswick, demolished many of the riverfront mills, and washed logs worth some $10,000 belonging to Porter & King out to sea—for a total loss to the firm estimated at $80,000. As one of the leading local businessmen in the area, Porter had been treasurer of Bowdoin since 1805 and had, as college treasurers of that day frequently did, mingled the College's funds with his own. There is no evidence that he had done anything unethical—John Hancock had annoyed James Bowdoin II in the same manner as Harvard's treasurer—but the college officers were alarmed at the thought of all of Porter's creditors seizing his assets in the aftermath of the collapse of his business.

They sent Benjamin Orr to get there first. It did not help matters that Orr was a fervent Federalist, while Porter and King were leading Republicans.[33] Nor did the fact that King was guarantor of Porter's bond as treasurer. In a tactless move, Orr attached all of King's holdings in Bath, which not only halted vessels ready to go to sea but served to question King's integrity. The money was quickly paid, but King now had a personal reason to hate Bowdoin College to add to his political doubts about the place.[34]

The Benjamin Porter affair intensified King's interest in Bowdoin's rival. Through his influence, Waterville, on the Kennebec, was chosen as the site in 1817 for what was named the Maine Literary and Theological Institution. According to one of its trustees, King took the opportunity of a committee meeting in 1818 to declare (italics in original):

Bowdoin College must go down—It is conducted upon too narrow principles to live; and will die a natural death. This Theological Institution is to be a substitute for Bowdoin College, and conducted upon more liberal principles. . . One of the classes of graduates at Bowdoin College had turned out to be, principally, drunkards; and another appeared to be religiously mad.[35]

Although "Baptist" did not appear in the new college's name, the petition which King presented to the Legislature in 1819 pointed out that "neither a professed Baptist nor Methodist is now to be found among the instructors at Harvard, Williams or Bowdoin. Considering ourselves pointedly excluded from the government of these institutions, and believing that the religious instruction afforded is of a kind not the most correct, we humbly petition for aid to our own Institution."[36]

The new professor of divinity, Jeremiah Chaplin, was as stern a Calvinist as anyone in Brunswick, and as unbending a disciplinarian as Bowdoin's William Allen (and, like Allen, he was to leave office amid a near-revolt of the students). He, too, believed strongly in a learned ministry. He knew that the new institution had little support in Boston because "so many men of influence in the state are engaged to support the University at Cambridge and the two colleges already established."[37] Moreover, most people expected Maine soon to leave Massachusetts. Chaplin appreciated King's friendship enough to know that too rigid a denominational stance would not please the Jeffersonian party; the charter of 1820 proclaimed that the college would be open to students of all denominations. And since most of King's fellow trustees were also Republicans, there was no opposition in Waterville to the control over colleges given to the new state's Legislature in the acts of 1820 and 1821. Maine Literary and Theological Institution became Waterville College in 1821 (a name that it was to keep for forty-six years, before it was renamed Colby College), and the next year Chaplin was chosen its first president.

LITERARY INSTITUTIONS

As we have seen, in the 1790s there was considerable support among the elite, particularly in Portland, for the idea of separation of the District of Maine from Massachusetts. The founding of Bowdoin College had been, among other things, a step toward creating a separate identity for Maine. A people who had their own essential civic institutions—banks, academies, militia companies, an agricultural society, a college—would no longer look to Boston for leadership. But the failure of the first separationist effort in the decade after the Revolution and the increasing identification of its spokesmen with an anti-democratic Federalist Party had rendered the cause suspect in the minds of many of the district's voters. When separation became a popular cause again, in the second decade of the century, the political situation had shifted. An awareness that Maine now had a majority of Democratic-Republicans who would keep the Federalists out of office in any new state government led many of those who had lobbied for separation in 1785 or 1794 to champion the long-standing link with the Commonwealth of Massachusetts. Culturally as well as economically, the district depended on eastern Massachusetts, a state of affairs that reassured the few while distressing the many.[38]

Whatever the intention of its founders, by 1816 the College was perceived as a party to this dependence. Already known as a rallying point for Federalists and orthodox Congregationalists, Bowdoin was soon identified as a center of anti-separatist feeling as well.[39] As Ronald Banks, the chronicler of Maine's arrival at statehood, points

Silhouette of Cullen Sawtelle, Class of 1825, who pursued a career in law and government, serving one term in the Maine Senate in 1843-44 and two terms as a member of Congress.

out, the only anti-separatist meeting held in the district before the crucial 1819 referendum on statehood was held in Freeport and attended by such "Federalist friends of Bowdoin" as Samuel Fessenden, Stephen Longfellow, Jr., Benjamin Orr, Joseph McKeen, William Vaughan, and Robert Hallowell Gardiner.[40]

One way to look at the College's history through the 1820s and early 1830s is to consider how it dealt with this "crisis" of statehood. The second and successful phase of the movement to break away from Massachusetts began about 1803, writes Banks, when the Democratic-Republicans started to dominate the political landscape. Politicians like William King and William Widgery knew how to tap anti-Boston and anti-elitist feeling among the electorate, especially among those who had recently settled in the district. Enthusiasm for separation waxed and waned, depending on which party controlled the Massachusetts state government, but the War of 1812—and Boston's evident lack of concern for the district's safety—proved a major turning point. By the May election of 1816, the separatists had amassed a 4,000-vote majority and, when even this did not convince the General Court, King looked forward to another vote in September. This proved a disaster, though only a temporary one, because worry about the fate of coastal shipping drove Republican voters in maritime towns to reject statehood. The vote in July of 1819, however, was a tribute to King's political skills. By revising the Coasting Law affecting local shipping and promising some jobs to Federalists in a new state government, he led his forces to triumph. The Constitutional Convention in Portland that soon met represented, in Banks's words, "a movement to democratize political and economic life in Maine. Without this important element, separation would have had much less appeal to the average citizen. . . ."[41]

What had been a regional issue now became a national one, for the addition of another New England state to the union threatened the uneasy balance of North and South in the U. S. Senate. To Jefferson, the debate came "like a fire bell in the night." But the famous compromise in 1820 that allowed Missouri to enter the union as a slave state, and Maine as a free one, proved the alarm had been premature, by some forty years. The new free state extended from the Piscataqua River and New Hampshire on the west, along more than 200 miles of Atlantic coast from Kittery to Quoddy Head, eastward to the Passamaquoddy and "a yellow birch tree marked in the year 1797. . . and incircled with an iron hoop" at the source of the St. Croix, and north to touch the British province of Lower Canada (though exactly where would take another generation to determine).[42]

The notion of including a section on higher education in a state constitution was nothing new; James Bowdoin II had made sure that Harvard's rights and privileges were protected in the 1780 constitution of Massachusetts. Given Bowdoin College's symbolic importance in the civic sphere, and King's animus against its government, it is no surprise that Article 8 of Maine's new constitution was drafted with the College in mind. The Republican-controlled New Hampshire Legislature had been quick (in the words of the *Argus*) to pry Dartmouth College loose from "the thralldom of an oppressive hierarchy and aristocracy"[43] and to turn it into the more egalitarian (or, at least, legislatively controlled) Dartmouth University. But as long as Maine was part of Massachusetts, the Federalist influence had been strong enough to prevent "popular" interference in the affairs of the commonwealth's three colleges.

Silhouette of John Crosby, Class of 1823. Crosby was a clergyman in Castine from 1828 to 1832 and died in Barbados, West Indies, in 1833.

U.S. Supreme Court Chief Justice John Marshall put an end to Dartmouth University by holding in a landmark decision that a college charter was a contract and therefore exempt from legislative interference. But the *Dartmouth College Case* did not help the friends of Bowdoin in 1819 (except in a way no one had anticipated: the president of the ill-fated university, William Allen, was to succeed Appleton at Bowdoin). Section 16 of the Bowdoin College charter of 1794 gave the Massachusetts Legislature power to alter the document. To head off any Republican attempt to take advantage of this clause after statehood, the college party persuaded the General Court, over King's protest, to insert a safeguard in the Act of Separation. It said that "the President, Trustees, and Overseers of the College, shall have, hold and enjoy their powers and privileges in all respects; so that the same shall not be subject to be altered, limited, annuled, or restricted, except by judicial process, according to law." This was qualified, however, by another article providing that any of the terms of the Act of Separation might be modified or annulled by the agreement of the legislatures of both states. The act further provided that Bowdoin would receive the accustomed $3,000 a year, until 1824.

According to Banks, King set immediately to work to dismantle this wall around Bowdoin College. The rationale of his policy was bluntly stated in a letter that Judge Judah Dana sent King during the summer of 1819. "In a country like ours," he wrote, "where its learning is mostly to be found in the desk [i.e., the pulpit] and at the Bar, those orders of men have an extensive, steady and increasing influence over the public mind, hence the necessity of having them filled with Gentlemen friendly to the Government; this can only be done by that wisdom and foresight, which shall enable us to establish, pure fountains of literature, so that the daily streams issuing forth, to replenish those professions, may not only be salubrious and healthful to the community; but also add strength and stability to the government." Since youths destined for public duties were likely to absorb the principles embraced by their instructors, he went on, "it becomes very necessary for the welfare of government, as well as the community that these Instructors should possess sound principles and unbiased tastes & feelings." With Bowdoin surely in mind, Dana pointed out that "the literary Institutions of a Country, when arrayed against its government are the most powerful engine to batter it down; but when favourably disposed, are its firmest and most desirable pillars."[44]

In October of 1819, the debate moved from the newspapers into the Constitutional Convention, meeting at First Parish Church in Portland. The original draft of Article 8 ("Literature"), as written by John Holmes,[45] gave the governor and his council a veto over the actions of governing boards of any "Literary Institution," it being quite clear which institution the Republicans had in mind.[46] Ether Shepley of Saco proposed amending the provision to give this power instead to the Legislature, saying that he thought its use ought to be restricted to financial oversight.[47]

The important thing, said Judge Judah Dana, was that such institutions be under *public* control. In a speech filled with classical allusions, he set forth his ideas on a system of public education in which the young would learn that "merit alone is the passport to preferment" and that "talents are not hereditary" and "greatness is not of lineal descent." If the public good required colleges, he declared, then legislators must take care "to shape the general course of instruction, and see that nothing therein should be taught contrary to the principles of our government." Left to their own devices, he feared that boards of trustees would be converted into "political junta or religious hierarchies" or "twisted up into indissoluable knots of family connections, who will consult their own gratification and interest, rather than the public good." Dana said

that common law rules protecting charters reflected British institutions—"theirs being shaped and modelled to monarchical, and ours to popular government"—and hence were inadequate in a republic. He warned that, in the absence of a provision to the contrary, the *Dartmouth* decision would apply to Maine's colleges. While the New Hampshire Legislature had failed, he said, "yet their discussion of principles has excited a spirit of inquiry throughout the nation, which will not be extinguished, I trust, till salutary reformations take place in our literary institutions." Give the visitorial power to the Legislature, not the governor, he implored the convention, to protect the people and the colleges from the exclusive control of either one man or a small board.[48]

Judge Albion K. Parris, who opposed the idea of direct legislative interference, said the same end would be met if officers of the state government were appointed to the Board of Overseers, to serve as watchdogs of the public interest. "It is Bowdoin College which is the object of this provision," he pointed out, "and we may as well name it, as keep it out of sight." Until the state had some connection with the College's Overseers, he added, "I would not grant them one acre of land, or give them a dollar in money." Admitting to "some attachment" to the College and a willingness to help it in the Legislature, Parris nonetheless threatened that "nothing will be given, until the people have in some way the control over this institution." He suggested having the Overseers meet in the capital at the same time as the Legislature's annual meeting.[49]

Holmes spoke up, reminding the delegates that the charters of Harvard and Bowdoin allowed legislative restrictions on the governing bodies and that the real problem was "the odious provision" in the Act of Separation putting Bowdoin beyond the reach of the state. "Ought there to be a literary institution in a state," he asked, "not subject to the control of the laws, nor subservient to the government that protects it? Why should this institution, more than any other, be beyond our reach?" The state should never grant any money to a college, he said, "unless we could in some way have a voice in its expenditure." He added: "If the College at Brunswick prefers to proceed on its present basis, it has its choice. I am for letting it alone, until it shall come forward and ask for aid, and if it will couple its request with a relinquishment of this odious provision, I would grant it."

Holmes played skillfully on several powerful themes. The convention had an opportunity, he reminded the delegates, to "preserve our republican institutions." Appealing to their anti-Massachusetts sentiments, he said he was "mortified" by the commonwealth's attempt in the act of separation to tell Maine how to deal with its colleges. ("Sir, are we in leading strings?" he asked.) And he warned of the "dangerous result" of the *Dartmouth* case. If institutions were beyond the control of legislatures, he concluded, "the time may come when creeds may be established, sects created, and parties built up, dangerous and destructive to the safety of the State and the liberties of the people."[50]

The Shepley amendment was adopted, 151 to 18, and still forms part of Article 8 of the Maine Constitution ("the only article that has never been amended," Banks points out). Dependent on the state subsidy for its continued existence, Bowdoin was for the time being effectively under state control.[51]

PUBLIC OR PRIVATE?

The 1830s produced a *Kulturkampf* of sorts in Maine, a struggle between two religiously based ways of looking at the world, in which higher education became entangled in politics. The immediate question was whether to continue the Legislature's subsidy of the College, but the answers given reflected the generation of struggle that had opened with Jeffersonians pitted against Federalists and now saw Jacksonian Democrats competing with anti-populist Whigs. It was often a contest between Baptists, Universalists, and other dissenters against Congregationalists—or, to put it in somewhat broader terms, between a largely rural majority that still felt left out of power and a more urban, rather high-minded elite which made up in eco-

nomic strength what it lacked in numbers. This is an oversimplification, to be sure—there were Whigs in the country, and Jacksonians in town (especially in Portland)—but it is clear that one area of contention between the two forces was for control over higher education.

Bowdoin was an easy target. "I will now point out some of the abuses tolerated in our principal College," wrote a critic under the pseudonym of "H" in Portland's *Eastern Argus*, the state's leading Democratic newspaper, on 15 February 1831. "The government of Bowdoin may be denominated a Theocratic-Oligarchy, a union of the two most odious forms ever imposed on man." Specifically, he charged that students could be dismissed without knowing their offense—a measure "worthy of an Inquisitor in the golden days of Papal supremacy"—and were subject to intense indoctrination by the college authorities.[52]

A lad upon entering this Seminary, instead of parental care and confiding tenderness, soon finds himself regarded with coldness and suspicion. He looks about among the higher classes and presently comes to the conclusion, that to conciliate the favor and gain the confidence of his instructors, he must not only resign the freedom of action, but of thought. He is not long in ascertaining that they act upon the position of total depravity [i. e., orthodox Calvinism], and must necessarily distrust all, who will not submit to the regenerating process, they kindly offer to direct. Nothing is more withering to an ingenuous and noble spirit—nothing more effectually damps the bold and daring aspirations of youth, than the relics of monastic discipline, still tolerated in our literary institutions.[53]

In further installments, "H" went on to catalogue other abuses. The government of Bowdoin had excessive powers, he complained, in violation of "the spirit of our Constitution." Its officers could enter a student's room at any hour, "notwithstanding the general principle that a man's house is his Castle." Too much power had been given to tutors and proctors. "Are they not often mere book worms—boys, who know nothing of human nature—nothing of the refined delicacy of intercourse expected in general society?" Even worse, the College violated the First Amendment's guarantee of the right of assembly by decreeing in its laws of 1824 that "no class meeting nor assemblage of students for consultation shall be held without permission of the President."[54]

When a friend of the College writing in the rival Portland *Gazette* accused the *Argus* of hostility toward Bowdoin, its editor called the charge unjust. Nonetheless, he took the opportunity to chastise the College for allowing students to recite partisan—i.e., anti-Democratic—speeches in their public declamations, "calculated to wound and irritate the feelings of a large part of that community upon which the college is dependent for its maintenance and support." The *Argus* was not hostile to Bowdoin as such, the editor explained, but toward "every thing in it which shall give it the colouring of a sectarian or partisan character." He added: "We hold that it is a public, a State institution, and the conduct of it open to discussion."[55]

In 1831, there were many who agreed with him. Yet the notion that some "literary institutions" were public and others private was a relatively new one. It was a distinction that would have been meaningless to an eighteenth-century American, who would have assumed that all colleges and academies served a public purpose, and hence fell within the public sphere, regardless of the circumstances of their founding. It was not the fact of a legislative chartering or grants of land or money that made these institutions public; it was the fact that outside the household a private sphere for education scarcely existed. In theory and in practice, Bowdoin—like Harvard or Williams at this period—was a state institution, a civil corporation, for the first three decades of the nineteenth century.[56] The efforts by the Maine Legislature to control Bowdoin between statehood in 1820 and the events of 1833 were not simply a grab for power; they were the logical result of a rather old-fashioned but widely held perception of the nature of the commonwealth and its civic institutions.[57]

But much had changed by the 1820s. The sheer number of new colleges, most of them fervently denominational, after the Revolution had challenged the monopoly of the state. The lack of ideological sympathy between the conservatives who ran the colleges and the Jeffersonian Republicans who controlled many state legisla-

tures added to the breach. Whether Marshall was more concerned about the future of the business corporation or the future of higher education in New Hampshire, his decision in *Dartmouth College v. Woodward* in 1819 had unmistakably declared Dartmouth a private eleemosynary corporation safe from the predatory grasp of state legislators.

By an interesting twist of fate, the Congregationalist minister who "lost" his university as a result of the Dartmouth case was to find himself its beneficiary some fourteen years later. William Allen had attracted the attention of William King and John Holmes—who had represented Allen's side before the Supreme Court—when the sudden death of Jesse Appleton left the Bowdoin presidency vacant. Despite his affluence—Allen had married well and was to awe Brunswick by the magnificence of the carriage in which he rode into town—the ex-president of Dartmouth University was known to be Jeffersonian in his political sympathies and a very likely candidate to inaugurate an era of cooperation between Bowdoin and the new state's leadership.

At first, this worked quite well. In 1820, Allen got the state-supported medical school for Bowdoin that King had promised him. In the following year he agreed to an act increasing the number of Boards members so as to allow King to place men of his own party among the Trustees and Overseers. However amenable in politics, Allen proved anything but conciliatory in religion, though; he was an evangelical Congregationalist, adept, in the words of his most famous student, at giving "a red hot Calvinist Sermon."[58] His denunciations of Universalists in particular gave offense.[59] An able but overbearing man—his signature alone can dominate a page—he alienated both students and legislators. The situation reached a crisis in 1831, when the Legislature passed an act declaring "that no person holding the office or place of President in any college in this State shall hold said office or place beyond the day of the next commencement . . . unless he shall be re-elected." Since no one at Waterville objected to President Chaplin, who would easily be re-elected, it was clear on whom the axe was descending.

As expected, no candidate at Bowdoin achieved a majority when the Trustees voted, and in September of 1831 Allen was dismissed.[60] He left town and established himself at Newburyport, in Massachusetts, which allowed him to turn to a federal court in the suit which he promptly brought against the treasurer of Bowdoin, Joseph McKeen, to recover his $1,200 salary—due him, he contended, as *de jure* president of the College—and the $5 fee paid for each diploma presented at Commencement (a traditional perquisite of office).[61]

Sitting as judge in the May of 1833 term of the United States Circuit Court held at Portland, Supreme Court Justice Joseph Story heard the arguments of the very able counsel for both the ousted president and the College.[62] The College was represented by Story's Harvard classmate, the Portland lawyer and Bowdoin Trustee Stephen Longfellow, Jr., who was a very competent, if not brilliant, advocate known for his gentlemanly manners. Allen was represented by Longfellow's good friend—whose son was soon to marry Longfellow's daughter—the learned Simon Greenleaf, who was about to be hired at Story's suggestion to begin a famous teaching career at Harvard Law School. Whatever passions the case raised, it was argued by two men of Federalist sentiments before a judge who, after a youthful fling with Jeffersonianism, had grown as conservative as Marshall.[63]

Greenleaf began with the distinction so important to the *Dartmouth* case: Bowdoin is "in its nature a private eleemosynary corporation." This could be seen, he said, in the fact that the Maine Legislature had reserved for itself certain powers. Had the College been public, "such reservation would be superfluous." After reviewing the nature of corporations, he pointed out that the

In 1833, in William Allen v. Joseph McKeen, *Judge Joseph Story held that Bowdoin College was a private, not a public, corporation, thus setting the College free of the control of the Maine Legislature. Chester Harding (American, 1792-1866),* Portrait of Joseph Story.

property which the state had granted to the College had become private property, "and the contract thus created could not be rescinded, nor the rights vested under it be devested, by any Act of the Legislature." More specifically, Allen's acceptance of the office of president had "created a private contract of service between the plaintiff and the College, which neither party, nor the Legislature could annul or impair."

Greenleaf went on to examine those legislative acts which purported to modify the charter of 1794. In allowing alterations to the charter from time to time—provided its consent was given—the Massachusetts Legislature, he argued, had contemplated actions "remote from the influence of popular excitement and the strife of party." The Maine legislators, nonetheless, had concluded that the Boards had "sold out" in 1820 the trust confided to them in 1794, "thus exposing the College to all the storms of political and sectarian violence." But Massachusetts had never consented to the law of 1820, "hence all the subsequent legislation of Maine in relation to the College is merely void, and the College still enjoys the immunity secured to it by the Constitution." Nor did it matter that Allen had consented to these acts. He could not give the state a jurisdiction it constitutionally lacked nor surrender rights that properly belonged to Massachusetts. And even if the 1820 law were valid, Greenleaf added, it would not give the state the right to act on behalf of the corporation: "It could neither make by-laws, nor create Trustees nor Overseers, nor displace any member of the corporation. If it might *limit* powers, it could not assume to *exercise* them. If it might invigorate the arm, it could not cut it off."[64]

Longfellow began with a more technical argument: that Allen was suing the wrong party.

86

McKeen was merely the agent of the corporation, he said, whose "situation involves no other responsibilities than those of a cashier of a bank." Moreover, even if an action could lie against the treasurer, Allen could not maintain it, for he was not president of the College. He had been removed by the 1832 act, which was constitutional, "for the College is in every respect a public institution. It was originally established and endowed by the State; the Legislature reserving the right to modify and even annul its charter. In each of these essential particulars," Longfellow continued, "it differs from Dartmouth College; and therefore the case of that College furnishes no analogy for the decision of this." When the Bowdoin family made its munificent gifts, he said, "these gifts were made to an institution already established by the public, and do not, in any degree, make it a private corporation." Nor did the appointment of trustees to manage it make it private: "this power must be vested somewhere; and the effect is the same whether it is exercised immediately by the Legislature, or more remotely by agents of its appointment." Ignoring *Dartmouth*, Longfellow went on:

Every institution, whether hospital or college, created and endowed by the government, as this was, for purposes of general charity, is a public corporation. The subsequent gifts of private benefactors, without Statutes directing their employment, are engrafted into the original foundation, but do not change its character. The State, as the founder, still retains the visitatorial power. . ."

Looking more specifically at the legislation, Longfellow could not resist pointing out that Allen himself helped obtain passage of the 1820 act. Any argument that Massachusetts had not consented to it failed to take into account that the corporation itself had vested the power of control in the Maine Legislature upon statehood and that this action had been ratified by Massachusetts. Longfellow made two other arguments: since no one at Bowdoin had objected when the Boards were enlarged by the 1821 act, hence "twelve years of profound acquiescence by all parties have already elapsed, affording the strongest presumptive proof of assent to the Statute." And since the 1832 act was "nothing

more than a legitimate exercise of the powers vested in the State by the Statute of 1820," Allen could claim no violation of vested rights; after all, he had accepted the office subject to the state's right of modification. He had not been removed from office, added Longfellow, a bit disingenuously; the act "merely declares that no President shall hold his office unless re-elected." Greenleaf replied that Allen's "supposed acquiescence" in the 1832 act was "merely a silent submission to superior force. . . nothing more than the bending of the rush before the tempest."

Story knew that he could have decided the case on the narrow question of whether McKeen had been the correct party to sue. But that would have allowed the challenge to *Dartmouth* to go uncontested and, he said, was not wished by either party in the case, because a decision on the whole merits of the controversy was "essential to the good order and prosperity of the College." Story was not only an energetic and scholarly jurist; he was also an economic nationalist who believed that the private business corporation would be the driving force in the expansion of the American economy, and he was determined to use his position on the bench to sweep away any legislative hindrance or relic of the common law that stood in the path of this economic nationalism. Although *Allen v. McKeen* is usually regarded as merely a footnote to *Dartmouth*, it gave Story an opportunity to refine his theory of the private corporation and the satisfaction of rapping the Democratic-dominated Maine Legislature on the knuckles.[65]

After rehearsing the legislative history of the various acts by which the Legislature had attempted to assert control over Bowdoin, Story moved quickly to the heart of the case. In what light, he asked, is the 1794 charter granted by Masssachusetts to be viewed? "Is it the erection of a private Corporation for objects of a public nature, like other Institutions for the general administration of charity? Or is it in the strict sense of law a public corporation, solely for public purposes, and controllable at will by the Legislative power, which erected it, or which has succeeded to the like authority?" In popular usage, it might be in some sense a public institu-

Henry Wadsworth Longfellow in his study in Craigie House in Cambridge, Massachusetts, ca. early 1870s. Longfellow, Class of 1825, returned to Bowdoin as professor of modern languages and librarian from 1829 to 1835 before moving to Cambridge to teach at Harvard and to become one of America's favorite poets.

tion, he admitted, for it benefited the public at large; but the sense of the law is far more limited, he said, as well as exact. Here he cited at some length Marshall's conclusions in the Dartmouth case. To which he added: "That a college, merely because it receives a charter from the Government, though founded by private benefactors, is not thereby constituted a public corporation, controllable by the Government, is clear, beyond any reasonable doubt." (Only fourteen years earlier it had not

been clear at all, at least until Marshall's bold and creative decision.) Bowdoin, said Story, was a private and not a public corporation. Massachusetts had entrusted its visitorial power to the Governing Boards, and while the Maine Legislature could enlarge or abridge the powers of those Boards, it could not tamper with their essential nature, such as would occur if the powers and privileges vested in them by the charter were given to the Legislature's appointees. Story held that the acts of 1821 and 1826 enlarging the Boards and making the governor a Trustee *ex officio* were unconstitutional, as was the 1831 act seeking to remove the College's rightful president from office.[66]

Allen returned to Brunswick, where the Boards accepted him as president and paid his back salary and fees. But Story, in an afterthought of sorts, had foreseen the problem that awaited: "It is impossible in any aspect of the case not to feel, that the decision is full of embarrassment," he had written in his decision. "On the one hand the importance of the vested rights and franchises of the literary institution have not been exaggerated; and on the other the extreme difficulty of successfully conducting any literary institution without the patronage and cordial support of the Government, and under a head, who may (however undeservedly) not enjoy its highest confidence."[67]

Nor could Allen be assured of support within the College. For example, the young professor of modern languages, Henry Wadsworth Longfellow 1825, took time from work on his *Outre Mer* sketches to write to a friend in Boston, in the summer of 1833: "You will see by the papers that Pres. Allen was received with some glee by the students; I suspect it was only for the fun of it. I was not present at his *entree*, being then on a visit to Portland. Things have taken their old course; and matters move on smoothly. We are all very glad to be beyond the reach of further Legislative interference, though some of us would not be sorry to have Dr. Allen resign."[68]

Allen remained president until 1839, but he grew more irascible in the conduct of his office, and increasingly the target for student discontent. "A meeting of the senior class was held in Dan'l Dole's room to take into consideration the expediency of taking some measures for ousting Pres Allen," noted Cyrus Woodman, Class of

Silhouette of Edmund Bridge Bowman, Class of 1823. Bowman was typical of those Bowdoin graduates who remained in the new state; he made a career for himself as a lawyer in Pittston, Dresden, Bowdoinham, and Wiscasset, Maine.

1836, in his journal for 1835. "Nothing definite done. Adjourned to next term. The Class were unanimous in thinking & saying that he is not fit for office."[69] Samuel Hazen Ayer 1839 reported a more public incident in May of 1837. The Senior Exhibition—an evening of recitations and orations by the class—began routinely:

. . . but when Scammon of Saco ascended the stage, and happening to have a part which was exceedingly witty, the President ordered him to leave the stage. . . No sooner had the words escaped from the President's lips, than every student and the whole audience filled the meeting house with groans, hissings and scraping. The President was as pale as death and almost fainted. . . After the performances were closed, the President left the chair and passed down through the isle [sic], when nothing but curses met his ear. Scammon is a great favorite among the ladies of Brunswick and they all of their own accord joined in the hissing.[70]

Allen's final departure in the spring of 1839 was cause for exuberance, on both sides. "Last evening we illuminated Pierce hall [a boarding house] in seven of its windows very brilliantly with about fifty candles," wrote a medical student, William Hawes 1837, to his friend Edward Daveis 1838:

. . . and the hint being taken from it the colleges [Maine and Winthrop Halls] both were prettily illuminated at about ten o'clock in the evening the freshmen & sophomores making huge noises with diverse cornets and sackbutts & psalteries, ringing the college bell etc. etc. uninterrupted by the office[r]s of the college;—for Mr. Allen yesterday left town, after having on the previous day (Sunday) assembled a large concourse of people at 1/2 past 4 p.m. to hear a farewell address, and uttering the most violent tirade and jargon of foolishness and impotence & wrath that the man's capabilities and the time and place collectively, would admit. He scourged the students, the faculty, the overseers, the legislature, all with much bitterness, and rehearsed in his own peculiar manner all the college offenses & crimes which he could remember. . .

Allen, according to Hawes:

. . . finally thanked the Lord that as he had only remained here for the sake of the good moral influence which he knew he had exercised in the chapel on sunday afternoons, he had by this means been enabled to save some souls. He charged everybody with everything, spoke hastily and rejoiced that he was biting the biters; and when he read the last hymn for singing, the choir rose and departed without performing this part of the service. He astonished all by his entirely absurd and childlike desire to get this opportunity of venting his last spite at all who he knows have long seen his inferiority. . . As to his religious character I not being orthodox may not be allowed to judge, but it is a rare thing to find a preacher prefacing with a hymn and a prayer on Sabbath such a collection of abuse and malicious snarling as that of this Wm. Allen.[71]

The air of promise that had characterized the new state to which the Allens had moved in 1820 had vanished; the feverish timber land speculation of the early 1830s had abruptly collapsed.[72] There were many causes for the Panic of 1837, the most significant leading across the Atlantic to the fiscal policies of the Bank of England, but Americans blamed their own banking system and the laxness of its credit practices in the boom years. It may have been of some satisfaction to Allen to know that among the victims of the crash were his old Democratic foes in the Legislature; economic unrest brought a desire for change, and the Whig Party triumphed in the 1838 elections.[73]

IN SEARCH OF FUNDS

The 1837 crash proved devastating to an institution which had invested more than 80 percent of its endowment of approximately $100,000 in bank stock. Those banks to survive did so by suspending payment of dividends, and the College had to borrow heavily to keep its doors open. The sale of College-owned lands had proved far less of a boon than anyone had expected at the time of the grants, and since *Allen v. McKeen* in 1833 there had been no further subsidy from the Legislature. The Visiting Committee for 1837 submitted a gloomy estimate of a $2,115 deficit, based on "diminution" of dividends. They added: "In the present unsettled state of business, the derangement of the currency, the novel situation

of all the banks, it seems difficult to predict with much accuracy what will be their future course and policy, as to the amount of dividend, they may declare." The Committee for 1838 reported even worse news: a $3,500 deficit—"rather more than a third of our whole expenditure"—and a shrinking of tuition income, also due to the condition of the nation's banks:

Unless . . . there should be a decided improvement in the college finances in these respects, it is apparent that if the institution can escape a reduction of expenditure, it will demand a great economy and carefulness in the application of its means with the strictest fidelity and attention to its most important interests and objects, and the utmost improvement of its resources from tuition.[74]

The Trustees contemplated reducing salaries and replacing a professor with a less expensive tutor, but they decided first to seek support among the philanthropic public. In 1841 the faculty issued a circular appealing to alumni and friends for money. During the winter vacation, President Woods and three professors visited potential donors throughout the state; in spring, the Winthrop lawyer Samuel Page Benson 1825 was hired (and promised 5 percent) to serve as agent in the same quest. But the depression had hurt more than the country's colleges, and, as Packard writes, "the result of these efforts was so meager that the project was abandoned."[75]

Meanwhile, Woods had persuaded the Boards to proceed with plans for a long-awaited new chapel, a structure estimated at this point to cost $15,000. A windfall from the Bowdoin estate arrived just in time to justify so monumental an undertaking.

James Bowdoin III's lack of a direct heir, which had benefited the College in so many ways, complicated its affairs in others. Bowdoin had made the College residuary legatee of the property he had bequeathed to his nephews, James Temple Bowdoin and James Bowdoin Winthrop, raising the interesting prospect that still more valuable real estate might revert to the College should those two young men produce no direct heirs. Winthrop, a member of the College's Class of 1814, took the name James Bowdoin and in 1823 persuaded the College to sell him its contingent remainder to a large tract in what is now Richmond, Maine, for $2,000—a sum a college historian aptly calls "a mess of pottage."[76] Had the College waited ten more years, it would have received the increasingly valuable land, for the new James Bowdoin died unmarried in Havana.[77]

James Temple Bowdoin had received the Beacon Street mansion-house and Naushon Island, among other land, but—despite a minor dispute in 1819 over the cutting of wood on the island—the College had little reason to expect anything from that quarter: the nephew lived in England and had a son. When this Bowdoin died at Twickenham in October of 1842, however, Woods moved with uncharacteristic speed. Claiming that Bowdoin had lost his rights to the property by failing to acquire American citizenship—a view supported by several distinguished members of the Suffolk County Bar—he authorized a symbolic "taking" of the Beacon Street property on behalf of the College.

What followed was a legal comedy worthy of Charles Dickens. As Packard remarks, "Great was the astonishment of neighbors and passers-by to find one morning in March, 1843, that the vacant Bowdoin lot on Beacon Street had been enclosed during the previous night, and already contained an inhabited shanty."[78] Where James Bowdoin II had entertained the royal governors and corresponded with the savants of two continents, and where his son had assembled one of the best collections of European paintings and drawings in the New World, the College that bore their name had hired a tenant to squat. Polite Boston was scandalized, the newspapers reacted with glee, and even some of the College's Trustees "pronounced it all moonshine." Representatives of the British Bowdoin's estate hastened to force their way in, knocked down the shanty, and chased the tenant away. As

Leonard Woods, Jr. (1807-1878), Bowdoin's fourth president (1839-1866), took office two years after the crash of 1837 substantially reduced the College's income. When fundraising solicitations were less than successful, he persevered in building the new Chapel and paid for it with a settlement from James Bowdoin III's estate.

planned, this "dispossession by violence" on the part of the estate allowed the College's legal advisers—Peleg Chandler 1834, Simon Greenleaf, and Benjamin Curtis—to seek a repossession in court.

The uncertain fate of an alien's cause in a Massachusetts court may have persuaded the other side to settle. The Bowdoin estate agreed to give the College three-tenths of the property, if it relinquished its claim to the rest. A quick sale followed, bringing the College $31,696.69. The intricate legal question of contingent remainders had appealed to the medievalist in Woods, but rarely has scholarly curiosity been so expeditiously rewarded.

Woods could proceed with his chapel, the price of which was rapidly climbing and would eventually reach $46,000. But the College still faced an uncertain financial future. There had been no state grant since 1831 and little prospect of any help from the Legislature ever again. Private support was proving negligible, despite the efforts of the College's partisans. At least another $10,000 was thought to be needed to complete the chapel, the cornerstone of which had been laid in 1845. Woods had sent Professor Thomas Upham to Boston and other cities in search of donations, but to no avail. Upham reported back that he could have raised $50,000 — but for one problem. The Baptists had their college at Waterville, he told Woods, and the Congregationalists had Yale, the Episcopalians had Trinity, and the Unitarians, Harvard, but otherwise sympathetic friends were puzzled by Bowdoin. "[I]f they felt a little more confident as to its denominational position," Upham wrote, ". . . the Congregationalists of Maine would cheerfully, I think, make a similar effort and would be likely to succeed in it, if they could be made to see that the responsibility of sustaining Bowdoin College rests on them, much in the same way and for the same reasons that the responsibility of sustaining Waterville College rests upon the Baptists."[79]

Upham knew that the Board of Overseers, dominated by orthodox clergymen, would agree, but no one knew how the more independent-minded Trustees would react; among their number were several of the state's leading Episcopal and Unitarian laymen. To test the waters, Upham circulated among the Boards members a draft of a formal adherance to orthodox Congregationalism on the part of the College. Trustee George Evans 1815 questioned whether the charter allowed the Boards to endorse such an affiliation and, joining with Robert Hallowell Gardiner, suggested an alternative: "a Declaration or expression of opinion binding in honor the parties and effectually securing the end desired."[80] Whether due to Upham's skills as a diplomat or to the Trustees' sense of financial realism, the document was approved. It was signed by eleven of the thirteen Trustees and by thirty-four of the forty-four Overseers.

The document, which came to be known simply as "The Declaration," made these seven points:

1) The 1794 charter had mandated that the College's funds be appropriated not only for improvement in "the liberal arts and sciences," but also in "such a manner as shall most effectively promote virtue and piety." Therefore, the drafters of the Declaration argued, it was "a permanent principle in the administration of the College, that science and literature are not to be separated from morals and religion."

2) The Boards were "of opinion, this object can be most fully accomplished, and at the same time the pecuniary ability of the College increased, by a known and established denominational character and position."

Silhouette of Richard William Dummer, Class of 1823. Dummer was typical of the many graduates who sought a fortune in the "West." He practiced law in Springfield, Illinois, and was involved in agriculture and teaching in Kansas.

3) While the charter specified no particular denomination, "yet, from its foundation, [Bowdoin] has been, and still is, of the Orthodox Congregational Denomination—as indicated by the state of the religious community in Maine when the College was established—by the religious instruction which has heretofore been given—and by the opinions of its former and present Presidents, and of a large portion of those who have been engaged in its government and instruction."

4) Any attempt to change this character now would be "unwise, and inexpedient."

5) Consequently, the Boards and faculty "should be composed of those who are competent and willing to perform their respective duties, in a manner not to impair or restrain or in any degree conflict with the moral and religious instruction . . .—care being taken that such instruction be given by officers of that religious faith."

6) Some further change in these arrangements was not ruled out.

7) Meanwhile, it was hoped that the Declaration "will not only furnish a basis for pecuniary aid, but will also effect a conciliation of different views and interests, and thus present the College in the most favorable and satisfactory light before the public."

It was, in other words, a sensible document in the minds of its signers, affirming the religious *status quo* but not in a rigid fashion. While falling short of late twentieth-century notions of pluralism, it nonetheless did not impose a religious test on undergraduates or even on faculty members, other than the president and the Collins Professor. Any constitutional questions were avoided by presenting the Declaration as a gloss on the eighteenth-century language of the charter—ignoring the possibility that the meaning of "piety" might have changed since 1794—and not as an attempt to amend it. The denominational conflicts of the past half-century were not forgotten, but a truce of sorts had been achieved in New England. Each persuasion had been allotted its recognized sphere of influence, and the sort of energies that William Allen, say, had devoted to combating the belief in universal salvation were being channeled by a younger generation into the benevolent social reforms—antislavery and temperance chief among them—championed by mid-nineteenth-century Protestantism. (The Baptists, a radical sect in the eyes of Bowdoin's founders, had grown respectable in both their Calvinist and Free Will branches by the 1840s, a decade when a new "enemy"—Roman Catholicism—was to remind the Protestant churches that they had more in common than they had once thought.) The Declaration brought no abrupt change to the College in the eyes of the public, and it is a tribute to its efficacy that it remained in force for almost another fifty years.[81]

The immediate results were impressive: by 1852, some $70,000 had been donated, mostly by Congregationalists in Maine and Massachusetts. Disaster had been averted; as Professor Ernst Helmreich points out, the Declaration "provided money for the payment of salaries, the completion of the chapel, the payment of loans contracted for the erection of Appleton Hall (in 1843 at a cost of $9,000), and the establishment of the Collins Professorship of Natural and Revealed Religion."[82] The only thing it did not do, however, was to resolve the internal denominational controversy at the College.

The orthodox were satisfied: as Woods wrote, "it leaves the Boards as they are and only provides that the religious instruction of the College should be in accordance with the sentiments of the Orthodox Congregationalists."[83] These points having been settled, he expected "a relaxation of the jealous and bitter spirit of sect." The result was the contrary. In referring to the College's early religious history, Upham had failed to note—perhaps on purpose—that in the

1790s New England Congregationalism was on the verge of being split by theological controversy and reshaped by evangelical strivings. The liberal, Arminian side of Samuel Deane and Joseph McKeen would have been of purely antiquarian interest to Congregationalists of the 1840s, but the orthodox "ascendency" at the College was still not beyond challenge. The immediate problem concerned the Board of Trustees. Most of the signers of the Declaration had assumed that as its older Episcopal and Unitarian members resigned or died, they would be replaced by "safe" Congregationalists. But several of the Trustees who had signed the Declaration, while bound to accept an orthodox president and Collins Professor, insisted that they were at liberty to choose their own members as they saw fit. The Overseers strenuously disagreed. Bowdoin was to be the Congregationalists' college, to be sure, but was it to be exclusively so, in terms of its governance?

On a rainy June day in 1855, the still-not-quite-finished Chapel was dedicated. The ceremony included a sermon by Roswell Hitchcock, the Collins Professor. The Chapel had been named for Bowdoin's old enemy and occasional friend, William King. When King died, leaving an estate insufficient to cover his pledge of $6,000 for the building, the College continued to call the building King Chapel. The evidence of the fruits of Upham's and Woods's labors—the professorship, the Romanesque building soaring above the pines—and the healing gesture of the honor given King seemed to bring to fulfillment the struggles of half a century. In his speech, a veteran of those battles, the aged Charles Stewart Daveis, of the Class of 1807, rejoiced that "I have lived to see this day, when clouds have passed away, and we see this symbol, as it were, ascending like an arch in the sky, to betoken as we trust the future smiles of heaven upon this cherished institution."[84]

But in a day so filled with symbols, one more deserves mention. The ceremony was held on a Thursday, because that was one of the days when the train ran from Portland. A very new age had begun.

NOTES

BCSC is Special Collections, Hawthorne-Longfellow Library, Bowdoin College.

1. Eliza Southgate Bowne to Miranda Southgate, New York City, 14 January 1806, Clarence Cook, ed., *A Girl's Life Eighty Years Ago* (London, 1888), p. 206. "Mr. Abbot is here from Brunswick and will take a letter for me to any of my friends. I should not have been surprised any more to have seen the cupola of the college itself walk into the room than I was to see Mr. Abbot, I could hardly believe me eyes; but I could not but *know* him, as I know nobody like him. . ." This confirms, incidentally, that Massachusetts Hall originally had a cupola, later removed because of structural weaknesses.

2. John Abbot to the Reverend Abiel Abbot, Brunswick, December 1812, Abbot Papers, BCSC. For another account of the same "ramble in the forest," see John Abbot to Jesse Appleton, Williamsburg (No. 6, 8th Range), 7 October 1812, Appleton Papers, BCSC.

3. Among those who explored the district in this period, the goal was not to see the forest, but to see beneath it—viz., to imagine the land cleared and turned to agricultural and pastoral use. On the problem of "how to subdue the land" (to use Jeremy Belknap's phrase), see "Clearing the Forest and Making a Farm," in Michael Williams, *Americans and Their Forests* (Cambridge, 1988), pp. 112-118. Abbot had been educated in an eighteenth-century tradition which saw no conflict between an "arcadian ideology," much influenced by the Virgil of the *Eclogues,* and an "imperial ecology," based on a desire to master nature in the spirit of Baconian science. On this tradition, see Max Oelschlaeger, *The Idea of Wilderness from Prehistory to the Age of Ecology* (New Haven, 1991), pp. 104-105. He lived into an age which distinguished between a "scientific nature" which was "devoid of taste, light, sound, and feeling" and a "poetic nature" which "in contrast, was alive, subjective, capricious, a riot of colors and sounds, and a source of aesthetic delight and philosophical inspiration." Oelschlaeger, p. 113. For a fuller account of this Romantic view of wilderness, see Roderick Nash, *Wilderness and the American Mind,* 3rd ed. (New Haven, 1982). There had been some notion of "romantic primitivism" among eighteenth-century Americans—William Byrd II's *History of the Dividing Line* (1728) is, Nash says, "the first extensive American commentary on wilderness that reveals a feeling other than hostility" (p. 51)—but "most of their contemporaries shared the pioneer aversion to wilderness" (p. 55). A typical reaction was the distinction the Anglican missionary Jacob Bailey drew in 1764 as he contemplated the Kennebec Valley: "here a gloomy forest presents with all its native horror, there a large field covered with corn, grass, and all the various productions of the climate." Quoted in Charles E. Allen, *History of Dresden, Maine* (Augusta, 1931), p. 739. Puritan "hatred" of the forest has probably been exaggerated, but even much of Hawthorne's work as late as the 1840s replicates the seventeenth-century view that the forest is an ungodly, disordered place. Abbot's reactions, which would have been commonplace to the next generation, were rather advanced for 1812.

4. Frederick S. Allis, Jr., *William Bingham's Maine Lands 1790-1820, Publication of the Colonial Society of Massachusetts: Collections,* vol. 36 and vol. 37 (Boston, 1954). Details on how the book came to be written are found in the introduction to vol. 36.

5. Allis, vol. 36, pp. 6, 7, 14-15, 23. Allis's initial chapter, "Background for Speculation," is a masterful overview of the district's economy in the 1790s, splendidly written.

6. One of the ironies of *William Bingham's Maine Lands* is the fact that a man who received so many letters about conditions in the district could remain so ignorant of reality there. Like most absentee proprietors, Bingham assumed much of Maine could be developed as rich agricultural land; it was not until the Barings sent John Black as their agent in 1820 and the lumber boom began, that the true source of wealth in the region began to be tapped. Black's handsome house at Ellsworth, open to the public, stands as a monument to that second age of speculation. Allis, pp. 1252-1255. The emphasis on agricultural improvement was very much a part of the program of the Kennebec Proprietors as well; see, for example, Charles Vaughan to James Bowdoin III, Hallowell, 15 January 1801, Kennebec Proprietors Papers, Maine Historical Society, Portland, Maine, and (on the Kennebeck Agricultural Society) Allis, vol. 36, p. 1043.

7. For an analysis of this instability, see John R. Howe, Jr., "Republican Thought and the Political Violence of the 1790s," *American Quarterly* 19 (1967), pp. 147-165, and the essays in Robert A. Gross, *In Debt to Shays: The Bicentennial of an Agrarian Revolution* (Charlottesville, Va., 1993).

8. Alan Taylor, *Liberty Men and Great Proprietors* (Chapel Hill, 1990), p. 272.

9. John Merrill and Benjamin Jones Porter to the President and Trustees, Topsham, 18 May 1798, BCSC.

10. Henry Adams, *The United States in 1800* (Ithaca, 1955; originally published in 1889 as the first six chapters of his *History of the United States,* vol. 1), p. 56.

11. Reverend Paul Coffin, "Some Remarks on the Methodists," in "Memoir and Journals. . . 1796," *Collections of the Maine Historical Society,* 1st ser., 4 (Portland, 1859), pp. 335-336. Coffin's travel notes, 1796-1800, are a particularly rich source for backcountry Maine life. For the best survey of the topic to date, see Stephen A. Marini, "Religious Revolution in the District of Maine, 1780-1820," *Maine in the Early Republic* (Hanover, N. H., 1988), pp. 118-145.

12. John Pierce to Jesse Appleton, Brooklin, 7 October 1804, Appleton Papers, BCSC, mentioning McKeen as a possible successor to Samuel Willard.

13. Appleton was not the Boards' first choice. Isaac Parker, who was to be chief justice of the Massachusetts Supreme Court and a Harvard Law

School professor, was elected 7-3 by the Trustees but rejected by the Overseers. The second candidate, the Reverend Dr. Eliphalet Nott, was chosen 8-1 and also rejected (he had already begun what was to be a famous, sixty-two-year presidency of Union College in New York). Appleton was sufficiently well-known to have been an unsuccessful orthodox candidate for the Hollis Professorship at Cambridge in the famous election of 1805 by means of which the Unitarians "captured" Harvard.

14. See "The Presbyterian Schism. 1792-1807" in Joseph Dow, *History of the Town of Hampton, New Hampshire* (Salem, 1893), vol. 1, pp. 419-439.

15. [A. S. Packard], "Memoir," in *The Works of the Reverend Jesse Appleton, D.D., Late President of Bowdoin College, Embracing His Course of Theological Lectures, His Academic Addresses, and a Selection from His Sermons. . .* (Andover, Mass., 1837), pp. 23-24.

16. "Memoir," pp. 36, 39.

17. "So-called" because recent scholarship suggests that the "Great Awakening" of the 1740s was a later invention or, at best, a surge of revivalism that did not extend beyond New England. For an explanation of this "interpretive fiction," see Jon Butler, *Awash in a Sea of Faith: Christianizing the American People* (Cambridge, Mass., 1990), pp. 164-165, and Joseph Conforti, "The Invention of the Great Awakening, 1795-1842," *Early American Literature* 26 (1991), pp. 99-118. The reality of the first "Great Awakening" had been uncritically accepted for some 150 years, further evidence of the degree to which New England dominated the writing of American history.

18. "Memoir," p. 53.

19. Reverend H. S. Burrage, "Capt. John Wilson in the War of 1812," *Collections of the Maine Historical Society*, series 2, vol. 10, pp. 418-429; George A. Wheeler and Henry Warren Wheeler, *History of Brunswick, Topsham, and Harpswell, Maine*, vol. 2 (Boston, 1878), p. 694. The sixty-seven men at Phippsburg, most of them militia draftees, remained in the garrison until January of 1815. The coastal defenders would have been no match for experienced British forces. The only Brunswick-area residents who did find themselves in a war zone were the three Sinnett brothers of Bailey's Island. According to the Wheelers' account, they boarded a vessel in the fog under the impression that it was an American man-of-war only to find themselves prisoners of the British aboard HMS *Rattler*. They were not harmed; the captain simply wanted use of their fishing boat for a week to reconnoitre the coast without arousing suspicion.

20. Rev. William Jenks to Rev. Jesse Appleton, Bath, 20 June 1814, Appleton Papers, BCSC.

21. There was some worry about the coasting trade, too; James Bowdoin III's widow, upon shipping his paintings to the College, was relieved to learn that they had arrived safely. "I should have been *extremely sorry* that they should have fallen *into the hands* of *our Enemy*: and am much gratified that they are disposed of, agreeable to the wishes of the donor—although the parting with them cost me a few melancholy reflections. . ." Sarah Bowdoin to Jesse Appleton, Boston, 9 March 1813, Appleton Papers, BCSC.

22. Louis C. Hatch, *Maine, A History* (Portland, 1919), pp. 73-78.

23. Barry J. Lohnes argues that the British failure to capture Portland, Portsmouth, and other coastal towns, where they would have met little resistance, was a strategic failure. "A New Look at the Invasion of Eastern Maine, 1814," *Maine Historical Society Quarterly* 15, no. 1 (1975), pp. 4-18. In "A Comment," pp. 26–29 of the same issue, Ronald Banks doubts, however, that the British could have gone much beyond the Kennebec, for he believes they would have met much stronger resistance and would have had to pull troops from the Chesapeake or Canada. It served British purposes to treat New England with "salutary neglect," he says. Eastern Maine was another matter, for the British saw it as a part of Canada that had been temporarily lost in the 1783 peace treaty. One interesting feature of the politics of the time is that areas with Republican majorities, such as William King's Topsham-Bath stronghold, had been provided some defenses; the Federalist areas were more or less neglected by the Madison administration. As it turned out, eastern Maine proved not important enough to bargain for; the Treaty of Ghent in 1814 restored the district's borders to the *status quo ante bellum*.

24. Hatch, p. 78.

25. Working in the King Papers at the Maine Historical Society, Alan Taylor found evidence that King was actively involved in trading with the enemy, as his political opponents in the 1820s were to charge. King, who had lost an estimated $5,558 a month when his ships could not leave port during the embargo, knew that his financial survival as a merchant depended upon taking advantage of the ineffectual enforcement of wartime restrictions on trade with Britain, Bermuda, and the West Indies. He had no choice, Taylor concludes, however hypocritical this rendered his public stance. "While the *Eastern Argus* vigorously adhered to the party line, blasting wartime trade with Britain as a treasonous Federalist plot, its principal financial backer was deeply involved in the trade." "The Smuggling Career of William King," *Maine Historical Society Quarterly* 17, no. 1 (1977), p. 35. Most of his colleagues were doing the same regardless of their politics, says Taylor, making Bath second only to Eastport as the smuggling capital of northern New England.

26. One possible explanation is that Appleton was mistaken for whoever it was that Governor Caleb Strong of Massachusetts sent in 1814 to sound out the commander at Castine, Sir John Sherbroke, on the prospects for a separate peace. Herbert T. Silsby argues that George Herbert was the envoy. "A Secret Emissary from Down East," *Maine Historical Society Newsletter* 2, no. 4 (1972). The mission produced no result before the war ended that winter. As for Brunswick, sentiment regarding the war is difficult to gauge, other than to note that the town meeting censured Rep. William Widgery for voting in favor of the declaration of war. Hatch, p. 72.

27. On the Federalists' influence in Maine, see James M. Banner, Jr., *To the Hartford Convention: The Federalists and the Origins of Party Politics in Massachusetts, 1789-1815* (New York, 1970), passim. For their reaction to the war, especially their fear of a strong central government, see Lawrence Delbert Cress, "'Cool and Serious Reflection': Federalist Attitudes Toward War in 1812," *Journal of the Early Republic* 7 (1987), pp. 123-145. Being in opposition made at least some Federalists appreciate civil liberties in a way they had not shown in the days of the Alien and Sedition Acts. Details of Stephen Longfellow, Jr.'s career are found in David Hackett Fischer, *The Revolution of American Conservatism: The Federalist Party in the Era of Jeffersonian Democracy* (New York, 1965), pp. 267-268. He was the father of the poet.

28. Ernest C. Marriner, *The History of Colby College* (Waterville, Me., 1963), pp. 2-7, 603-604.

29. John Adams to Daniel Cony, 1 February 1819, quoted in Jeremiah Perley, *The Debates, Resolutions and Other Proceedings of the Convention . . .* (Portland, 1820), p. 300. Adams was replying to a query regarding his views on statehood, which he opposed.

30. Order from Mark Dyett, merchant, Montserrat, to Porter & King, 4 December 1800, King Papers, Maine Historical Society, Portland, Maine.

31. Eliza Southgate to Moses Porter, 13-16 September 1801, Bath, *A Girl's Life Eighty Years Ago* (London, 1888, and Williamstown, Mass.: Corner House, 1980), p. 73. "All the navigation belonging to the different ports on this river above Bath, passes directly by here, and several times I have seen 12 or 14 [vessels] at a time. To one who has been brought up amidst salt marsh and flats, this large fine river affords much novelty and amusement, and I cannot confess but the sensations I feel in viewing it are more pleasing than those produced by a stagnant water in a Scarborough salt-pond."

32. The best account to date of King, at least as a politician, is found in Banks, passim. Some useful genealogical material appears at the end of Marion Jaques Smith, *General William King: Merchant, Shipbuilder, and Maine's First Governor* (Camden, 1980). Henry Wilson Owen, *History of Bath, Maine* (Bath, 1936), p. 139.

33. Orr was an exception to the usual pattern by which the newly successful became Republicans, while the established were Federalists. He began his career apppprenticed to a housewright in New Hampshire, took to the road, and after many hours of observing courthouse business, decided to became a lawyer. He worked his way through Dartmouth, then settled in 1801 in Topsham, where he became one of the district's leading attorneys and one of the College's most energetic Boards members (Overseer, 1808-14; Trustee, 1814-28). He was "a truly original character," according to Nehemiah Cleaveland and Alpheus S. Packard, *A History of Bowdoin College* (Boston: James Ripley Osgood and Company, 1882), pp. 41-42.

34. Hatch, pp. 42-43. Porter resigned in 1815 as treasurer but served again as a Trustee from 1821 to 1844. Porter's house on Elm Street, today part of a retirement complex, is still the most handsome building in Topsham.

35. Reverend Sylvanus Boardman, quoted in *A Vindication of the Character of Alfred Richardson Against the Aspersions of Governor King* (Portland, 1822), pp. 31-32.

36. Perhaps with Bowdoin in mind, the future Waterville president, upon writing to congratulate King on passage of the Coasting Law by Congress, urged caution in any attempt to raise funds for the new college through the newspapers: "We fear that to address them in that manner at the present juncture would have a tendency to give a *political character* to our Seminary, which ought, if possible, to be avoided . . . " Jeremiah Chaplin to William King, Waterville, 20 April 1819, King Papers, Maine Historical Society.

37. Jeremiah Chaplin to William King, Waterville, 1 March 1819, quoted in Marriner, p. 34.

38. The political polarities in the Maine of the early Republic were not rural labor versus mercantile capital, or even coastal elites against backcountry radicals. Voters seem to have adhered to one party rather than the other on the basis of their feeling of "arrival"—Federalists tending to be men well-established in their communities, Republicans "new" men seeking an economic foothold and a right of participation in civic life. Some evidence for this view is found, for example, in an election report sent to King from Lisbon, Maine, in the spring of 1819: "I am sorry to find the storm the night before opperated verrey un favourable for this Town. the snow was so deep and slumpey that Horses could not Travail and the main body of the Federalists reside in near the middle of the Town abought the Corner where we hold our T[own] Meetings. and they took oportunity to raise all their horses. I am satisfied that their would have been a large majority on the Republican side had the Roads been pasable Many of the Republicans living in the remote parts of the Town, whom I road amongst & had their promise to attend Town Meeting, were not present. . ." Ezekial Thompson to William King, Lisbon, 6 April 1819, King Papers, Maine Historical Society. In terms of village geography, at least, the Federalists were at the center, the Republicans on the fringe.

39. The College could hardly have ignored the statehood debate, even had it wanted to. On 30 September 1816, 185 delegates from 137 towns convened at the Congregational Meeting House in Brunswick—in other words, practically on campus—for what Banks calls a "decidedly un-Christian" encounter between Republican separatists and their Federalist opponents. President Appleton stayed busy receiving a stream of visitors. High-handed efforts by William King and his followers to "steal" the Brunswick Convention were so bungled, it is a tribute to the strength of separationist sentiment that the movement triumphed only three years later. Banks, pp. 103-115.

40. Banks, p. 143.

41. Banks, p. 207. "Coasting" was transporting fish or fuel, say, from Maine to Boston or other seaports.

42. Moses Greenleaf, *A Statistical View of the District of Maine. . .* (Boston, 1816), p. 9.

43. *Eastern Argus*, 7 October 1817.

44. Judah Dana to William King, Fryeburg, 30 July 1819, King Papers, Maine Historical Society.

45. John Holmes, a celebrated lawyer from York County, had begun his career as a Federalist but converted to King's party during the War of 1812. He represented the district in Congress and, as counsel for the university, opposed Daniel Webster in the *Dartmouth College Case* of 1819. In 1820, the new Maine Legislature elected him to the U. S. Senate.

46. Banks, p.175. An amendment to replace this veto clause with a power of removing the Trustees if they misused the institution's funds was quickly defeated, after Holmes pointed out that such power already existed under common law and that the funds in such a case could be forfeited to the state. Jeremiah Perley, *Debates and Journal of the Constitutional Convention of the State of Maine, 1819-20* (Portland, 1820), p. 278.

47. Once it had been ascertained that the funds were being properly applied, Shepley argued, then a college should be managed "by those to whom it properly belongs"—the trustees—for "Legislatures as well as Executive officers are continually changing and can know nothing of the mode of study and discipline pursued in Colleges." Perley, pp. 279-280. This view was not widely held among Republicans, even though his amendment succeeded.

48. Perley, pp. 280-286.

49. Perley, pp. 286-288.

50. Perley, pp. 288-290.

51. According to Samuel Benson's reminiscence, King testified to a legislative hearing in 1834 that Thomas Jefferson had inspired Article VIII of the Maine Constitution. "Origins of Article VIII, Literature. . .," *Collections of the Maine Historical Society* 7, 1st series (Portland, 1876). This has been confirmed, Banks says, by King's letter to Jefferson of 3 November 1819, which states that the "Literary Article we are indebted to you for. . . . when at your hospitable mansion the last winter you may recollect naming the article of the kind to me as of the first importance, as calculated to perpetuate our Republican systems." Banks writes: "It is more likely that King outlined generally to Jefferson what he, Dana, and others had contemplated doing to bring Bowdoin under state control, and that Jefferson, already excited about the probable establishment of the University of Virginia along nonsectarian lines, nodded his approval and perhaps made a few tactical suggestions. . . . Article VIII would not have been significantly different had King never gone to Monticello." Banks, pp. 178-179.

52. The reference to Catholicism was surely not accidental; Irish immigration to New England in the 1830s and 1840s gave rise to intense, occasionally violent anti-Catholic reaction. "A majority of the people of this State," writes "H," exploiting this prejudice, "would not more deeply regret the conversion of their children to Popery, than to Calvinism. . .," *Eastern Argus*, 11 March 1831. The implication is that both Romanism and authoritarian Congregationalism are dangerous to Republican values.

53. *Eastern Argus*, 15 February 1831. The author returned to this theme, with relish, in discussing revivals at College. "Some one of the officers relates his *experience*—exhortation and prayer ensue—some of the lads in the freshman or possibly sophomore class, are wrought up to a high pitch of excitement—there is a prayer meeting in one of the recitation rooms in the evening—those who are under concern are visited in their rooms, tortured into fearful apprehension, by lectures on original sin, total depravity and final decrees. Panic struck, desponding, and with countenances clouded by gloom; the regular exercises are neglected, the excitement spreads like a contagion, and some are wrought up to a wild and feverish enthusiasm, while others sink into irremediable despair. I have seen lads of fifteen or sixteen, under those impressions, wander about for months, without hope or consolation; while their friends witnessed their mental aberration, with excruciating agony, expecting daily to see them become raving maniacs." *Eastern Argus*, 11 March 1831.

54. *Eastern Argus*, 22 February 1831.

55. *Eastern Argus*, 8 March 1831. Writing in the same paper on 18 March 1831, "H" was even blunter. "Speeches, orations and essays, steeped in the gall of party spirit, scurrilous attacks upon the South, slavery, slave representation and republican principles, are recommended as models of American eloquence. Everyone knows how captivating are the corruscations of genius. Bolingbroke, Hobbs and Hume have converted their thousands, and Voltaire his tens of thousands to infidelity; and is it supposed that political sophists are less successful? May not young men be modelled into Tories or Aristocrats, with as much facility as they can be made Atheists or Deists? . . . The General Government is often libelled, at the semi-annual exhibition, by beardless boys, who mistake flippancy for wit and cavilling for wisdom."

56. The case of Williams College is especially apposite. As Frederick Rudolph writes, "the conclusion is inescapable that the 'independent, privately supported' American college has perpetrated a fiction upon itself and upon society by ignoring the degree to which it is a creature of the state," *Mark Hopkins and the Log: Williams College 1836-1872* (New Haven, 1956), p. 190. Between 1793 and 1823, for example, Massachusetts gave Williams College $53,000 (including $19,000 from the sale of its townships in Maine), a sum equal to what the college had been able to raise on its own in that period. Anti-elitist sentiment may have discouraged further support in the decades that followed, but state grants in 1859 and 1868 brought an additional $100,000. Such subsidies were the difference between survival and failure until the day

when the post-Civil War fortunes of various alumni could be tapped for donations. Although the 1868 grant was the last, there was no formal break between the state and the college. Rudolph, pp. 188-200.

57. For a close examination of the question of state control, see Jurgen Herbst, *From Crisis to Crisis: American College Government 1636-1819* (Cambridge, Mass., 1982). On Bowdoin's status as a public institution, see pp. 214-218, 248. Of the forty-four institutions operating in 1820, nine were colonial foundations and the others were divided more or less evenly between public and private (p. 241). "The decades following the Dartmouth decision," he writes, "were to witness an unprecedented increase in the number of private colleges, and they established the private college as one of the country's most characteristic and unique institutions" (p. 242). For an analysis of a more narrow sample, see John S. Whitehead, *The Separation of College and State: Columbia, Dartmouth, Harvard, and Yale, 1776-1876* (New Haven, 1973). He argues that the public/private distinction was still not well defined even after *Dartmouth* nor would be until after the Civil War. States, he writes, did not want control of colleges lest they have to pay for them; colleges, while valuing their "inviolability," still asked for state grants (p. 6, 83-87). But the debate in Maine would seem to disprove his conclusion that *Dartmouth* attracted little attention (p. 83). For a more recent summary of their disagreement on these questions, see Whitehead and Herbst, "How to Think about the Dartmouth College Case," *History of Education Quarterly* 26, no. 3 (Fall 1986), pp. 333-349.

58. Nathaniel Hawthorne to his sister Elizabeth, Brunswick, 28 October 1821,Thomas Woodson *et al.*, ed., *Nathaniel Hawthorne: The Letters 1813-1843*, p. 159.

59. By asserting that all people would receive salvation through the goodness of God, the Universalists rejected Calvinist doctrines of damnation for those who were not among the elect.

60. Press reaction to the controversy reflected party and denominational alignments. *The Christian Mirror*, the Congregationalist newspaper in Portland, called the legislation "an act of *attainder*" and noted, "One atrocious feature of the bill (and one which makes us tremble for our future liberties) is, that it was meant to have full operation upon one person, upon the President of Bowdoin College, alone," 5 May 1831, reprinted at Allen's request in the *Eastern Argus*, 3 June 1831. On the other hand, the *Gardiner Chronicle*, a Universalist newspaper, said, "And especially are we grateful to the Legislature for a law, which will have the effect to remove Dr. Allen from the Presidency of Bowdoin College." 15 April 1831.

61. McKeen was the son of the College's first president.

62. Story heard the case in Maine because in his day U. S. Supreme Court justices traveled around the country on three circuits each spring and fall, Portland and Wiscasset being the northernmost towns on the Eastern Circuit. These federal circuit courts consisted of two justices and the district judge, any two of whom constituted a quorum. It was a particu-larly demanding chore, given poor roads and bad accommodations. For details of the system, see Maeva Marcus, ed., *The Documentary History of the Supreme Court of the United States, 1789-1800*, Volume Two: *The Justices on Circuit 1790-1794* (New York, 1985). Story heard the case alone because the district judge, Ashur Ware, was a Bowdoin Trustee.

63. For details of the two lawyers' careers, see William Willis, *A History of the Law, the Courts, and the Lawyers of Maine* (Portland, 1863).

64. Story's decision along with the arguments of both lawyers is printed in *Charter of Bowdoin College together with Various Acts of the Legislature, and the Decision of the Circuit Court and the By-Laws of the Overseers* (Brunswick, 1850); for Greenleaf, see pp. 26-31, 34-35; for Longfellow, pp. 31-34.

65. Story's role in helping create the American business corporation is masterfully presented in R. Kent Newmyer, *Supreme Court Justice Joseph Story: Statesman of the Old Republic* (Chapel Hill, 1985); see especially the chapter "Judge-made Policy and Economic Progress," pp. 115-154. On the ideological mood of the Marshall Court and the impact of republicanism on its economic thought, see G. Edward White, *The Marshall Court and Cultural Change 1815-35* (New York, 1988), passim.

66. The intellectual ancestry of *Allen v. McKeen* goes back to a seventeenth-century English precedent cited by Marshall in the Dartmouth case: *Philips v. Bury*, which dealt with the power of visitation over charitable foundations. More to the point were the Yazoo land scandal case, *Fletcher v. Peck* (1810), in which Marshall held that states may not make laws negating contracts, and *Terrett v. Taylor* (1815), in which Story held that the state of Virginia could not take back property granted the Episcopal Church before it had been disestablished: a religious institution enjoyed the same vested rights to property as an individual.

67. *The Opinion of Judge Story in the Case of William Allen v. Joseph McKeen* (Boston, 1833), p. 19.

68. H. W. Longfellow to A. H. Hill, Brunswick, 16 July 1833, Andrew Hilen, ed., *The Letters of Henry Wadsworth Longfellow*, vol. 1 (1814-1836), p. 419.

69. Cyrus Woodman Journal, vol. 2, 7 December 1835, Maine Historical Society.

70. Samuel H. Ayer to Issac Hill, Brunswick, 23 May 1837, BCSC.

71. William Hawes to Edward H. Daveis, Brunswick, [1839], BCSC. Allen had already been the butt of several student pranks. Henry Ingalls 1841 wrote to his sister in South Bridgton, for example, that during the president's levee for the seniors students had slipped a goose into the house, which spoiled the new presidential carpet—"The joke was perpetrated partly as a cut on the President and partly to probe the Seniors who are despised by most of College"—and had taken Allen's hat ("worth six dollars") and put it on the lightning rod of the Chapel. "The 'President's man' came to take it away just as the bell was tolling for prayers amid the shanks of the assembled Collegians." Henry Ingalls to Clara Ingalls, Brunswick, 22 July 1838, BCSC. Almost a month before Allen officially

resigned, Ingalls told his sister of the rumors that he would soon leave. "If so *good* if not why there will be verified the adage viz. 'hardly ever any great loss without some small gain,' or, in other words we shall have some sport with the old man." Ingalls predicted the Boards would offer the post to Dr. William Sprague of Albany, N. Y., one of the most famous preachers of the day. "He is a fine looking man and I should have no hesitation in predicting the rapid rise of this College to the first rank in the Union if he became President. He is handsome and dignified two rare qualities in combination and at the same time very easy and affable in manners." Brunswick, 19 August 1838, BCSC. No one would have written of Allen in those terms. But as a letter writer, Ingalls was later to regret the president's absence: "When Allen was here there was always something to write about, some disturbance, rebellion, suspicion, rustication etc but now under the happier yet more monotonous rule, no such interesting matters come in to help the empty brain to fill a sheet. . ." Ingalls to Clara Ingalls, Brunswick, 10 May 1840, BCSC.

72. "The timber lands of Maine had become a favorite habitat for the speculator of the East. The rumor that 'the timber of Maine was diminishing so rapidly that the supply must soon be exhausted' precipitated the scramble to engross what remained. 'The rage to purchase these lands became excessive, and most extravagant prices were paid.' Building lots in Bangor, Maine, which heretofore had sold for $300, now brought $800 and $1,000, while woodlands, instead of selling at their normal price of $5 and $10 an acre, were snatched up at the fanciful figures of $15 to $50 per acre." Reginald C. McGraw, *The Panic of 1837* (Chicago, 1924), p. 47.

73. By contrast, the Panic of 1819, which grew out of the aftermath of the Napoleonic wars, seems not to have made a great impression in Maine, possibly because its banking system was so undeveloped, possibly because statehood and the Missouri Compromise distracted public attention.

74. Reports of the Visiting Committee for 1837, 1838, BCSC. The College had enjoyed a surplus of approximately $1,730 for 1836. The treasurer estimated expenses of $9,260 and income of $7,145 for 1837, the deficit to be covered by a $2,100 loan.

75. Cleaveland and Packard, p. 21. Between 1841 and 1845, about $6,000 was pledged in subscriptions, of which only about $2,000 was collected. See Visiting Committee Reports for 1840-44, especially August 1842, BCSC. This was not the first public campaign for funds for Bowdoin. In addition to the appeals that had accompanied the opening of the College, there was a circular sent in 1818 to "the friends of good morals and good education" and signed by subscription committees in each Maine county seeking annual donations of $5 in support of a professor of languages. The response must have been modest, for there was not to be such a professorship until 1825, when James Bowdoin III's widow partially funded it. The response to the fire in the original Maine Hall in 1822 was more gratifying, thanks to the efforts of John Holmes in

Washington, D. C. President James Monroe gave $50, John Quincy Adams $100, John C. Calhoun $25, and Stephen Van Rensellaer $150. Many other subscribers were recruited in New England. As Nehemiah Cleaveland noted afterwards, "The damage was estimated at $6,513.44. The amount received was $9,735.32. The fire, it appears, was not ultimately ruinous." See "Account of College Funds," c. 1832, p. 4, College Records: Financial, BCSC.

76. Cleaveland and Packard, p. 108.

77. The sad story of the scholarly James Bowdoin Winthrop and his miserable death from tuberculosis at age thiry-eight in Cuba is told in Lawrence Shaw Mayo, *The Winthrop Family in America* (Boston, 1948), pp. 289-299.

78. Cleaveland and Packard, p. 109.

79. Quoted in Hatch, pp. 74-75.

80. Their text reads, in part: ". . . as religion of some kind was recognized in the Charter, and as all religion has its *form*, it was their duty to say, what method or form of religion was, in their opinion, contemplated by the founders. In this way it was possible, that the denominational position of the College could be satisfactorily settled, disputes and collisions prevented, the course of religious instruction indicated with sufficient clearness, and also a permanent basis for pecuniary support secured." *To the Friends and Patrons of Bowdoin College,* [1846?].

81. In the absence of such a denominational identity, it is possible the College would not have survived the 1850s; few, if any, small antebellum colleges were able to attract funds or students without clearly allying themselves to a denomination—and not just any denomination, but one with sufficient numerical strength in the college's "catchment" area. A Unitarian Bowdoin, say, might have been an intellectually more adventurous place, especially in the 1860s and 1870s, but there were simply too few Unitarians, even in Portland, to have supported it.

82. Ernst C. Helmreich, *Religion at Bowdoin College: A History* (Brunswick, Me.: Bowdoin College, 1981), p. 77. (Helmreich, Thomas Brackett Reed Professor of History and Political Science Emeritus, taught history at the College from 1931 until his retirement in 1972.) Leading the list were a $6,000 donation by Mrs. Amos Lawrence of Boston and a like sum from Professor Upham. Those giving $1,000 each included Benjamin Tappan of Augusta, John W. Ellingwood and George F. Patten of Bath, John McDonald of Bangor, Joseph McKeen ("for himself & others") and President Woods of Brunswick, Robert Appleton of Boston, and Ether Shepley of Portland. There were 397 other subscribers, whose gifts ranged from $1 ("a youthful friend") to $800, including $100 from Henry Wadsworth Longfellow in Cambridge. A separate subscription raised $16,600 for the Collins Professorship. "List of Subscriber names in aid of Bowdoin College 1847-'8," College Records: Financial, BCSC.

83. Helmreich, p. 77.

84. C.S. Daveis, "Address, delivered at the laying of the corner stone of King Chapel Bowdoin College," C.S. Daveis papers, BCSC.

Professor Parker Cleaveland (1780-1858), called the father of American mineralogy, taught chemistry, mineralogy, and natural philosophy from 1805 to 1858 at Bowdoin and the Medical School of Maine.

AN

ELEMENTARY TREATISE

ON

MINERALOGY AND GEOLOGY,

BEING AN

INTRODUCTION TO THE STUDY OF THESE SCIENCES,

AND DESIGNED

FOR THE USE OF PUPILS,—FOR PERSONS, ATTENDING LECTURES
ON THESE SUBJECTS,—AND AS A COMPANION FOR
TRAVELLERS

IN

THE UNITED STATES OF AMERICA.

ILLUSTRATED BY SIX PLATES.

BY PARKER CLEAVELAND,

PROFESSOR OF MATHEMATICS AND NATURAL PHILOSOPHY, AND LECTURER ON
CHEMISTRY AND MINERALOGY, IN BOWDOIN COLLEGE, MEMBER OF THE
AMERICAN ACADEMY, AND CORRESPONDING MEMBER OF THE
LINNÆAN SOCIETY OF NEW ENGLAND.

.............................itum est in viscera terræ ;
Quasque recondiderat, Stygiisque admoverat umbris,
Effodiuntur opes.................   Ovid.

BOSTON :

PUBLISHED BY CUMMINGS AND HILLIARD, NO. 1, CORNHILL.

PRINTED BY HILLIARD AND METCALF, AT THE UNIVERSITY PRESS,
CAMBRIDGE, N. ENGLAND.

1816.

Parker Cleaveland's An Elementary Treatise on Mineralogy and Geology, *published in 1816, was the first American text in the emerging field of geology and made its author internationally famous.*

This vacuum pump, used in the early nineteenth century by Parker Cleaveland in his chemistry lectures, is on permanent loan to the Smithsonian Institution.

CHAPTER FOUR

Amid the controversies brought by statehood, religious ferment, and economic and
social upheaval, the daily work of the College went on. This was not simply
a matter of memorized recitations and laboratory demonstrations, of student orations
and daily prayers. It included a variety of cultural, civic, and
intellectual projects—from Parker Cleaveland's mineral-hunting to Leonard Woods's
medieval revivalism—which had an impact far beyond the town of Brunswick.
The Medical School of Maine, affiliated with the College, demonstrated
the power of formal education to give authority to an emerging profession,
that of the scientifically trained physician.

AMERICA, THOU HAST IT BETTER

Seeking to recreate the mental world of backcountry Maine in the early years of the nineteenth century, Alan Taylor has explored what he calls "the supernatural economy" of rural New England. This took the form of a widespread belief between about 1780 and 1830 that the ground was full of buried treasure. "Why did such astute people cherish incredible fantasies?" he asks, and finds the answer in a complex of economic and psychological factors that drove people in the early Republic to yearn for quick wealth and a sense of power over the supernatural world.[1] With such treasure-hunting on so many minds, it is hardly surprising that lumbermen from Brunswick and Topsham sought out the young man from Harvard who had just arrived in 1805 to teach mathematics and "natural philosophy"—the study of the created world—at the new college on the hill. They brought him the bright and eye-catching stones they had found in the riverbanks where they were building mill-dams and sluiceways. He often did not know what they were but resolved to find out.

They were not buried treasure or precious gemstones, but they did prove a source of infinite scientific richness for Parker Cleaveland. He had already read law, come close to going into the ministry, tutored at Harvard (where he had

graduated in 1799), and undertaken to teach chemistry at Bowdoin. But with his discovery of the uncharted field of American mineralogy he had found his true vocation. The result, in 1816, was his *Elementary Treatise on Mineralogy and Geology*, the pioneer American work on the subject. From his house on Federal Street, copies of his treatise (and of its second edition in 1822) went out to the learned societies, royal libraries, and renowned men of science in Europe as well as to his fellow collectors and scientific colleagues in the United States. There can be few other instances in which a new college in a remote location so quickly made its name known throughout the learned world.[2]

One of the most remarkable tributes to Cleaveland's work came from the poet Goethe, who was also a keen scientist and at one time director of mines for the Grand Duchy of Weimar. Goethe was fascinated by mineralogy and thought the character of a country was shaped by its rocks and minerals. Given a copy of Cleaveland's book, with its descriptions of New World phenomena presented within the terminology of European science, Goethe was ecstatic. He had Cleaveland made an honorary member of the Jena Mineralogical Society. And in 1830 he published a poem beginning "Amerika, du hast es besser" and entitled "Den Vereinigten Staaten," or "The United States." It was *translatio* in reverse, a great European's tribute to the

Members of the Chandler family on the side porch (since removed) of the Parker Cleaveland House (built 1806), at 75 Federal Street, ca. 1900. Parker Cleaveland's daughter, Martha Cleaveland Chandler, and her husband, Peleg Whitman Chandler '34, bought the house from the College after Cleaveland's death in 1858. Peleg Chandler, who became a Trustee in 1871, financed the remodelling of Massachusetts Hall and the installation of the Cleaveland Cabinet in 1873. The College repurchased the house in 1991 for use as a president's house. The white-haired man in the chair on the right is Melville Weston Fuller '53, a Trustee after 1894 and chief justice of the U.S. Supreme Court from 1888 to his death in 1910.

freshness of the new nation. In the slightly inaccurate English translation that was soon published in *Fraser's Magazine*, it reads:

America, thou hast it better
Than our ancient hemisphere;
Thou hast no falling castles.
　　Nor basalt, as here.
Thy children, they know not,
Their youthful prime to mar.
　　Vain retrospection,
　　Nor ineffective war.
Fortune wait on thy glorious spring!
And, when in time thy poets sing,
May some good genius guard them all
From Baron, Robber, Knight, and Ghost traditional.

It sounds much better in German. As Thomas A. Riley explains, Goethe's reading of Cleaveland's *Mineralogy* had reinforced his idea

that it was more important first to understand a country's minerals and rocks than to know its written history, the structure of the earth being entwined with human destiny. The lack of basalt in the eastern United States meant to him that America had missed the tortured "volcanic" upheavals that had marred the Italian character, for example, and had perhaps escaped the burden of tradition altogether. Goethe's theories of natural science may strike the modern reader as no less eccentric than those of the New England "treasure-seekers," but the point is that he wanted to believe in a fresh and vigorous new nation untouched by the tragedies of Europe. "The man who taught him the most about the possibilities of the United States," says Riley, "was the mineralogist Parker Cleaveland, Professor of

Mathematics and Natural Philosophy at Bowdoin College in Massachusetts."[3]

In retrospect, Cleaveland's book is primarily a work of classification and organization, in the spirit of the Baconian science he taught for more than half a century. He did not do research in the modern sense, and his field work did not take him very far from Brunswick (for one thing, he was terrified of lightning, as students loved to relate, and would take shelter on a feather-bed at any sign of a thunderstorm). He was an energetic exchanger of specimens, and there was steady traffic in boxes of minerals between his house and those of his learned friends.[4] There is so much surviving correspondence, it is surprising no one has written his biography (although there is a very good one about his Revolutionary War grandfather, Christopher M. Jedrey's *The World of John Cleaveland*, the life and times of a Massachusetts clergyman). The starting point in any such future biography ought to be an observation Michael Chandos Brown makes in his recent biography of Cleaveland's more famous contemporary, Benjamin Silliman of Yale: the importance of scientists of the early Republic like Cleaveland and Silliman is not in their originality but in the role they played *as men of science*.[5]

In that sense, Cleaveland's career at Bowdoin takes on new meaning, for in truth he did not follow up on his early success as a mineralogist, and as a practicing scientist he was extremely conservative. His treatise had a strong pedagogical tone, for he was a man who loved teaching. In the splendid eulogy that Leonard Woods, Jr., wrote after his death in 1858, he tells of Cleaveland's meticulous devotion to his chemical lectures:

After an early breakfast, it was his invariable custom, continued to the last years of his life, to go to his laboratory, and employ the whole intervening time in preparing for the lecture of the day, laying out his topics, performing beforehand every experiment, and practicing every manipulation. These preparations were interrupted only by the frugal repast sent to him from his house in a small basket, when the dinner hour had arrived . . . When at length the hour of the lecture had arrived, and the eager and punctual audience had assembled, and, after seven minutes by the watch, the door was closed, and silence prevailed, and the Professor stood forth amidst his batteries and retorts, master of his subject and of the mighty agents he had to deal with, he was then indeed in his element and in his glory.[6]

His tenacity, love of routine, and "intense conservatism of character," Woods noted with approval, had an effect beyond the lecture hall:

It is owing very much to his persistent adherence to the old college system, as he found it at Harvard, and as he brought it with him from thence, that Bowdoin College has been able effectually to withstand the spirit of change at some points, where some other colleges have yielded, it may be to their hurt.[7]

Although the modern College remembers Cleaveland chiefly for his book and his chemistry lectures—a remnant of his "philosophical apparatus," or laboratory equipment, hangs in the fireplace of the McKeen Study of Massachusetts Hall, where it is mistaken by many visitors for cooking utensils—those achievements do not begin to exhaust his activities. He was an early practitioner, for one thing, of what today might be called adult education, for he traveled frequently between Hallowell and Portland giving public lectures; he was a master of the dramatic explosion and the galvanic twitch, at a time when demonstrations of basic chemistry and physics were a popular and genteel entertainment. He assembled the vast treasure of minerals, sea shells, stuffed birds, Indian artifacts, and other curiosities that filled what came to be called the Cleaveland Cabinet, now sadly lost or thrown away but for much of the second half of the nineteenth century a much-visited tourist attraction in Brunswick and a country cousin of the great *Wunderkammern* of the Renaissance.[8] He founded the local volunteer fire department. When William Allen was thrown out of office, Cleaveland took over much of the sensitive negotiations with the Legislature and the Boards and ran much of the everyday business of the College. He lobbied Congress and the Legislature energetically but in vain for an observatory and a hospital in Brunswick. Above all, from 1820 to his death he was one of the major figures in establishing and running the Medical School of Maine, where he served as professor of

Between 1873 and the renovation of Massachusetts Hall in the 1930s, visitors entered the Cleaveland Cabinet by way of the portico shown on this early twentieth-century postcard.

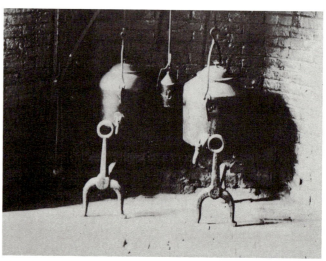

Part of the "philosophical apparatus" that Professor Cleaveland used in fifty-three years of chemistry lectures is still in the fireplace in President McKeen's study (which President Sills used as an office) in Massachusetts Hall.

The Cleaveland Cabinet contained the mineral collections of James Bowdoin III and Professor Parker Cleaveland, the Shattuck Shell Collection, and an assortment of other natural history specimens. Installed in 1873 in the top floors of Massachusetts Hall, it was a major public attraction. The space was needed for other uses, however, and the top floor was converted into the Faculty Room in 1936-1938. The architect for the renovations was Felix A. Burton '07.

materia medica. In his leisure, he corresponded with his good friend Dr. Benjamin Vaughan, the Hallowell polymath, on subjects ranging from the techniques of "heroic medicine" (usually, drastic purging and bleeding) to the weather (both were keen meteorologists).

Parker Cleaveland was a representative figure at the antebellum College in another sense: he impressed himself upon his students not simply by his erudition, which was broad if conventional, but by the force of his character, a model of teaching that was to shape the College in many ways. His former student and faculty colleague, Henry Wadsworth Longfellow, for one, recognized how special he was. Visiting Brunswick in the summer of 1875, he reflected on how much he missed him:

Among the many lives that I have known,
None I remember more serene and sweet,
More rounded in itself and more complete,
Than his who lies beneath this funeral stone.
These pines, that murmur in low monotone,
These walks frequented by scholastic feet,
Were all his world; but in this calm retreat
For him the teacher's chair became a throne.
With fond affection memory loves to dwell
On the old days, when his example made
A pastime of the toil of tongue and pen;
And now, amid the groves he loved so well
That naught could lure him from their grateful shade,
He sleeps, but wakes elsewhere, for God hath said,
"Amen!"

THE WORLD OF THE BOOK

At only their second meeting in Portland in 1795, the Trustees outlined the duties of the College's librarian: Bowdoin, in other words, had a library before it had a president, faculty, buildings, or students. What books if any were at hand is unknown, but donors soon appeared. For example, rather than give money or land, as the Trustees surely hoped, General Henry Knox responded to the College's published solicitation in 1797 with the six weighty volumes of the sumptuous elephant folio of Louis Ferdinand Marsigli's *Danubius Pannonico-Mysicus* (The Hague, 1726), a *de luxe* geography of the Danube basin. Samuel Deane, a former librarian of Harvard (1760-63), added the post of

This manuscript fair copy of Henry Wadsworth Longfellow's poem to his old teacher is in Special Collections, Hawthorne-Longfellow Library.

Bowdoin librarian to his duties as vice president of the Trustees and contributed a second edition of his *New England Farmer* to the collection. By the opening of the College in 1802, Deane had accumulated between 300 and 500 books and arranged them on the second floor of Massachusetts Hall. Governor Bowdoin's widow, Elizabeth, mother of James Bowdoin III, gave £100 for the purchase of more books in London, a benefaction which roughly doubled the size of the collection. In the fall of 1803, the Boards appropriated a further $1,000 for books and named John Abbot, the College's single faculty member, to succeed the seventy-year-old Deane as librarian, beginning a tradition of professor-librarians that would last until the 1880s. Among his many other duties Abbot found time to prepare four catalogues of the collection, three in manuscript (1808, 1811, and the "Alcove Catalogue"—so called for its listing by shelf—of 1819) and a fourth printed in 1821.[9]

Later writers have made much of the alleged inaccessibility of early nineteenth-century college libraries, and in some ways Bowdoin's was no exception. It was open only from noon to 1 P.M.

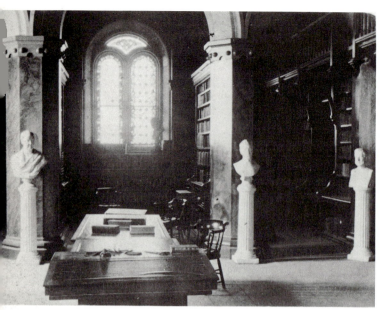

The interior of the library in Banister Hall.

one day of the week, in an unheated and poorly furnished room, on the second floor of the wooden chapel built in 1805 (where the books were to remain until 1848). Its contents did not necessarily reflect the intellectual interests or classroom pursuits of either students or faculty. Yet it is anachronistic to expect such a collection to have provided the services of a circulating library or research collection of the twentieth century. From the surviving records, it is clear that many of the books did circulate among a wide portion of the College community—faculty, students, and alumni living nearby. Moreover, in a locale that still seemed a frontier, *any* collection of books had a symbolic force beyond the mere fact of being read. A number of American colleges—including Harvard, Yale, and William and Mary—had been founded by gifts of libraries, and throughout the Federal period the identification of a gentlemanly standard of learning with a tangible assortment of appropriate titles was a cultural given. Judging by their letters and diaries, students at antebellum Bowdoin had ample time to read, but they found most of the material to read in the excellent circulating libraries of their undergraduate literary societies and did not feel too inconvenienced by the restrictions on the College collection.

Throughout the century, the library depended more on private gifts than on institutional funding. Some of these gifts were exceptional. The Vaughan family—Benjamin in nearby Hallowell, William in London—was especially generous. The arrival in 1811 of James Bowdoin III's bequest of books (about 775 titles in 2,035 volumes, plus more than 2,000 pamphlets) meant that the College had for a time the third largest institutional collection in the country, surpassed only by Harvard and the Library of Congress. Contrary to the earlier view that the new arrivals represented a "gentleman's library" of the time, Kenneth Carpenter has persuasively argued that James Bowdoin purchased most of these books with a specific pedagogical purpose in mind, namely to create a library useful in fulfilling the cultural mission of the College that bore his family name.[10] The collection also reflected the younger Bowdoin's own political and diplomatic career and his interest in contemporary history, particularly recent French history. As the *General Repository and Review* of Boston noted in 1812, "of many of the books . . . a few copies, or perhaps in some cases but a single copy . . . can be found in this country." Perhaps because of their rather specialized nature, many of the James Bowdoin III books sat undisturbed on the shelf, despite the fact they were available for circulation for more than a century. The condition of many of them indicates minimal use. It was not until the 1950s, and again in the early 1960s, that the Bowdoin volumes that had escaped pilfering were pulled from the general stacks and housed in Special Collections.

The next major windfall came courtesy of President Allen. When he had been president of the short-lived Dartmouth University in 1817, he accepted the offer of an old family friend to take whatever books from his library that Allen thought the new institution might need. The friend was Thomas Wallcut of Boston, the leading book collector in New England and a great admirer of Allen's father-in-law, the Rev. Eleazer Wheelock, who in addition to running Dartmouth College had been a missionary among the Native Americans. Among the 558 books chosen was a first edition of John Eliot's

"Indian Bible" of 1663, one of the rarest pieces of Americana, even at that time. With Wallcut's permission, Allen brought the books with him and gave them to Bowdoin in 1820, a major bibliophilic coup for the College.[11] The same year Benjamin Vaughan turned over 1,067 volumes in the name of "a friend of the College." The collection had been brought by Samuel Vaughan to Jamaica, where it is said that the cockroaches were so attracted to the leather bindings, that it was necessary to send the books to a cooler climate if they were not to be destroyed. A second Vaughan deposit, smaller but perhaps even more valuable, followed in 1823 from London. By the time Henry Putnam wrote his promotional *Description of Brunswick* in 1822, the College could boast of a library of about 6,000 volumes. The collection grew slowly through the rest of the century. The building of Upjohn's chapel between 1844 and 1855 meant a safe—though, as it turned out, inconveniently arranged—space to house the library at last.

But the world of the book in early nineteenth-century Brunswick extended beyond the College. In 1819, a young printer from Andover, Massachusetts, set up shop in town, in response to an invitation from Professor Samuel Newman, and soon was setting the late Jesse Appleton's final Baccalaureate address into type. "It was required that the work should be printed in the best manner, without regard to expense," the printer was told. It was the beginning of a long association of the College with Joseph Griffin. Unfortunately he had taken the commission too literally and despite 70 subscribers to the memorial, it took him ten years to clear the debt he faced on the edition of Appleton's sermons.[12]

With a new printing press in 1828, Griffin put himself on better financial footing by being able to undertake publishing on a broad commercial scale. President Allen and Professors Upham, Smyth, and Longfellow brought him their books, "the printing of which, with the other usual work, kept Mr. Griffin's press in constant use for about 25 years, and was the means of placing him in very comfortable pecuniary circumstances." He did particularly fine work—elegantly simple and clean—on twenty-nine annual edi-

Alpheus Spring Packard '16, librarian from 1869 to 1881, in the library in Banister Hall, 1879. Packard taught classics, mathematics, languages, and religion at the College from 1819 to 1884 and was acting president for a year between the Chamberlain and Hyde administrations. His sixty-five years of service to the College may be the longest of any faculty member to any American college. Professor Packard was also a key figure in the Maine Historical Society from its founding in 1822 until his death in 1884.

tions of the *Catalogue of Bowdoin College* and forty-two biannual editions, plus sixteen editions of the *Triennial Catalogue*. About the time he began his press, Griffin also opened a bookstore where from the 1820s on he sold textbooks (previously, students brought their texts with them, or purchased them at cost from the professors or secondhand from fellow students.) Griffin was a small-town printer, but the work produced— Appleton's *Works* (1837); Allen's second edition of his popular *American Biographical Dictionary* (1832); Cleaveland's *Mineralogy* (1816 and 1822); Harris's *Christian Doctrine of Human Progress* (1870); Longfellow's *Proverbes Dramatiques* (1830) and textbooks for Spanish, Italian, and French (and parts of *Outre-Mer*, 1833); Newman's *Practical System of Rhetoric* (1827, the first of 65 editions!) and *Elements of*

Bowdoin's collection of plaster casts from antique classical statues was displayed in the library in Banister Hall before 1894, when they were installed in the rotunda of the Walker Art Building. A picture of Nathaniel Hawthorne is in the center, with the Laocoön *to the right of it. The* Hermes of Praxiteles, *given by Professor Henry Johnson '74, is behind the* Laocoön, *and further right, in the niche, is the* Primaporta Augustus, *given in 1882 by the Hon. W. W. Thomas h '13.*

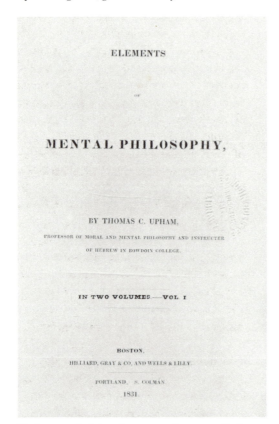

ELEMENTS

OF

MENTAL PHILOSOPHY,

BY THOMAS C. UPHAM,

PROFESSOR OF MORAL AND MENTAL PHILOSOPHY AND INSTRUCTER
OF HEBREW IN BOWDOIN COLLEGE.

IN TWO VOLUMES.——VOL I

BOSTON,
HILLIARD, GRAY & CO. AND WELLS & LILLY.

PORTLAND. S. COLMAN.
1831.

In addition to printing the college catalogue, Brunswick printer Joseph Griffin published widely distributed textbooks by Bowdoin faculty members in such fields as languages, mental philosophy, rhetoric, and mathematics.

Used as a textbook in colleges across the country, Professor Thomas Upham's Elements of Mental Philosophy *was still in print in 1888. The earliest editions (1826, 1827, and 1828), titled* Elements of Intellectual Philosophy, *were printed by Joseph Griffin in Brunswick.*

Political Economy (1835); Packard's *Xenophon* (1839); Smyth's *Elements of Algebra* (1830); Tucker's admirable 1863 *Catalogue of the Library*; Upham's *Mental Philosophy* (1827) and *Practical Treatise on the Will* (1834); and Woods's *Address on the Life and Character of Parker Cleaveland* (1860), to mention only a few of the titles from Bowdoin pens—carried the name of the College throughout the English-speaking world.[13]

THE WORLD OF THE EYE

There are any number of unanswered questions about the life of James Bowdoin III, and one of the more interesting ones is why did he become a Jeffersonian Republican? He had commercial ties with Virginia dating back to the Revolution, to be sure, and he admired Jefferson's range of interests, some of which he shared, such as political economy, agricultural improvement, and the cultivation of the eye. (The marble statue of a reclining woman, thought at the time to be *Cleopatra* but actually *Ariadne*, can still be seen at Monticello, the gift to Mr. Jefferson by his Boston admirer.) Yet one suspects that the younger Bowdoin's political unorthodoxy had more to do with some long-term act of rebellion against his father. By the first years of the new century, it must have been clear to everyone concerned that the son had not lived up to the Governor's expectations for him. As the scion of a family with a strong dynastic sense, he had not produced an heir. As the only child of a very shrewd politician who had wielded enormous power in the 1780s, he had managed to accumulate only a few local honors around Boston. And as the witness to his father's decisive action that may have prevented full-scale civil war at the time of Shays's Rebellion, he knew how much of his own life had been spent in a passive and unheroic state of ill health, some of it possibly self-willed.[14]

Much of that is speculative, of course, but it is unfortunately the case that when his only significant moment to prove himself on the world stage came, he flubbed it. This was not entirely, or even principally, his fault—the United States was too feeble to be taken seriously by Napoleon and Talleyrand—but it must have been a dispiriting experience. Instead of appointing him to the London embassy he had lobbied for, Jefferson sent him in 1805 on a rather ill-defined mission to the Court of Spain, in hopes of settling border disputes arising from the Louisiana Purchase and claims by American merchants against the Spanish and of possibly even buying Florida for the United States. Forced to operate from Paris rather than Madrid, Bowdoin made little progress. He had to spend much of his time guarding himself against a hostile colleague, General John Armstrong; their exchange of angry notes is one of the oddest episodes in U. S. diplomatic history. Bowdoin's diplomatic venture came to naught.[15]

The journal (now in Special Collections) in which Sarah Bowdoin recorded on an almost daily basis the events of their sojourn in Paris and London from the fall of 1806 to the winter of 1808 is the fullest account to have survived of the domestic life of James Bowdoin III. It is also valuable for its behind-the-scenes look at one of the new republic's diplomatic missions in Europe. Much of the journal is a matter-of-fact record of who came to dinner—the Bowdoins often fed a dozen or more of their fellow citizens, there being more Americans in Napoleonic Paris than one might expect—and of daily constitutionals in the gardens of the Tuileries palace, not far from the Bowdoins' lodgings at the Hôtel de Rome. But Mrs. Bowdoin also weaves in shrewd observations about French life and customs, as well as lamenting her husband's chronic ill health and their distance from her Boston friends in Milk Street. When "Mr. B—," as she calls him, feels well enough, they ride out in their carriage to see Versailles (which, though stripped of furniture, still "evinces great marks of magnificence") and Marly (where, as a young man, Bowdoin had seen the late queen "in *all her beauty & glory*"). In good weather, they walk on the boulevards: "the vanity you there see, is very amusing, it seems as though there was *a procession* passing *all* the *time*, & every kind of Article is exposed for sail, & every kind of Amusement is going on, & some are eating & drinking" (24 October 1806).

ADVICE TO SHEPHERDS

AND

OWNERS OF FLOCKS,

ON THE

CARE AND MANAGEMENT OF SHEEP.

TRANSLATED FROM THE ORIGINAL FRENCH OF

M. DAUBENTON,

BY A GENTLEMAN OF BOSTON.

To which are added,

EXPLANATIONS OF THE PLATES,

AND A

TABLE OF CONTENTS.

BOSTON,
PRINTED BY JOSHUA BELCHER.

1811.

James Bowdoin III was the "Gentleman of Boston" who translated Daubenton's Advice to Shepherds and Owners of Flocks *from the French.*

Another contrast with Boston that she notices is the independence of married French women. (She and her companion, her eighteen-year-old great-niece, Sarah Bowdoin Winthrop, walk frequently in the gardens, but always accompanied by a footman.) "Women here are very useful kind of beings. They are shop, & store kepers, also box-keepers at the Theatre, when you are there they unlock the box door, & put you in & keep the key in their pocket, but you can open the door withinside—the women are also *drivers* of Carts, carriers of large burdens, & work also in the field" (13 December 1806).

One woman in particular who excites Mrs. Bowdoin's curiosity is the Empress Josephine. One February day in 1807, she follows the Empress on her walk, noting details of her dress and hat. "We followed *so very near,* that we might have *almost* been supposed to have been *in her train.*" On a visit with Mr. B to the Jardin des Plantes, she notes how much Napoleon has improved the appearance of Paris in six years. The Emperor, she adds, is "indeed a *most wonderful Character,* he is *not* only great in his *Military skill,* but in Civil establishments, & the *most minute things* do not *escape* his *observations,* & *attention.* The more one hears, & knows of him, the more wonderful his Character appears" (27 June 1807). Mrs. Bowdoin's second husband was to be a general. She had noted more sharply, however, how skilled Napoleon's regime was in keeping the populace diverted with festivals, parades, and victory celebrations "executed with all the Stile, *Magnificence & Pomp,* which the french give to public Exhibits" (17 May 1807).

Much of Mrs. Bowdoin's day is spent in writing letters and entertaining the American colony in Paris—guests come for the mid-day dinner and stay or return for evening tea—as well as receiving such friends of America as the Marquis de LaFayette and General Kosciuszko. *La vie diplomatique* does have its perils: the ambassador of Morocco and his suite move into the rooms directly below, and "not being *acquainted* with the *European* customs, & manners they come several times to look into our appartments, to the *no small fright* of my *maid Polly*" (3 September 1807). She and her husband find time to order furniture and draperies made "for our Salon in Beacon-Street" and to buy a clock, wallpaper (for the Beacon Street house and the house they plan to build on Naushon Island), silk and linen, and carpets, all to be boxed up and shipped to America. There is, alas, no mention of buying pictures, and not much indication that Mrs. Bowdoin was particularly interested in art, other than one reference to going to the Louvre to see paintings of Napoleon and his battles (24 October 1806) and another to her cousin's visit a year later to see a famous portrait, presumably David's, of Mme. Recamier "but the maid who

110

shew it to them, said it was a *flattering likeness* of her Mistress." The Bowdoins do enjoy the Cabinet of Curiosities at the Jardin des Plantes: "indeed a most magnificent establishment, and every thing is arranged in the most beautiful order, & manner, one could pass several days here with great pleasure, & satisfaction" (5 October 1807). A cabinet on a more modest scale, including Bowdoin's collection of minerals and crystal models, was to be a feature of the new college in Maine.

The most dramatic passages of the journal describe the miserable ten days it took in the fall of 1807 to cross the Channel en route to London. The weather is so bad, they almost are shipwrecked within sight of Portsmouth (the ship's cook is swept overboard and drowned); the gale blows them back to France; when they finally reach Southampton Harbor, the wind dies down and they have to be rowed for two hours in a small boat to shore. Life at 42 Conduit Street, Hanover Square, is more tranquil, although Mrs. Bowdoin is disappointed in her hope of seeing George III at court. She is pleased to attend the fashionable church of St. James, Piccadilly—in Paris, she had had to confine her devotions to reading Blair's *Sermons*—and finds it "very full, so much so that Mr. Sullivan was obliged to stand in the Ile, where a great number were also standing, it seemed really full like *our Commencement* [at Harvard]" (31 January 1808). Among her callers are a Miss and a Mrs. "Copely"—perhaps the family of the painter Copley, who was then living in London—but whether the Bowdoins' friendship with them was artistic or simply based on shared Boston origins is not spelled out. The journal ends as the Bowdoins prepare to leave to take the waters at Bath; she thinks the unhappy business with General Armstrong and others in Paris has ruined her husband's health.[16]

Upon their return to Boston in 1808, her husband seems to have resolved to live a more retired life on Naushon Island, where among several rural pursuits he raised prize Merino sheep—a great status symbol among gentlemen farmers at the time—and translated Daubenton's *Advice to Shepherds and Owners of*

The Trustees named the Sophia Walker Gallery in the Chapel for the mother of Theophilus Wheeler Walker, a cousin of President Woods's who had concerned himself with the state of the College's art collection. Most of the paintings had been left to the College by James Bowdoin III and his widow, Sarah Bowdoin Dearborn.

Flocks, on the Care and Management of Sheep. (He had brought a shepherd-boy with him from France.) His health began to fail more rapidly, and on 11 October 1811, at the age of fifty-nine, he quietly died, having guaranteed the longevity of his name by attaching it to a struggling institution in the District of Maine. After a decent interval of two years, his widow, Sarah, married General Henry Dearborn.[17]

As a youth Bowdoin had spent part of a year at Christ Church, Oxford, where he surely would have seen the collection of Old Master paintings and drawings given to that college in 1763 by an eccentric *dilettante*, Colonel Guise. His own Grand Tour through Italy would have exposed him to many famous collections, and perhaps he had inspected Napoleon's loot in Paris, and it is at least arguable that the Guise donation in particular stuck in his mind.[18] There is no evidence that he bought any art while in Europe, and not

111

The Chapel, looking southwest, along what is now the Class of 1895 Path.

Some of the paintings left to the College by James Bowdoin III and his widow, Sarah Bowdoin Dearborn, are shown in the Chapel in 1893. Recognizable are: (top center) Brigadier General Samuel Waldo, *by Robert Feke; (middle center)* Elizabeth Bowdoin and James Bowdoin III, *by Joseph Blackburn; (top left)* The Reverend Samson Occom, *by Nathaniel Smibert, and (middle left)* William Bowdoin as a Boy, *by an unknown artist. Space was also allocated to the library and collections, or "cabinet," of the Maine Historical Society until 1881, when the society moved to new quarters in Portland. This photograph was taken in what is now the organ loft.*

The north and south walls of the Chapel were gradually decorated with copies of Old Master paintings and scenes from the Old and New Testaments. The murals were done as funds became available; the first two were completed in 1856, the last in 1915. This picture was taken between 1877 and 1886.

much in his letters—which mostly concern family and diplomatic business—even to indicate he was particularly interested in painting. Yet the collection he left to the College is an important one. If Kenneth Carpenter is correct that the younger Bowdoin's library was assembled specifically with the College in mind, then it seems logical that he acquired the paintings out of a similar motive. If so, it was a remarkable step for the time and place.

However and whenever Bowdoin acquired his collection, the College was pleased to have it. Professor Alpheus Spring Packard, in his "College Reminiscences," remembered seeing the paintings hung as a collection in 1812 in the western half of the second story of Massachusetts Hall.[19] While older colleges typically displayed portraits of benefactors and presidents, this is very likely to have been the first collegiate art gallery whose primary purpose was simply aesthetic. It may also have been the first *public* collection of Old Master paintings in the United States—public in the sense of being regularly available for inspection by any respectable-looking visitor. And there are ample references to people going to see the pictures, although to many visitors they may have been regarded simply as one more curiosity, perhaps less interesting than what was in the natural history cabinet. How they were displayed when the Medical School took over much of Massachusetts Hall after 1820 is unclear.

When the new Romanesque Revival chapel was ready for occupancy in the early 1850s, the pictures were moved to the upper chamber at the east end and hung in several rows up the walls. Woods, who was well traveled and well read on art matters, had at least some of the pictures professionally cleaned and restored; several whose subject matter seemed a bit too free for a chapel—a *Jupiter and Danaë*, for example—were quietly sold.[20] The fact that photographic reproductions of some works in the collection were available for purchase in the 1880s indicates that visitors did continue to come, despite the steep stairs.

As badly lighted as the gallery was, the paintings had in one sense found an appropriate home. Richard Upjohn's Chapel was a major innovation stylistically—for all its medieval revivalism, it was in fact an advanced design, and one which, as Kathleen Curran has pointed out, was to have considerable impact on later Romanesque Revival churches in this country. It was a triumph for President Woods, who knew the work of both the British Ecclesiologists of the 1840s and the German theoreticians of the *Rundbogenstil*, or "round arch style" movement. Woods knew that a plain, severe exterior of native stone required a dazzling interior, and a plan evolved—probably with Gervase Wheeler's help—that combined polychrome decorations and huge murals on the broad expanse of walls. It was an attempt to create a college that would "teach" not only through lectures and recitations but by the very nature of its fabric. The world of ivy-covered cloisters was about to arrive in North America.[21]

THE MEDICAL SCHOOL OF MAINE

Of all the cultural forces exerted by the College on the people of the new state of Maine, none was quite so direct as the influence of the Medical School, founded in 1820, in what could have been the first step toward developing Bowdoin into a small university. This was not simply a matter of turning out young doctors—more than 2,000 of them in the century that the school endured, many of them taking up practice in small towns and villages that might otherwise not have seen an educated practitioner. In the first decades of the school's existence the influence on the state had more to do with the idea of medical professionalism itself. Accustomed as we are to the prestige and ability to command high fees of the medical profession of our own day, it is difficult to imagine how modest and under-appreciated a calling the practice of medicine was in the Early Republic. Almost anyone could call himself a doctor—a scholarly practitioner like Benjamin Vaughan, trained at Edinburgh and conversant through his journals and correspondence with the most advanced medical thought of two continents; an illiterate, self-taught healer, handing out herbs

The Sophia Walker Gallery (the south wing of the Chapel, now laboratories of the Department of Psychology) housed the College's collection of plaster casts of Greek and Roman sculptures until the Walker Art Building was built in 1894. Copies of European art, thought to be superior to modern American originals, were prized for their ability to inspire as well as to instruct.

This view toward the Chapel in the 1890s was probably taken from the window of 204 Adams Hall, now the office of Professor of Mathematics Charles A. Grobe, Jr. On the extreme left is the first Sargent Gymnasium, now the Heating Plant, finished in 1886.

and folk remedies; or a quack with a gift of gab and some acquaintance with pseudo-sciences like phrenology and homeopathic medicine. The title often was simply honorary, in recognition of a self-taught skill. In some communities the mere fact of having *any* formal education was sufficient basis for setting up a medical practice; Eliza Southgate's father, Robert, for example, had been a physician in Scarborough before he decided to become a judge instead. One statistic bears witness to the state of the profession: of the 109 established practitioners listed in a biographical dictionary of Maine physicians in 1820, at least seventy-four of them had no known college or medical school degree. In New England as a whole in the early nineteenth-century, more than half of the practicing doctors neither belonged to a medical society (an early attempt at licensing) nor had graduated from a medical institution; they had learned their business by serving an apprenticeship and by trial and error. Indeed, because of a popular suspicion of elite professional groups, in the Jacksonian period several state legislatures—including Maine's—passed legislation refusing to require degrees or certified licenses of physicians.[22]

Most histories of American medicine tacitly deplore this state of affairs and present the gradual triumph of professionalism as a victory of science over superstition. Yet many people in the Early Republic would not have seen this process as an entirely benign or inevitable one. The early history of the Medical School of Maine cannot be understood, then, without some appreciation of the state of the healing "arts" in the early nineteenth century and the popular resistance to the idea that the only good doctor was an educated one. Fortunately, a remarkable document chronicling the life of an uneducated healer has recently been published in full, with a brilliant commentary by Laurel Thatcher Ulrich. *A Midwife's Tale: The Life of Martha Ballard, Based on Her Diary, 1785-1812,* is the story of a woman who over twenty-seven years attended 816 births in and around the Kennebec Valley towns of Hallowell and Augusta. In recreating Martha Ballard's career from the rather laconic entries

By the time Parker Cleaveland died in 1858, the College was overdue for modernization in the sciences. Under the leadership of Professor Paul A. Chadbourne, Adams Hall was built in 1861 to house the Medical School of Maine and to provide laboratories for undergraduate study. This view (1884) is looking northwest, with the Delta on the right and Rhodes Hall (1867) across the street in the background.

in her diary, Ulrich brings to life the community in which Ballard played a role as healer and organizer far larger than the mere practice of midwifery might suggest.

Two rather paradoxical facts are of significance here. First, if you were pregnant, your chances of a safe delivery were considerably greater with the experienced midwife, as Ulrich shows in comparative statistics comparing Ballard's record of live births with that of the region's trained physicians. In fact, if you had almost any ailment, short of a broken bone that needed setting, you were more likely to survive her herbal remedies and gentle counseling than the "heroic" medicine of purges and bleeding and generally intrusive treatment considered state-of-the-art by the educated profession. Obstetrics in particular was in a crude state, and the chances of puerperal fever (an often fatal infection caused by a wound during delivery) were far greater with a male doctor than with an experienced midwife. Second, in Martha Ballard's own lifetime, the craft of the midwife began to be neglected as the work of the doctor

Fred L. Varney, Herbert W. Hall, Magnus G. Ridlon, Roland B. Moore, Alfred L. Sawyer, and Karl B. Sturgis dissecting a body at the Medical School of Maine in 1905. Hall graduated in 1908, the rest in 1907.

grew in prestige and indispensability. In the Hallowell region at least, this did not necessarily mean hostility between traditional healers and college-educated physicians; Ulrich shows, for example, close cooperation between Ballard and such medical luminaries as the Augusta physician Daniel Cony, a founder of the Kennebec Medical Society and a charter Overseer of the College. But the notion took firm root that if you were ill or in any life-threatening situation, you should turn to a professional (which is to say a male), despite the profession's lack of diagnostic skill and feeble grasp of the etiology of most diseases in this period. Latter-day Martha Ballards practiced, of course, but on the fringe of Maine village life—at least until the modern revival of midwifery—and the finest tribute they ever received came, ironically, from the daughter of a Bowdoin-educated physician: Sarah Orne Jewett's depiction of the herbalist Mrs. Todd in *The Country of the Pointed Firs*.[23]

It was the Medical School of Maine, above all, that produced several generations of Maine doctors as well as helping to establish popular acceptance of medicine as a profession in the state. Founded "for the instruction of students in Medicine, Anatomy, Surgery, Chemistry, Mineralogy and Botany"[24] by one of the first acts of the new legislature in 1820, with a $1,500 grant and the promise of $1,000 more each year, the school was a tribute to the cooperative efforts of Governor King and Bowdoin's new president, William Allen. Having seen a successful medical school in operation at Dartmouth, Allen sought the assistance of its founder, Dr. Nathan Smith, who had also founded the medical school at Yale and was probably the most highly esteemed medical educator in the country. Smith replied enthusiastically to Allen's inquiry:

I think after what experience I have had, we could form a medical school that would, in point of real utility, equal any in the country. In a new state like Maine, where neither habit nor parties have laid their ruthless hands on public institutions, and where the minds of men are free from their poisoning influence, everything is to be hoped for. Such a field would be very inviting to me, and such a place I take Maine to be. For though they have heretofore been divided into parties, I am disposed to think they have become a state unto themselves, party spirit will in great measure subside, and they will be ambitious to promote the honor and welfare of the state.[25]

This, as we have seen, was an optimistic assessment of the political situation in the new state, but with Smith's help the school became a reality. He taught anatomy, surgery, medicine, and obstetrics—during a summer course, for he remained on the faculty at Yale—with Parker Cleaveland lecturing in chemistry and Dr. John Wells assisting in the dissecting room. The school opened in 1821 with twenty-two students; in its second year, there were forty-nine; and by 1829, nearly 100 (a year when the College itself granted only thirty degrees). The school moved into the unused portions of Massachusetts Hall—where it was to remain until Adams Hall was built in 1861—and operated as a distinct yet closely affiliated part of the College: the same Governing Boards and president controlled the

This engraved view of the campus from 1856 includes the new Chapel, which had been finished a year before.

operations of both institutions. Undergraduates in the 1820s were allowed to attend anatomy lectures, but there was frequently some degree of tension between the college students and their rather more loosely supervised medical counterparts. Partly this was the result of intellectual elitism: entrance to the Medical School was notoriously easy. Many students stayed only a term or two before going into the traditional—and, in the early period at least, possibly more useful—apprenticeship with an established physician. The school's teaching was based solely on lectures and demonstrations—it was not until well after the Civil War that clinical work became a central part of the training—and it is some indication of the intellectual rigor of the discipline that the first thesis presented for an M.D. was a three-page work on the subject of "water." Much of the faculty's time was spent trying to acquire "subjects"—i.e., the corpses of condemned criminals or paupers—for the anatomy theater.[26]

In organizational terms, one of the most important developments had been the founding of a state medical society in 1821. Joining with the medical faculty, the society's examining committee participated in the decisions on degrees, thereby serving as a licensing body. The notion of a professional elite of trained practitioners was eventually firmly established. Unfortunately, the College's resources were never sufficient in the later nineteenth century to keep up with the advances of a more scientifically based system of medical education, and the legislature could not be persuaded to come to the rescue. The Medical School of Maine—like many other "country" medical colleges—was severely criticized for its clinical inadequacies in the famous Flexner Report of 1909 on conditions in American education, and in 1921 the Governing Boards voted to end its existence rather than see its national rating downgraded. Yet the idea of a medical school in the state has never completely vanished, a ghost of the ambitious effort of the Bowdoin of the 1820s.[27]

NOTES

BCSC is Special Collections, Hawthorne-Longfellow Library, Bowdoin College.

1. Alan Taylor, "The Early Republic's Supernatural Economy: Treasure Seeking in the American Northeast, 1780-1830," *American Quarterly* 38 (1986), pp. 6-34.

2. The most complete account of Cleaveland's life is found in Leonard Woods, Jr., "An Eulogy on Parker Cleaveland, LL. D.," *Proceedings of the Maine Historical Society for 1859*, article 20, pp. 375-435. For the background of the period, see, for example, Trevor H. Levere, "The Rich Economy of Nature: Chemistry in the Nineteenth Century," in U. C. Knoepflmacher and G. B. Tennyson, eds., *Nature and the Victorian Imagination* (Berkeley, 1977), pp. 189-200.

3. Thomas A. Riley, "Goethe and Parker Cleaveland," *Modern Language Association* 67B (June 1952), pp. 350-374. (Riley, Class of 1928, taught German at Bowdoin from 1939 until his retirement in 1973.) See also Rudolf Magnus, *Goethe as a Scientist* (New York, 1964), pp. 200-221.

4. The house, at 75 Federal Street, was owned by the College during Parker Cleaveland's lifetime and stayed in the family of his daughter, Martha Cleaveland Chandler, until 1951, when it was bought by Robert B. Miller, Bowdoin's swimming coach. It belonged to Professor and Mrs. William Shipman from 1960 to 1991, when the College bought it back for use as a president's house. President Robert H. Edwards and Blythe Bickel Edwards took up residence there in December 1992.

5. Christopher M. Jedrey, *The World of John Cleaveland: Family and Community in Eighteenth-Century New England* (New York, 1979); Michael Chandos Brown, *Benjamin Silliman: A Life in the Young Republic* (New York, 1989).

6. Woods, pp. 414-415.

7. Woods, p. 425.

8. For American college and university museums and their relationship to the *Wunderkammern*, see Clifton C. Olds, "The Intellectual Foundations of the College Museum" in *The Legacy of James Bowdoin III* (Brunswick, ME: Bowdoin College, 1993).

9. The material in this section is largely based on Roger Michener, "The Bowdoin College Library: From Its Beginnings to the Present Day," (M.A. dissertation, Graduate Library School, University of Chicago), 1972. This is the most thorough study of the Bowdoin library to date, although some of its conclusions about twentieth-century developments should be treated with caution. Other sources include the various catalogues (the 1808 one was discovered after Michener had written) and the Trustees' Minutes, all in BCSC.

10. Kenneth E. Carpenter, "James Bowdoin as Library Builder" in *The Legacy of James Bowdoin III* (Brunswick, ME: Bowdoin College, 1993).

11. Edwin Wolf II, "Great American Book Collectors to 1800," *Gazette of the Grolier Club*, No. 16 (New Series), June 1971.

12. Joseph Griffin, ed., *History of the Press of Maine* (Brunswick, 1872), pp. 71-85; "Works by Officers of Bowdoin College," 223-228.

13. For a more complete bibliography, see *Publications of the Presidents and Faculty of Bowdoin College, 1802-1876* (Brunswick, 1876).

14. The standard account of his life is Clifford K. Shipton, "James Bowdoin," *Sibley's Harvard Graduates 1768-1771*, vol. 17 (Cambridge, Mass., 1975), pp. 487-500. There is no full-scale biography.

15. For a very detailed account of the diplomatic mission, see Isaac Joslin Cox, *The West Florida Controversy, 1798-1813* (Baltimore, 1918).

16. Journal of Sarah Bowdoin (Mrs. James Bowdoin III), 1 October 1806-14 February 1808, BCSC.

17. For insight into the social and cultural context of Bowdoin's final years, see Tamara Plakins Thornton, *Cultivating Gentlemen: The Meaning of Country Life among the Boston Elite 1785-1860* (New Haven, 1989); on the sheep-breeding craze in the Early Republic, see Carroll W. Pursell, Jr., "E. I. duPont and the Merino Mania in Delaware, 1805-1815," *Agricultural History* 36, no. 2 (April 1962), pp. 91-100.

18. For an overview of the Guise Collection, see James Byam Shaw, *Drawings by Old Masters at Christ Church Oxford*, vol. I (Oxford, 1976), pp. 1-30. For background on Bowdoin's student days, see William L. Sachse, *The Colonial American in Britain* (Madison, Wisc., 1956) and Richard H. Saunders, "James Bowdoin III, 1752-1811" in *The Legacy of James Bowdoin III* (Brunswick, ME: Bowdoin College, 1993).

19. A. S. Packard, "College Reminiscences," Packard and Nehemiah Cleaveland, *History of Bowdoin College* (Boston, 1882), pp. 83-102.

20. On the Bowdoin paintings at Bowdoin College, see Susan E. Wegner, "Copies and Education: James Bowdoin's Painting Collection in the Life of the College" in *The Legacy of James Bowdoin III* (Brunswick, ME: Bowdoin College, 1993).

21. Kathleen Curran, "The Word, the Book, the Building: Bowdoin Chapel Reilluminated," lecture delivered at Bowdoin College, 29 October 1992.

22. James A. Spalding, *Maine Physicians of 1820, A Record of the Members of the Massachusetts Medical Society Practicing in the District of Maine at the Date of Separation* (Lewiston, 1928); Barnes Riznik, "The Professional Lives of Early Nineteenth-Century New England Doctors," *Journal of the History of Medicine and Allied Sciences,* vol. 19, no. 1 (January 1964), p. 1.

23. Laurel Thatcher Ulrich, *A Midwife's Tale: The Life of Martha Ballard, Based on Her Diary, 1785-1812* (New York, 1990). Sarah Orne Jewett, the first woman to receive an honorary degree from Bowdoin (in 1901), was the daughter of Theodore Herman Jewett '34, a professor and lecturer in obstetrics and diseases of women and children at the Medical School of Maine from 1866 to 1869.

24. "An Act to Establish a Medical School in this State," 27 June 1820, *Special Laws,* vol. 1, p. 23.

25. Nathan Smith to William Allen, quoted in Samuel E. Kamerling, "Bowdoin's Old Medical School," unpub. talk to the Town and College Club, 13 February 1976, p. 3. Kamerling taught chemistry at Bowdoin from 1934 until his retirement as Charles Weston Pickard Professor in 1952.

26. For a more detailed account of the school, see Richard Kahn, "An Historical Sketch of Medical Education in Maine," *Journal of the Maine Medical Association,* vol. 62 (1971), pp. 212-216; Avanelle P. Morgan, "The Medical School of Maine at Bowdoin Colledge (1820-1921), *Journal of the Maine Medical Association,* vol. 68 (September 1977), pp. 315-319; and K. C. M. Sills, "The Bowdoin Medical School," *Bowdoin College Bulletin,* no. 105 (October 1920).

27. One very useful tool for further research is [Dianne Gutscher], "Resources for the History of Medicine in Maine: Survey" in Stephen Trent Seames, "Bibliography for Medical Research," Maine Historical Society, 1991. Special Collections, for example, has copies of all the theses submitted for the M.D., biographical files on the Medical School of Maine's students and faculty, and lecture notes from various medical courses.

Thomas Curtis was an eccentric Englishman known to students as "Diogenes." He earned a living doing chores for the College and the students, including running errands, carrying water and wood, and building students' fires in the morning. An obituary described him as unschooled but widely read: "Quotations from the best authors were at his tongue's end, and were brought forward on occasions appropriate and otherwise."

When Diogenes died in 1868, his obituary described him as "an exceedingly eccentric character living by himself in a miserable hovel." Nonetheless, Diogenes was an enthusiastic bibliophile who spent all his earnings on books. On his death his house on the edge of campus was said to contain some 2,000 volumes.

The lure of pastoral life in mid-nineteenth-century New England is captured in Winslow Homer's wood engraving The Strawberry Bed, which appeared in Our Young Folks in July 1868. Bowdoin College Museum of Art. Museum purchase, Hamlin, Quinby, and Special Funds. 1974.1.133.

CHAPTER FIVE

*Outside of the recitation room and the libraries, a well-documented student culture
flourished at antebellum Bowdoin, reflecting both the tensions and the aspirations
of Jacksonian America. At first centered in the rival literary societies, this subculture from the
1840s on eagerly absorbed the new "secret societies" identified by Greek letters.
The search for "the self" on the part of two students in particular—James Hanscom 1846
and Charles Clifford 1849—reveals some aspects of collegiate life that did not always
find their way into the institutional record.*

A SUMMER'S DAY

For much of the nineteenth century, students in Maine colleges attended class in the summer, fall, and spring, taking a long winter vacation and a briefer one in the spring. It was a schedule that had much to recommend it. Fuel was saved, and students and faculty were spared each others' company in the bleakness of the shortest days of the year. Yet it must not have been easy sitting in a recitation hall on a Maine summer day. From Hawthorne's time on, the almost lyrical references on the students' part to blueberry fields and the shaded glen called "Paradise," to swimming in the still-clean river and boating in Casco Bay, serve to remind us that boys were still boys, however often they were told they were scholars and young gentlemen.

For example, take one afternoon in July of 1856. An elderly man named Fields, "of temperate habits, and a little inclined to be crazy," had disappeared from the village and had last been seen some four miles away. After several days of futile search, the authorities asked the students for help. "So Sunday morning at eight o'clock about sixty of us started," recorded Henry Melville King, Class of 1859, in his diary.[1] "We rode out in all kinds of carriages imagineable. About forty of us got into a rack to which two horses were attached, and rode out in this manner, expecting every moment to see the old thing break and 'drap' us in the road." The students formed search parties with the villagers,

King taking care to join the group whose guide was related to a young woman in town who had caught his eye ("[I] strove to initiate myself into his favor"), and they began to search the rain-dampened woods. "We made it a rule to look under every raspberry and blueberry bush so that we could see plainer," King explained.

When the crazy old man still had not been found by dusk, the faculty told the students that they could return to the hunt after the next day's recitation. "We all voted to go but only about one third went," wrote King. "The others kept back out of the way so as not to be seen." King and his party left at 8 A.M.—recitation had been, as usual, before breakfast—and "travelled through woods and swamps and mire knee deep, through bramble and brake, over rail-fence and stone-wall, up hill and down, indeed in every place wherever man went or can go." When they met up again, they learned the alarm had been premature—Fields had wandered forty miles away, but had sent a letter which had just arrived revealing his whereabouts. "But we did not mean that this should spoil our fun," said King, "and not wishing to come back to Brunswick to go into recitations . . . we started, some for the salt water, and others for the blueberry plains, and all arrived safely home sometime in the evening, having been unsuccessful in one respect, that is, in finding the lost man ourselves, but having been very successful in having a good time."

The image of the young Henry Melville King eating berries and avoiding class, wandering out-doors almost as aimlessly as mad old Fields him-

A turn-of-the-century view of a path through the Bowdoin pines.

self, his hands and tongue stained blue, the wind off Maquoit Bay in his hair—it is a pastoral, a New England genre scene of the kind Winslow Homer was about to celebrate in his wood engravings for *Harper's Weekly*. It is not an unflattering picture, nor a deceptive one, of the life young men found at Bowdoin in the generation before the Civil War.

If it seems timeless, perhaps that is because so many generations of students experienced it. Thirty years earlier, Horatio Bridge 1825 and his friend Nathaniel Hawthorne 1825 had sought the same kind of escape. The uninhabited land adjoining the College, Bridge recalled late in life, was filled:

with foot-paths running deviously for miles under the shady trees, where, in their season, squirrels and wild pigeons might be found in sufficient numbers to afford good sport. The woodland gave a charmingly secluded retreat, and imparted a classic aspect to the otherwise tame scenery of the Brunswick Plains . . . . In our day one could wander for miles through this forest without meeting a person (except a stray student or two) or hearing a sound other than the occasional chatters of a squirrel, the song of a bird, or the sighing of the wind through the branches overhead.

Bridge also remembered the brook behind Parker Cleaveland's house where "we often fished for the small trout that were to be found there; but the main charm of those outings was in the indolent loitering along the low banks of the little stream, listening to its murmur or the whispering of the overhanging pines."[2] Some of this scenery found its way into Hawthorne's first novel, *Fanshawe* (1828), which he may have begun writing as an undergraduate.

There is a certain gilding to this kind of reminiscence—the roads of nineteenth-century Brunswick were for much of the year either mud-sodden or dusty; there is ample student testimony to bed-bugs and mice in the residence halls; for much of the early spring, the snow beneath their windows was a disgusting collage of tobacco juice and much worse—but the notion of college as an idyll was a powerfully sustaining one, especially amid the tensions of Jacksonian America. The moments in the "classic" shade—a *translatio* of Theocritus and the Virgil of the *Eclogues* to the local pine woods—were real enough, to be sure. They were in fact all the more cherished because they stood in such contrast to the unavoidable conflicts of everyday student life.

The faculty, for example. One could write an extracurricular history of Bowdoin simply from the pages of the *Records of Executive Government,* which is to say, the unedifying list, year after year, of the minor fines and occasional rustications imposed on those students unlucky enough to get caught. (Outright expulsions were less common; the College for much of the century depended on tuition to stay open.) It is a chronicle of youthful high spirits and low-grade wrongdoing—of people who sleep in chapel or fail to prepare for recitations or slip off to the neighboring taverns. (For much of the antebellum period the closest was Estabrook's, which was on the site of the modern College gate at the intersection of Maine Street and the Bath Road; when it was torn down shortly before the Civil

FANSHAWE,

A TALE.

"Wilt thou go on with me ?"—SOUTHEY.

BOSTON:
MARSH & CAPEN, 362 WASHINGTON STREET.

PRESS OF PUTNAM AND HUNT.
1828.

FANSHAWE.

CHAPTER I.

Our court shall be a little academy.
SHAKSPEARE.

IN an ancient, though not very populous settlement, in a retired corner of one of the New-England States, arise the walls of a seminary of learning, which, for the convenience of a name, shall be entitled 'Harley College.' This institution, though the number of its years is inconsiderable, compared with the hoar antiquity of its European sisters, is not without some claims to reverence on the score of age ; for an almost countless multitude of rivals, by many of which its reputation has been eclipsed, have sprung up since its foundation. At no time, indeed, during an existence of nearly a century, has it acquired a very extensive fame, and circumstances, which need not be particularized, have of late years involved it in a deeper obscurity. There are now few candidates for the degrees that the college is authorized to bestow. On two of its annual 'Commencement days,' there has been a total deficiency of Baccalaureates ; and the lawyers and divines, on whom Doctorates in their respective

Feeling embarrassed by his first novel, Nathaniel Hawthorne bought back and destroyed as many copies of Fanshawe *as he could find. Bowdoin owns one of the approximately twenty-five copies of the first edition known to have survived. Hawthorne may have begun writing* Fanshawe, *which is set at a fictional "Harley" College, as an undergraduate in 1825.*

War, the local joke was that they found that its original pump was in perfect working order—water being the one beverage no one had ever requested there.) Occasionally a hint of something more serious appears: on 5 March 1832, the faculty noted that:

Whereas it is currently reported, that a house of ill fame has been established in Bath near the Turnpike bridge, presenting temptations to the students of this College, therefore Voted, that the Treasurer of College be requested to ascertain the facts, and to take such measures as to him may appear expedient.[3]

Joseph McKeen was, in other words, sent off, like Emil Jannings in the film *The Blue Angel,* to investigate the vice, but unlike Professor Unrat he seems to have returned calmly to his duties.

On the whole, Bowdoin students were unruly—but so was the entire country. Outside of the home, the only other institutions of the Jacksonian era in the North in which large assemblies of young men were successfully kept under strict discipline were those situations—the army, ships at sea, prisons, perhaps lumber camps—where far more drastic methods of coercion could be employed. At colleges like Bowdoin, until the 1850s, the obligations of *in loco parentis* seem to have ended at dusk, save for the gravest offenses. The residence halls were the kingdom of the young, and their very architecture—clusters of rooms on staircases—encouraged a certain independence of movement. One result was relentless hazing, usually of freshmen by the sophomores. Playing on the Biblical allusion to "the cities of the plain" (Brunswick's flat, sandy landscape being much commented upon at that time) the students at

For all its dignity, the Chapel was nonetheless the scene of frequent student pranks in the late nineteenth century. The entire campus was often decorated on Halloween.

Fire walls divided Winthrop and Maine Halls into two "ends." For much of the nineteenth century, the north end of Winthrop Hall (1822) was known as "Sodom," the south end as "Gomorrah."

either end of Winthrop Hall, for example, renamed the two "ends" of the building Sodom and Gomorrah. Until Civil War days, "Sodom County Court" regularly meted out punishments to freshmen, and some of the earliest photographs of the building from the 1870s reveal SODOM painted (albeit faintly) on the north entry, a label that must have puzzled more than one visitor to campus. The hazing—which ranged from pranks like holding someone's head under the pump or having one's room filled with cigar smoke to intense psychological harassment—continued, despite faculty disapproval, until a very independent-minded undergraduate, Cyrus Hamlin 1834, brought charges for assault against some fellow students. Interclass rivalry—perhaps an important bonding rite—continued in less actionable forms well into the twentieth century.

Aside from the singular "drill rebellion" in post-Civil War days, students rarely took on the faculty directly. The one grave exception to this occurred in the spring of 1842, when Endicott King '44 was expelled after having thrown sulphuric acid onto the clothes and into the face of Professor Goodwin. The incident arose from a scuffle over the building of a bonfire—a custom students regarded as their sacred right, but which worried the faculty members, who remembered the two Maine Hall fires and doubtless thought of all those books in the wooden chapel. (The custom of bonfires probably explains why virtually no furniture survives from antebellum Bowdoin.) Happily, the students found other ways to act out their generational differences with the "Government." Much of this involved carnivalesque mockery—notably, the raucous "May Training," which was a noisy parody of the short-lived militia drill which the State Legislature had required of collegians in the early 1830s, and the elaborate mock-funerary cult (complete with printed programs and titles in parodied Latin) devoted to "Anna Lytics," namely the burning and burying at the end of the year of their mathematics texts.

The townspeople were also a source of irritation to many students, a feeling that appears to have been reciprocated. Student pranks ranged from nocturnal pilfering of local poultry to the elaborate charade in 1824 when the Marquis de Lafayette was expected to visit Brunswick for an honorary degree. He changed his mind, and the degree was brought to him in Portland, but a student (John Cleaveland 1826) dressed up like the aged hero and rode in a carriage into town, where a large and unsuspecting crowd paid him homage.

Much of the town-gown friction was channeled into the so-called "yagger wars." The term, according to B. H. Hall's *A Collection of College Words and Phrases* in 1856, was unique to Bowdoin and Brunswick. The most plausible derivation is from the German *Jäger*, meaning huntsman, and perhaps in the local context loosely referring to lumbermen and other backwoodsmen who gathered each year in Brunswick and Topsham at the time of the spring freshet on the river. How this usage came to be taken up by the students is unclear, but by the 1820s the young Longfellow was referring to Brunswick as "Yaggerheim"—a play on Brunswick's origin as Braunschweig?—and by the Civil War period "yagger" was synonymous with any non-collegiate townsperson. The "yagger wars" were more bark than bite—and for both sides were doubtless an exercise in camaraderie—but there was occasionally some serious bruising and no small touch of class warfare between those who lived "up" and those who lived "down" the hill.

From the 1840s on, students began to find the new "secret societies"—the origins of modern social fraternities—a more fulfilling experience than these less structured diversions. For an institution that was to shape the lives, over more than a century, of so many college-educated American males, there is surprisingly little written about their origins. Judging by their rapid appearance at Bowdoin—first, Alpha Delta Phi in 1841, then Psi Upsilon in 1843, and Chi Psi and Delta Kappa Epsilon in 1844—they met some intensely felt need for smaller social units within the College. Tocqueville had commented a decade earlier on the American propensity for association, and by the 1840s the competitive pressures of the Jacksonian market economy and the individualistic mood it encouraged had

A view of still-unpaved Maine Street looking from the college hill to the fortress-like Cabot Mill. On the right is the town mall, which, like much of Brunswick in the late nineteenth century and the first half of the twentieth century, was heavily shaded with elms.

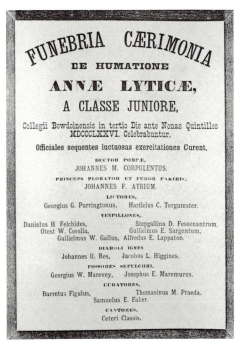

Students held mock funeral services, complete with printed programs in mock Latin, for "Anna Lytica," in which they "cremated" and buried their analytical geometry textbooks. Two headstones, one from 1877 and one from 1878, survive on the campus.

taken hold in New England. The fraternities in this context played a paradoxical role: they allowed a young man to formalize close and trusting ties with a small group of initiates, to whom he was bound by brotherly oaths for eternity, yet they allowed these small groups to become intensely competitive with each other. (At Bowdoin, this at first took the form of politicking for office in the Peucinian and Athenaean societies; contrary to the traditional explanation that fraternities emerged to replace the declining debating clubs, here they seemed to coexist comfortably for about twenty years.)

They also drew on a number of sources for both their imagery and their structure, Freemasonry most obviously, but also the romantic medievalism of Sir Walter Scott, the widespread notion of "brotherhood" found in many other fraternal groups in the early nineteenth century, and the appeal of the *Burschenshaften*, the German university student clubs that had played an important role in the German nationalists' opposition to Napoleon. From the start Bowdoin's fraternities were literally secret organizations, which tried to hide their places of meeting (usually, a room rented in town) from the rest of the student body. From an early date, the Governing Boards and Executive Government were suspicious of them, but no one at Bowdoin in their first two or three decades of existence imagined what a central role they and the newer chapters would play during the second century of the College.

EN AVANT! COURAGE!

Living in an age before the college decal or the pep club banner had been imagined, James Hanscom 1846 nonetheless surrounded himself with the emblems of a collegiate life. He had to confine them to a diary which he began keeping in November of 1844, when he was a seventeen-year-old junior living at 29 Maine Hall, and which he continued, at home and at college, through his graduation in the fall of 1846 and beyond. *En avant! Courage!* was the motto he chose for the opening page. He appended an untranslated quotation from Schiller—his

recently acquired German was a source of great pride to him—along with the usual tags from Latin and Greek. He added a few swirls to show off his not especially expert penmanship, and he told himself, in firm letters: "Never Say Die" and "Stiff Upper Lip." It was his way of whistling in the dark.[4]

The diary begins in a sunny enough fashion; for all the troubles that are to befall him, Hanscom's unfailingly cheerful nature is one of his most endearing qualities. His chronicle of daily life at Bowdoin seems uneventful: he writes themes and studies German; he hears Elijah Kellogg preach in Topsham and is impressed; he sets out to read on his own the four volumes of Roddeck's *History of the World*. He has joined one of the new secret societies, Alpha Delta Phi, and is happy to receive a letter from "brother Talbot"—who is Thomas Talbot 1846, of East Machias. "I have never received a kinder, more brotherly letter from a friend than from him. My heart is rejoiced," Hanscom writes to himself. "I shall most certainly avail myself of the opportunity this presents of cultivating the finer feelings of the heart. I see more and more reason to rejoice that I am as I am—'*an ADP,*'" He has been lonely, homesick for his large family in Eliot, Maine, and has found a surrogate home of a sort in his new secret society.

But he does not dwell on such things; he is too busy. "In the morning I get up at 4 o'clock, and build a fire in the furnace in this end," for he supplements his funds with a campus job. He frets about over-eating; he is living in a country that is rapidly becoming more faddish about diet. And he lets no opportunity to learn escape him. Laying a fire in President Woods's office, he finds a German newspaper wadded up in the fire box and asks to have it, and this leads to a conversation with the president on the language and literature of Germany. Whenever depression creeps up on him, Hanscom writes, "[I] say to myself, as I often have in difficulty, *En avant! Courage!*"

He would need it. On 5 February 1845, while at home in Eliot, he writes: "At 6 o'clock in the evening, we received a letter from Saco, informing us of an event, which has for a time deprived

A tug of war on the Delta. The buildings in back are (l to r) 84-86 Federal Street (now student housing), Copeland House (also student housing), and Cram Alumni House.

us of our kind friend and protector, our dear father—that he was in Limerick in a deranged state. Our feeling on hearing the news of this affliction I cannot describe, but shall long remember . . . to Mother and Grandmother it was only the realization of fears constantly entertained. He has been so 3 times before, and they were constantly in fear of his being overtaken by his old malady."

Despite the intense cold, Hanscom's father is taken by one of his brothers to the state insane asylum at Augusta. There is an eerie calm about him, James Hanscom reports: "Father was very thoughtful sometimes—asked about his pocketbook, his watch, his valise, which he said contained some shirts. . . ." The family, though, are in turmoil. The sudden incapacity of the man who was not only father and husband and financial support but the moral center of any Victorian family was a catastrophic event. The circumstances—the reappearance of an early bout of madness—were especially cruel.

Hanscom knows that he must give up college; he will miss the Class of '46, he writes, but he knows he will never give up the learning he has grown to love. "I can dig as well as ever I could, and my books are still left." He hopes a family conference will result in some arrangement by which they can all survive. "I shall come out right yet— *En avant! Courage!* Cheer up! Press on!" His older brother Daniel rescues his prospects; taking over the family's expenses, he tells James to return to Bowdoin and gives him $50 to pay his bills in Brunswick.

The figure of his father—who is in some ways worse off than were he dead—continues to haunt the boy. Yet the more than 200 remaining pages of his diary are, with a few exceptions, the story of a young man piecing back together his everyday life, testing his strengths, discovering his nature. They are also one of the most remarkably detailed accounts of day-to-day life at an antebellum New England college to have survived. Such diaries are not uncommon, and some are better written, or perhaps more useful in what they tell us about events beyond the confines of quiet college towns. But what emerges from the pages written each evening by James Hanscom is not just the portrait of an institution but a self-portrait of a mind, an identity taking shape. Through his eyes we see the strengths and weaknesses of a country college—as they appeared not to the later champions of university reform but to the intelligent and quite capable young men who in the decades before the Civil War turned to such places for an education.

Let us catch up with Hanscom at the end of winter vacation in 1845. He has left Eliot, where he had taught school for six weeks, and we can accompany him back to Brunswick, by rail and by horse:

At last the train came, and we were soon puffing and rattling along over the swamps and through ledges, on our way to Portland. Then came the wearisome tarry of an hour or more at the Elm House—and again we were on our way, in crowded stage, for Bowdoin's sandy plains.

Prof. Goodwin was in the stage, and a Bath merchant (an Abolitionist & Temperance man, I think)—I was the only Bowdoin Student in our stage, the other being full of them. A Vermonter, an Andover Student, a lady & gentleman, & a Medical Student, completed our 3 on a seat. The conversation was more entertaining than I have before heard in a stage.

After a ride, *passablement* comfortable, we arrived at the 'Tontine' about 6 1/2 o'clock. And after stepping up to the captain's office and paying $1.25, we were landed 'on the hill'.

Hanscom, like many of his contemporaries who left diaries behind, was a relentless self-improver—indeed he pushed himself as hard, if not harder, than anyone he knew. Early in the new term, for example, he pledges:

I will endeavor constantly: —

German student customs were widely emulated by nineteenth-century American collegians, most notably in the secret fraternal societies that began appearing in the 1840s. Henry Wadsworth Longfellow made this sketch of himself on the trip he took in 1829 to prepare for his duties as professor of modern languages (1829-35).

1st. To exercise in the open air 2 hours every day.

2nd. To be sparing in my diet. For surely if any one has cause to be careful to preserve health, I, who have so many obligations resting on me, ought to endeavor to.

3rd. To study hard enough, and not too hard.

4th. To read all I can, and read all I read carefully.

5th. To go to bed at 9 o'clock, and get up early.

6th. To be economical in my expenses.

7th. To bathe in cold water at least twice or 3 times a week, and use the flesh brush every day.

8th. To do things up as nearly right as I can; and "never say die."

The routine of term quickly sets in. "Calculus, which we have been studying, seemed to me at first like a parcel of nonsense. It was not at first very hard, but I saw no sense in it at all. We have had only one lesson that could be called difficult. Now I do not have the least idea what calculus is, what its object is; if I did I should be as willing to study it as I could be. But I do not like to study anything of which I know not the advantage, proposed to be gained. However I do not mean to give up studying it, for I may find this out." His classical studies are more fulfilling—he is reading that term in Latin the Fourteenth Satire of Juvenal and Cicero's *De Oratio* ("On Public Speaking")—but it is German that captures his imagination. "In William Tell, we are pressing on quite rapidly. We stay in a whole hour, and we have to take a thorough drilling from the Prof. I suppose Prof. [probably Daniel Raynes] Goodwin goes on the presumption that we all use *ponies*—which may in many cases be true. . ." (A "pony" was a translation.)

Nevertheless, Hanscom reserves his highest praise for old Bowdoin's most famous classroom experience:

Prof. Cleaveland's Chemical Lectures have for us a charm, which no other exercises have—that of novelty . . . . He gave us a short lecture on *punctuality* at the

Diarist James Hanscom 1846 lived at 29 Maine Hall. Built in 1808 and destroyed by fire in 1822, Maine was rebuilt in 1837. This early twentieth-century photograph was taken from the approximate location of the woodyard that burned in 1846, the site of the present-day Polar Bear statue.

A groundskeeper in front of a Maine Hall doorway, probably about the turn of the century.

Maintenance man with pruning clippers, probably about the turn of the century.

beginning of the first lecture. He commences at precisely seven minutes after the bell strikes. These lectures open to us a new world of ideas. It is taking a great step in knowledge, to enter upon the science of Chemistry.

Acquiring in the course of a day far more knowledge than his journal can hold, he buys a blank book and has the words *Thesaurus Omnium* put on it. "My plan is to note down in this every thing of importance in such a way that I can refer to it at any time. Many advantages will be gained by following this course. The facts & passages will be at hand, and I shall have to read with more care and thought." Again like many Americans of the 1840s, he is increasingly anxious about his health, especially his weight, no small concern in a culture whose cuisine depended heavily on pork fat. "I have made to day some clubs to exercise with. I took 2 pieces of cord wood, and shaved down one end, leaving the large. The thing is to swing them around over the head, one in each hand. It is excellent exercise—for the arms and chest." It was not only in regular exercise that the body could be made to move: "Prof. Cleaveland had his Galvanic Battery on the *tapis* to day, and the result was some contortion & twisting of the limbs. The lecture was a very interesting one."

Through the 1830s an annual rite of spring had been the pre-Fast bonfires, but there had been none for three years, presumably at the insistence of the faculty. But, Hanscom notes, on 17 April 1845—Fast-Day, the Congregational observance of Good Friday—someone set fire to the "Temple," the College privy.

"When I got there the fire was nearly out, though more fellows were constantly arriving at the scene of the conflagration. The roof continued to smoke, and a ladder was brought, a hole cut in the roof, and some water throwed down. This was about half past three. I waited a few minutes and then came off, with my pail." It was a "mean" trick, Hanscom writes. "There is not *wit* at all in it." He speculates that perhaps the culprit was not a student at all. And he notes that the result will be an assessment of $4 or $5 and to be "destitute of the useful building a month or two."

The next day, there is more purposeful demolition: "To day at about 12 o'clock, the steeple of the old church was pulled down," he writes of Brunswick's Federal-style meeting-house that had stood since 1806 where Richard Upjohn's new Gothic church was about to rise. "All the students, and a large number of the town's people were collected near. Two ropes we fastened to two of the pillars—at a given word, we all pulled—the steeple slowly started—pitched over—increased in velocity—came to the ground with a loud crash, breaking it into thousands of pieces. The pillars that supported the steeple were very much rotted— I should think it would have fallen of itself soon."

The year rolls on, Hanscom returning home for spring vacation, at the end of which (8 June 1845) he has an epiphany of sorts, on the train:

On the way in the cars, a gentleman, who sat behind me, remarked that I had a pin on, which was very familiar to him—the ADP—he gave me his hand and told me his name—said his name was Sherwood, that he graduated at Yale in '39, that he had been abroad nearly ever since, and was then on his way to the White Mountains and the Lake Champlain etc. Jo. Titcomb came in to the car just then and I introduced him to Mr. Sherwood—and we had quite a brotherly talk for a few minutes, till Titcomb got out but I continued to converse with him till we got to Saco, and then, after shaking hands we parted. Perhaps we may never meet again. But still it is pleasant and cheering to meet a brother thus, with whom though a stranger we are united in the fraternity of ADP. We are brothers, can each say with truth on meeting one another:—"*Warum geht das Herz mir auf bei Eurem Anblick.*"

Whatever solace Hanscom finds in identifying a fraternity brother in the crowd, the thought of his father's plight is never far from his mind. He receives a letter from him and from his doctor, who reports that the patient is "generally rational but is very excitable." Perhaps triggered by these reminders, one night he sketches this reverie in his journal:

My thoughts and imagination carry me to scenes dear to me—home. I can feel the latch on my hand—I am among them—mother reading, and thinking, and sighing as she thinks, and silently praying for what would make her heart leap with joy, for the recovery of her husband and our father—John reading a newspaper, a magazine, or a book of some kind as busy as

Students kept fit with a variety of exercise regimens. These photos from later in the century show a gymnastics team with a more sophisticated version of James Hanscom's wooden dumbbells and a crew on the Androscoggin River.

can be, and as happy too—George reading aloud to any who will hear, or else laying down in the grass. . . Abby, little stirring restless sis Abby, she is holding her kitten and fondling over it or looking at her flowers. . . [He continues, describing the whole family, including his grandmother.] Daniel, my good brother Daniel, I should like to see again, and why can't I? All looks strange here—there is Dan there—I grasp his hand—he is the "same old sixpence," as kind, as affectionate as dear to me as ever—say nothing. I'll come back to 29 M[aine] H[all]—and here is my chum just got home, to our home, and he don't know I have been away so many miles.

In his senior year, he again allows himself to indulge from time to time in such rhapsodizing, interspersed with the details of everyday life as Commencement approaches. The fifteenth of February 1846, for example, finds him back in Brunswick and glad of it. "I have never been so long away from College, since I entered, as now. The stillness, the quiet comfort, that reign around & within these walls of my old room, are dear to me, and even the stones and trees now covered with a mantle of snow, seem like friends long absent met again. I feel as if study would come easy here again. O long shall I remember the quiet joys & true pleasure of the years now passing . . . Will not the merry laugh, the glad tones so familiar to our ears, the joke, the softer voice of feeling, still steal into the listening ear? Will it not be one of the pleasures and the touching, stirring joys of manhood, and white-haired, watery-eyed old age, to live over again our college days?"

The pleasures of comradeship remain one of college's greatest boons. "O I have had one of the best talks with John Waterman [1846] all this evening! We have talked of the past, the present, the future. He is a fellow I love; warmhearted, affectionate, generous, kind. When he does get married his wife will be a happy woman—in my opinion. How glad I am we are so near to each other this last—pleasantest—year of our four years' stay! O memory!" College also offers less familiar experiences [8 April 1846]: "A Mr. Berk has been lecturing here on the Jews, his countrymen. Very interesting. He calls our land the land of protection & liberty. No! land with the stretched-out wings! America was never made to be exclusive." Hanscom admits, "My

political knowledge is exceedingly small, my opinions unformed—except that it seems to me the duty of every freeman to work for the abolition of the accursed system of slavery in some way." It would be interesting to know if that subject had come up on 15 April 1846, when "in the afternoon Pres. Woods gave us seniors a Lec. on *the origin of civil institutions*—a beautiful Lec., prepared for a more important occasion, I think. I did not believe all he said."

Yet visits with the president make a considerable impression on him. [24 April 1846] "8 1/2 P.M. I have just returned from the President's room in the village, have had a fine talk with him. He is quite affable, as I have long known. He seems pleased with my Literary Farmer; & half inclined to believe there is some truth in the ideas—the only thing I hesitate on is the duty of going out & taking the thickest of the fight of life. . . . One familiar, friendly talk with a student, by the Professors, does more to keep matters harmonious than a dozen faculty meetings." Woods approves of Hanscom's "Literary Farmer" essay—a topic that would have pleased Samuel Deane, too, half a century earlier—and encourages him to write on a more ambitious theme.

For the past two decades, students at Bowdoin had been complaining of what seemed to them an arbitrary system of "ranking" scholars for each class. Each time a student was called on to recite, he was given a number from one to ten, in ascending order of success. At the end of the year, these numbers were tabulated and made public, occasionally producing results that surprised even the faculty. Commencement honors—a far greater distinction then than now—were based more or less entirely on this ranking. What bothered many students was not the fine distinction between various levels of winners but the very idea that classmates should be in competition with one another. It was an objection that touched upon both older republican fears of "striving" men and a more recent emphasis on the equality of all citizens. It was a cause that appealed to an idealistic youth like Hanscom, and he got right to work [9 May 1846]:

Been very busy for a few weeks—have studied as much as usual, written a forensic against our ranking system,

Class Day exercises were held under the Thorndike Oak. This photograph was taken after 1894, when the Searles Science Building was built.

The Quad, with its dirt paths and roughly clipped grass, presented a more meadow-like appearance in 1884.

of the evil of which I am convinced. It produces envy, jealousy, malevolence, hatred, feelings that poison the heart. . . . The college gauge of merit is a false one—as time too often proves. There is no need of any distinction of merit here in college—it is unfair to those who are in spite of effort inferior to their fellows—it is time enough to make distinctions in active life. Here let us be as near as nature will admit, on a level, a harmonious equality. I confess these objections to the system of rank in college seem so unanswerable, and I would gladly see the whole system abolished at once, leaving the natural, proper desire of esteem to produce its legitimate influence on all. I shall get Prof. Upham's views on this matter.

A few days later, with the medieval towers of Richard Upjohn's College Chapel rising near his window, he reflects on what seems a less pernicious age. "What a stirring scene those old tourneys must have been! We, with our corrected notions, our cold, money-making, selfish spirit can hardly conceive of the feeling which filled the hearts of those chivalrous knights of olden time. . . And we think of those men of doughty valor as strangely infatuated; for so they seem to us of the nineteenth century with our utilitarian spirit." This notion of chivalry was to reappear so often, less than twenty years later, in the mental landscape of the Civil War, it is interesting to read what Hanscom writes three days later [16 May 1846]: "I am no believer in war—except for civil & religious Liberty, like our forefathers. Let all means be tried before the sword. Then, look to Heaven for a blessing on a righteous cause, grasp the sword with a stout heart & a strong arm, and use it manfully! And yet 'tis a fearful thing, to cut down one's fellow men in battle! Only a clear, strong cause, in my opinion, can justify it."

He is acutely aware that College is drawing to a close [21 June 1846]. "We are passing our last & most pleasant term. We begin to talk of separation, of Commencement. Schemes are laying for the future. Albums begin to pass. We'll be happy while we may—separation will come soon enough." Again, some of his most appreciative observations are of the sixty-six-year-old scientist [27 June 1846]:

Our lectures from Prof. Cleaveland are interesting & exceedingly valuable. Not many more Bowdoin classes can be trained under him, to become enthusiasts in the study of Nature; he is an old man now.—In the morning we have a lec. on Mineralogy etc., at 8 1/2; in the Cabinet [in Massachusetts Hall]. This Cabinet is a rare & pleasant place—large, airy room, tables & chairs instead of crooking-back benches; an invaluable collection of minerals,—a more than invaluable Lecturer. The Lec. usually lasts about three qr's an hour; then the specimens pass, conversation is free; movement permitted—in short we do "hold a sort of literary levee." "*O nos fortunati!*"

The more conventional routine of recitation continues:

Have Nat. History, [Professor] Smellie, in the morning; Anatomy also; & a lesson on Mineralogy once in a few mornings, from our best text Book, P. Cleaveland's Lec's—Upham on the Will—easy & interesting, common-sense, plain thus far. Wayland's Mor. Sci Lec, in afternoon, to Pres.—argumentative, pointed, simple, unvarnished, true—but goes too far in a few instances.—No themes.

Thus we are let, all of a sudden, into the secrets of Nature. Glorious Nature,—& her God!

True enough, one cannot tell how much interest he will take in Nat. Sciences, till he studies them. They are the pills, & the bitters, & the exercise, & the diversion, which should preserve students' capital, health.

Early in July, he notes: "Got my Com. coat & vest today—am to pay $20, for the *tout ensemble*. . . I do not like to spend money not my own. But a good suit I must have if possible—Com. comes but once in a lifetime. I want a good coat when I perform at *Com.*, & one when I am *married*—further than that I care not." From his room he can hear the click of the hammers of the stonemasons working on the Chapel. By the eleventh, it is 96 degrees in Brunswick—"turn *in* on floor these nights." He gives a speech at his fraternity, which has opened a "room" in town, and he learns that his father has escaped from the asylum. The year is about to end. The president gives the seniors a levee at his house, and later delivers a farewell sermon to them on the text "blessed are the peacemakers." On the twenty-eighth, final examinations arrive, and the collegiate rites of parting.

All are recommended to have the sheepskin, without exception—as Dr. Gillett announced—the same who made *'remarks somewhat more discriminating'* last year.—Then Mr. Clement, who has frequently been, on the Exam. Com at Dartmouth & elsewhere, spoke in high terms of our examination—paid us some high compliments—congratulated us on having fairly & safely fin-

Unlike his predecessors, President Leonard Woods, Jr., a scholarly bachelor, chose to live off-campus. At Class Day the seniors called on the president at his lodgings in the Weld House, at 7 Federal Street, where he received them with refreshments and an exchange of speeches. The class then proceeded to call at the homes of the other professors, where further food and drink was offered.

ished our course—urged us to continue thro' life habits of industry in study here acquired.—Judge Goodenow, a noble-looking man, with a white hand and a clear voice.—then advised us in a very appropriate manner—told us we must not believe our young days our best days, & think the world all care & darkness *(my views exactly!)*

Then came the ring and the run around the graduating tree—glad faces—glad voices—glad hearts.

Our Supper came on in the evening, or rather in the night,—for we kept it up til 3 in the morning. This Supper is the last meeting of the Class, as a Class,—a mixture of joy and sorrow—anticipation and retrospection—a "meeting of the Past and the Future."

After an oration and a poem:

Next came an hour or two of toasts &—rather boisterous—some circumstances over which I would fain draw the mantle of charity. However, about 1 1/2 we all got calmed down, and a sort of short-speeches followed—some felt what they said—some, I fear, will soon forget their confessions.

After singing the last ode, we formed a ring around the table in the old "Commons Hall"—agreed to meet in 3, 10, & 20 years from now; that is in '49, '56, and in '66—chose secretaries from various parts to keep record of the changes of time.—The ring was formed,—we shook hands all round—and left the Hall in silence—never again to meet as a class entire. A few eyes filled, and a few lips quivered—I controlled my feelings—under other circumstances I might have given away to them more, perhaps. . . . I can bear the parting till the last minute, when we take leave of a friend, say in a carriage just starting.

Most of his classmates leave, but Hanscom plans to stay at College until Commencement and to read Schiller's *Jungfrau von Orleans* with Talbot. He is also studying French with M. F. P. Girard (12 lessons for $2)—"the only difficulty is, Monsieur will drink; and a great pity it is too." He feels closer than ever to Talbot:

"Thom" sticks it out like a man, as he is. He is as independent as I like to see one; does what he thinks proper, let people say what they will. He will adorn our

Congress before years have passed away in great numbers—and, he will not sacrifice principle to "the party." *Ein treuer, tapferer Mann ist mein Freund Thomas!*

And, as ever, he seeks to reassure himself:

The shades of evening fall calmly on trees and scaffolding and stone. The moon rises over the pines yonder, full, large, and round; a bar of blue across its yellow disk. That same moon looks upon a wandering father; a cheerless home once cheerful with his presence; a mother with sadness & thoughts that wander.—Fear not for the Future! Thy duty is with the Present! It will unfold as the Future comes to thee! See how the moon has e'en now emerged from the cloud, and smiles in orbed brightness! So shall my Future be. Up! Then, and on with a brave heart!

In early August, he attends a temperance lecture, reads Longfellow and the Bible, and attends the Episcopal Church, for which Upjohn has designed a small wooden Gothic building. He is not impressed by the liturgy. "I believe no religion without prayer, and can hardly see how there can be much spirituality,—much fervor of desire & emotion, in repeating the same form over and over again." But Hanscom is no materialist: "I sometimes feel within me stirrings of something I cannot grasp, flitting thoughts of great things. And so doubtless does everyone. We are a mystery to ourselves." As College begins to dissolve for him, he finds himself trying to "seize upon as many old associations as possible. . . . Thom & I make a team together."

At Commencement, his speech criticizing "ranking" is well received. Someone present "teased the President: His attempt, long persisted in, to resist all female charms, and live a life of single [bliss] was made the butt of several good hits." The Athenaean "collation" was "as usual, fertile in wit, sentiment, and song; manhood, grace, and beauty."

After the Collation, I walked with Mr. Kimball a few minutes. And then a feeling of loneliness & alienation came over me. I lingered about our door with Thomas a few minutes, and then, fatigued with the tiresome days, sought repose.

He has one final setback; he is blackballed for Phi Beta Kappa by one person—there is no indication in the diary of a reason—but "this is no disappointment to me," although Professor Upham offers sympathy. (Bowdoin's chapter of

Classes held dinners at the end of the year with elaborate menus, toasts, singing, and the declamation of poetry written for the occasion. This freshman dinner was held in Portland in 1861.

Phi Beta Kappa, established in 1825, was for most of the century an alumni organization, to which one was elected upon graduation or afterwards.) He describes his final departure in almost cinematographic terms:

Friday 4th. Rose (with a stiff neck) and prepared for my final departure from old Bowdoin. Parted with classmates; glad & sad; with only a dim, unreal, feeling of departing for so long a vacation, as the world's strife must be, from college quiet & college happiness. Promises to write—enquiries of where will you be?—hasty looks—hasty shakes of the hands of tried friends and true—rattling of carriages—hurrying of trunks—mirth & melancholy—cries from a distance of good bye to you—such & of such sort was our final parting from Bowdoin.

James Hanscom soon found a job as preceptor of Thornton Academy in Saco, a post which should have allowed him a few years of paying off his college debts while considering the career—in law, journalism, college teaching—

which his talents, and his Bowdoin connections, would have opened for him. But three days short of a year after he delivered that Commencement part, he died from a severe attack of dysentery, aged twenty-one. At the request of his friends, his brother Amos reprinted the address "as a memento of the deceased." The family saved his college diary, the record of the Bowdoin career of a young man as likable as he was exemplary.

THE WOODYARD FIRE OF 1846

The burning of the Workman's shed and of the Wood Yard has impressed us all very much with the necessity of a new Law of the State relating [to] civil offenses comitted in Literary Institutions, and I beg, dear Sir, you would turn your thoughts to this subject. The very guarded and careful introduction of legal measures in this case seems to have had a salutary effect.

Leonard Woods, Jr., to Charles S. Daveis
Brunswick, 1 December 1846[5]

Newcomb had walked to Topsham but was in bed by 10 P.M. Frye and Stinson were roasting potatoes in the fireplace. Bulfinch had to go out to "the Temple" about the same time. A record survives of how every Bowdoin student spent the evening of 29 October 1846: it is as if the facades of North and South Colleges (Winthrop and Appleton) and Maine Hall had been peeled back, the activity in each chamber revealed.

In 15 South College, the room of Lewellan Deane 1849 of Portland, a "convivial gathering" was assembling. Around eight that evening, while Orville Jennings 1849, of Leeds, Indiana— one of the few non-New Englanders at Bowdoin that year—was preparing for recitation the next day, Deane came to his room to invite him to the party. Sometime between nine and ten, after he

Professor Samuel P. Newman taught rhetoric and oratory from 1818 to 1839 and was acting president during William Allen's absence from 1831 to 1833. The story of the twelve friends from his textbook, A Practical System of Rhetoric, *inspired the North Yarmouth friends to pledge themselves to yearly reunions.*

had completed his lesson in Horace, Jennings walked from his room at 32 Maine, past the site where the granite walls of the new Chapel were rising, and entered South College, where he soon found himself in this scene:

"They were all seated around the room, engaged in conversation, excepting Wakefield, who was taking some potatoes from the fire, & Deane, who was setting the table," Jennings recalled later.

We had chicken, turkey, potatoes, & sauce, also coffee. After this supper a second table was set, consisting of apples, nuts, raisins, &c. and there were also set on three small bottles, two of which were pint flasks, I should judge, & the other a half pint bottle. One of the two larger was full of Brandy, the other about half full of [port] wine, the smaller one contained lemon sirup. I did not know of the liquor until it was brought forward. . . I turned myself out some lemon sirup, & mixed with it some wine, while I was mixing it Clifford, who stood by the table, took up the Brandy & poured some into my tumbler, at the same time remarking that 'it would be much better,'. . . The remainder of the evening was passed in smoking, talking, & laughing, upon various subjects, the principals of which were topics of our Freshman year, & of the time we passed together at N. Yarmouth Acad.[6]

During the supper, another student, David Wasson 1849, had likewise noted the North Yarmouth connection. "Having in mind the story of the twelve friends, in the appendix to Newman's *Rhetoric,* I proposed that we agree to meet yearly on the anniversary of that evening, so many of us as were able, and relate to each other what had passed during the intervening period."[7]

At about half past eleven, as a student living elsewhere in college, Isaac W. Case 1848, noted in his diary, "chum and I were waked from a

A later Temple, ca. 1897-99, is inscribed with graffiti of the hazing society Phi Chi. Blowing up the Temple was considered particularly amusing by some students.

sound sleep by the alarming cry of 'Fire! Fire!' At first, we thought little of it, as that is a very common cry about college whenever the students feel a little merry—but very soon our room was illuminated by the glare of a real fire, sure enough—and jumping out of bed, we observed the 'Wood Yard' all enveloped in flames."

Case and his roommate threw on their clothes and rushed "to the scene of conflagration, where had already assembled a large No. of the students, and some of the professors. As no efforts could save the wood, except a small lot at the north end. . . the attention of those disposed to *save anything* was directed to the preservation of the 'Temple.'" [8]

While some brought buckets of water from the college pump, others ran down to the village's Engine House and dragged the engine and hose carriage up the hill. By running its hose from the pump to "the Temple," writes Case, "that *necessary* edifice" was preserved. He and most of the others were back in bed by 2 A.M. "How this fire originated, and what was the object of the incendiary, is entirely enveloped in mystery," he writes:

There were about one hundred and fifty cords of hard wood in the shed, of which all but the merest trifle was consumed. The value of the shed and wood could not have been less than six hundred dollars.

If the fire was set by a student, it shows a degree of depravity and recklessness which I can hardly imagine in a college student. At any rate, I hope the offender will be discovered and brought to justice.[9]

In the crowd of amateur firemen was Charles E. Clifford 1849, a sophomore from Newfield, Maine, and one of the North Yarmouth alumni who had attended the convivial supper (and filled Jennings's glass for him). He had already been in some difficulty with the faculty for

In the days before fraternities had houses of their own, they often took over groups of rooms in residence halls. The letters over this Appleton Hall doorway belong to the Delta Kappa Epsilon fraternity.

misbehaving in chapel. After the evening of 29 October, his life took a new and troubling turn.

"The faculty have bored us more than a little with their examinations about '*the fires,*'" Charles B. Merrill 1847 noted in his diary later that term, referring not only to the destruction of the 150 cords "sawed split and piled" but also to the unsolved case of arson involving a temporary "shop" erected by the stone cutters working on the new Chapel.[10] The outrageousness of the two offenses, which in terms of audacity as well as physical loss far exceeded any student prank to date, inspired an equally unprecedented effort on the part of the Executive Government—the faculty and president—to identify and punish whoever had set the fires, the woodshed fire in particular. (From the start, there seemed to be

no presumption of accident or misdeed on the part of outsiders.) Each student was required to present a written affidavit explaining his movements on the night of 29/30 October and assuring his interrogators in these or similar words: "I had no participation whatever in causing the fire. I have no knowledge direct or indirect in relation to it; and no suspicion in regard to its origin." Each student then had to sign his name below this final phrase: "The above is the whole truth in this case, so far as my knowledge extends; of which I am ready to make oath before a magistrate, when required." The survival in the College Archives of these affidavits and a great deal more documentation regarding the case is what allows us to know what everyone was doing—or said he was doing—that night.[11]

To no one's surprise, the first round of investigation led nowhere. But it did allow the faculty to compare different accounts of the same activities, and there survives an extraordinary schema, in President Woods's hand, in which the movements of each of the North Yarmouth friends are traced. It was the age of Poe's detective Auguste Dupin (*Murders in the Rue Morgue* had been published two years earlier), and the notion that crimes might be solved by sheer ratiocination had wide appeal. Perhaps anticipating this, most of the students had well-established alibis and were quick to describe in detail their efforts to contain the fire or rescue the unburned wood.

Early in the course of the interrogations, it became clear—though the records do not show exactly how—that Clifford was behaving as if he had something to hide. A second round of questioning of those present in Deane's room—this time by a group of Trustees and Overseers, including a distinguished member of the Bar, Judge Reuel Williams h 1855 of Augusta (a Trustee from 1822-1860), formerly the College's land agent—produced enough, albeit circumstantial, evidence to "indict" Clifford and cast strong suspicion on William C. Ten Broeck 1849. Clifford was dismissed from college on 10 November and sent home to Newfield. President Woods wrote to his father, who was out of state at the time, describing the steps taken to identify the incendiary:

"It is with extreme regret that I have to announce to you, that the whole body of the evidence thus obtained pointed generally to a convivial company of students with wh. your son was connected on that evening, and then more particularly towards himself." Woods described a visit by the examining committee to young Clifford's room:

As your son had not left his room the week previous on account of ill health but still professed himself well enough to sustain an examination, these Gentlemen with myself, after spending most of the day and evening in examining others who had been suspected, went to his room. I am sorry to be obliged to add that his appearance at this examination was very far from being satisfactory. He denied facts wh. were established by abundant testimony, and advanced statements, wh. were not only contradictory to what he had

subscribed before, but wh. he afterwards acknowledged to be fabricated for the sake of covering up circumstances wh. appeared suspicious. The result of the examination tended to confirm the suspicions wh. had existed before.

Declaring himself in the father's absence young Clifford's "adviser and protector," Woods said he would prefer to handle the case as a matter of college discipline. "There are, however, many in our Boards and in the Community who think that offenses of this nature committed by students should be dealt with according to the Laws of the Land." Several citizens, he added, were ready to commence a prosecution on their own. For several years, the Boards had been urging the College to prosecute for civil offenses, "but they have always been opposed by me, and hitherto successfully, as repugnant to the relation in wh. we stand to young men committed to our charge, and over whom, even when they are offenders, we are called to exercise, a parental, rather than a judicial authority." Woods said he had sent the boy home with the advice to confess or face trial.

Some days later, Woods added more than a page to this letter, saying in part:

New facts were disclosed by persons who were in company with your son during the evening of the fire, placing it entirely beyond doubt that the fire was set by him. And every day since that time the evidence has accumulated, so that the hesitation I felt in communicating to you suspicions of so grave a nature. . . has been at last removed.[12]

Ten Broeck's father had been called to Brunswick and asked to examine the evidence, which at that point seemed to implicate his son as well. How young Ten Broeck talked his way out of that is unclear, but by 14 November the young man and Wasson could write to their absent classmate in these terms: learning of some "new facts," they tell Clifford that they are:

satisfied you did set it. It becomes my duty [the draft of the letter preserved is in Wasson's hand] to inform you of this change of feeling and opinion, and to urge you to adopt the only course of conduct which can save you from utter ruin. . . . [I]f this case goes to court you are a lost man. No jury can resist the mass of testimony accumulated. . . . The Trustees to a man had no doubt of your guilt.

They add that Ten Broeck's father and a former mayor of Portland likewise "have the strongest conviction that you are the man." Warming to his subject, Wasson envisions the eighteen-year-old Clifford standing before a jury made even less sympathetic because they will know he has perjured himself to the faculty. "Your name will become a bye-word of reproach; it will ring from one end of the Union to the other. . . ." There is but one way to escape such "damning infamy." "You must confess, or make up your mind to wear the parti-colored garb of a *State Prison Convict* and pick stone at Thomaston for the three years to come." The letter is signed "Your Friends"—Wasson and Ten Broeck.[13]

Four days later, Jennings wrote him: "Why did you come to my room, in the manner you did? . . . It must have been the result of a guilty conscience." Then he got to the point: "Now if you have any respect for yourself, if you have any honor, if you have any regard for your former College companions, I conjure you by all that is great & good to come forward & confess. . . ." Only a confession by Clifford, in other words, would completely clear the names of his fellow revellers, who might otherwise find themselves included in the indictment. "Now I am authorized by the Government," Jennings went on, "to say to you, that if you will make your confession by Letter to me, they will compromise with you." It would be his last chance, Jennings said—not only to avoid a prison term but to restore his good name at Bowdoin.

Clifford would have none of this. He replied from Newfield to Wasson that he was "perfectly innocent of any participation in the fire" and that "there'll be a day when you believe me." As for the threat of criminal charges, "I've thought of all these things and I'm prepared for the worst." He added a postscript: "My next will probably be from state's prison." Five days later, he sent the same protestation of innocence to Jennings, adding "I've not a person or a thing to go to. You three hold my destiny." He also asked Jennings how he could have had enough time, between leaving Deane's room and returning to their floor of North College, to have set a fire

that had advanced so far, "for you know that when the smoke didn't hide it, it would shine as bright as the brightest sun and even brighter on the wall of Wasson's room." He asked what the "new" evidence was and if the College was investigating the previous fire as well.

In the early stages of the investigation, the case against Clifford had lacked either a motive or much evidence of premeditation. His account of how he had spent the earlier part of the evening—he said he had taken a walk down the Town Mall and back—was a bit vague, and unsubstantiated, but this would hardly link him to a fire that was not discovered until past 11 P.M. The fact that several of his friends remembered seeing him look for something on the mantel just as the party was breaking up suggested the possibility of matches—the group had been smoking "segars"—but there was no proof that he found any. The fact that he lingered behind the others as they parted did not look good, but there was a very real question as to whether anyone could have started the fire in the brief time between Clifford's leaving Deane's room and returning to his own. Even the attempt to concoct a story to throw suspicion off the group might be excused as nervous overreaction on the part of a youth who had already been in some disciplinary trouble.

What persuaded the examiners, it seems, in reviewing the students' depositions and Woods's lists of questions for them, must have been two things: 1) Clifford's somewhat odd behavior in the time between leaving Deane's room and the discovery by the rest of the College of the fire and 2) a remark he had made earlier to Wasson.

The lengthy written statements by Wasson and Jennings to Woods in mid-November rehearsed the events of the evening. Wasson remembered returning to his room, building a fire, and settling down to read. Within six to eight minutes, he said, Clifford came in. He sat quietly for fifteen minutes then said "he wished to use a certain article of furniture" in the bed room. Wasson had finished his Horace and was about to turn in when he heard Clifford call "Wasson,

Wasson, look here!" He and Ten Broeck hurried into the room and found Clifford pointing out the fire. "It won't do for us to give the alarm, for we have just been out," Wasson recalled Clifford's saying. Ten Broeck agreed that it was "unlucky" but wanted to give the alarm. Clifford insisted that it was a bad idea—"the fire had already got too strong a hold to be extinguished." Wasson said nothing had happened to make him suspect Clifford was the cause of it. Wasson himself turned down the lamp lest someone outside should see them looking out the window. He then told Clifford to go to his room and await the cry of fire, which followed in a moment. The friends rushed into the crowd and soon lost sight of each other.

The next morning, Wasson remembered that Clifford had pulled aside the curtain before calling to the others. He asked him why. Clifford said that, upon bending down to pick up the chamber pot, he had seen bright light under the lower edge of the curtain. That satisfied Wasson, but "still he would not agree that we should tell the whole story," despite his friends' protestations. "He continued to protest against it, saying we had nothing to do with the fire, we knew very well, and that withholding the circumstance of his being in my room would be the best way to make this apparent." This seemed reasonable enough to Wasson, who suppressed this fact when called before the faculty. But he had a pang of guilt and told Clifford he wanted to go back and tell the truth, whereupon Clifford said "it would not do."

"What can I say?" Wasson asked his examiners. I have no mother, but let my Father be asked if he can remember when I ever told a falsehood. I do not say this boastingly; but if for twenty three years I have adhered to truth can I but curse the hour in which I departed from it? All this is horrible—a humiliation to which I never expected to be subjected.

There were other circumstances that seemed at first to clear Clifford of any suspicions. Wasson had noticed that the fire was burning from the ground, its flames licking up and through the roof of the shed. "According to the best computation of time I can make this was not above 17 or 18 minutes after Clifford set the fire, suppos-

ing he did set it. But is it possible that in this short space of time the fire could penetrate this mass of wood, mount to the roof and burst through?" Moreover, Clifford seemed to Wasson an unlikely incendiary. "I have always considered him anything rather than daring, with a certain off-hand air of independence it is true; but timid, even cowardly, in matters involving actual danger. And I find this to be the common feeling of the class."

On the other hand, "his mode of accounting for the time between leaving Deane's room and coming to mine differed at different periods." Clifford had told his friends that even if they knew who was guilty they should not tell.

In his account of the evening, Jennings practiced the lessons of Newman's *Rhetoric*: he made "a skillful selection and arrangement of the circumstances," as the professor had suggested in his textbook. After the description of the supper quoted earlier, he retraced his friends' steps back to their neighboring rooms. He remembered that Clifford had his hat and cloak on and had paused as if he were looking for something on the mantel. On the way, Wasson told Jennings and Ten Broeck a long story about his falling twice down the steps in the dark—distracting them enough so that Jennings could not recall where Clifford had wandered off to. His chum already asleep, Jennings reviewed an ode in his Horace once more and in a quarter of an hour was undressing to go to bed. Someone knocked. "I should not have gone at all to the door," Jennings said, "had I not heard a voice in a sharp whisper, calling my name." It was Clifford, "who appeared somewhat excited. This was the first time I saw him after I left him in Deane's room, with his hat & cloak on. The first words he spoke were 'You will not say anything! Will you Jennings?' which somewhat startled me, and I asked him what he meant, to which he replied 'You *will* keep still, now, *won't* you Jennings?'. . . Said I, 'Clifford tell me what you mean!' He then answered, 'the wood pile is on fire.'" Jennings rushed to the window and was about to give the alarm, but Clifford caught his arm. "Don't give the alarm! if you do they will suspect us, as we have been out this evening." He escorted him instead to Wasson's room. "All this passed in a short space of time," wrote Jennings, "shorter than I have been writing its account. . . . I cannot tell what was said [there], but think I heard Clifford mention something about 'lowering the light.'" The room was dark, the young men very still. Soon the alarm was given by someone in South College, followed by the college bell.

"I never had the least suspicion of Clifford until Monday last," Jennings went on. "Clifford said to me that Faculty would not think otherwise than that he set the fire, unless he could make out that he came up from Deane's room, directly behind us." He looked "very anxious" when Jennings hesitated. "[T]he peculiar manner of his making the enquiry caused my first suspicion of him." Jennings remembered that Clifford still had his hat on when he had come to his room. Nor could Jennings remember hearing his footsteps on the landing in the interval between leaving Deane's and the discovery of the fire, which at least suggested the possibility that Clifford had been outside the entire time.

Once started, this speculation as to Clifford's state of mind seems to have been what persuaded the College to move so rapidly ahead in singling him out as the culprit. Asked why he thought Clifford had come to his room, Wasson told the president that Clifford was "not self possessed" at the time—"Liquor easily affected him, and made him mischievous." Questioned again on 19 November, Wasson remembered that Clifford had "said to me two or three times that he wished some one would burn the Wood Yard." Woods's notes of Wasson's answers continue:

This was after the other fire. I rebuked him. . . . Do not know of his having said this to others. Have an impression that TenB. heard something of the sort. Thought it seemed to be pure lowly mischief. He had no good will toward the College, or the Faculty; but know of no particular occasion of revenge.

With this evidence in hand, Woods felt confident enough to approach Clifford's father. The president, usually the most lenient and complaisant of men, found himself in a particularly difficult spot. The wantonness of the damage, the insult it represented to the College's govern-

ment, could not be passed over merely with the expulsion of the most likely miscreant. The Governing Boards—some of whose members already suspected Woods was too mild a disciplinarian—were angered by the destruction; the leading men in town were also aroused.[14] At a time, moreover, when funds were being sought for the architecturally ambitious new chapel and when Bowdoin was still seeking to win supportive friends among New England Congregationalists, the incident had to be taken seriously. The misdeed itself—the destruction in a few hours of a winter's supply of fuel—may also have stirred some unspoken, ancestral unease on the part of people who respected the value of human labor and appreciated the dangers of a northern climate. The case against Clifford represented more than the ants' disdain for the grasshopper. It is difficult to imagine the marshalling of quite so many forces had not some deep offense been felt by the community.

On the other hand, Woods must have known that the evidence against Clifford was at best circumstantial. There were no eyewitnesses nor a clear motive or method. Above all, there was no confession.

Woods's letter was plainly an offer to negotiate. On 14 December, Clifford senior—acting through his agent, John Anderson, a well-known Portland lawyer and Democratic politician—paid the College $400.67 by way of settlement of damages.[15] Three days later, the Executive Government voted to dismiss Charles Clifford on the grounds of his having attended "a convivial party" on the evening of 29 October. No mention was made of the fire.

In outlining for his father the facts that pointed to young Clifford's guilt, Woods did not need to explain the law that applied: Clifford senior was attorney-general of the United States. A lawyer soon to become a diplomat, Nathan Clifford had received the Cabinet post in September of 1846—a few weeks before the fire—not so much in recognition of his legal acumen (which was unremarkable) as because of President Polk's desire to reward his Democratic supporters in New England.[16] The son's prob-

144

lem could not have arisen at a worse time. The elder Clifford had had serious misgivings about accepting the job, which he said had come "unsought by me" even though "well meant toward Maine." The country lawyer turned politician had suddenly found himself transported to the wartime cabinet of a president whose expansionist policy in the Mexican territories had raised new legal issues that had to be mastered in little time. The thought of representing the administration's interests before the U. S. Supreme Court in particular almost unnerved Clifford; in Polk's diary, the president records the extraordinary visit before church on Sunday, 13 December, of his new attorney-general bearing a letter of resignation. "I at once expressed my astonishment to him, and told him I should greatly regret it," writes James K. Polk. "I told him that I was entirely satisfied with him, and hoped he would retain his place." The president tried to reassure him while warning of the difficulties his quitting so abruptly would cause. "I think Mr. Clifford an honest man and a sincere friend. He feels in his new position somewhat timid, fears that he will not be able to sustain the reputation of his predecessors, and had therefore brought himself to the conclusion that he had better resign."[17] Polk talked him out of it. Clifford proved an acceptable advocate in court and a diplomat of far more than average skill when, in 1847, he was sent to Mexico to negotiate the peace settlement that was to bring the United States, as spoils of war, an expanse of territory larger than the Louisiana Purchase.

Sometime between 10 November (when young Clifford was expelled) and 14 December (when Anderson paid the damages), Clifford senior learned of the events back in Maine, and one wonders if the knowledge that respectable people thought his eldest son an arsonist might not have undermined his self-confidence as much as any professional self-doubts. That can only be a conjecture; Nathan Clifford's surviving papers include no mention of the incident. But they do provide evidence to clear young Clifford of any suspicion that he was a rich young wastrel out to exploit a famous and well-connected

Unlike his predecessor, William Allen, President Leonard Woods, Jr. (shown here ca. 1860), was known as a mild disciplinarian, although, as the woodyard fire incident showed, even his patience could be tried.

father. Nathan Clifford's family never had money to spare. In his dutiful letters to "Dear Wife" in Maine, the new attorney-general complains not only of his exhausting duties but of the expense of living in the capital. "The people here would bankrupt us if we went to House keeping here," he writes, by way of explaining why she and the family must remain in Newfield.[18] The payment of $400 to the College, in other words, must have strained resources that already were barely adequate.

An interesting and unresolved question is whether Clifford paid so quickly to avoid a politi-

145

cal, or at least personal, scandal at a time when Maine's Democrats were already in disarray and when Polk's Mexican War was unpopular in New England. Some hint of this appears in Wasson's poignant remark warning young Clifford not to be another "Spenser's son"—a reference to the secretary of war in the Tyler administration whose midshipman son had been executed in 1842 for attempted mutiny. It was in Woods's interest as well to avoid too public a controversy, for he was known for his Democratic sympathies. "The President evidently felt great relief," Anderson reported to Nathan Clifford, and promised, in return for the damages paid, that "no vote injurious to your son would be passed."

Whatever may have inspired it, the quick settlement ended the controversy. Woods's chapel continued to rise. The Boards bought more firewood and erected a more secure yard for it. The southwest territory was made safe for the Anglo-Saxons and, in the view of many New England Whigs, for the slave-owning Southern expansionists. Nathan Clifford returned to practice law in Portland and in 1858 was named by President Buchanan to be justice of the U. S. Supreme Court. He was Maine's first (and to date only) justice, though one of the court's less distinguished jurists. Bowdoin gave him an honorary degree in 1860.

Reviewing the fires and the catalogue of other disorders of the day, the Visiting Committee for 1847 found a remedy. "The want of moral instruction to a greater extent, and at an earlier period, is believed to be a prominent cause of the existing irregularities and vices, among the students," the visitors concluded. The first three years of college are devoted to classical and mathematical studies, without "any instruction upon moral or religious subjects." As a result, the College was failing "to impress upon the student, just sentiments and principles of action, or to inculcate moral precepts in his heart." By senior year, when such instruction was traditionally offered in American colleges by their presidents, "it is quite too late to repair the mischief which have resulted to the college, by the irregularities of the previous years."[19] One result was to

be Bowdoin's Collins Professorship, which three years later was to bring the Stowe family to Brunswick.

For all practical purposes, the woodyard incident was soon forgotten—except by Charles Clifford. The young man continued his studies under a private tutor at home, expecting to be admitted to some other college as a junior. On 24 August 1847, Woods prepared the following certificate for President Edward Everett of Harvard: "This may certify that Charles E. Clifford pursued the course of study prescribed by the Laws of the College to the beginning of the Sophomore year, and is hereby honorably dismissed from that standing at his Father's request." Feeling cheated of a year by Bowdoin, Clifford entered Harvard, graduating with the Class of 1850. By 1853, he was admitted to practice law in Maine and began a highly respectable—and by comparison with the events of 1846—a rather uneventful career as an attorney. His marriage in 1866 produced five children. He traveled widely and spent four years on the West Coast and one in Iowa. Upon retiring from practice, he supervised a farm six miles from Portland. There is no indication, in looking at the later records of his life, that the charge of arson in his student days had had any impact on the course of his career. In his 50th Class Report to Harvard, the only negative note is that he has been "a sufferer from asthma now for 30 years."[20]

And yet the evening of 29 October continued to haunt him. His file at Bowdoin includes an extraordinary twenty-four-page manuscript, which appears to have been deposited by his son, Charles H. Clifford, in 1908 in response to Librarian George T. Little's request for biographical data. The memorandum rehearses the events that followed the fire, beginning in a calm, lawyerly fashion, then turning into an impassioned attack on Leonard Woods's integrity. Why did Woods tell his father the case against him had not been "strictly" proved, he asks. Does Woods not know the plain meaning of words?

Where punishment is to follow an act, there is no half way between guilt and innocence. If a charge of crime is not maintained by evidence it is wholly defeated. . . It cannot be that it was not well known at this time in Bowdoin College that one is to be held innocent until proved guilty, and that before inflicting a penalty the evidence of guilt must rise to the full point of strict or exact and precise proof.

This detestable proceeding shows an unmistakable utterance of sentence to punishment in one breath and in the next one a statement, clear, authentic, that there is no proof of guilt.

After speculating that Woods and the faculty feared the Trustees' wrath, Clifford grows angrier:

Trump up a suspicion—guess—guess—guess—where there is no trustworthy evidence filch the father's purse and the son's good name. . . .The most pitiable part of this money-making transaction is that this eager, thankful obsequious acceptance of the $400.67 is accompanied by an acknowledgement that no proof exists of a cause for taking it.

It is not clear to whom this document—half of it a reasoned attempt to assert his innocence, half of it a diatribe against the Bowdoin of his youth—was addressed; possibly the Governing Boards, for in 1902 Clifford was granted a Bowdoin A. B. "as of 1849."[21]

Charles E. Clifford died in 1907, aged seventy-eight. In 1922 his nephew, Philip G. Clifford '03, published a biography of Nathan Clifford, the Supreme Court justice, and in 1969 his great-grandnephew, Roger Howell, Jr. '58, was inaugurated as the College's tenth president.

Clifford's story is one of those moments when the placid surface of a traditional society is broken by an untoward event whose psychological shocks expose patterns of behavior otherwise hidden in the routines of daily life, and whose legal (or, as in this case, quasi-legal) record is as densely textured as a novel. The story is not so much one of youthful folly or institutional misjudgment as it is of the use and misuse of the notion of human accountability. "Oh they should have taken your word for it," Joshua Chamberlain, many years later, told Charles Clifford.[22] Why "they" did not is a question worth pausing over.

It was not, simply, that Clifford's lie about what he and his friends had been doing that evening had destroyed his credibility. The college authorities knew a lesson found in one of Professor Upham's treatises on the human mind, namely that friendship easily taints testimony (and should be allowed for by the investigators) and that Clifford (in his own mind) could have been lying as much to protect his fellow revellers as to cover his own tracks.[23] This would hardly have been unprecedented in the College's experience of dealing with undergraduate wrongdoing. Where the case became something exceptional—really a battle of wills between the eighteen-year-old Clifford and the college elders—is when, in the face of so much incriminating evidence and the conclusion reached by so many worthy men that he was guilty, the youth still refused to confess. The "crime" could be quantified—$400.67 worth of wood—and the damage indemnified by a parent, yet the offense against the community required some admission of guilt before the offender could be allowed to resume his previous status. The payment and Clifford's absence from Brunswick allowed the incident to be "lost" as new classes followed and new crises arose, yet there remains a suggestion, which can be teased out of the documents, that Clifford got the better of Woods, though at a great price.

Was all this a peculiarly New England way of dealing with such things? Had such an incident arisen at a Southern college or university, for example, might not the outcome have been very different? Refusal to accept a gentleman's word would have had more potentially serious consequences than damage to college property.[24] A small part of Clifford lived in that genteel and chivalric world—his friend Deane was reading one of Scott's Waverly novels, and Clifford can sound as touchy about his honor as any Southerner—but the other part dwelt in the world of Nathan Clifford and John Anderson, a pragmatic, even prosaic place, in which a threatening situation was more comfortably dealt with by quiet recourse to cash, rather than by some heroic defense of face. Perhaps that is a final, if remote, lesson to be extracted from Clifford's misadventure: that the South and New England, for all their ties of blood and commerce, had grown by the late 1840s into two irreconcilable peoples.

NOTES

BCSC is Special Collections, Hawthorne-Longfellow Library, Bowdoin College.

1. Henry Melville King Diary, Maine Historical Society, Portland, Maine.

2. Horatio Bridge, *Personal Recollections of Nathaniel Hawthorne* (New York, 1893), p. 8

3. Records of the Executive Government, 1832. BCSC.

4. James Hanscom Diary, BCSC.

5. C. S. Daveis Papers, BCSC.

6. Orville Jennings to Leonard Woods, Jr., 14 Nov. 1846, "Burning of the Woodyard 1846" Box, BCSC, pp. 1-2.

7. David Wasson to Leonard Woods, n.d., Woodyard Box, p. 2. BCSC. The story referred to is Exercise V: "The first and last dinner," in Samuel P. Newman, *A Practical System of Rhetoric* (Andover and New York, 1835), 5th ed., pp. 235-237.

8. Isaac W. Case Journal, 25 Oct. 1846, BCSC.

9. *Ibid.*

10. Charles B. Merrill Diary 1844-47, 13 Dec. 1846, New York Public Library Special Collections.

11. The documents are available in BCSC in the box marked "College Records—History; Burning of the Woodyard 1846." No other nineteenth-century disciplinary incident at Bowdoin is so thoroughly documented.

12. Leonard Woods to Nathan Clifford, n. d., Woodyard Box.

13. The threat of being stripped of one's social identity was a very real concern in antebellum America, according to Karen Halttunen, *Confidence Men and Painted Women: A Study of Middle-Class Culture in America, 1830-1870* (New Haven: Yale University Press, 1982), p. xv. Two social problems faced an ambitious youth, she writes: "the problem of establishing and recognizing social identity in a republic based theoretically on the boundless potential of each individual, and the problem of securing success in the anonymous 'world of strangers' that was the antebellum city," p. xvi. One social role the antebellum college may have played was in helping to secure this identity— e.g., through bonding with a class and otherwise playing the alumnus.

14. The most favorable account of Woods's style as disciplinarian is to be found in Robert H. Gardiner's Visiting Committee Report for 1845: "The President spends most of the afternoons in his room in the College, where he is in the habit of sending for such scholars as seem by their inattention to study or by any slight irregularity to give indication of approaching dereliction from duty. There he converses with, advises, and if necessary admonishes, and if the case requires it informs the parents that their son is failing to derive benefit from being a member of College and advises his temporary removal. It is not necessary to speak of the great superiority of this mode of discipline to that formerly adopted [i. e., by President Allen] of allowing follies to ripen into acts of a graver nature and then to visit them with heavy punishment. It however imposes an arduous and severe duty upon the President which cannot be appreciated by those who do not enter into the spirit of the system."

15. John Anderson 1813 was one of the state's leading "Jeffersonian" Democrats, as he styled himself. After reading law with Stephen Longfellow in Portland, he served in the Maine Senate in 1824 and the U.S. Congress 1825-33, served three terms as mayor of Portland, was U.S. Attorney for Maine 1833-36, and at the time of the Clifford incident was in a second term in the patronage post of collector of customs for Portland. He was also active in establishing the Atlantic & St. Lawrence Railroad. He was, in other words, a figure to

reckon with, should the College have decided to prosecute young Clifford. He was also a lineal descendant of the Reverend Thomas Smith of Falmouth, Samuel Deane's elder colleague, suggesting how small a world formed Portland's elite. And he was no stranger to college disciplinary problems: his own son, Samuel J. Anderson 1844, had been in and out of trouble at Bowdoin, including one incident that produced a classic in the long history of undergraduate self-exculpation.

In 1844, Samuel Anderson wrote to the faculty: "In the afternoon, in company with two others, I started for Topsham with the intention of going to church. But as we were passing the tavern I asked the others to go in and drink with me—feeling myself justified *at the time* in so doing by the attack of an illness which is constitutional and for which spirituous liquor has formerly been prescribed as a remedy. . ." S. J. Anderson File, BCSC. There was an interesting parallel with the woodyard incident; one of Anderson's companions also tried at first to lie to the faculty to cover for him. John Anderson wrote to Woods insisting that in the future his son and his ward attend meeting in Brunswick "where they will remain under the eye of yourself or some officer of the College." *Ibid.*

Samuel went on to become one of Portland's most notable citizens. A lifelong Democrat and opponent of the Civil War, "General" Anderson, as he was usually called because of his rank in the state militia, came within 117 votes of defeating Thomas Brackett Reed 1860 for Congress in 1880 (the closest Reed ever came to losing in his long career). The "General," too, was a railway president (Portland & Ogdensburg Railroad). Another son of John Anderson, Edward W. Anderson 1848, Harvard M.D. 1852, was at the College at the time of the woodyard fire.

16. For details of his career, see Philip G. Clifford, *Nathan Clifford, Democrat* (New York: G. P. Putnam's Sons, 1922), and the more critical essay by William Gillette in Leon Friedman and Fred J. Israel, eds., *The Justices of the United States Supreme Court 1789-1969*, vol. 2 (New York: Chelsea House Publishers, 1969), pp. 963-975.

17. Milo Milton Quaife, ed., *The Diary of James K. Polk during His Presidency, 1845-1849* (Chicago: A. C. McClurg & Co., 1910), pp. 274-275.

18. Nathan Clifford Papers, 1846, Maine Historical Society, Portland, Maine.

19. Visiting Committee Reports, 1847, BCSC, pp. 20-21.

20. *Class of 1850* (Cambridge, MA: John Wilson and Son, 1895), p. 9.

21. *Ibid.*

22. *Ibid.*

23. Thomas C. Upham, *Elements of Intellectual Philosophy* (Portland: Shirley and Hyde, 1828), 2nd ed., p. 337.

24. For the contrast between New England and the South on the question of presentation of self, see the chapter "Male Youth and Honor" in Bertram Wyatt-Brown, *Southern Honor: Ethics and Behavior in the Old South* (New York: Oxford University Press, 1982), pp. 149-174, and, more generally, William R. Taylor, *Cavalier and Yankee: The Old South and American National Character* (New York: Doubleday & Company, 1963). An interesting essay remains to be written on the concept of honor and the value of truth-telling among antebellum college students in the North. Two models for such a study are Jennings L. Wagoner, Jr., "Honor and Dishonor at Mr. Jefferson's University: The Antebellum Years," *History of Education Quarterly* 26 (Summer 1986), pp. 155-179, and Kenneth S. Greenberg, "The Nose, the Lie, and the Duel in the Antebellum South," *American Historical Review* 95 (Fall 1990), pp. 57-74.

The bronze plaques in the lobby of Memorial Hall commemorate 288 Bowdoin alumni who fought for the Union in the Civil War. A smaller plaque in the west staircase commemorates the eighteen who served the Confederacy.

Memorial Hall, built between 1867 and 1882 to honor those who had served. The entrance was significantly changed in 1955, when the building was renovated and Pickard Theater installed.

The Brunswick home of Professor Thomas C. Upham and his wife, Phebe Lord Upham, now the Elks Club, at 179 Park Row.

Lower Maine Street, Brunswick, taken before 1866. On the left, the Universalist Church; on the right, the Maine Street Baptist Church; in the distance, the spires of the First Parish Church and the College Chapel.

CHAPTER SIX

Although the Civil War had little immediate impact on the College,
the lives of many people associated with Bowdoin were shaped by the debate over slavery
and the fight over preserving the Union. The war changed the College, they
were to discover afterwards, because it changed the country. By examining portions of the
lives of two novelists, a senator, a president, six black students, several generals,
and other alumni in battle, we can begin to piece together some understanding of why
Americans sacrificed so much for the cause in which they believed.

63 FEDERAL STREET

Years later they would boast that the Civil War had begun and ended in Brunswick, Maine. Harriet Beecher Stowe had written her great novel there, inflaming the Christian North to fight; Joshua Chamberlain had returned to live in Brunswick after receiving the Confederate surrender at Appomattox Court House. It might be more accurate, however, to say that Stowe's Civil War had begun years earlier when she had seen at first hand the cruelties of slavery in Kentucky. And when did the war end? Perhaps at Selma or Montgomery in the 1960s, for Chamberlain's heroism in the field, like Oliver Otis Howard's labors for the Freedmen's Bureau, ultimately failed to guarantee the citizenship of their black fellow countrymen. But nonetheless there is some truth to the old chestnut, for Brunswick is a town saturated with Civil War memory. You feel it still, when you stand in front of the Chamberlain House or First Parish Church, or cross the Bowdoin Quad, with Memorial Hall and its bronze plaques at one end and General Thomas Hubbard's tower at the other. Were the war a film, it could begin with Jefferson Davis going into the church at the Commencement of 1858 and end with Ulysses S. Grant coming out the same door in 1865.[1]

Harriet Beecher Stowe arrived in Brunswick on 25 May 1850, happy to return to her native New England—she had been born in Connecticut—after eighteen years in Cincinnati,

in those days a rough riverfront city. It had not been an easy journey. She was seven months pregnant. She was grieving over the death of her youngest son in a cholera epidemic in Ohio. Her husband could not join her until later in the summer. She had their other five children in tow. Upon arriving at Bath on the Boston steamer, she discovered that William Smyth, the Bowdoin mathematician who had played a large role in persuading her husband to return to teach at his old college, was not waiting as promised. As she told her husband later:

Proff Smith had written that he should be at the landing to wait on me to the cars—It was a drenching running rain & fog when the boat stopped. Proff Smyth was there umbrella in hand waiting in anxious expectation he says—but I also waited on board the boat hoping to hear somebody enquire for me—I waited till all the baggage was taken out & seeing or hearing no one I went on shore & took a hack & was driven up to the [street] cars took my ticket saw my baggage put in & then waited patiently for the cars to go off—Meanwhile Mr. Smith after rambling over the boat in search of me came to the cars in despair to go back to Brunswick . . . He went into the front car—I & the children into the back & in fifteen minutes we were in Bath—I wondered when I got there that nobody came to the cars to look for me—he got out [in Brunswick] quite disappointed & walked up to Mrs. Upham's who had her breakfast table all waiting & announced the [grim?] fact that I was not coming & then directly on the heels of this while he & Mrs Upham were wondering over their coffee what could have become of me I came bag & baggage to the door—What way did you come was the astonished cry—From Bath says I quite cool—Impossible says Proff Smyth how could you have got there you were certainly not on the Bath

An enlargement of a cabinet card-size photograph of Lyman Beecher and his children by the Matthew Brady Studio, ca. 1859. Front row: Isabella, Catherine, Lyman Beecher, Mary, Harriet. Back row: Thomas, William, Edward, Charles, Henry Ward.

boat—But indeed I was says I—& then such a laugh as Mrs Upham & Mary & Susan railed on the poor Professor—it has been a standing joke ever since—he laughs & shakes his sides talks about it incessantly himself—begs nobody will mention it to him—for it hurts his feelings to have it alluded to—What was the matter yet remains a mystery—I am quite sure that I stood a long time in a very conspicuous situation with my children drawn up before me—& he is sure that he came on board—looked every where & did not see me.[2]

Stowe arrived bearing two well-known names and a fair amount of literary ambition: the Beecher family included four of the most famous preachers in the country (her father and three brothers); her husband, Calvin Ellis Stowe '24, was a distinguished theologian, and she had some small reputation of her own, as the contributor of sketches and stories to several national publications.[3] But her first task was to set up house. Perhaps to make up for having missed her at Bath, Smyth planted a garden for the Stowes, so that the family would have summer vegetables that year, and he found her a cow. Mrs. Upham, who lent her bedding until her delayed belongings arrived, found her a house-

keeper-nurse and promised her a round of entertainments—which, to everyone's surprise, was Professor Upham's idea, despite his notorious shyness ("Mr Smith & Mrs Upham say that this proposition from him is one of the latter day wonders & shows that he thinks a new era is commencing," Harriet told her husband.) For $125 a year, the Stowes had rented the Titcomb House, now 63 Federal Street, the former home of the newspaperman-turned-Baptist minister who had rented rooms in Calvin Stowe's student days to the Longfellow brothers. Expenses were greater than anticipated, but Harriet promised her husband that "as I mean to raise a sum myself equivalent to the rent this year it only imposes the labour of writing an extra piece or two on me."[4] Unlike the Upham's "princely house" on Park Row, the Titcomb property was showing its age and proved a constant source of inconvenience to the Stowes during their two years in Brunswick.

Early summer saw the arrival of Calvin (who was already looking for another job), her sister Catharine (who was to take over much of the housekeeping), and on 8 July a son, Charles

Edward. Although she had a slow recovery, Harriet managed to help Catharine start a school in town and began sending pieces to *The National Era*, a new abolitionist paper in Washington, D. C., edited by Gamaliel Bailey.

Financial worries continued to plague the family. The $1,000 salary that Calvin Stowe received as Collins Professor was inadequate to support a family, he had warned his friends at Bowdoin, and he made little secret of the fact that, at age forty-eight, he would much prefer, for personal and professional reasons, to accept the post waiting for him at Andover Theological Seminary in his native Massachusetts. "My worldly circumstances are very trying and demand relief," he wrote to a friend that fall. "I have no property and no house. At an age when most men begin to see their children off their hands & settled in life, I have a family of six between the ages of 14 and 1. At my death they are roofless and penny less, without a friend on earth with property to help them. My wife is also feeble & unable to endure much of labor or hardship."[5] Stowe tried to persuade Smyth and Upham to arrange a salary of $1,200 plus a house, reminding them that they had urged him to return to New England as an experiment. The Titcomb House had been an expensive disappointment, he told Upham: "most miserably out of repair, and certainly unfit to offer for rent to any body. The door latches were all broken except one or two, of all the panes of glass in the house four out of every five are broken—the fences, the gates, every thing corresponds faithfully to the doorlatches and window panes, and [stands] in amazing contrast with a $40,000 chapel." His wife had told him their expenses for the year would exceed his salary by $200 or $300, adding: "I do not want to feel *obliged* to work as hard every year as I have this. I can earn 200 dollars by writing, but I do not want to feel that I must; and when weary with teaching children, tending baby, buying provisions, settling bills, cutting out clothes, still to feel that I must write a piece for some paper."[6]

Yet she had already begun that winter to write a series of sketches "to illustrate the cruelty of slavery," as she explained to her brother, Henry

Harriet Beecher Stowe and Calvin Ellis Stowe 1824 in 1852.

Ward Beecher. By 9 March 1851, she alerted her editor, Bailey, that she would be sending him a story painting both "the lights and shadows of the 'patriarchal institution,'" which "may extend through three or four numbers." It took longer than the two or three weeks promised, but on 5 June 1851, filling most of the front page of *The National Era*, was the first installment of *Uncle Tom's Cabin, or Life Among the Lowly*. Neither the nation nor the Stowe family was ever to be the same.[7]

The book became the bestseller of the century. For various reasons, however, Stowe's international celebrity and *Uncle Tom's Cabin*'s political reverberations were not to win her a place in the traditional canon of major nineteenth-century American writers. There were several reasons for this. Alongside Hawthorne, Melville, Whitman, Emerson, and Twain, she seemed to most twentieth-century critics amateurish, writing in a voice that was perceived as shallow, thin, sentimental, "feminine," parlor-bound. She lacked the cool, serious, ironic tone of her famous male contemporaries. Moreover, the infantilization of her saintly Uncle Tom at the hands of popular dramatists and minstrel show performers turned him from the Christ-like figure of her imagina-

The Stowe family lived in the Titcomb House, at 63 Federal Street (then called Back Street), during the two years when Calvin Stowe 1824 was Collins Professor of Natural and Revealed Religion at the College.

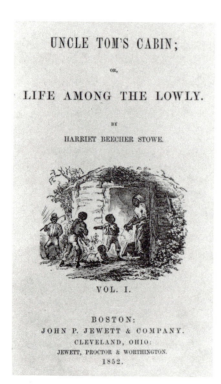

The first edition of Harriet Beecher Stowe's Uncle Tom's Cabin *appeared in 1852, after its serialization in an antislavery newspaper the previous year. The novel quickly became an international bestseller and one of the most influential books of its century.*

Richard Upjohn's First Parish Church after 1848, when the tower took its present form, and before the spire was blown off in 1869.

154

tion into a caricature of unmanly servility. The racists had triumphed. By the mid-twentieth century, an "Uncle Tom" had become a symbol to blacks of all they were fighting against.

This century has also seen an effort—still very much under way—to rescue Stowe from her detractors. It began in 1962 when Edmund Wilson called attention to her work in *Patriotic Gore* and compared her to Dickens and Zola.[8] After gaining strength among revisionist feminist critics in the 1970s, her rehabilitation took off in 1985 with Jane Tompkins's chapter on Stowe and "sentimental power" in *Sensational Designs: The Cultural Work of American Fiction, 1790-1860*. Rather than try to win Stowe a place in the male-dominated canon, Tompkins set forth an alternative canon, one in which women writers had restored to them the cultural authenticity that male critics had denied them. "*Uncle Tom's Cabin,*" wrote Tompkins defiantly, "was, in almost any terms one can think of, the most important book of the century."[9]

Much of this new scholarship was energized by the feminists' discovery of nineteenth-century America's construction of a special "sphere" in which women could enjoy a rich culture of their own. But could a claim to a place in any canon be justified for a writer like Stowe, who depended so much on the conventions of popular sentimentality? And could a late twentieth-century feminist accept with enthusiasm a writer who clearly thought that a woman's place was in the kitchen and parlor? As of 1992, these matters were not settled; a suggestion, for example, that Stowe be honored as part of Bowdoin College's celebration of the twentieth anniversary of coeducation in 1991-1992 got nowhere.[10] But whatever her book's place, if any, on the reading lists, it seemed clear that *Uncle Tom's Cabin* was a work which yielded an extraordinary richness of levels of interpretation—as religious parable, proto-feminist tract, devastating critique of the patriarchy, sado-masochistic Gothic thriller, celebration of the female sphere of home and family and church—and that Stowe could never be taken for granted again.[11]

One approach to her work returns us to 63 Federal Street. In explaining the genre of "par-lor literature," the Stowe scholar Joan Hedrick describes a now-vanished tradition, on the boundary of the public and the private spheres, in which white, middle-class women wrote a variety of works for themselves, their close friends, and their families—and read them aloud. The parlor in which much of this work was created and consumed was, she says, "a shaper of public opinion as potent as the 'press' and 'pulpit'"— the warmest room in the house, where women and children, sometimes with adult male company, gathered to tell stories, write letters, sing and play the piano, sew, exchange recipes, read silently, or read aloud to each other the sketches and poems of fellow non-professionals. Instead of the distance between author and audience that developed after about 1860 when "high" culture divorced itself from "low," there was a sense of domestic intimacy to this creativity— one that, in Stowe's case, allowed her to judge what moved an audience. Her son's famous account of her vision at First Parish Church of Tom's death—she rushes home to write it down, then reads what she has written to her children, who break into tears—may be an extreme and sentimentalized example of what Hedrick is talking about, but the social context rings true. "When *Uncle Tom's Cabin* burst on the national scene in 1851," writes Hedrick, "the intimate narrative voice of that book, its appeal to domestic institutions and reader emotions, had had a long foreground in Stowe's apprenticeship in parlor literature."[12]

In fact, 63 Federal Street plays a double role in the life of Stowe in her Brunswick years of 1850 to 1852: as a place to realize her ideal of Christian homemaker and as a place to escape from. Trying to reassure her absent husband, shortly after arriving in Maine, she paints a picture—a favorite trope of hers—of a bracing climate, "a fine grassy yard" for the children to run in, pine woods not far away, and the "handsomest & largest room in the house" awaiting Calvin's arrival. By winter, though, when Calvin again is away for long periods, the reality of the climate is felt: "Everyone says that we have not had so severe a winter for fifteen years. . . In the evening the girls sit in my room & put out the

A mid-nineteenth-century view of Appleton Hall, built in 1843 by Samuel Melcher and Sons and named after Bowdoin's second president, the Reverend Jesse Appleton. Harriet Beecher Stowe wrote parts of Uncle Tom's Cabin *in her husband's study, 7 Appleton Hall.*

fire in the kitchen—The children shiver dolefully about going up to their cold rooms nights—I was bred to such hardness from the cradle & so did not mind it but they feel it." Two months later, complaining of her headaches, she reports that:

the pail of water has frozen solid in the room when I have kept fire all night & [the housekeeper's] biscuits have frozen to the board while she was rolling them out close by the cook stove. . . . The children keep trying to get up from table at meals to warm feet & fingers & tis not a very comfortable business.[13]

Yet the house was made an acceptable home, for a feeling of domestic empowerment was at the heart of the Beecher sisters' family ideology. Her sister Catharine Beecher must have been a great help in this; after all, she was the author of several of the most widely read housekeeping manuals of nineteenth-century America.[14] When

it was clear early in 1851 that Stowe had taken on a book, not a series of sketches, Beecher took matters firmly in hand: "I am trying to get Uncle Tom out of the way," Catharine wrote another sister, Mary Beecher Perkins, on 27 September 1851. "At 8 o'clock we are thro' with breakfast and prayers and then we send Mr Stowe and Harriet both to *his room in the college.* There was no other way to keep her out of family care and quietly at work and since this plan is adopted she goes ahead finely."[15] In what was then chiefly a residence hall for young men—Calvin Stowe's presence there was supposed to be, among other things, disciplinary—his wife wrote at least part of that attack on the patriarchy which is *Uncle Tom's Cabin.* In Appleton Hall she had found a room of her own, even if she had to share it with Calvin. (As of 1992, no plaque marks the scene; and since the 1920s, the house on Federal Street which the Stowes found so uncomfortable has been a popular inn.)

Wherever the book got written—some of it possibly during visits to Boston and Andover, other passages on the Brunswick kitchen table—Stowe returned with it to her parlor. We know that from a remarkable fragment of an evidently unfinished memoir that Joshua Lawrence Chamberlain 1852, a pious and musically inclined young man from Brewer, Maine, wrote very late in his life. Recalling his junior year at Bowdoin, the future general told of how "a great new orb had risen on the eastern horizon in the person of Professor Calvin E. Stowe, with his Hebrew literature, and his genius of a wife—surely a double-star, this!" By his senior year (1851-1852), he had befriended the family and become part of their "Saturday Evenings."

On these occasions a chosen circle of friends, mostly young, were favored with the freedom of her house, the rallying point being, however, the reading before publication, of the successive chapters of her Uncle Tom's Cabin, and the frank discussion of them. It was manifest that the author was the least impressed with their merit, and surely no one there dreamed of the fame that was to follow. The sweetness of her spirit, and her genuine interest for others, and her charming hospitalities, even when the preparations for them fell mostly upon her own hands, were what drew to her the hearts of all.[16]

The Stowe home received not only Calvin's students. An undated letter survives describing another visitor, a black man on his way to Canada. Writing to one of her sisters who shared her indignation over the Fugitive Slave Act of 1850, Stowe tells of her running debate on the subject with the colonizationist and peace advocate Thomas Upham.

Joshua Lawrence Chamberlain 1852 taught logic, natural theology, rhetoric, oratory, and modern languages from 1855 until 1862, when he joined the 20th Maine Infantry Regiment. From a Class of 1864 Album.

Professor Thomas Cogswell Upham, who taught at Bowdoin from 1825 to 1867. He was a pioneer in his discipline, mental philosophy, the forerunner of modern psychology.

He has got his mind filled with an idea of the negroes having been brought into this country in order to acquire civilization & christianity & be sent back to evangelise Africa & that our nation ought to buy them with the public money & send them off—& until that is done he is for bearing everything in silence & stroking & saying "pussy"—"pussy" so as to allay all prejudice & avoid all agitation!

Stowe reports that she had been arguing with him over the tea-table one night, trying unsuccessfully to get him to admit he would break the law to aid a fugitive.

Well the next day there comes along a fugitive bound for Canada & Proff Smyth sends him right up to Proff Upham who takes him into his study & hears his story, gives him a dollar & Mrs Upham puts in bountifully in the provision line & then he comes here for lodging—Now our beds were all full & before this law passed I might have tried to send him somewhere else. As it was all hands in the house united in making him up a bed in our waste room & Henry & Freddy & Georgy seemed to think they could not do too much for him—There hasn't any body in our house got waited on so abundantly & willingly for ever so long—these negroes possess some mysterious power of pleasing children for they hung round him & seemed never tired of hearing him talk & sing. He was a genuine article from the "Ole Carliny State"[17]

By the time she left Brunswick in the fall of 1852—Calvin had taken the tempting job at Andover—Harriet Beecher Stowe was internationally famous. She was soon to meet Queen Victoria, and reportedly to be greeted by President Lincoln as "the little woman who wrote the book that made this great war." Her parlor had become the world, and—as her sister Isabella wrote to her husband, John Hooker, from Brunswick on the Fourth of July 1852—"she wends on her way patiently, for the most part hopefully & always with a heart full of

The families of Professors Alpheus Spring Packard and William Smyth 1822 shared this double house at 6-8 College Street, built in 1827, which was later the home of Professors Wilmot Brookings Mitchell 1890 and George Thomas Little 1877 and of his son, Noel C. Little '17. It is now the John Brown Russwurm Afro-American Center.

Professor William Smyth 1822, a staunch abolitionist, taught mathematics and natural philosophy. He oversaw the construction of the First Parish Church and, after the Civil War, raised money to build Memorial Hall.

Thomas Ridgeway Gould's 1864 marble portrait bust of John Albion Andrew 1837, now in the collection of the Massachusetts Historical Society. As a young lawyer, Andrew represented accused slave-rescuers and raised money for John Brown's defense after his raid on Harper's Ferry. As governor of Massachusetts during the Civil War, he organized the Union's first black regiment, the 54th Massachusetts.

158

benedictions for the erring & suffering of every nuance & hue. In the belief of her immense & sudden wealth she is already beseiged with applications for pecuniary assistance." Stories of her wealth were exaggerated, for she had not made a good bargain with her publisher over royalties and she never received anything from the numerous stage adaptations of her novel. But her fame was for the moment secure. Calvin—who grew more eccentric with age—played his role gracefully; he and Prince Albert were the only two Victorian husbands of note who had to be content to be less famous than their wives. Harriet's half-sister Isabella, however, viewed the situation in 1852 with some trace of envy. She told her husband:

I find in sister Harriet a very beautiful mind & soul—if her face were only the true outter [sic] to these what a face it would be. . . It is distressing however to see her crowded upon & worn down by common cares which could so much more easily be met by a worldly wise lady—And the imperfections in family management are so clearly traceable to the very qualities which render her so superior to most, in thought & deed. . . Mr Stowe's health is miserable & the children have nearly every one already received an inheritance of physical infirmity, sufficient to endure their whole lives. . . . I never saw so many strong points in any one family—father, mother & every child have as marked & unique a character as if there were no other human beings created. . . .[18]

THE CAUSE OF THE SLAVE

It is difficult to know what impact Stowe and the abolitionists had on the willingness of young men in Maine to go to war in the spring of 1861. The political arm of the antislavery cause—the short-lived Liberty Party (1841-1848)—never polled more than about 15 percent of the vote in Maine gubernatorial elections, for example, and sometimes had trouble attracting more than 5 percent. The large number of people who opposed slavery in principle were not necessarily willing to express that distaste in political terms, at least well into the 1850s. Even when, in that decade, the new Republican Party became a majority party in Maine, its origins were so mixed with nativist, anti-Catholic, and pro-temperance elements,

that it could not be considered a purely abolitionist force.[19] Democrats dominated the state's political life from the 1820s through the 1840s, and they tended to be complaisant about the distant plight of the slave and sensitive to the feelings of their Southern political allies. In the words of the Reverend Austin Willey, an abolitionist, the Democratic Party was "the absolute tool of the slave-power"; the Maine economy was "bound to the South by political and commercial bands of steel. Let any shipowner or master, or commercial parties be suspected of any sympathy with antislavery, and their chance for southern freight was at an end." Moreover, the traditional guardians of the public's conscience—the Congregational clergy—tended until the 1850s to be lukewarm, if not hostile, toward the antislavery campaign. (Baptist ministers, on the other hand, tended to welcome it.)[20]

Nonetheless, between William Lloyd Garrison's visit to Maine in 1832 and the firing on Fort Sumter in 1861, anyone in the state who took the least interest in public and religious affairs would have been exposed to a withering critique of the "Slavocracy," and of the North's complicity in it. As a writer in the *Advocate of Freedom* in Hallowell pointed out, commercial connections with the South had turned too many Northerners into slavery's "apologists if not its abettors." Moreover, New England Christians should exercise their influence, he urged, "upon the hundred thousand of our southern brethren, who, during every warm season, either for the purpose of pleasure or health, or business, resort to our various cities, villages, and watering places, and mingle with us in our stage coaches, [and] attend our commencements, and other literary festivals."[21] Much of this attack was framed in the language of evangelical Protestantism, which intensified its power. Advocates of immediate abolition—as opposed to those who favored colonization (i.e., returning the blacks to Africa) or gradual, evolutionary emancipation—called for radical action. Theirs was but one cause among many, to be sure—this was a time of fervent temperance movements, campaigns for foreign missions, attempts to enforce Sabbath observance or to abolish flogging in the Navy, peace campaigns, and a handful of other "benevolent" reforms—but none of these other causes struck so dangerously at the constitutional and economic underpinnings of the existing social order. One result of this critique was to "demonize" the South in the popular imagination of the North, to suggest that however similar the two peoples might seem, there were profound moral differences between the two societies, and that a just God would judge them accordingly.[22] Few of the young men who went to war from Maine in 1861 and 1862 had any notion of freeing the slaves, but they were determined to crush the rebellion; surely the emotional residue of a generation of attacks on the Southern way of life helped them persuade themselves to risk their lives for the Union. Commenting in his daybook on the course of the war in 1862, the Brunswick insurance broker Henry Merritt summed up these feelings:

William Pitt Fessenden '23 was a member of the Maine Legislature and then of the U.S. Congress (1841-43) and Senate (1843, 1845, 1854-64, 1865-69) and served as Lincoln's secretary of the treasury in 1864-65. He was making public speeches against slavery as early as 1827. His father, Samuel Fessenden, and half-brother, Samuel Clement Fessenden '34, were also active in the antislavery movement; all three were Overseers.

We are being punished for national sins, the most prominent of which are, the Sin of Slavery. . . . [T]he African slave will have redress for his *aggrievances*; there is an overruling *Providence*, that takes cognizance of all that passes and that *retributive* justice will take place and altho, the present appearance of things seems to point to a different direction, yet in the End it will come out right; *right will prevail.*[23]

In his history of the antislavery impulse in Maine, Edward O. Schriver singles out four "stalwarts" who were at the heart of this agitation: Samuel Fessenden, a militia general and Portland lawyer and an Overseer of the College from 1822 to 1829; the Reverend David Thurston, a Congregationalist minister in Winthrop who was an Overseer from 1833 to 1864; Professor William Smyth 1823, the "ferocious" Bowdoin mathematician; and Willey, a minister and abolitionist editor. Most especially it was Smyth who kept the flame—small, but very bright—burning at the College, despite the general conservatism of the Governing Boards and most of the leading townspeople. Indirectly, he was aided by several alumni whose professional distinction added respectability to the cause—among them, the Reverend George Barrell Cheever 1825, a well-known reformer in New York; U. S. Senator John Parker Hale 1827 of New Hampshire; U. S. Senator William Pitt Fessenden 1823 of Maine (Samuel Fessenden's son), and John Albion Andrew 1837, later governor of Massachusetts and, before the war, a leading defender of the legal rights of Boston's black community. A man of great energy and conviction, with the fierce look in his photographs (and, students said, in the classroom) of an Old Testament patriarch, Smyth made certain that the subject of slavery remained before the eyes of the Brunswick public, however uncomfortable it made them.[24]

Smyth was also well known throughout the state for his exchange of letters in 1836 and 1837 in the pages of the Portland Congregationalist newspaper the *Christian Mirror* with a Northerner, the Reverend Rufus W. Bailey, who had moved to South Carolina and rapidly adopted its values. (Bailey later reprinted his side of the debate under the title of *The Issue*, a minor classic of proslavery apologetics.) Appalled that any sincere Christian could condone keeping another human in bondage, Smyth attacked Bailey with Pauline vigor. Always addressing Bailey as his "brother" who may have strayed but could be brought back, Smyth hammered, week after week, at his opponent's weakest point: Bailey's insistence that slaves were taught the Bible (orally) and allowed to practice Christianity. Smyth had read too much evidence to the contrary:

The general ignorance, which is the inseparable attendant of slavery, the utter confusion of moral distinc-

The public rooms of Brunswick's Tontine Hotel were the scene in 1838 of a debate over abolition, a touchy subject in a town with many commercial ties with the South. The hotel, built in 1828 and destroyed by fire in 1904, stood on the site of the present Tontine Mall, on Maine Street.

tions which it induces, its stupefying effects upon the conscience, and especially the want of the Bible in the hands of the slave, to which the preacher may appeal, and by whose authority he may enforce his exhortations, must it is easy to see be an almost insuperable barrier to the success of a preached Gospel among the slaves.[25]

In Brunswick, many of Smyth's fellow citizens did not share these views. According to the *Advocate of Freedom*, when a public meeting was held at Stinchfield's Inn in the fall of 1838 to discuss the cause of the slave, "when any one who was known to be an abolitionist attempted to speak, he was constantly interrupted by hisses, 'down with him,' 'down with the nigger,' 'hustle him out,' etc." When the meeting reconvened the next evening at the Tontine Hall, it was resolved that "any attempt by the people of the non-slaveholding states to interfere with slavery in the South, is unjust, inexpedient, and an unwarrantable encroachment upon the rights of a portion of the citizens of our country." Furthermore, the townspeople "deeply regret that efforts are being made in this town and vicinity . . . to prejudice the minds of the citizens

against our brethren of the South, and to mislead them in regard to the institution of slavery . . ." The resolutions—which proclaimed themselves "in accordance with the sentiment of a vast majority of the citizens of this community"— were rushed through without debate and adopted, 163 to 117. Meeting in Topsham the following night, "the friends of free discussion" deplored the gag rule that had been passed and reassembled two nights later at the Second Baptist Meeting-House in Brunswick as, in Smyth's words, "friends of unfettered thought and free inquiry." They in turn passed a resolution affirming freedom of thought and of speech as "the natural right of every human being," by a unanimous vote of 205, including twenty to twenty-five Bowdoin students.[26]

The passage in Michael Schaara's popular Gettysburg novel, *The Killer Angels*, about Joshua Chamberlain's having rarely seen a black man is fanciful; blacks may have been scarce in nineteenth-century Maine, but they were hardly unknown. Out of a population of 583,169, the U. S. Census of 1850 counted 1,356 "free col-

161

ored" residents in the state. Very little is known about them; some worked in Portland as sailors and laborers; some lived with other blacks in isolated rural settlements, including one on the New Meadows River, between Bath and Brunswick. Maine was exceptionally progressive in offering the full rights of citizenship, including the suffrage, to blacks—but, given the degree of racism prevalent throughout the country, that liberality may have reflected how tiny a minority they formed. When nativist sentiment became strong—and violent—in Maine in the 1850s, it was directed primarily against Irish Catholics, whose willingness to work for low wages was seen as an economic threat to the Yankee population.[27]

In retrospect the one black resident of pre-Civil War Maine who stands out most vividly is, as might be expected, the one who conformed most closely to a white Protestant notion of ideal minority behavior. She was Phebe Ann Jacobs. She had begun life as a slave in New Jersey presented to the wife of President Wheelock of Dartmouth as a maid for her daughter, who grew up to marry Bowdoin's President William Allen. Free but still a domestic servant, Jacobs had come to Brunswick in 1820 with the Allen family. Sometime after Mrs. Allen's death in 1828, she went to live on her own, supporting herself until her death in 1850 by taking in washing and ironing for Bowdoin students (including, possibly, Chamberlain, who matriculated in 1848). Her piety was a local legend. In telling her story after her death, Mrs. Thomas Upham shapes it to embody the Christian paradox that the last shall be the first. She did so persuasive a job of it, that Jacobs has been suggested as one source for Stowe's Uncle Tom. Mrs. Upham's eight-page "Narrative of Phebe Ann Jacobs" was published by the American Tract Society soon after the black woman's death, and

John Brown Russwurm '26 was the first African-American to graduate from Bowdoin. Russwurm cofounded and edited the country's first black newspaper, Freedom's Journal, *and served as governor of the Maryland Colony of Liberia from 1836 to 1851.*

would surely have been read by every pious Christian in town.[28]

The tract is an affectionate and admiring account of Jacobs's piety; it is also an example of how well-meaning whites could cope with the strangeness of poor blacks by "shaping" them into something no longer quite human. Sainthood is a particularly compelling form of non-identity. There is no reason to think that Upham falsified the outlines of Jacobs's life, but she presents it to make her own points about piety, acceptance of one's lot, and daily devotion. The attributes assigned to Phebe—she is "contented and happy"; she "loved the Scriptures," "loved the house of God," "loved to pray," "prayed for the college," "was humble," "had no fear of duty"—disembody her further and further until she is almost pure spirit (and hence out of her black skin). Jacobs is also an intensely feminized "saint," whose love of "the church and female prayer-meeting" reminds us of Stowe's well-known views on the power of female influence in the fallen world of men. By a nice coincidence, Phebe died on the same night as Sarah Folsom Adams, the wife of the Reverend George Adams h 1849 (an Overseer from 1830 to 1872), who was pastor of First Parish Church and, a few years later, Chamberlain's father-in-law. "We may think of them," writes Upham, "as ascending together to the mansions of the blessed. To die with Phebe was a privilege; and the pastor remarked . . . that if his wife had been permitted to choose a companion to accompany her through the 'dark valley,' and into the open portals of heaven, she would have chosen Phebe."[29] William Allen and his daughters came from Northampton to the funeral, and Phebe was accompanied to her grave next to Mrs. Allen's at Pine Grove Cemetery by the officers of the College.

Not all blacks in Brunswick were laborers or domestics. There were six students of color at

162

Bowdoin between 1824 and 1864. The best known by far was John Brown Russwurm, Class of 1826, later co-editor in New York City of the country's first black newspaper, *Freedom's Journal*, and governor of the colonizationists' Maryland Colony (1836-1851), which was later joined to Liberia. Born in Jamaica in 1799, the son of a white Virginian who had settled on the island and a black woman, he was sent to school in Quebec and then rejoined his father when the elder Russwurm moved to Portland, Maine, and married a widow there. When his father died, the widow married again, accepting the sixteen-year-old Russwurm into her extended family. After several years at Hebron Academy, he went to Boston, where he taught school. Returning to Maine and entering Bowdoin from North Yarmouth Academy at age twenty-five, he spent a somewhat lonely two years in college, though he was well-enough accepted by his fellow students to be elected to the Athenaean Society. In his reminiscence of Hawthorne at Bowdoin, Horatio Bridge commented:

[Russwurm] was a diligent student, but of no marked ability. He lived in a carpenter's house, just beyond the village limits, where Hawthorne and the writer called upon him several times, but his sensitiveness on account of his color prevented him from returning the calls. Twenty years later I renewed the acquaintance pleasantly in Africa, where—as Governor of Cape Palmas—he received, with dignity and ease, the Commodore and officers of our squadron, myself all the more cordially because we had been college associates and fellow-Atheneans.[30]

At Commencement in 1826, Russwurm delivered an oration on the Haitian revolution. He was later criticized for his cooperation with white colonizationists, many of whom did not want to help black Americans so much as simply get them out of the country. But his great accomplishment, according to the historian of the Maryland Colony, was in proving in the nineteenth century that blacks were capable of self-government, without the supervision of paternalistic whites.[31]

For many years it was believed that Russwurm was the first black to graduate from any American college, but in fact Amherst had given a degree to Edward Jones two weeks earlier, and

Dr. John V. De Grasse, an 1849 graduate of the Medical School of Maine at Bowdoin, served as assistant surgeon of the 35th U. S. Colored Troops during the Civil War. One of five black medical students at Bowdoin before 1864, he is believed to be the first black physician to be elected to the Massachusetts Medical Society.

Middlebury had graduated Alexander Twilight in 1823.[32] It is perhaps of greater significance that five other blacks were enrolled at antebellum Bowdoin, all of them in the Medical School, since so few other Northern colleges enrolled non-white students until this century. The medical students included John Van Surley de Grasse and Thomas Joiner White, two New Yorkers who were among the fifteen students in the Medical Class of 1849. De Grasse, who is believed to be the first black to join the Massachusetts Medical Society, served as assistant surgeon of the 35th U. S. Colored Troops before his death in Boston in 1868, aged forty-two. White evidently returned to New York City and practiced there. Also at the Medical School in this period were Peter William Ray 1848, who went on to get his M. D. from Castleton Medical College in Vermont in 1850 and practiced in Brooklyn, New York, and William Miller Dutton 1847-1848, about whom little is known other than that he returned to New York from Bowdoin.

A more complete account exists for a fifth black medical student, Benjamin A. Boseman, another native of New York City, who after studying at Dartmouth got his Bowdoin M. D. in 1864, in time to serve as a U. S. Army assistant surgeon for the last year of the war. Boseman moved to Charleston, South Carolina, where he practiced medicine for sixteen years, served in the state's Reconstruction Era legislature, and was appointed U. S. Postmaster by Presidents Grant and Hayes.[33]

Franklin Pierce '24, fourteenth president of the United States (1853-57), rewarded Nathaniel Hawthorne '25, his old college friend, by appointing him as U. S. Consul in Liverpool. Hawthorne had written Pierce's presidential campaign biography in 1852.

Nothing is known of how these students were treated by their classmates or professors at Bowdoin. Some idea, however, of the sentiment of the day comes through in this passage from a letter to Professor Parker Cleaveland written at Castleton by William Sweetser, who at various times between 1833 and 1861 was professor of the theory and practice of medicine at Bowdoin:

We have Ray & another coloured student here. They behave very modestly, & no exception has, I believe, as yet been taken to them, even by our Southern pupils—at least no open objections have been made, though I think many of the class, would a little rather, have them away. Indeed I much doubt the policy, under the present state of prejudices in regard to colour in this country, however wrong such prejudices may be, of receiving blacks at our medical schools—I feel convinced from cautious observations that, in the end, they would lose more than they would gain by it. Such I believe, unless I received wrong impressions, to be your opinion & I hope you will act in strict accordance with it. Mr. Thomas, who attended at Brunswick last spring, & is now here had got the idea that Dutton was graduated with the other blacks at Brunswick—I told him it was not so, & hope I told the truth. I understand, though not officially, that only White & De Grasse received diplomas.[34]

PEACEABLE MEN

The summer of 1852 saw the publication not only of *Uncle Tom's Cabin* but of a book by one Bowdoin alumnus about another alumnus that touched, as delicately as possible, upon the subject of slavery. Nathaniel Hawthorne's campaign biography of Franklin Pierce revealed more about his loyalty to a close college friend (Hawthorne was in the Class of 1825, Pierce of 1824) than about his understanding of the depths of sectional feeling that, within a decade, would lead to civil war.

As an official biographer, Hawthorne faced several problems. Pierce, though very successful in state politics, had no major achievements to boast of on the national scene. He was also known to drink heavily—not particularly unusual among antebellum politicians, but potentially damaging among temperance voters—and to have a wife with emotional problems (he had married one of the daughters of President Appleton). From the Democratic Party's point of view, however, General Pierce, as he liked to be called, had two major advantages: a moderately successful Mexican War career, which could be played up in the book, and a reputation for being sensitive to the feelings of the touchy Southern branch of the party. He also looked like a president.

In writing *The Life of Franklin Pierce*, Hawthorne could not avoid the debate over slavery. Dismissing reformers lost in "the mistiness of a philanthropic system," he goes on to say:

[Abolitionism] looks upon slavery as one of those evils which divine Providence does not leave to be remedied by human contrivances, but which, in its own good time, by some means impossible to be anticipated, but of the simplest and easiest operation . . . it causes to vanish like a dream. There is no instance, in all history, of the human will and interest having perfected any great moral reform by methods which it adopted to that end; but the progress of the world, at every step, leaves some evil or wrong on the path behind it, which the wisest of mankind, of their own set purpose, could never have found the way to rectify.[35]

Although critical of the Fugitive Slave Act, Hawthorne seemed to share the views of the many Northern Democrats who thought like Pierce: slavery ought someday to disappear, they contended, but it was not within their rights or moral responsibilities to interfere with its operation. He admitted to Bridge that he had tried to avoid the commission and that his heart "absolutely sank, at the dearth of available material," adding that "though the story is true, yet it took a romancer to do it." Despite his earlier disclaimers, Hawthorne confessed he hoped some political patronage would come his way—he wanted the consulship at Liverpool, and got it—because Pierce "certainly owes me something; for the biography has cost me hundreds of friends, here at the north, who had a purer regard for me than Frank Pierce or any other politician ever gained, and who drop off from me like autumn leaves, in consequence of what I say on the slavery question. But they were my real sentiments, and I do not regret that they are on the record."[36]

The Hawthornes spent the years 1853-1857 in England and 1858-1859 in Italy, returning briefly to England in order for him to finish *The Marble Faun*. In studying the attitudes of American writers toward the war, Daniel Aaron suggests that Hawthorne's rather confused and contradictory views on that conflict and his lack of sympathy with the abolitionists may reflect the fact that, having been abroad, he missed the great public debate on slavery and national unity in the 1850s. By what may have been an uncomfortable coincidence, however, the Hawthornes shared the boat home in the summer of 1860 with his Bowdoin acquaintance Calvin Stowe and Stowe's famous wife. Hawthorne had written to his publisher, William D. Ticknor, from Liverpool five years earlier that one reason he liked living abroad was because "America is now wholly given over to a d—d mob of scribbling women, and I should have no chance of success

Jefferson Davis, at the time a U.S. Senator from Mississippi, received an honorary degree from Bowdoin while visiting Maine in 1858. Half-plate daguerreotype, ca. 1853.

while the public taste is occupied with their trash."[37] He specifically had in mind Maria Cummins's *The Lamplighter* (1854), which had sold 100,000 copies in its first year, at a time when *The Scarlet Letter* and *The House of Seven Gables* were selling 6,000 to 8,000 copies, and which, like *Uncle Tom's Cabin*, was competing with Hawthorne's novels for the attention of English readers. Hawthorne congratulated his own wife, Sophia, for having "never prostituted thyself to the public" by writing a book. "Women are too good for authorship," he told her, "and that is the reason it spoils them so."[38] The shipboard conversation with the Stowes must have been interesting.

Back home in Concord, Hawthorne seems to have gone out of his way to offend progressive and patriotic Northern opinion. His ambivalence about the issues at stake had already been widely noted; as early as 1853, Theodore Parker had observed in a letter to Thackeray that Hawthorne and Carlyle were "the only two men of Genius in the age [who] have appeared on the side of slavery . . . on the side of the enemies of mankind."[39] In 1862, by dedicating his collection of essays on England, *Our Old Home*, to Pierce (who, after all, had made them possible through the consulship), Hawthorne further offended Cambridge and Boston; Emerson is said to have torn the dedication page out of his copy. (Hawthorne had written: "To Franklin Pierce, as a slight memorial of a college friendship, prolonged through manhood, and retaining all its vitality in our autumnal years. . .") That summer, in the pages of the *Atlantic Monthly*, Hawthorne went a step farther. In his essay "Chiefly About War Matters," under the signature of "a peaceable man," he wrote a mocking description of his visit to the front and to Washington to meet Lincoln. He not only criticized those "sacrificing good institutions to passionate impulses and impracticable theories" — i. e., the abolitionists—but also the administration ("there never existed any other Government against which treason was so easy . . .") Expressing sympathy for the view that allegiance to one's state was more compelling than to a vast country, he regretted that the war had "converted crowds of honest people into traitors, who seem to themselves not merely innocent, but patriotic, and who die for a bad cause with as quiet a conscience as if it were the best." Hawthorne's views were no more extreme than those being expressed by thousands of "Copperheads" (anti-war Northern Democrats) and other critics of Lincoln's war effort, but having them voiced by a leading representative of New England's literary establishment was a special affront.[40] (Longfellow, by contrast, as early as 1842 had written his seven "Poems on Slavery," thereby allying himself in public with the antislavery cause.)

These views were certainly widely shared in Brunswick, although by the late 1850s abolitionist sentiments were treated with more respect than they had been early in Smyth's career as an antislavery activist. President Woods, for one, had little sympathy for reformers of any kind (other than ecclesiologists), and was widely assumed to be, if not pro-Southern, then at least a lukewarm Unionist.[41] The Bath-Brunswick shipowners depended heavily on the cargoes of cotton that their Maine-built vessels transported from New Orleans or Savannah to Liverpool or Le Havre. In Brewer, Maine, in 1838,

Chamberlain's father had admired the most famous Southerner of the day enough to name his youngest son John Calhoun Chamberlain (Class of 1859). The spirit of friendship between sea-faring northern New England and the slave-owning, agricultural South was especially evident in the triumphal progress through Maine in the summer of 1858 by Calhoun's successor as the leading spokesman for the Southern way of life, Senator Jefferson Davis of Mississippi.

Davis's New England holiday was ordered by his doctor, but he did not fail to take advantage of the fact that so many Mainers were willing to listen to his views on politics. Despite the sectional tensions, Davis was still among those—and would remain so well into 1860—who thought that reasonable men on both sides would reach an accommodation, as they had in 1820 and 1850, to hold the country together. Toward this end, it was especially important to hold the Democrats together as a national party, in the face of the increasing sectional threat from the Republicans. In his public remarks during the visit, Davis was so accommodating, so smoothly confident that peace would prevail, that he evidently had to answer critics back in Mississippi who, he claimed, had misrepresented his reported words. His speeches from the visit were accordingly published as a small pamphlet in 1859.[42]

As the pamphlet indicates and local newspapers confirm, Davis was greeted by enthusiastic crowds in Portland and elsewhere, and returned the compliment with fulsome praise of the Maine air, Maine trees, Maine seacoast, and Maine hospitality. (He had visited the state once before, to inspect its forts when he was secretary of war.) He reminded his northern friends of the Revolutionary heritage both parts of the United States shared, and of the commercial and personal ties that linked their regional interests. Denying that he was on a political mission— Davis said he would not "imitate the mischievous agitators who inflame the Northern mind against the Southern States"—he proceeded to explain in lucid detail the Southern point of view on the expansion of slavery into the territories and the relevant constitutional questions in dispute. At

166

the State Fair in Augusta in late September, he invoked the Jeffersonian ideal of an agrarian republic and flattered everyone in the audience who had ever left a farm to go to sea:

Yankee is a word once applied to you as a term of reproach, but you have made it honorable and renowned. You have borne the flag of your country from the time when it was ridiculed as a piece of striped bunting, until it has come to be known and respected wherever the ray of civilization has reached; and your canvas-winged birds of commerce have borne civilization into regions, where . . . but for your prowess it would not have gone.

Nor did he fail to compliment the horsemanship of the ladies.

Among the interesting features of the exhibition I shall remember the equestrianism of the ladies. Though it was beautiful in every sense of the word, it was not regarded as mere sport, but the rather looked upon as part of that mental and physical training which makes a woman more than the mere ornament of the drawing-room—fits her usefully to act her appropriate part in the trying scenes to which the most favored may be subjected—to become the mother of heroes, and live in the admiration of posterity.[43]

Davis's holiday, in other words, began to take on the air of a state visit, and it is not surprising that Bowdoin College gave him an honorary LL.D. at Commencement that fall. It was an easy day-trip from Portland. Davis would have pleased the Democrats on the Boards by his presence; the award of an honorary degree on that same occasion to U. S. Senator William Pitt Fessenden, an abolitionist from Portland, would have placated at least some of Davis's critics. The Mississippi senator already had a Bowdoin connection of sorts: he had been secretary of war in Pierce's cabinet (and a dominant influence on the hapless president). As embarrassing as the degree was to prove in a few years, it made sense at the time, and the College never rescinded it.[44]

THE TRUMPET CALLS

Almost thirty years before the Civil War began, Harriet Beecher Stowe had written to a friend that teaching belonged in female hands:

To govern boys by moral influence requires tact and talent and versatility . . . But men of tact, versatility, talent and piety will not devote their lives to teaching. They must be ministers and missionaries, and all that,

Brevet Major General Joshua Lawrence Chamberlain.

and while there is such a thrilling call for action in this way, every man who is merely teaching feels as if he were a Hercules with a distaff, ready to spring to the first trumpet that calls him away.[45]

Joshua Lawrence Chamberlain 1852 had been promised in 1861 a paid leave of absence in Europe for two years, similar to the sabbatical voyages Longfellow and Goodwin had taken to prepare themselves for the professorship of modern languages. The death of his brother Horace from disease had shaken him, however, and he delayed the trip. Perhaps thinking, like so many other volunteers in 1862, that the war would soon be over, he decided to postpone the European visit and answer instead the call to help save the Union. He telegraphed Governor Israel Washburn: "I have leave of absence for two years to visit Europe, but I wish to know whether I have a country. Can you make any use for me?" The governor replied: "Come and see me. I am organizing a regiment."[46]

Chamberlain had to overcome the opposition of his father (who told him it was "not our war"), his wife, Frances (they had recently purchased

George Beaman Kenniston '61 spent his graduation day in a Confederate prison. After the war he returned to Maine to become a lawyer and a coastal real estate developer.

Stephen Hart Manning '61, with pistol and sword. On the page of a class album where other graduates put "Law" or "Teaching," he wrote "War." He entered the U. S. Army as a quartermaster sergeant in the 1st Maine Volunteers.

Kingman F. Page

To the President and Trustees of Bowdoin College, Dr

TO HIS THIRD TERM BILL, ENDING SEPTEMBER 3d 1851

Interest to be paid, if not discharged within one month after the commencement of the next term.

	Dolls.	Cents.
Tuition	8	00
Chamber rent	6	67
Repairs		16
Average of Repairs *Floor 18—Entry 23—G. av. 44*		85
Sweeping and Bed-making	1	00
Library		50
Monitor		21
Catalogues, Order of Exercises, & Commencement Dinner		50
Books		
Bell		20
Reciting room and Lights	1	19
Chemical Lectures		25
Wood		
Library Fine		
Assessment for absence from College		
Diploma		
Music		
Advance standing		
Commons	15	45
	34.98	

College bill for Kingman Fogg Page '53, great-great-grandfather of David S. Page, who has taught chemistry and biochemistry at Bowdoin since 1974. Page was a Washington, D.C., attorney in whose box at Ford's Theater President Lincoln was shot.

the small house on Potter Street in which Longfellow and his bride had lived in the 1830s), and his faculty colleagues, who had not known of his plan until they read about it in the newspapers. As Chamberlain explained in his memoir:

The "faculty" objected. They remonstrated with the governor assuring him that the young professor had no military stuff in him. They even sent a representative to the capital to demonstrate that he was no fighter, but only a mild-mannered commonplace student. It was indeed a strange exhibition of affection. But this was not the ruling motive. The professors were men of military experience in the religious contests for the control of the College. They had learned grand tactics. The young professor held for them a strategic position. This chair was much sought for; and those competent to fill it were for the most part, not of the strict orthodox persuasion. In case this chair should become vacant, as the experiences and prospects of war rendered highly probable, the chances were that it would be filled by one of the adverse party.[47]

Any number of young officers could fight the rebels, in other words, but Smyth and Upham feared that without Chamberlain a Unitarian would win the field at Bowdoin.

Defense of the Union, not a desire to free the slaves or reform the South, compelled Chamberlain and so many others to leave their civilian tasks and take up arms. It is not clear at just what point he made up his mind to go. Among his papers in Special Collections is an envelope marked "Notes of my little speeches & doings which led to my going into the army in the war 1862." This would seem to indicate that Chamberlain was already giving patriotic speeches, perhaps even recruiting volunteers, before he actually was commissioned as lieutenant colonel of the 20th Maine. Perhaps he talked himself into going. Inside the envelope are two sheets with fragmentary notes for several speeches. "Fellow Citizens," one passage begins,

I have been used to dealing in words most of my life but I never wasted any that I know of. But I feel now like laying aside words for deeds. . . . Still I have a few more words for such occasions as this, & they shall be brief. I believe, fellow citizens, & friends, that we are all agreed in this that we must show our strength now whatever may be our theory of the war—the origin or conduct of it. Whatever we may think of the adminis-

tration & of the commander in chief (& for me I have confidence in both) we cannot shut our eyes to the facts now before us—we must strike a blow. This war can only be quelled by a swift & strong hand. Gentleman may cry peace, peace, but there is no peace. . .

He goes on to urge immediate seizure of the chief rebel cities. He warns that the British were standing by for "the two quarreling cats" to exhaust themselves. He exhorts his audience to "come out for your country—answer her call." What is especially noticeable is the simplicity of his language. Chamberlain, as the excerpts from his memoir showed, could produce a dense and knobby prose. But in these notes his spoken voice comes through:

I believe the war would have been ended by this time, if we had gone heartily into it at first, & had not given time for other issues to get at work & complicate & mix up matters so that men. . . seem hardly to know what they are fighting for. I feel that we are fighting for our country—for our flag—not as so many stars & stripes but as the emblem of a great & good & powerful nation—fighting to settle the question whether we are a nation, or only a *basket of chips*—whether we shall leave to our children the country we have inherited—or leave them without a country—without a name. without a citizenship among the great powers of the earth. [48]

On 1 September 1862, the citizens of Brunswick presented him, as a token of their esteem, "the Staples horse," a gray stallion, dappled white. The thirty-four-year-old officer in the 1862 photograph has acquired a drooping moustache and a fiercer gaze. By the twelfth, he was riding the horse through northern Virginia. The commander of the regiment—a West Point-educated colonel named Adelbert Ames, who was later to be a Reconstruction Era governor of Mississippi—took advantage of the four-day voyage from Boston to the Potomac to teach Chamberlain and his other volunteer officers tactics.[49]

Chamberlain's commission was perhaps the most publicized departure from civilian life of anyone associated with the College, but it was a far from singular event in terms of personal sacrifice. By the time Chamberlain volunteered, Oliver Otis Howard '50, West Point Class of 1854, had lost his right arm at the battle of Fair

Taken from an upper window of a house on Maine Street, this is believed to be the earliest photographic view of the campus. Adams Hall (1861) has not yet been built, and the trees lining Maine Street are still staked. The cow (center foreground) may help explain the fences and staking.

Oaks. Among the other alumni who went to war, the oldest was Luther Bell, Class of 1824. Aged fifty-five, a widower with four children, he saw duty at the first battle of Bull Run in 1861 as surgeon of the 11th Massachusetts. As he wrote afterwards, "The whole volume of military surgery was opened before me on Sunday afternoon with horrid illustrations. Sudley Church with its hundred wounded victims will form a picture in my sick dreams so long as I live." But the unanswered question that drove him on, he explained, was "whether or not our children are to have a country."[50] He died the next year of disease. Among the youngest volunteers was Lieutenant George Kenniston, Class of 1861. In May he had enlisted in the 5th Maine; in July he was wounded and taken prisoner at Bull Run. On Commencement Day—he was Class Orator—he was in Libby Prison in Richmond.[51]

Other Bowdoin graduates served behind the scenes, none more notably than Governor Andrew '37 of Massachusetts, who was responsible for forming Colonel Robert Gould Shaw's famous 54th Massachusetts Regiment of black soldiers. Promptness in raising and equipping regiments was of crucial importance in the Union war effort, and in this regard Andrew proved the best of the wartime governors. Equally well-known to contemporaries was Maine's Senator William Pitt Fessenden '23, who served as Lincoln's secretary of the treasury in 1864-1865 and who, in 1867, was to cast the decisive vote that saved President Andrew Johnson in his impeachment trial. At the Treasury, Fessenden was succeeded by Hugh McCulloch '29, a leading midwestern banker. Otherwise, it was a young man's war. Of the twenty-four alumni who rose to the rank of general by 1865, their average age at the time of the battle of Gettysburg was twenty-nine.[52]

Not all of the activity was on the Union side. There were three Southerners, for example, in the Class of 1860: the two North Carolinians, Sidney Finger (who became a leading school reformer in his state after the war) and Manuel Shell (who was killed in 1862), fought for the

Confederacy, but a Floridian, Albion Howe, served the North as an artillery officer, helped guard the captured Jefferson Davis, later fought the Ku Klux Klan in post-war Georgia, and in 1873 was ambushed, killed, and scalped by Indians while leading troops in the Oregon Territory. Altogether, at least eighteen Bowdoin graduates fought for the South (although, contrary to a widespread tradition, none of them rose to the rank of Confederate general).

The College itself on the eve of the war was a relatively quiet institution of 269 students (fifty of whom were in the Medical School) and nineteen faculty members (nine of whom taught medicine). The curriculum had not changed in its essentials for half a century; some of the faculty seemed less pedagogues than landmarks on the local landscape. Parker Cleaveland's death in 1858, more than the semicentennial observances of the opening of the College six years earlier, reminded observers that even landmarks vanish—he had taught fifty-three classes of Bowdoin students and had been memorialized as an enduring symbol of learning in a Longfellow poem. A year's expenses at the College were about $185, including $30 for tuition and $10 for room rent, with board estimated at $2 or $3 a week. The political agitation of the 1850s had left its mark on the students; in 1860, when three political clubs were formed, 135 students supported Lincoln, 30 Douglas, and 7 Breckenridge (a "peace" Democrat).[53]

In May of 1861—about a month after Fort Sumter fell—students organized a volunteer company known as the Bowdoin Guards, whose first accomplishment seems to have been unnerving the faculty by firing explosive caps in the "colleges." In June a second company, the Bowdoin Zouaves, was formed and as a drill captured the Topsham bridge. Somewhat in the jaunty spirit of the old "May Training," the Zouaves were a particularly eye-catching unit: their Franco-Algerian costume of baggy trousers and short red jackets led John J. Pullen, historian of the 20th Maine, to compare them to "a parade of Shriners." Before the news of Bull Run traveled north in July, the war seems to have been regarded, as least by some students, as a bit

of a lark. All things considered, Hatch's conclusion still holds: "the immediate effect of the war on the college was not as great as was that of the [First] World War," when the campus was to turn into an armed camp.[54]

In fact there is a remarkable dearth of war commentary on the part of faculty and students. Similarly, in town: although Henry Merritt's daybook for those years includes brief, almost telegraphic reports of the war's progress, he pays far more attention to corn prices and the weather than to the great events of his day.[55] And while the Conscription Act of 1863 was to preoccupy the selectmen (who had to find the money to pay bounties), for many people, on and off campus, the conflict must have seemed distant. Until late 1863, only a certain nervousness about Confederate raiders in Casco Bay or fears that Britain might enter the war on the Southern side (hence interrupting New England's commerce) brought the Civil War directly to much of the coastal populace. Eventually the casualty reports and the appearance back home of maimed and crippled men made their impact, especially in the poorer communities whose sons could not buy their way out of service. Yet there was no concerted opposition to the war—except in Kingfield, where there was a draft riot—and fewer signs than one might expect of any great enthusiasm for it. Meanwhile, hordes of deserters from several states filled the towns near the Canadian border.

After the war, the College took great pride in pointing out that a larger percentage of its alumni had fought for the Union than those of any other college in the North. When a Dartmouth graduate made a similar claim for his college in 1910, the newspaperman Edgar O. Achorn, Class of 1881, leaped to his alma mater's defense. In a long letter to the *Boston Transcript*, he tabulated the relevant figures and confirmed that, in proportion to its size, Bowdoin had outperformed Dartmouth by 25.02 percent to 22.82 percent (based on counting living graduates in 1867 who had seen Civil War service).[56] Such statistics are not entirely reliable, for war records were not complete (at least for Bowdoin) and it is difficult to know whether to

Members of the Class of 1866 in front of the Chapel. Wearing a tall hat was a badge of senior status.

count various non-combatant jobs, such as Civil War government clerkships, or students who transferred to other colleges. But the fact that such a reckoning was attempted (and much publicized) is itself significant. For several reasons, it was important after the war to the College's self-esteem to stress its loyalty to the Union—and the self-sacrifice by its sons for the cause.[57]

In truth, the record is more ambivalent. Civil war service, especially for sons of the elite, was notoriously easy to avoid: you paid a $300 commutation fee or hired a substitute. While it is not possible to reconstruct the draft histories of every Bowdoin graduate of military age, it is striking how low the absolute percentages of military service are for the late antebellum classes. For example, of the forty-two members of the Class of 1840, only one fought in the Civil War—perhaps not surprising for a group of men who would have been middle-aged by 1861-1865. But of the Class of 1850 (which produced generals Howard and Hyde), only five of its thirty-six members served; of the Class of 1860, twenty-nine of its sixty-three members, slightly less than

half. Enthusiasm for the war diminished over time. For example, of the fifty-one students enrolled as seniors in the fall of 1861, twenty-four went to war (two of them for the Confederacy), or 47 percent. Among the forty-four juniors, twenty-three would eventually serve (52 percent). Of the fifty-two sophomores that fall, however, only eighteen would serve (35 percent), and of the fifty-two freshmen, only fifteen (29 percent). Twenty-four alumni who were not students at the time of the war were killed or died in service, sixteen from the 1861-1865 student population; approximately 290 alumni of the undergraduate College served in the war.[58]

Even allowing for students who went into the ministry or had medical disabilities, there were clearly many Bowdoin men who chose not to fight. The psychological and demographic impact of the war, in other words, was by no means as devastating within the extended college community as it was, say, in the Down East farming and fishing town of Old Deer Isle, whose story was told so movingly in Vernal Hutchinson's *A Maine Town in the Civil War*.[59]

Hatch is, of course, correct in pointing out that a college history is a record of an institution, not of its graduates, yet nonetheless it is important to ask with what degree of enthusiasm those identified with the College prosecuted the war. The unimaginable price paid, for example, by Chamberlain (twenty-four battles, six major wounds) stands out all the more vividly against this background.[60] But the mythology of Bowdoin in the war that developed later in the century—with its implications for the College's civic identity, its moral claims, its students' concepts of manliness and duty—is also part of the story, as we shall see.

POOR NEW ENGLAND!

That you could be enthused about the war but not about the Union is a lesson from the picaresque life of Arthur McArthur, Class of 1850. Born in 1830 in Limington, Maine, the son of a lawyer and temperance leader also named Arthur McArthur, of the Class of 1810, the younger McArthur had been the black sheep—at least as a student—of a rather distinguished Cumberland County family. The extremely pious Oliver Otis Howard, who roomed with McArthur in their final term at North Yarmouth Academy, remembered him as "a splendid specimen of a youth, having a perfect physique, with mental talents above the ordinary." But "fearful headaches and depression followed his frequent indulgences, and I did my best to care for him. His example . . . was a constant warning to me and I think deterred me from giving way in those days to temptation." At Bowdoin, McArthur was in frequent difficulty with the faculty because of his heavy drinking, and Howard thought it was chiefly "the eminence and worthiness of his father" that enabled him to get a degree.[61] With vague notions of becoming a lawyer, McArthur, like many graduates of his day, spent a few years in various teaching posts, one of which took him south in 1853.

Wanderlust seemed a family trait. A remarkable archive of a century of the McArthur family's life (1790-1890) survives in Special Collections—some 8,000 items—and we can trace in some detail the travels of the Civil War generation of siblings. Like all good Victorians, they wrote each other devotedly; the cumulative effect of spending several days with this correspondence is not unlike that of reading a sprawling nineteenth-century novel. One brother runs off to California in search of gold; another (the family favorite) goes to sea and drowns off the coast of France; another has a successful West Point career; a fourth—William McArthur, Class of 1853—becomes a Union general (and, later, a Limington eccentric); their sister graduates from Holyoke Seminary and has a rather unhappy teaching career.

One of Arthur's first jobs is as tutor for two prosperous families near St. Louis, where he gets his first close look at slavery. He likes what he sees. Reflecting on how hard his mother and sister worked at home on the family farm, and noting how much genteel leisure his Missouri friends enjoyed, he quickly internalizes Southern attitudes toward race and labor. The following years find him traveling through Georgia (evidently working as a debt collector), joining a "filibustering" expedition headed for Nicaragua (only to be shipwrecked on a sandbar), persuading some friends back home to join him in the California gold fields (only to have to turn around at Panama because of near-fatal dysentery), and trying unsuccessfully to start a business in Wisconsin (whose "cold" and "grasping" people he disliked). In 1860, en route to Texas, he finds himself in Sabine Parish, Louisiana, near Natchitoches, on the Red River. Several local families invite him to start a school, and within months he has established himself as a highly esteemed member of a pious, friendly community of small plantation owners, many of them devout Baptists. As he tells his father, he had at last, after so many false starts, found a place to which he felt he belonged. (He also assures his father he had adhered to his temperance pledge.)

On the last day of 1860, he wrote his father a seven-page letter explaining his position in life, for he feared "the mails will be still further interrupted by the political disturbances of the next few months." The elder McArthur had just writ-

173

ten that despite Lincoln's election he thought no state would actually secede and that sectional differences would be "amicably adjusted." He was wrong, his son warned him; "you misjudge the spirit in this section."

There is no power under Heaven that can prevent the separation of these two sections of country who entertain opinions moral political & religious, some diametrically opposed to each other. The heart of the Northern people is wrong their education is in the wrong direction upon the political institutions of the country. . . . The last fifty years' history of this country has proved conclusively that the present system of African slavery is closely interwoven with the interests of this country & with the whole world. . . It is mutually beneficial to the master & slave, & I cannot conceive how labor & service could be better regulated. And that great insidious plan of Black Republicanism to strangle it by nonextension is now most beautifully going to fail. Twenty years will see these seceeding States, with the rich tropical countries west & south west of us, & perhaps the rich islands of the West Indies annexed, a most flourishing & powerful nation—the most powerful on the Globe . . .

Poor New England, what a share in this glorious future History has she lost by her mistaken humanitarianism. They have made many mistakes. Harr[ied] Quakers, burnt witches, banished Baptists, & now they have aimed a blow at the pap that gave them suck.

On page five of his letter, he delivered a blow that must have crushed his parents:

Companies are forming all over the country. In the Parish we have formed one, & at the election of officers your unworthy son was honored with the position of Captain, which he accepted. This you can tell to any of my acquaintances about Maine, especially any who might have supported Lincoln.

After more fulmination against the abolitionists, he closes with love to all the family and best wishes for the New Year.[62]

When the war starts in April of 1862, McArthur and his "Sabine Rifles" become part of the 6th Louisiana Regiment, which sees action in Virginia. He sends his parents a copy of a New Orleans newspaper announcing his company's passage through that city. It was the last they would hear from him. The family had reports of his death in battle that summer, but it was many months before they could confirm this, a cruel repetition of the ordeal his parents had undergone a decade earlier trying to piece together

the details of their son Duncan's death at sea.[63] On 12 December 1862, William McArthur—by then, a captain in the 8th Maine—wrote his brother Malcolm at West Point: "He died a soldier's death, but in what a cause! Yet he was sincere and conscientious in the stand he took. Why should he have been so misguided. And yet I love and respect his memory and ever shall."[64]

In his last months as a civilian, Arthur McArthur had lived among kind, earnest people who, once the war began, were as convinced as Chamberlain and Howard that they were doing God's will on earth. McArthur felt at home with them, as he felt at home with their ideology. He spoke with the conviction of the convert, but there was so much anger in his letter to his father that one can speculate that in more than an intellectual sense, he was in revolt against the evangelical, moralizing New England of his youth. Had his treatment at the hands of the Bowdoin faculty had something to do with this? Possibly, among the other experiences of disappointment and renewed expectation he had crowded into his thirty-two years. What Arthur McArthur reminds us is that not only could the Civil War be literally fratricidal, but that within the same family, and the same College, brothers could in all moral seriousness go such different ways.

A GOOD WAR

Like many of his classmates, John Deering, Jr., of the Class of 1864, had taught school during the winter vacation of his sophomore year. Urged by an old schoolmate to join him in the 13th Maine, a regiment forming under the command of Colonel Neal Dow, the famous temperance leader, Deering decided not to return to Bowdoin from his home in Saco for the spring term but to go instead to Augusta and enroll as an infantryman. "I have determined to become a soldier, chiefly because I feel that it is my duty to." In those last nine words, in his diary entry for 31 December 1861, he sums up in lapidary fashion the range of emotions that compelled so many young men of his generation to go voluntarily to war.[65]

174

President Joshua Lawrence Chamberlain's house, which he and his wife, Frances Adams Chamberlain, had moved from 4 Potter Street to its present location at 226 Maine Street. The year he became president of Bowdoin he had the house raised and the present lower story built under it. The house is operated as a museum by the Pejepscot Historical Society.

The new year finds him in camp in the snow at Augusta, sharing a warm tent with twelve others, ages sixteen to forty-five. On furlough the following week, he goes home. "Found Mother well though rather tearful at the prospect of my having enlisted." He sets out to recruit more friends in the neighborhood and flirts with the young women he meets at church. A few weeks later, on the way to Boston by train, he stops briefly in Brunswick, where evidently many of his college friends came down to the station to see him in his new uniform. From quarters at Fanueil Hall the regiment embarks for New York, where amid the ringing of bells and firing of guns to celebrate Washington's birthday, he and some 1,600 others board the steamship *Fulton* for the long voyage south. "The soldiers are contented and joyful," he writes. "Ah! how many of them shall return alive!"

From his diary, found years later in an attic in Saco and given to Special Collections, we can recreate something of the Civil War of this Bowdoin sophomore. His first ordeal is two days of seasickness, but he marvels at the porpoises and flying fish, the sunset on the Virginia coast, and the lushness of the Florida landscape, "very beautiful to us accustomed to the snows of New England for the past three months." In early March of 1862, they reach Ship Island, off Biloxi, Mississippi—a seven-mile-long sandbar with "a few stunted pines." Many of his fellow soldiers were soon to hate the place; weeks of drilling in the hot sun exhausted them, and disease and a wave of suicides would follow. But nineteen-year-old Deering, perhaps because he had had some collegiate training, is given a clerkship on General George F. Shepley's staff. In May, when the staff, leaving Deering's regiment behind, goes to join the Federal troops who have just taken New Orleans, he goes, too.

In his dress uniform, the young man stands on the deck of the steamer as it moves upriver past the captured forts that had failed to stop Farragut's fleet ten days earlier. He sees:

the most delightful country my eye ever feasted upon. On each bank as far as the eye could reach, extended large and fertile plantations covered with cane, [and] orange and banana groves and dotted with the little white huts of the slaves or the stately mansions of the planters. The slaves ceased from their work and taking off their hats, cheered us as we steamed by. . . . The lights of New Orleans in the form of a blazing crescent, came into view at eight o'clock, and an hour later we anchored near the levee of the "Crescent City."[66]

General Benjamin Butler had already "infused a wholesome fear into the brave hearts of New Orleans," Deering noted, following several insults to the American flag. (He had hanged one of the offenders.) While Butler and Shepley enjoyed the comforts of the St. Charles Hotel (the most celebrated hostelry in the South, and owned by one of the McClellans of Portland), Deering and his fellow clerks set up shop in the neoclassical U. S. Customs House on Canal Street. He obtained the services of two "contrabands," or runaway slaves, as cooks, and by 20 May 1862 could report "Our situation now is very comfortable. We have good sleeping quarters upstairs and a plenty to eat and feel much better in general than do private soldiers."

He was tempting fate. Between that last entry and 21 June 1862 is a long blank. When Deering is finally able to write again, he explains: "About a month ago I fell in the Custom House near my room a distance of 25 feet striking my head. The blow was so severe that I was taken up for dead. But I gave signs of life shortly after and was conveyed to the St. James General Hospital." He had fractured his skull and for two weeks lay unconscious. He finally was able to "pencil" a letter to his mother; "it will be a great surprise to her to receive it, as she doubtless supposes me fatally injured." As he grows stronger, and his dizzy spells abate, Deering begins to help out around the hospital, which—to his horror—is beginning to fill up with the wounded from the campaigns

up the river. He is eventually medically discharged and returns to Saco; the 13th Maine, meanwhile, after the misery of Ship Island sees action in the Red River campaign (for the war had come home to Arthur McArthur's adopted Sabine Parish) and later in the Shenandoah Valley.

There was something chivalric, even archaic, about Chamberlain's heroics and McArthur's sacrifice of himself in Virginia. But with Deering we see modern war emerging from that backward-looking Southern act of rebellion—war that is bureaucratic, full of creature comforts for those lucky enough or clever enough to find them, marked by a "fortunate fall" (in both the literal and Miltonic sense) for some, senseless ruin for others. John Deering, Jr., who never returned to Bowdoin, ended his days as a lawyer in Washington, D. C., specializing in pension claims.

TOUCHING THE MYSTIC CHORDS

After his unlamented departure from Brunswick in 1839, William Allen returned to his native western Massachusetts, where from his house in Northampton he devoted the next three decades to a variety of literary and devotional projects. In 1844, for example, he produced for his fellow Congregationalists a *Report on Popery*, in response to the rapidly growing numbers of Irish immigrants in the state. In 1856 he published *Wunnissee, or The Vale of Hoosatunnuk, A Poem, with Notes*, an original, if somewhat unlyrical, production drawing together the history of Pittsfield and of his family, Christian piety, Indian lore, and denunciations of slavery. He followed it four years later with *A Book of Christian Sonnets*, including poems on the deaths of his daughter and wife that show the more tender side of his nature. In retirement he enjoyed receiving calls from former students, such as Governor Andrew and a white-bearded Calvin Stowe, who told Allen that children in Boston had called him "Santa Claus." ("Owing to my deafness," Allen wrote in his journal, "I thought he said not S. C. but *Anti-Christ!*") In his eightieth year the former president could still ride horseback. The entries in that journal include much Civil War news amid accounts of his orchard and his neighbors, his trips to nearby Amherst, and his frequent dreams of death.[67]

In early April of 1865, he writes: "Great news of capture yesterday of *Petersburg and Richmond* was received here about noon and the bells were long run . . . . Gen. *Weizel* then entered Richmond with his *negro army* of 25,000 men from N. side of the James, having discovered the enemy was leaving his front—fitting humiliation for the rebels, that black men should do this, the war having been for slavery!" When a torchlight victory parade is held in Northampton, Allen hangs colored paper lamps before a portrait of Lincoln on his piazza.

Sat, April 15 Rose at 7

Heard this morning at 1/4 past 10 that president Lincoln was assassinated at the theatre last night at 10, or 9 1/2 and died this morning at 7 o'clock 22 minutes! I was then lying in bed, looking at my poetic writings relating to the celebration of yesterday! He was murdered by J. Wilkes Booth, at the theatre, a drunken stage actor. Great God! let this most awful event of thy holy providence be made conducive to the good of the whole country . . .

In Brunswick, John Furbish had noted in his journal that spring was coming. The snow had melted, the earth had absorbed the water, rather than letting it run into the river as usual. "The air has been very good and farmers are busy plowing, some even planting potatoes. Everything now bids fair for a favorable season, and we may well thank God for his many blessings to us." When the news of Lincoln's death arrives, "people only looked and thought for hours. Feelings were too deep for utterance." By 3:00 P.M., First Parish Church is filled. "It does seem that the death of our President has united our people even more than before. Party lines disappear, and we see all paying tribute to his greatness, and universal goodness." People are so

General Oliver Otis Howard '50 was chosen by President Lincoln to head the Freedmen's Bureau in 1865. In this capacity he helped found Hampton Institute and Atlanta, Fisk, Lincoln, Straight, and Howard universities and later served as Howard's first president. He was a Bowdoin Overseer (1866-74) and Trustee (1892-1909).

eager for news, they cannot wait for the *Telegraph*, but ask the editor, Albert Gorham Tenney '35, to read the morning's telegrams in church.[68]

Almost four months later, the church was to be filled for another communal rite.

If the Civil War did not really begin and end in Brunswick, there is a way of bracketing the conflict that is flattering to local sensibilities: Jefferson Davis's honorary degree in 1858 was followed, after some interruption, by U. S. Grant's in 1865. In 1858 Davis had been one of the most respected politicians in the country, a defender of Southern interests yet moderate enough, by Mississippi standards, to hold out some hope of compromise. By Commencement 1865, he was in prison, discredited as a leader, possibly facing execution as a traitor, and humiliated by the reports (wildly exaggerated) that he had been caught while fleeing disguised in his wife's clothing.[69] Grant, who in 1858 had been a failed businessman and alleged drunkard, after Lincoln's death was the most famous living American. (The Robert E. Lee legend took a few more years to coalesce.)

In July of 1865, Chamberlain returned to his house in Brunswick, "brown and fit-looking" but suffering from the wound in his groin that was to afflict him most of the rest of his long life. In the admiring words of his most recent biographer, "with his intelligence, education, and character, he epitomized the best of America's citizen soldiers, a volunteer standing with millions of other volunteers risking all for their country's cause."[70] Grant had offered him a signal honor: at Appomattox, Chamberlain was selected to receive the formal surrender, by General John B. Gordon, of what was left of Lee's army. Chamberlain's magnificent gesture—having his men salute as the defeated foe marched by—was pure Sir Walter Scott. It was also an ambiguous symbol, as some of Chamberlain's radical critics

A turn-of-the-century view of Chamberlain's library at 226 Maine Street, showing a portion of his collection of Civil War memorabilia.

immediately saw, for it suggested that the wound to the Republic had begun to heal, that restoration of the Union was the simple act that justified the war's terrible pain. General Gordon, only a few years later, would be terrorizing blacks and their white supporters as head of the Ku Klux Klan in his native Georgia.

When Grant came to Brunswick on 8 August 1865, he called at the Chamberlains' house on Potter Street (it would not be moved to its present location on Maine Street until 1867) and joined the officers of the College for what turned out to be a splendid reunion of many of the alumni who had fought in the war. Chamberlain's biographer, Alice Rains Trulock, says that Grant came at Chamberlain's invitation; Grant's biographer, William S. McFeely, tells a slightly different version of the Commencement story, namely that Howard, as head of the controversial Freedmen's Bureau,

had persuaded Grant to attend in an effort to link him in the public eye with Howard's campaign to save the abandoned Southern farmlands for the ex-slaves.[71] Chamberlain, like Grant, had no particular sympathy for the freedmen; like many others who had fought for the North, they expected social relations in the South to return more or less to their prewar patterns, but with wage labor or tenant farming replacing the discredited institution of slavery, and the blacks allowed some small public role.[72] Howard, who understood what would befall the freedmen if they were left without federal protection, was to see his far-reaching goal of radical social reform in the South abandoned by Lincoln's successors. But for the moment, as McFeely writes, the one-armed Howard shared the platform at Bowdoin with Grant:

His empty sleeve was a badge of sacrifice familiar throughout the land; his proud record in the war was

178

known to all who came to Brunswick to salute the first postwar generation of graduates. To stand honored with the greatest of the Union heroes was surely a sign of visible election.[73]

Howard had of course to share the platform with Chamberlain, too; already their disagreement over how to deal with the blacks was souring their relationship.[74] By coincidence, the only other professor to leave Bowdoin for the war was Howard's close associate Eliphalet Whittlesey, a Yale graduate who had been a clergyman in Bath before the war and an Overseer (1859-63). He had succeeded Chamberlain as professor of rhetoric and oratory in 1861, but had taken a leave in 1862 to serve as a chaplain. A man of great energy whose horsemanship was admired by Lincoln himself, Whittlesey returned briefly to Bowdoin after Chancellorsville, then left again in 1864 to serve on Howard's staff in Tennessee. (Chamberlain, upon his return to Brunswick, was elected to Whittlesey's post, which had been declared vacant.) Whittlesey, who later taught at Howard University—the predominantly black institution named for the general—was to have a controversial career as an official of the Freedmen's Bureau.[75]

The Brunswick event was reported in great detail—including a paragraph lauding the beauty of the ladies present—in the *New York Times* of 9 August 1865. The paper said that, under Smyth's direction, funds would be raised to erect a Memorial Hall honoring those who had served; it would include portraits, captured battle flags, and other war memorabilia. A gala banquet followed, at which the modest Grant declined to speak. It marked more than the end of the war. As Chamberlain already realized, the old college—not just Bowdoin, but the whole antebellum notion of the small, semi-rural classical seminary—was in decline. While it would take another decade or more for the full implications of this process to be understood, for Bowdoin a new and uncomfortable time was at hand.

For all their differences, the Old South and New England shared more than their citizens may have realized. The war forced the Union together again, but it was to be a very different United States. New England, still comfortable

General Joshua Lawrence Chamberlain on horseback at the Eastern Promenade, Portland, ca. 1900-1904. Chamberlain served four terms as Maine's governor before becoming president of the College from 1871 to 1883.

with the republican values of the Federalist elite, and the South, which had never entirely lost its claim to the heritage of Jefferson and Madison, would see severely weakened their cultural and political authority to define what it meant to be an American.

One of the things they had shared, however superficially, was a belief in the cultural values of the eighteenth-century classical curriculum. The teaching of Latin and Greek was never to disappear completely, but classical learning—and the related notion of classical civic humanism—was to be a casualty of the new industrial and urban age. Yet a few enclaves of classical learning survived, making all the more touching a souvenir, now at Bowdoin, that washed ashore at Port Royal, South Carolina. It was a volume of Virgil's poetry, printed in the South during the war, containing half of the *Aeneid* and the *Georgics*. It had floated to the beach in 1864 from a wrecked Confederate gunboat.

O nimium caelo et pelago confise sereno,
nudus in ignota, Palinure, jacebis harena.

You trusted too much, my pilot, in a peaceful world

And now you lie naked on an unknown shore.[76]

NOTES

BCSC is Special Collections, Hawthorne-Longfellow Library, Bowdoin College.

1. For students of Civil War trivia, Brunswick has another claim to closure. In 1827 the Skolfields, the best known of the local shipbuilding families, launched their first ship, the *Brunswick*. Converted into a whaler in 1833, the ship was still in service during the Civil War. In June 1865, two months after the fall of the Confederacy, the raider *C. S. S. Shenandoah* (not knowing the war had ended) put the vessel and seven other Yankee whalers to the torch in a Siberian bay. The last to be burned was the *Brunswick*, which thus became the last maritime casualty of the Civil War. Erminie S. Reynolds and Kenneth R. Martin, *"A Singleness of Purpose": The Skolfields and Their Ships* (Bath, Maine, 1987), pp. 101-102.

2. Harriet Beecher Stowe to Calvin Stowe, Brunswick, [May 1850?], Stowe Collection, Schlesinger Library, Radcliffe College, folder 74.

3. Her brother Charles Beecher, Class of 1834, was a Congregational clergyman who in 1851 published *The Duty of Disobedience to Wicked Laws, a Sermon on the Fugitive Slave Law*. Her brother Edward Beecher, Yale 1822, was during his presidency of Illinois College a close friend of the editor Elijah P. Lovejoy, who was killed by an anti-abolitionist mob in 1837; in the 1850s Edward was pastor of the Salem Street Church in Boston and editor of the *Congregationalist*. The most famous of the brothers was Henry Ward Beecher, Amherst 1834, one of the greatest preachers of the century; in the 1850s he attracted crowds that averaged 2,500 persons to his Plymouth Church in Brooklyn, N. Y. Their father was Lyman Beecher, president of Lane Theological Seminary in Cincinnati, at which Calvin Stowe was teaching before returning to Bowdoin.

4. Harriet Beecher Stowe to Calvin Stowe, see note 2.

5. Calvin Stowe to the Reverend W. Adams, Brunswick, 20 September 1850, Stowe-Day Foundation, Hartford, Connecticut.

6. Calvin Stowe to Thomas Upham, Walnut Hills, Cincinnati, 19 February 1851; he had used much the same language in writing to William Smyth on 17 January 1851. Although some biographers later described the Stowes not just as pinched for cash but as "impoverished," his $1,000 salary placed them solidly in the middle class in mid-nineteenth-century Maine.

7. E. Bruce Kirkham, *The Building of Uncle Tom's Cabin* (Knoxville, Tenn., 1977), pp. 65-67. Kirkham provides as thorough a reconstruction of the steps by which the novel was written and published as we are ever likely to have. The book's subsequent history as a cultural icon and its misappropriation by racists is explored in detail in Thomas F. Gossett, Uncle Tom's Cabin *and American Culture* (Dallas, Texas, 1985). The novel traveled quickly, and in all directions. Living briefly in Milledgeville, Georgia, where she was teaching music, Chamberlain's future wife, Fanny Adams, wrote to her sister, "I just glanced up to the mantelpiece in this room and what book do you suppose I saw there? no other than "Uncle Tom's cabin" in two volumes, well thumbed and worn out too!" Fanny Adams to Charlotte Adams, 10 January 1853, Chamberlain Papers, Maine Historical Society, Portland, Maine.

8. Edmund Wilson, *Patriotic Gore* (New York, 1962), pp. 3-58; on Calvin Stowe, see pp. 59-70. For an earlier attempt—sympathetic, though condescending—to do her justice, see Herbert Ross Brown, *The Sentimental Novel in America 1789-1860* (Durham, N.C.), pp. 241-280.

9. Jane Tompkins, *Sensational Designs: The Cultural Work of American Fiction, 1790-1860* (New York, 1985), p. 269. For a survey of recent work on Stowe, see Eric J. Sundquist, ed., *New Essays on* Uncle Tom's Cabin (Cambridge, 1986) and the introduction by Ann Douglas to the Penguin Books edition (Baltimore, 1981).

10. There have been only two recent public gestures on the College's part to honor Stowe: in 1978, to mark its own seventy-fifth anniversary, Masque & Gown staged George L. Aiken's 1852 adaptation of *Uncle Tom's Cabin*, with a program note by Professor Herbert Ross Brown; and in the spring of 1986, the *Bowdoin Alumni Magazine* published an essay by the magazine's former editor, Helen E. Pelletier '81, "Yearning for Freedom, Yearning for Home" (vol. 59, no. 4), pp. 2-7.

11. For example, if the creation by a writer of fiction of characters so vivid and representative that they become part of the general culture is a sign of genius—as it certainly is with Dickens and Balzac—then why is Stowe so underappreciated? However one-dimensional, can Tom, Legree, St. Clair, Eva, and Eliza be considered *minor* achievements?

12. Joan Hedrick, "Parlor Literature: Harriet Beecher Stowe and the Question of 'Great Women Artists,'" *SIGNS* 17 (Winter 1992), pp. 275-303. The account by Charles Edward Stowe (her son, born in Brunswick) and Lyman Beecher Stowe (her grandson) was based on family tradition. Whatever its accuracy, it catches the sort of scene Hedrick has in mind: "A daughter of Mrs. Stowe well remembered her whole life long the scene in the lit-

tle parlor in Brunswick when [the letter from Mrs. Edward Beecher describing the Fugitive Slave Law] was received and read. Mrs. Stowe read it aloud to the assembled family, and when she came to the words, 'I would write something that would make this whole nation feel what an accursed thing slavery is,' rising from her chair and crushing the letter in her hand, she exclaimed, with an expression on her face that stamped itself permanently on the minds of her children: 'God helping me, I will write something. I will if I live.'" *McClure's Magazine* 36 (April 1911), p. 611. Kirkham (pp. 72-75) examines the differing versions of the vision of Tom's death Stowe is reported to have had during a service at First Parish Church.

13. Harriet Beecher Stowe to Calvin Stowe, 3 February and 8 February [1851], [Brunswick], Stowe-Day Foundation, Hartford, Connecticut.

14. In 1841, for example, she had published *A Treatise on Domestic Economy for the Use of Young Ladies at Home and at School*, the first of a series of books incorporating brisk advice on home decoration, healthful cooking, personal hygiene, child care, calisthenics, and education. In 1861, she and Stowe were to collaborate on *The American Woman's Home*, which combined practical advice with a homily on "Christian home-making." The book has had a second life in a modern reprint because it includes so much data for historic preservationists seeking to recreate Victorian interiors.

15. Catharine Beecher to Mary Beecher Perkins, Brunswick, 27 September 1851, quoted in Jeanne Boydston, Mary Kelley, and Anne Margolis, *The Limits of Sisterhood: The Beecher Sisters on Women's Rights and Woman's Sphere* (Chapel Hill, 1988), pp. 346-347.

16. Joshua L. Chamberlain, "'Do It! That's How,'" *Bowdoin* 64 (Spring/Summer 1991), p. 10.

17. H. B. Stowe to "Dear Sister," n. p., n. d., Yale University Library. I am grateful to Professor Alfred H. Fuchs for calling my attention to this letter, the only contemporary account I have found of a fugitive slave in Brunswick.

18. Isabella Hooker to John Hooker, Brunswick, 4 July 1852, Stowe-Day Foundation.

19. Especially on the role of the "Temperance Question" in Maine, see William E. Gienapp, *The Origins of the Republican Party 1852-1856* (New York, 1987), pp. 129-133; and more generally, Richard R. Wescott, *New Men, New Issues: The Formation of the Republican Party in Maine* (Portland, 1986).

20. Edward O. Schriver, *Go Free: The Antislavery Impulse in Maine, 1833-1855* (Orono, Maine, 1970), p. 61; Austin Willey, *The History of the Antislavery Cause in State and Nation* (Portland, 1886), p. 155. Willey describes the movement vividly but, as a leading participant in it, much less than objectively. Two letters a Mr. Hyde wrote to Professor Parker Cleaveland in 1836, for example, convey what was a more common attitude of the time. Writing from Columbus, Georgia, on 4 April 1836, he reports that "every day's observation is deepening my conviction that the war which our 'abolition' neighbors are carrying against the good providence of the Lord, is not only absurd, but, as idle as the wind. The slaves themselves have more sense to appreciate their own condition & interest than they." And from Tallahassee, four days later: "I do not mean to intimate that slavery in every shape will not ultimately yield to the benign influences of Christianity; but that, passing as the negro now is from paganism & barbarity, he must be subject to despotic sway for a time." Parker Cleaveland Papers, BCSC.

21. "Five Reasons for Abolitionizing the North," *Advocate of Freedom* (Hallowell, Maine), 26 April 1838.

22. This "demonization" could take many forms. Speaking to the Maine Anti-Slavery Convention in Topsham in 1841, for example, the Reverend N. M. Williams, perhaps with a view toward the Bowdoin students in his audience, said that slavery's enfeeblement of the Southern intellect (as well as the Southern body and soul) extended even to collegians, including those who came north to study. They were superficial scholars and lazy to boot, he said. They "love to visit those regions of science which can be reached by riding, with folded arms, and reclining feet, and smoking pipe, in railroad cars; but, if they are to clamber up those rugged heights, *on foot*, they beg to be excused." *Advocate of Freedom*, 4 February 1841.

23. Daybook, Henry Merritt, Journal 1861-75. Pejepscot Historical Society Archives, Brunswick, Maine.

24. According to local tradition, Smyth's house on College Street (today, the John Brown Russwurm Afro-American Center) was a "station" of the Underground Railroad. Indeed, the shallow crawl spaces beneath many early nineteenth-century houses in Maine are often pointed out to visitors as hiding places for runaway slaves. There are two reasons for viewing these claims with skepticism: there is little evidence of the presence of fugitive slaves in coastal Maine (and in the one document, note 17 above, relating to Brunswick, it is the Stowes' house, not Smyth's, where the presumed runaway finds shelter), and the tradition of the Underground Railroad itself is largely mythical, especially in New England; see, e. g., Larry Gara, *The Liberty Line: The Legend of the Underground*

Railroad (Lexington, Kentucky, 1961). Willey (p. 70) quotes a long letter from the theologian Egbert Coffin Smyth '48 attesting to his parents' hospitality toward fugitive slaves in Brunswick, but Smyth's reminiscence was written forty years after the fact, and he may have conflated acts of charity toward local blacks or free blacks heading for Canada after the Compromise of 1850 with the presence of genuine runaways. It is true, as defenders of the tradition point out, that fugitive slaves would not have signed the guest book, but it is also true—as the story of Frederick Douglass, for example, reminds us—that successful escapes were usually achieved by the most intelligent and resourceful slaves, with a minimum of white assistance. (The notion that it was the *whites* who were being especially brave is further evidence of post-Civil War racial bias even among abolitionists.) For a fuller discussion of the question, see the exchange of letters between Professor Ernst C. Helmreich and the author, *Bowdoin* 63, no. 2 (Summer 1990), p. 36. Pending further research on Maine's pre-Civil War African-American population, there is no evidence now available to suggest that a large population of fugitive slaves passed through or settled in the state.

25. *Christian Mirror* (Portland, Maine), 19 May 1836. For the background of Bailey's position, see Larry E. Tise, *Proslavery: A History of the Defense of Slavery in America 1701-1840* (Athens, Georgia, 1987).

26. *Advocate of Freedom*, 8 November 1838. The next year, the student abolitionists sent $50 to the Maine Anti-Slavery Society and called for further contributions from their fellow students: "Let the dollar, which he spends for the disgusting weed, or puffs away in smoke, be consecrated to the great work of emancipation." The *Advocate of Freedom* had been established by Smyth and Willey in Brunswick (and later moved to Hallowell) in 1838 to present the immediate abolition point of view. Its editors admitted that Maine was difficult ground to plow: "Our ship owners, the masters and mariners employed in the carrying trade, forming a most important part of our population, have an interest to be on good terms with southern planters." 8 March 1838 (inaugural issue).

27. Michael Schaara, *The Killer Angels* (New York, 1974), p. 168. Schaara's highly readable account of the battle of Gettysburg begins with one misstatement (that Lee did not "believe in slavery," p. xvi) and ends with another (that Chamberlain "de-emphasized" religion as president of Bowdoin, p. 355). On demography, see Randolph Stakeman, "The Black Population of Maine 1764-1900," in *The New England Journal of Black Studies* 8 (1989), pp. 17-35. Stakeman has taught history and Afro-American studies at Bowdoin since 1978 and is now associate dean for academic affairs and director of the Afro-American Studies Program. Slavery had been officially abolished by judicial action in Massachusetts (including the District of Maine) in 1783, based on the human rights language of the state's new constitution. By 1830, slavery had been virtually abolished in the North, but except for the four northernmost New England states, the rest of the "free" states denied blacks the right to vote on an equal basis with whites. For details on this and the various forms of economic and social prejudice, see Leon F. Litwack, *North of Slavery: The Negro in the Free States, 1790-1860* (Chicago, 1961). On nativist bigotry aimed at the Irish, see James H. Mundy, *Hard Times, Hard Men: Maine and the Irish, 1830-1860* (Scarborough, Maine, 1990).

28. Theodore R. Hovet, "Mrs. Thomas C. Upham's 'Happy Phebe': A Feminine Source of Uncle Tom," *American Literature* 51 (May 1979), pp. 267-270. Jacobs died on 28 February 1850. Stowe said that soon after arriving in Brunswick in May 1850 she read "a small religious tract" on the life of a "coloured woman named Phebe." H. B. Stowe, *A Key to Uncle Tom's Cabin* (Boston, 1853), pp. 40-41. A reference to Jacobs's piety also appears in a letter to his mother by Henry H. Boody '42, professor of rhetoric and oratory, who said she was "the most spiritual, consistent, devoted follower of Christ I have ever known"; quoted in the *Bowdoin Alumnus* 34, no. 1 (October 1959), inside cover.

29. Mrs. T. C. Upham, "Narrative of Phebe Ann Jacobs," American Tract Society, no. 536 (New York, [1850?]), p. 8.

30. Horatio Bridge, *Personal Recollections of Nathaniel Hawthorne* (New York, 1893), p. 30. There is no adequate biography of Russwurm.

31. Penelope Campbell, *The Maryland State Colonization Society 1831-1857* (Urbana, Ill., 1971), passim. For the more general context, see P. J. Staudenraus, *The African Colonization Movement 1816-1865* (New York, 1961).

32. Twilight had reportedly "passed" as white, "leaving only an ambiguous census return and a whispered legend to document his racial background." David Stameshkin, *The Town's College: Middlebury College, 1800-1915* (Middlebury, Vt., 1985), pp. 108-109.

33. For further details on the five students, see the Medical School Biographical Files, BCSC; the information is scanty except in the case of Boseman, who was a leading black citizen of Charleston, S. C. On the difficulties facing aspiring black medical students in nineteenth-century America, see James L. Curtis, *Blacks, Medical Schools, and Society* (Ann Arbor, 1971), pp. 1-27.

34. William Sweetser, M. D., to Parker Cleaveland, Castleton, Vt., 5 October 1849, Cleaveland Papers, BCSC.

35. Nathaniel Hawthorne, *The Life of Franklin Pierce* (Boston, 1852; reprinted, New York, 1970).

36. *The Centenary Edition of the Works of Nathaniel Hawthorne*, vol. 16, pp. 604-605. The letter to Bridge contains a shrewder assessment of Pierce's abilities than appeared in the campaign biography.

37. *Centenary Edition*, vol. 17, p. 304. For comment on this much-quoted remark, see Brown, *The Sentimental Novel in America, 1789-1860*, pp. 100-112. See also John T. Frederick, "Hawthorne's 'Scribbling Women,'" *New England Quarterly* 48 (June 1975), pp. 231-240, and Henry Nash Smith, "The Scribbling Women and the Cosmic Success Story," *Critical Inquiry* 1 (September 1974), pp. 47-70.

38. *Centenary Edition*, vol. 16, March 1856, pp. 456-457. Edwin H. Miller notes Hawthorne's "deep-seated anger toward women," quoting another comment of his on female authors: "I wish they were forbidden to write, on pain of having their faces deeply scarified with an oyster-shell." *Salem Is My Dwelling Place: A Life of Nathaniel Hawthorne* (Iowa City, 1991), p. 384; Hawthorne to J. T. Fields, Concord, 11 December 1852, *Centenary Edition*, vol. 16, p. 592.

39. *Centenary Edition*, vol. 16, quoted in notes, p. 608.

40. [Nathaniel Hawthorne], "Chiefly About War Matters," *Atlantic Monthly* 10 (July 1862), pp. 43-61. Seeking to distance themselves from Hawthorne's views, the editors inserted several disclaimers, saying of one passage that they were "inclined to think its tone reprehensible, and its tendency impolitic in the present stage of our national difficulties," p. 49. They excised his very unflattering sketch of Lincoln. On Hawthorne's position as a "lonely dissenter," see Daniel Aaron, *The Unwritten War: American Writers and the Civil War* (New York, 1973), pp. 41-55.

41. There is no evidence that Woods was proslavery. In a note in his translation of *Knapp's Theology* in 1831, he said "the least traces" of rational and moral powers should be regarded as evidence that African slaves were men bearing "something of the image of God, however low the degree in which they may possess those powers, and however widely they may differ from us in the incidental circumstances of color, feature, and temperament" (p. 130).

42. *Speeches of the Hon. Jefferson Davis of Mississippi, Delivered During the Summer of 1858* (Baltimore, 1859). On the reasons for the trip, see Clement Eaton, *Jefferson Davis* (New York, 1977), p. 103.

43. "Speech at the Portland Serenade," 9 July 1858, pp. 13-16; "Banquet after the Encampment at Belfast," (n. d.); "Speech at the Portland Meeting," p. 17; "Speech at the State Fair at Augusta, Me." (reprinted from the *Eastern Argus*, 29 September 1858), pp. 23-29.

44. Despite demands that the degree be rescinded—one alumnus at the 1865 Commencement said Davis's LL.D. might soon prove to mean "Long Let him Dangle" (Hatch, p. 123)—the Governing Boards stood firm, whether from principle or simply because they did not wish to be seen as admitting an error. Soon after Davis was elected president of the Confederacy in February of 1861, the Bangor *Whig* urged that the "traitor's" degree be expunged; the rival Bangor *Union* defended him and the College. Hudson Strode, *Jefferson Davis, Confederate President* (New York, 1959), p. 22. In 1889, four months before his death, Davis wrote from his retirement at Beauvoir, Mississippi, to thank Joseph Williamson 1849 of Bangor for having sent him a *Bowdoin College Catalogue* that listed his name: "Some newspapers had circulated a report that Bowdoin College had revoked the honorary degree conferred by it upon me & it was with no small gratification that I found in the catalogue evidence that the Administrators of Bowdoin were incapable of such spite which could only originate from sectionalism." Jefferson Davis Papers, BCSC. For a recent assessment of Pierce's administration and Davis's major role in it, see Larry Gara, *The Presidency of Franklin Pierce* (Lawrence, Kan., 1991). With evidently unselfconscious irony, the United Daughters of the Confederacy in 1973 established a Jefferson Davis Award at the College, awarded annually to the best student—in constitutional law.

45. H. B. Stowe to Georgiana May [1833], *Letters of Harriet Beecher Stowe*, pp. 72-73.

46. Chamberlain, "'Do It! That's How,'" p. 12.

47. Ibid. "I have always been interested in military matters," he told the governor, "and what I do not know in that line, I *know how to learn*." Chamberlain to Gov. Israel Washburn, Brunswick, 14 July 1862, Maine State Archives, Augusta, Maine.

48. Chamberlain Papers, BCSC.

49. Alice Rains Trulock, *In the Hands of Providence: Joshua Lawrence Chamberlain and the American Civil War* (Chapel Hill, N. C., 1991), pp. 64-65. Trulock's long-awaited biography is an excellent survey of his career, though stronger (as its subtitle suggests) in describing battles than in analyzing his peacetime pursuits. For details of the regiment, see William E. S. Whitman and Charles H. True, *Maine in the War for the Union* (Lewiston, Maine, 1865); John J. Pullen, *The Twentieth Maine: A*

Volunteer Regiment in the Civil War (Philadelphia, 1957); Theodore Gerrish, *Army Life: A Private's Reminiscences of the War* (Portland, 1882), and the forthcoming edition of the diaries of Colonel Ellis Spear.

50. Quoted in John J. Pullen, "Bath, Brunswick, and the Civil War," typescript of speech, 29 October 1960, Pejepscot Historical Society Archives, Brunswick, Maine.

51. Kenniston spent thirteen months in various prisons until being exchanged in August 1862, in time to fight at Fredericksburg. He ended his service career as a lieutenant colonel and returned to his home in Boothbay, where he became a judge and pioneer real estate developer of summer vacation homes. He died in 1917. See his biographical file, BCSC, for more details.

52. For brief sketches of these generals, see Philip S. Wilder, "Stars on Their Shoulders," *Bowdoin Alumnus*, vol. 37, no. 3 (March 1963), pp. 2-6. For a brief account of Governor Andrew's role in establishing the 54th Massachusetts Infantry Regiment, see Russell Duncan, ed., *Blue-Eyed Child of Fortune: The Civil War Letters of Colonel Robert Gould Shaw* (Athens, Ga., 1992), pp. 20-39.

53. *Catalogue of the Officers and Students of Bowdoin College and the Medical School of Maine: 1860* (Brunswick, 1860); Hatch, p. 116.

54. For a reminiscence of the Guards, see Charles A. Curtis (1861), "Bowdoin Under Fire," in John Clair Minot and Donald Francis Snow, *Tales of Bowdoin* (Augusta, Maine, 1901), pp. 261-272; Hatch, p. 117. The 1863 Visiting Committee did note an anticipated decline in numbers, concluding that "the war has something to do with this. The establishment of Bates College is also to be considered." [J. W. Bradbury], 1863 Visiting Committee Report, BCSC. Attendance in the Medical School increased slightly, reflecting the new demand for military surgeons and hospital staff.

55. Henry Merritt Journal 1861-75, Pejepscot Historical Society Archives, Brunswick, Maine.

56. "Bowdoin and Dartmouth," undated clipping, Edgar O. Achorn File, BCSC. He counted 1,770 living Bowdoin graduates, of whom he reckoned 443 (including Medical School graduates) served; 2,800 living Dartmouth graduates, of whom 639 served. For Bowdoin, Achorn also lists two major generals (O. O. Howard and Francis Fessenden '58), a paymaster general (Hawthorne's old friend Horatio Bridge '25), a medical inspector general, a surgeon general, a medical director, seven colonels, eight brevet major generals (including Chamberlain), eighteen brevet brigadier generals, eigh-teen brevet colonels, and 188 other officers—for a percentage of alumni with commissions of 79.70, compared to Dartmouth's 67.33 percent. (A brevet rank is an honorary one, voted by Congress, giving an officer a higher nominal rank than the one for which he is paid.)

57. Phillip S. Paludan sees the enthusiastic reaction to the war among northern students as evidence of "deep patriotism" and as an affirmation on the part of the upper class that its moral values had held firm. *"A People's Contest": The Union and Civil War 1861-1865* (New York, 1988), pp. 132-133. More than 24 percent of Harvard's graduates from 1841-1861 served the Union; Yale, 23 percent, compared with 17.6 percent for the male population as a whole, aged fifteen to fifty, in the North. For obvious reasons, the sacrifices were even greater for Southern colleges and universities. The University of Virginia, for example, had an enrollment of 645 in 1856-1857; in the war years, the student population fell to forty-six to sixty-six. Virginius Dabney, *Mr. Jefferson's University, A History* (Charlottesville, Virginia, 1981), pp. 24-28. Two well-known Bowdoin graduates were identified with the pro-slavery cause: Nathan Lord 1809, a famous president of Dartmouth College who championed slavery on Biblical grounds (and finally was eased out by his embarassed trustees in 1863), and Seargent Smith Prentiss 1826, one of the great orators of his day and a member of Congress from Mississippi from 1837 to 1839.

58. The numbers come from the *General Catalogue of Bowdoin College 1794-1950* (Brunswick, Maine, 1950) and the *College Roll of Honor* (Brunswick, 1867), a detailed biographical account of those who served the Union.

59. Vernal Hutchinson's *A Maine Town in the Civil War* (Freeport, Maine, 1957) was drawn upon extensively in Ken Burns's television series *The Civil War* (1990) to show the impact of increasing casualties on a small New England town. But the book gives a slightly distorted impression of the impact of the war on the state as a whole.

60. For an interesting discussion of Chamberlain's war career and the psychology of battle, see Gerald F. Linderman, *Embattled Courage: The Experience of Combat in the American Civil War* (New York, 1987), pp. 163-164, 273-274.

61. *Autobiography of Oliver Otis Howard*, vol. 1 (New York, 1908), pp. 27-28. On their way to Bowdoin from Yarmouth, McArthur insisted on stopping at a tavern, saying to his roommate: "Howard, you are ambitious, you

would like to make something of yourself in the future; you do not expect to do it without ever taking a glass of liquor, do you?" The future general said he did not see the connection. "Then he gave me the names of several public men of distinction, both state and national; he said they all drank and in his judgment drink helped them to their greatness," Howard recalled. "I answered that I did not care to be great and that I was already on a pledge to my mother and would not drink," p. 28.

62. Arthur McArthur to Arthur McArthur, Sabine Parish, Louisiana, 31 December 1860, McArthur Papers, BCSC.

63. Duncan had fallen in 1853 from the rigging of the *A. B. Thompson*, captained by George B. Mustard, who later gave his name to a house in Brunswick that is now college faculty housing. Details of Arthur's death arrived in March of 1864 from a fellow Confederate officer who was a prisoner of war in Ohio. Major McArthur (he had been elected to the promotion) was killed by snipers hidden in an orchard outside of Winchester, Virginia. His comrade told of the elaborate funeral given him and sent along his few remaining possessions. "It will be a consolation to you to know that the ladies of Winchester adorn his grave with flowers annually. The Major often spoke to me of you, his brother in California & the one at sea & always very tenderly of his sister . . . . I heartily join with you in wishing for the speedy termination of the war." John Orr (Adjutant, 6th La. Reg.) to Arthur McArthur, Johnson's Island Prison, Ohio, 28 March 1864. McArthur Papers, BCSC.

64. William McArthur to Malcolm McArthur, Limington, Maine, 12 December 1862, McArthur Papers, BCSC. The story of the family based on their correspondence is found in Elizabeth Ring, *The McArthurs of Limington, Maine: The Family in America a Century Ago, 1783-1917* (Falmouth, Me., 1992).

65. John Deering, Jr., Diary, 1861-65, BCSC. Deering had been contributing articles on Bowdoin College to the *Maine Democrat*, the Saco newspaper edited by James Hanscom '46's brother, Daniel. Relatively little war news was included, other than a flowery tribute to the new cadet corps on 11 June 1861 ("For once it seems the martial fury of the devotees at the shrine of learning is fairly aroused, and woe to the enemy when we shall meet on the field of battle!") and this passage on 19 November 1861: "Our number has been thinned somewhat by the departure of several who have gone to fight our battles for us. All honor to the patriotism that moves them to leave the quiet retreats of Bowdoin for the perils of the camp and field!" Like other Democratic newspapers (e.g, the *Eastern Argus* and the *Bath Times*), the Saco paper also included much criticism of the war effort and of the abolitionists.

66. Deering Diary, 4 May 1862.

67. William Allen, *Report on Popery, Accepted by the General Association of Massachusetts, July, 1844* (Boston, 1844). He had not lost his gift for invective: "If, in the next village to ours, in enlightened New England, the inhabitants were all pagans, and bowed down daily in a temple of Venus or Jupiter, we are persuaded the Holy Majesty of Heaven would be less insulted, and less offended, than he is by the actual worship of Mary and the saints by a multitude among us, who bear the name of Christian," p. 20; William Allen Journals 1861-66, Forbes Library, Northampton, Mass. (Gov. Andrew, 2 October 1863; Stowe, 15 February 1866.)

68. John Furbish, "Facts About Brunswick, Maine" [1862-79], facsimile edition (Brunswick, 1976). The original of this valuable account of mid-nineteenth-century Brunswick is in the Pejepscot Historical Society Archives, Brunswick, Maine.

69. Among the occasional clippings he pasted into his journal, Henry Merritt, for example, included a cartoon of the cornered Davis wearing his wife's hoop skirt and insisting that he was a woman. Pejepscot Historical Society Archives, Brunswick, Maine.

70. Trulock, p. 333.

71. William S. McFeely, *Grant: A Biography* (New York, 1981), p. 236.

72. On Chamberlain's unsympathetic attitude toward ex-slaves, see Trulock, p. 315.

73. William S. McFeely, *Yankee Stepfather: General O. O. Howard and the Freedmen* (New Haven, 1968), p. 109.

74. The two generals were to be associated again, between 1892 and Howard's death in 1909, when they were both Trustees of the College; see photo, p. 186. Howard had also been an Overseer from 1866 to 1874, overlapping with the first years of Chamberlain's presidency, 1871-83.

75. Ibid., pp. 79-80.

76. *Virgilii Carmina: Aeneidos VII-XII et Georgica* (Wilmington, N. C., 1863), copy now in BCSC with note on its discovery. The passage from *The Aeneid*, book 5, lines 870-871, refers to Aeneas's drowned pilot, Palinurus.

The President and Trustees of Bowdoin College posed for this photograph in 1904 in what was called the Alumni Room, now a Computing Center laboratory, on the second floor of Hubbard Hall. l to r: General Thomas Hamlin Hubbard 1857 h 1894; General John Marshall Brown 1860; William Pierce Frye 1850 h 1889, U.S. Senator from Maine; Barrett Potter 1878, secretary of the President and Trustees; Edward Stanwood 1861 h 1894, editor and historian; President Hyde h 1886; William LeBaron Putnam 1855 h 1884, judge of U.S. Circuit Court; Samuel Valentine Cole 1874 h 1898, president of Wheaton Seminary; Melville Weston Fuller 1853 h 1888, chief justice of the United States Supreme Court; Andrew Peters Wiswell 1873 h 1900, chief justice of Maine; General Joshua Lawrence Chamberlain 1852 h 1869; General Oliver Otis Howard 1850 h 1888; Ira Pierce Booker, treasurer; Reverend John Smith Sewall 1850 h 187°

Thomas Brackett Reed 1860 of Portland—"Czar Reed"— was the most powerful speaker in the history of the U. S. House of Representatives, although he eventually left Congress in dismay over U.S. colonialism after the Spanish American War. At the same time between 1896 and 1899, Bowdoin graduates held three of the highest posts in Washington: Reed as speaker, Melville Weston Fuller 1853 of Chicago as chief justice, and William Pierce Frye 1850 of Lewiston as president pro tem of the U.S. Senate

The Reverend Samuel Harris, Class of 1833, Bowdoin's fifth president (1867-1871). Uncomfortable in the role of fund-raiser and disciplinarian, Harris left Bowdoin for Yale, where he continued his distinguished career as a theologian.

CHAPTER SEVEN

Within a few years of the end of the Civil War, it was clear to even the most loyal friends
of the College that the institution was suffering a decline. Overcoming their almost legendary
conservatism, the Boards first turned for reform to a war hero and popular governor,
General Joshua L. Chamberlain, Class of 1852. He reshaped the classical curriculum
to include engineering and more modern science instruction, but his tenure was marred by
ill health and the student "rebellion" of 1874 against his required military drill.
Where Chamberlain met frustration, the young William DeWitt Hyde met remarkable success.
He transformed the look of "Old Bowdoin," the quality of the faculty, and the outdated
curriculum, becoming in the process a national spokesman for muscular Christianity
and the cause of the small liberal arts college.

THE WOUNDED KING

In his Northampton retirement, ex-president Allen relished the gossip from Bowdoin relayed to him by various callers. The Reverend Charles Dame, Class of 1835, for example, brought him some particularly welcome news in September of 1866. Leonard Woods, Jr.—who had replaced Allen in Brunswick twenty-seven years earlier—was on his way out. He was "not acceptable to the orthodox . . . accused of utter indifference as to the late religious revival . . . rides to chapel at prayers—but no lectures—no preaching." His critics had long suspected Woods of being at heart a High Church Anglican who had never been brave enough to leave the Congregational faith; his enemies, Allen was told, reported "that when at Rome, [Woods] walked on his knees down stairs of V[atican] C[ity] and was proud of having sat in chair of St Peter. His reliance is on a majority of the Board of Trustees [that] is unitarian and democrats etc. . . . Also, has not shown himself a Unionist in public."[1]

In the wave of patriotic feeling and, in some quarters, desire for revenge on the South and its sympathizers that swept the North after Lincoln's death, it is not surprising that Woods—who on one notorious occasion in Chapel during the war had avoided praying for the Union until shamed into it by the students—

was eased into retirement in 1866. His replacement, the theologian Samuel Harris, of the Class of 1833, did not last long. Whatever Woods's shortcomings, he had been an accomplished fundraiser and overall a mild disciplinarian; Harris, though a popular teacher, doubted his own ability to be a "successful beggar" and, according to his biographer, found that the cares and vexation of the presidential office, particularly controlling the students' penchant for hazing, gave him the "jim-jams."[2] He resigned in 1871 and went on to a distinguished teaching career at Yale. A Brunswick newspaper editor concluded that Harris had been "strict, faithful, and conscientious in the discharge of duties," adding that "it is no fault of his that matters here are not in the state that the best friends of the college could desire."[3]

Chamberlain was the logical candidate to succeed him. Returning to Brunswick from the war restless and often depressed, troubled by his wounds and an unhappy marriage, he had found some satisfaction in state politics, where, thanks to his military fame, he was elected to four terms as governor.[4] Already a member of the Board of Trustees, he agreed to accept Harris's place as president—a fourth career, as it were, after being a teacher, soldier, and statesman. As Trulock observes, "His experience as a Bowdoin student and professor brought a particular insight to the requirements of the school, and

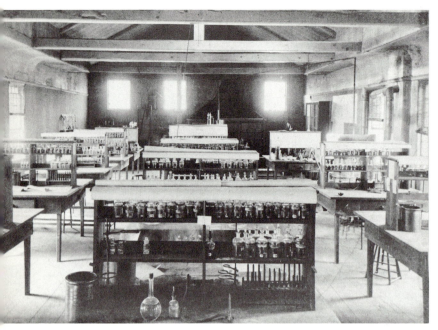

The chemistry laboratory in Commons Hall, now the Carpentry Shop, 1879. The hall had been built in 1829 to house a student-operated dining facility. The alternative, throughout the nineteenth century, was for students to board with families in town.

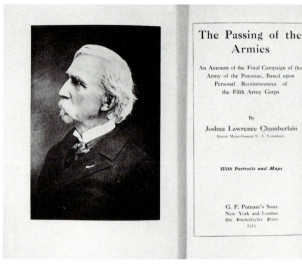

Published posthumously, The Passing of the Armies, *1915, describes the final campaigns of the Civil War in Virginia, and recounts General Chamberlain's controversial decision to order his troops to salute the defeated Confederates at Appomattox.*

A civil engineering class, 1877-1878, in Winthrop Hall. Part of Chamberlain's reform program was a short-lived science and engineering course, designed as an alternative to the classical curriculum. The most famous engineer to come out of this course was the Arctic explorer Robert E. Peary, who earned a B.S. in 1877.

his subsequent years of leadership in the army and state gave him the confidence, presence, and prestige to help carry out his ideas."[5] Before his term ended, he was to have to draw heavily on all three reserves.

Chamberlain had seen the future and knew that it did not look like the institution he had inherited from Harris and Woods. This was confirmed by some alumni, a group who, as their professional and commercial careers began to prosper in the post-war decades, expected to play a larger role in the College's affairs. (Traditionally, there had been no requirement that a Boards member had to be a graduate, an inheritance from the time when there simply were not enough alumni of the desirable age, prestige, and availability to fill the seats.) As an alumnus wrote Chamberlain from Minneapolis in 1874, the very rich W. D. Washburn, Class of 1854, on whom the College was counting for a large donation, had changed his mind: "He takes the ground that Bowdoin is too sectarian, that she is not out of the hands of *Old Foggies* and that you, Sir, are too strong a sectarian to manage its concerns. . . . What canvassing I have done convinces me that some radical changes yet remain before Bowdoin can command the monies of all persons."[6]

The new president was certainly aware of the need for reform. He struck that note immediately in his inaugural address on "The New Education," perhaps the best inaugural the College has ever heard in terms of a new president's willingness to express a vision in very concrete terms. He first paid a wistful tribute to "the dear old college":

It stood erect, though it moved not; apart from the people, its voice reaching not far into the din of the times; supported by few, yet not forlorn; proud even in its isolation. Yes, after all its glorious history, the high purposes of its character and fame of its Presidents and Professors, its most distinguished roll of graduates and most noble record of good works, something had gone. Men meant it all too much when they said "Old Bowdoin." Something about the tone seemed like the *Ilium fuit*, some *pius Aeneas* had borne off the old Anchises, and the story took on an antique, epic style, whereof in like fashion the first books were the best. . . . Yes, gentlemen something

had come between the college and the life of the people. . . .The college had touched bottom, not so much by the fault of men, as the fate of things.

He had several proposals to carry the College beyond "the cloister spirit." A greater emphasis on science was, for the moment, the most important of them; the Boards agreed to a new Scientific Department, which introduced, into an otherwise traditional curriculum, courses such as civil and mechanical engineering and drawing for those who sought the Bachelor of Science degree. The department was to last for ten years and attract about one-quarter of the undergraduates, by far the most famous of them Robert E. Peary, Class of 1877. (Its demise had a great deal to do with the growth of the State Agricultural College in Orono, with its free tuition and easier admission standards.)[7]

Chamberlain was even bold enough to suggest replacing Greek and Latin with more emphasis on French and German (both of which had been available since Longfellow's professorship, but in brief doses). He went on to deliver a line that must have startled much of his audience:

Woman too should have part in this high calling. Because in this sphere of things her "rights," her capacities, her offices, her destiny, are equal to those of man. She is the Heaven-appointed teacher of man, his guide, his better soul.

He left his endorsement of some form of coeducation at that for the moment, and, affirming the enduring importance of religion—Bowdoin should be "not a sectarian but a Christian college"—he declared:

This is my hope and ideal for the college—that it may be indeed a lofty seeker after truth, but more than all a lifter up of men. I fear not the age, with all its hot haste. Let it come and stir all minds and all hands. Let it be a new Elizabethan age—dazzling discoveries, broadening science, swift-following invention, arts multiplying, civilization advancing, new fields of thought and labor, new prizes of courage, new rewards of toil, new aspects and fashion of all things![8]

It was a splendid vision, yet somehow it failed. Writing seventy years later, in an engaging account of Brunswick's "Golden Age"—the last two decades of the century—Edward Chase Kirkland described Chamberlain's "harrassed administration" at a college that "after three-

"WARUP."   "THERE WILL BE NO DRILL AT BOWDOIN."   "DID."

'76

Office of the Corresponding Secretary of the

Class of "Seventy-Six," Bow. Coll.

JOHN A. MORRILL, *Pres.*

A. T. PARKER, *Treas.*   JOHN H. PAYNE, *Vice Pres.*

FRANK C. PAYSON, *Cor. Secy.*   *Box 764.*

Portland, Me.,   *187*

Letterhead of the Class of 1876, with the motto "There will be no drill at Bowdoin." Student opposition to required military training led to the "Drill Rebellion" of 1874, a major setback in Chamberlain's plan to reshape the College.

The staff of the student newspaper, the Bowdoin Orient, *1890. The paper was first published in 1871 as a biweekly; it has been a weekly since 1900.*

BOWDOIN COLLEGE, Nov. 12, 1873.

DEAR SIR:—

At the approaching meeting of the Boards of Trustees and Overseers, the Students of Bowdoin will ask leave to present the following petition:

"We, the undersigned, Students of Bowdoin College, would respectfully petition that the Military Department in this institution be abolished, for the following reasons:

First. Injury to the institution from loss of students.

Second. Abundant facilities for more popular and profitable exercise.

Third. Expense incurred in purchasing otherwise useless equipments.

Fourth. Loss of a large proportion of time devoted to study.

Fifth. Its intense and growing unpopularity, and other subordinate reasons."

This is signed by 126 out of the 133 persons to whom it was submitted—that is, by the three upper classes, with the exception of one senior, five juniors, and one sophomore.

They will also ask leave to send a committee to the meeting with this petition, for the purpose of more fully explaining just what is meant by its several propositions, and to give the reasons which have led to this extraordinary step.

Our high respect for our military instructor, our belief that the Faculty, Trustees and Overseers have the best interests of Bowdoin at heart, in this as in all other matters, and the supposition that previous knowledge of the petition will render them better prepared to discuss its subject, and to consider the earnest wishes of the petitioners, if so they shall choose to do, form our sole excuse for troubling you with this communication.

Very respectfully,

A. G. BRADSTREET, ⎫
M. W. DAVIS, ⎬ Com.
G. B. WHEELER. ⎭

Three members of the Class of 1874—Albion G. Bradstreet, Marshall W. Davis, and George B. Wheeler—sent a printed letter to the Governing Boards in 1873 urging the abolition of drill. Although some Boards members were sympathetic, they supported Chamberlain's emphasis on military science and agreed with him in deploring student insubordination.

quarters of a century [was] a provincial institution still, ridden with denominationalism, starved for funds, limited in curriculum."

He went on:

The eminent analyst of railroad finance, Henry Varnum Poor, departing from his fiftieth anniversary in sober mood, noted that there were fewer students in the college than in 1835, there was an air of apology about the campus, "an appearance of weakness on every side," and that the only thing that had grown was the campus trees.[9]

There were several burdens under which Chamberlain labored—the appearance of rival colleges in the state, the conservatism of the Board of Overseers in particular, the beginning of the state's century-long economic slump—but none that seems to have demoralized him so much as the famous Drill Rebellion of 1874. Student unrest had been a regular feature of American collegiate life since the eighteenth century, but the post-war era had seen much less overt rebellion—for one thing, Victorian notions of gentility had "tamed" the student population; for another, the gradual emergence of what was to be known as "campus life"—fraternities and organized athletics—was beginning to claim students' free time. The Drill Rebellion stands out all the more sharply, then, suggesting that it went beyond mere situational discontent.

The facts were simple enough. Remembering how ill-prepared his own generation had been for military duty, and concerned with the "softness" that a more comfortable way of life had brought to the middle classes, Chamberlain had instituted in 1872 a system of military drill, under the direction of Major Joseph P. Sanger, an officer assigned to the College along with twelve artillery pieces by the War Department. The drill was accepted at first without too much fuss; the students joked about aiming the cannon at the still-uncompleted Memorial Hall and created a great stir by scaring away the horses with their noisy salute at the Topsham Fair.[10] But when the novelty wore off, something about the drill—possibly Sanger's overbearing manner, possibly the required purchase of a partial uniform, possibly Chamberlain's long and detailed list of military regulations—began to irritate the "cadets." In November of 1873, the students

Students found gymnastics a far more healthful and invigorating activity than military drill.

petitioned the Boards to abolish the drill. They were ignored, and by May of 1874, feelings were sufficiently intense to lead to an incident on the parade ground (the students made rude noises—some said they "groaned"—upon being given an order; six were punished).

To the extent that the new biweekly, *The Bowdoin Orient*, reflected student opinion, a drastic change of mood had taken place. In June of 1872—the newspaper's second year of operation—an editor had reminded his fellow students of the important role that citizen militias had played in the nation's distant past. Yet the tradition had died out, and "when the rebellion broke out, the country—in the North at least—was wholly uninstructed in the science of war. . . . In the first battle they were driven back in disgraceful rout." The writer went on to acknowledge that a few people thought military drill out of place in a college and argued in reply that "considered merely as an exercise to alternate with the gymnasium, it is valuable." For example, it gave "an erect carriage, a manly bearing and precision and grace of movement."[11] Yet by July of 1873, the newspaper could report: "Many heartily like the 'drill'; many are carelessly indifferent; many, very many, are quietly but thoroughly restless and dissatisfied, many are openly and bitterly rebellious."[12]

The notion of "manliness," as employed by both sides, is a key to the quarrel. To Chamberlain and Sanger, manliness meant mili-

Rowing at Bowdoin goes back at least to 1858, when the Bugle *reported two boat clubs in existence. Bowdoin was an active participant in intercollegiate regattas in the 1870s and '80s. By 1894, however, when the last race was held, football had replaced crew in popularity and the Androscoggin River was becoming polluted. The activity was revived as a club sport in the 1980s. This photograph shows the crew in 1890.*

Varsity crew, 1882. The glass slide from which this photograph was taken is signed by Professor Leslie A. Lee, who taught natural history, geology, and biology from 1876 until his death in 1908.

Crew Field Day, 1889, on the banks of the Androscoggin, showing the boathouse that stood immediately east of the railroad bridge. The boathouse was moved on the ice in 1898 to Merrymeeting Park, where it became a bowling alley.

tary prowess and a willingness to make sacrifices in the name of duty. To many of the students, on the other hand, manliness meant independence and forthright expression of one's point of view. Stung by the Boards' refusal to treat with respect a petition signed and politely offered to the College authorities by 126 of the 133 students affected by the drill requirement, *The Orient* asked: "Were these not fair and manly steps? Did they not entitle the petitioners to be treated as men, and be met in a manly way?" On the contrary, "no more notice was taken of the petition than of the drifting of the snow about old Massachusetts. . . . Is it not natural that we feel indignant at this contemptuous treatment?"[13]

Henry Johnson 1874 h '14—a future professor of modern languages, librarian, and first director of the College's art museum—brought his father up to date in a letter a few days after the parade ground incident:

A crowd of students unknown have sometime in the last night painted some inscriptions in black paint on the front of the chapel and on the chapel door coming down profanely on the military department of this institution and the military officer placed here. They show a low sentiment enough but a true one on the part of the students. Such notices must gall Chamberlain as the military is his pet scheme.[14]

By 28 May 1874, the fathers of about three-quarters of Bowdoin's student body got a letter from the general himself, saying in part:

On Friday last, at the hour for drill, the greater part of the Sophomore and Freshman classes refused to report for duty. During the day it became known that a majority of the Junior, Sophomore, and Freshman classes had bound themselves by a written agreement to resist the drill at all hazards. . . . It was clearly the duty of the Faculty [on Monday] to deal first of all with concerted rebellion against lawful authority, and a rebellion, too, of no ordinary magnitude, for in addition to their demand to be exempted from drill, it was well known that the disaffected students had bound themselves to leave in a body if their leaders were sent away. The Faculty therefore decided as a first step to send home every man who persisted in his refusal to comply with all the requirements of the College. . . .[15]

To Chamberlain's generation, the notion of "rebellion" had particularly troublesome connotations.[16] He gave the absent students until 7 P.M. on 8 June 1874 to return to campus and

sign a document renewing their matriculation pledge to follow the College's rules, or to face permanent expulsion. All but three of the students capitulated. But it was a shallow victory for Chamberlain. As he was to write later, "the toil and trial to me [as president] has been far beyond anything I ever experienced in the field."[17] That fall the drill was made elective—with the far more popular gymnastics offered as an alternative—and only a handful of students turned out. By 1879, the faculty decided to recommend ending the program; the Boards agreed to do so in 1882, and the next year Chamberlain, suffering terribly from his unhealed wound from the battle of Petersburg and frustrated by the College's continued decline, resigned. He dabbled—not very successfully—in Florida real estate, as had Harriet Beecher Stowe.[18] (Whatever bitterness remained had dissipated by 1878, when Chamberlain returned from serving as United States commissioner of education at the Paris Universal Exhibition. The students met his train and, led by a band, escorted his carriage to his house. He made a speech of thanks, and "the air was rent with cheers for President Chamberlain and B-o-w-d-o-i-n.")[19]

Newspapers from as far away as New York published generally hostile accounts of the students' actions, but there must have been several points prior to May of 1874 when, given a little common sense and willingness to compromise on both sides, the whole thing could have been defused. This did not happen. To the students, the drill was an onerous burden that detracted from their studies, took time from sporting activities (such as the newly-popular crew) that were even more healthful, and in general did not belong at a liberal arts college.[20] Many of the Boards members agreed with them, but Chamberlain was not used to being disobeyed, and what was at first a reasonable protest turned into a clash of wills.

Given these circumstances, a question remains: why did the drill offend the students so grievously? Was there something in the very nature of military activity that prompted them to rebel? In other words, was there an unconscious

The President's House, built in 1860 at 77 Federal Street, before being moved to 85 Federal in 1874. The house was bought for Samuel Harris, then sold and repurchased in 1890 and rented to President and Mrs. Hyde. It served as the President's House for the next ninety-two years, and is today the college Office of Development.

Like most nineteenth-century college presidents, the Reverend William DeWitt Hyde (president 1885-1917) not only presided over the institution, but also hired its faculty, interviewed students for admission, dealt with the more serious disciplinary problems, courted prospective donors, and taught classes in moral philosophy.

Because of the presence of James Bowdoin III's art collections and the Walker Art Building, 1894, on the campus, Bowdoin was one of the first colleges to teach formal art appreciation courses as part of the curriculum. This turn-of-the-century classroom, in the basement of the Walker Art Building, is full of copies of European works.

Gentler pursuits than gymnastics or football also occupied the students' ample leisure time, as seen in this late nineteenth-century photograph of students playing tennis on the future site of Hubbard Hall.

repulsion at work beneath the very real list of complaints they had about what, to Chamberlain, seemed an essential reform? One possibility in this regard would be to consider the Drill Rebellion as a kind of delayed reaction to the Civil War itself. Many of the fathers, uncles, and older brothers of the Bowdoin students of 1872-1874 had fought in that war, often with traumatic consequences. There was too much emotion invested in memorializing the event for the students to oppose any aspect of the war openly. Yet how could so terrible a thing happen to a nation without some long-range psychological damage even to the victors? And, other than widows and orphans and the like, what group of civilians would have been more sensitive to this feeling than a cohort of men a little too young to have experienced at first hand the most cataclysmic event of the century? We do not know enough about the long-term impact of the war on the civilian population to make any categorical statements, but at least the possibility of a kind of war-weariness—half revulsion, half guilt—could help explain as singular an event as the rebellion against Chamberlain's militarization of Bowdoin.

THE YOUNG HERO

Viewing the situation at Bowdoin at the close of Chamberlain's presidency, the *Boston Post* suggested that what the College needed "is money and brains, the former with fat interest available, and the latter in the head of a big-headed, big-hearted, and well-informed president."[21] For the Boards' first choices, in Kirkland's nice phrase, "it was a distinction to be asked; it was a danger to accept." The candidate who accepted—after two years of searching on the College's part—was a twenty-six-year-old Harvard-trained minister who, after seminary at Andover, had been a pastor for two years in Paterson, New Jersey. It was an inspired decision, though some were skeptical at the time. William DeWitt Hyde was to transform Bowdoin from a failing country college into an examplar of a style of higher education that was to challenge the domination that the large universities exercised over American higher education in the last decades of the nineteenth century. Small colleges like Bowdoin were never to begin to match the intellectual capacities of the new German-inspired research universities, nor fulfill the range of social and econom-

Physical education was not a matter of informal games but, under the aegis of Dudley Sargent and Frank N. Whittier 1885 m 1889 h '24 (who, in his varied career at Bowdoin from 1886 to 1921 was director of physical training, taught hygiene and bacteriology, and was college physician), a medically calculated progression of exercises and drills designed to train specific muscles. These photographs, from about 1904, taken in the first Sargent Gymnasium, now the Heating Plant, show the progression over three years.

Sophomore Year—Dumb Bells.

Sophomore Year—Boxing.

Junior Year—Broadswords.

Senior Year—Foils.

196

ic roles played in the nation as a whole by the huge new land-grant institutions. But they kept alive the idea of a highly moralistic, highly personalized style of undergraduate teaching, and their graduates were to have an influence on the country out of all proportion with the colleges' size. In essence, Hyde took the disadvantages of the old-fashioned college—its small size, rural isolation, tradition of piety, and fondness for professors who taught by force of personality more than by intellectual example—and turned them into virtues.

In purely programmatic terms, Kirkland summed up Hyde's achievement well:

A pioneer in college athletics, Dudley A. Sargent 1875 h 1894 was performing with a circus when he was hired as Bowdoin's first director of gymnastics in 1870. He kept the position while studying for his degree and then taught gymnastics at Yale, where he received his M.D., and at Harvard, where he was director of gymnastics from 1879 to 1919.

. . . within a decade he had enlarged the faculty, raised its salaries, established separate professorships in history and government and a new one in economics and sociology, given a new status to science and modern languages, liberalized entrance requirements, and inaugurated, perforce, the elective system. For the old orthodoxy and evangelicalism, he substituted "muscular Christianity." Nothing demonstrated the liberalization of the college better than the fact that in 1888 Hyde was able to advocate the election of Cleveland before the Young Men's Democratic Club of Brunswick. Although he did not escape censure, he at least kept his job in a college whose visiting committee some thirty-five years before had condemned undergraduates for political activities.[22]

Hyde literally transformed the campus. The Bowdoin of Chamberlain had been, for the most part, a "row" of buildings—as were many early nineteenth-century colleges—facing the street across an open "yard." The first year of Hyde's presidency—1885—saw the addition of a modern gymnasium (later to be a student union, then the heating plant), named for Dudley Sargent, Class of 1875, who first at Bowdoin, then more famously at Harvard, more or less invented the modern idea of collegiate physical education. The architectural *annus mirabilis* of 1894 saw the opening of McKim, Mead & White's Renaissance Revival Walker Art

Building—to this day, the finest public building in Maine—and Henry Vaughan's eclectic Searles Science Building. With the addition of Vaughan's medievalized Hubbard Hall in 1903, the yard was turned into a quad.

It was a day of "hands on" college presidents, at least at small colleges—Hyde did everything from run admissions to give sermons around the state—but his two great loves were teaching and advocacy. Presidents of small colleges were still expected to conduct a senior course on ethics and philosophy, and there had been a tradition at least since Mark Hopkins's day at Williams to use this course to leave an indelible impression on the minds of earnest, though sometimes less than intellectual, students.[23] Hyde was a master of the art. His Teddy Roosevelt-style athleticism won the respect of students who might have ignored a more bookish teacher, yet his ability to popularize philosophical and theological ideas made his listeners feel that, yes, they finally *understood*. "The President's course in Philosophy is the deepest thing yet," Henry Hill Pierce '96 wrote to his mother. "We are studying Royce's *Spirit of Modern Philosophy* now and the president makes everything as clear and absorbing as possible."[24]

Hyde had been a promising student of Hegelian idealism under George H. Palmer at Harvard (and, as it turned out, a close observer—though not uncritical admirer—of President Eliot as an educational reformer), but his real gift, as his extraordinarily long bibliography suggests, was as a popularizer of the progressive ideas of his day. The country was full of half-educated people, many of whom had interrupted their studies in order to earn a living, and a good number of whom hungered for someone who could explain to them what they had missed. Hyde had the philosophical training and

The gift of Harriet Sarah and Mary Sophia Walker in memory of their uncle, Theophilus Wheeler Walker, the Walker Art Building was designed by Charles Follen McKim of McKim, Mead & White. The facade was modelled after the Villa Medici in Rome and several other Renaissance buildings.

World War I had a far greater impact on New England college campuses than did the Civil War. The presence of men in uniform became a regular feature of collegiate life, as suggested by this 1915 cartoon from Judge magazine, showing the Walker Art Building in the background.

This view of the east face of the Mary Frances Searles Science Building was sold as a postcard by the college bookstore in the early twentieth century. Designed in "Jacobethan" style by Henry Vaughan, the building was a gift in 1894 from Edward Searles in honor of his late wife, the heir to the California railroad empire assembled by her first husband, Mark Hopkins.

This 1896 view of the Delta shows the baseball diamond on the present site of Sills Hall. The name derives from the triangular shape of the lot, which could be flooded in winter for hockey. During World War I, the field became an army encampment.

This 1907 bird's-eye-view of the College is part of a series of American college and university campus drawings by F. D. Nichols. Searles Hall appears lighter in color, with its original surface of glazed yellow brick, later covered with paint. The streetcar is traveling on the Harpswell Road, which until 1948 ran between Adams Hall and the main campus.

the belief in a cheerful, forward-looking, not very doctrinal Christianity that made him perfect for the task. Among his most popular works were *Practical Ethics* (1892), *From Epicurus to Christ* (1904, and as *The Five Great Philosophies of Life*, 1911), *Self-Measurement* (1908), *Outlines of Theology* (1895), *Practical Idealism* (1897), *God's Education of Man* (1899), and *Jesus' Way* (1902).

In addition to dozens of religious and ethical essays in some of the leading magazines of his day, Hyde also published works that guaranteed him a place as one of the most popular theorists of higher education in late nineteenth- and early twentieth-century America. (These publications also helped carry the name of Bowdoin College across the country.) His famous "Offer of the College" expressed a Newmanesque faith in the broadening powers of a liberal arts education, an idea he expanded in *The College Man and the College Woman* (1906). Next to a benevolent Deity and a country run by upright Anglo-

Saxons, Hyde believed most strongly of all in the mission of the small college. He summed up this mission in the *Educational Review* in 1891:

For combining sound scholarship with solid character; for making men both intellectually and spiritually free; for uniting the pursuit of truth with reverence for duty, the small college, open to the worthy graduates of every good high school, presenting a course sufficiently rigid to give symmetrical development, and sufficiently elastic to encourage individuality along congenial lines, taught by professors who are men first and scholars afterward, governed by kindly personal influence, and secluded from too frequent contact with social distractions, has a mission which no change of educational conditions can take away, and a policy which no sentiment of vanity or jealousy should be permitted to turn aside.[25]

Bowdoin was the laboratory in which he tried out his theories, and it was clear by the gala Centennial of the chartering of the College in 1894 that both he and the institution were a success.[26]

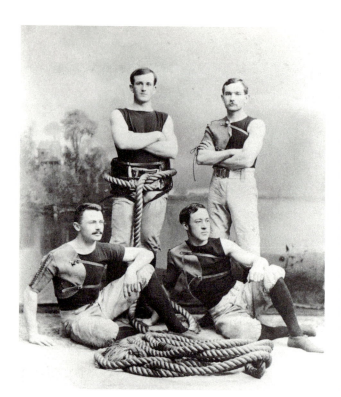

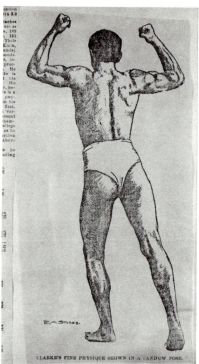

An article from an unidentified (Portland?) newspaper about Walter Bradley Clarke '99, who was the fourth strongest male New England college student, according to a table listing his measurements and those of his competitors. The Sandow pose is a reference to a famous German physical culturalist of the day.

CLARKE'S FINE PHYSIQUE SHOWN IN A SANDOW POSE.

Class "rushes"—attempts by the sophomores to push the freshmen through a door, for example—were a regular feature of antebellum collegiate life. In the later nineteenth century, efforts were made to channel these inter-class rivalries into athletic events like the tug-of-war. This photograph shows the tug of war team in 1891.

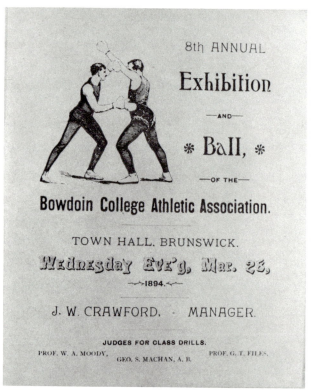

The program for the 8th Annual Exhibition and Ball of the Bowdoin College Athletic Association, Town Hall, Brunswick, Maine, 28 March 1894. The entertainment consisted of fencing, pole vaulting, tumbling, Indian club drills, and other gymnastic stunts. From the scrapbook of Herbert O. Clough 1896.

Date 10/12 '97.		7.30 o'clock	
Age	19	Depth Chest	19
Weight	69.7	" Abdomen	19
Height Standing	177	Breadth Head	15.3
" Sitting	89.6	" Neck	10.8
" Knee	48	" Shoulders	42.5
" Pubic Arch	90.5	" Waist	26.5
" Navel	109.5	" Hips	34
" Sternum	152.4	" Nipples	18.6
Girth Head	57.8	Shoulder Elbow R	38.5
" Neck	34.5	" L	37.5
" Chest	91	Elbow-Tip R	48
" " Full	96.3	" L	49.2
" Ninth Rib	86	Length Foot R	25.7
" " Full	91.2	" L	25.7
" Waist	76.5	" Horizontal	
" Hips	94	Stretch of Arms	
" Thigh R	57	Capacity Lungs	235
" L	56.7	Strength Lungs	14
" Knee R	37.5	" Back	155
" L	37.5	" Legs	340
" Calf R	35.5	" Chest	
" L	34.5	Up. Arms	90.6
" Ankle R	21.9	Fore Arms	83
" L	21.7	Total	682.6
" Instep R	24	Development	545.5
" L	24	Condition	134.1
" Up. Arm R	30	Vision	10
" L	30	Hearing	10
" Elbow R	25.5	Pilosity	3
" L	25.5	Color Hair	B Br
" Fore Arm R	26.6	" Eyes	Br
" L	26.6	Temperament	120-144
" Wrist R	16.5		
" L	16.5		

As part of the athletics program at the turn of the century, each student was measured and a sequence of exercises recommended to develop his physique toward a perfect standard. This is the card of Herbert L. Swett '01.

Student rooms before the Civil War had been sparsely furnished, but new standards of comfort, encouraged by the rapid increase in consumer goods, meant that students in the second half of the century could emulate the domestic interiors of the time in their dormitories. This is the interior of 15 Maine Hall in 1880.

Gender illusionism was an important element in student theatricals in the years before World War I. Here is Warren Eastman Robinson '10, dressed to play a female role in a student production of She Stoops to Conquer. Special Collections has a group of these studio photographs, which were exchanged among the actors. Lieutenant Robinson died in service in France in 1918. His wife, Anne Johnson Robinson, daughter of Professor Henry Johnson, donated in his memory the memorial gateway on the Hawthorne-Longfellow Hall corner of the campus.

In 1897, during renovations to Appleton Hall, some Delta Kappa Epsilon relics were found in the basement. The New York Evening Post ran this sensational "Chamber of Horrors Found Under a Dormitory at Bowdoin College" on 24 July, alleging that torture implements and human bones were among the finds. Its retraction was printed a short time later, but the story attested to public fascination with undergraduate secret societies.

The main living or reception room of the Delta Kappa Epsilon House, ca. 1900-1901. The appearance of well-appointed fraternity houses in the years 1890-1910 helped change the social character of student life at Bowdoin.

Maine Street, 4th of July, ca. 1890s. The Brunswick Town Hall (center), designed by John Calvin Stevens in 1883, was razed in 1961 and replaced by a Newberry's store. Its auditorium had been the scene of many student theatricals, concerts, and gymnastic exhibitions.

Parade float from Brunswick's 150th anniversary celebration in June of 1889, in front of the current Cram Alumni House at 83 Federal Street. The original entrance to the 1857 house was, as the photo shows, on the side.

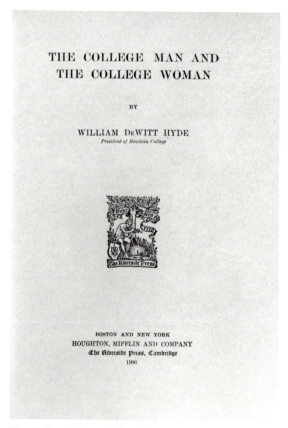

THE COLLEGE MAN AND
THE COLLEGE WOMAN

BY

WILLIAM DeWITT HYDE
President of Bowdoin College

BOSTON AND NEW YORK
HOUGHTON, MIFFLIN AND COMPANY
The Riverside Press, Cambridge
1906

The College Man and the College Woman, 1906, is a collection of essays by President Hyde, who wrote frequently for national publications on educational, religious, and ethical subjects. The standard version of Hyde's "Offer of the College" appears as the first chapter of this book.

A drawing from the 1906 Bugle depicting the Class of 1875 Gateway, designed by McKim, Mead & White in 1902. The columns and their flanking urns marked the entrance to the walkway toward the Chapel.

Football is first recorded at Bowdoin in 1869, although it had been played in some rudimentary form since the 1820s. The College's first intercollegiate contest, played in Portland on 12 October 1889, saw Bowdoin lose to Tufts, 8-4. By the end of the century, football had surpassed all other sports as the collegiate athletic activity. Among the members of Bowdoin's 1895 team was (first row, left) Donald B. MacMillan 1898, the author and Arctic explorer.

Not all the outdoor exertion was on the playing fields. In 1891, a group of students and young alumni led by Professor of Biology Leslie A. Lee sailed in the Julia Decker to Labrador. Austin Cary 1887 h '22 and Dennis M. Cole 1888 discovered and named Bowdoin Canyon, below Grand Falls, as members of the Bowdoin College Scientific Expedition to Labrador.

The first recorded baseball game took place on 29 September 1860 on the Delta; the juniors beat the seniors, 23-13. A college nine was formed in 1864, a forerunner of this later nineteenth-century team.

203

BCSC is Special Collections, Hawthorne-Longfellow Library, Bowdoin College.

1. William Allen Journal, 1861-1866, 25 September 1866, Forbes Library, Northampton, Mass.

2. Frederick William Whittaker, *Samuel Harris, American Theologian* (New York, 1982), p. 43. In 1871, Yale elected Harris to the Dwight Professorship of Didactic Philosophy, a chair that he was to hold for twenty-four years. He published little of consequence until his sixty-ninth year (1883), when there appeared his *Philosophical Basis of Theism*, a major work; he continued publishing until his eighty-second year, which saw the two-volume *God: The Creator and Lord of All*, an attempted summary of his moderate theological views. According to his nephew, Harris left Bowdoin because "administration was not to his taste, nor was he well fitted for it," and because he wished to return "to the more congenial work of teaching theology." Whittaker, p. 47.

3. Whittaker, p. 47. One victim of Harris's effort to stamp out hazing was Edward Page Mitchell, Class of 1871, a co-founder of *The Orient*, author of the hazing song "Phi Chi," and later the famous editor of the *New York Sun*. In 1870, the sophomores of Phi Chi stormed a room defended by several of the brawnier freshmen. Several men were knocked unconscious by clubs—one was feared dead—and the faculty expelled or suspended many of those involved. See Louis C. Hatch, *The History of Bowdoin College* (Portland, Me.: Loring, Short and Harmon, 1927), p. 128, for details. Mitchell recalled years later: "I was suspended for the greater part of one year. . . . Shall I go so far in candor . . . as to confess that the disgrace of this discipline to myself, my family, and friends appeared so ineradicable, so terribly blighting, that I thought for a while there was no way out of it but laudanum." His family was more sympathetic, and rather than kill himself Mitchell returned "at the end of the penal term" to enjoy the rest of his college career, although he admitted he should have entered at age nineteen, rather than fifteen. He got his start in journalism in 1871 as a result of a letter from Chamberlain on his behalf to Edward Stanwood, Class of 1861 (pictured with the Trustees on p. 184), later well known as editor of the *Youth's Companion*. E. P. Mitchell, *Memoirs of an Editor: Fifty Years of American Journalism* (New York, 1924), pp. 73-74.

4. A full account of the wound Chamberlain suffered at Petersburg, Virginia, on 18 June 1864 is to be found in *The Medical and Surgical History of the War of the Rebellion*, part 2, vol. 2, *Surgical History* (Washington, D. C., 1876), p. 363, a massive compendium of wounds interesting enough to the medical profession to be published. A minie ball had hit Chamberlain in the right hip and passed through to the other hip, slicing through his urethra and part of his bladder. The medical interest of the case arose from the catheter technique used by the Army surgeons (it is illustrated, fig. 286). A fistula formed, through which urine escaped, and its failure to heal properly caused Chamberlain severe pelvic pain for much of the next half-century and necessitated several more operations. His biographer, Alice R. Trulock, suggests, rather obliquely, that the injury may have left Chamberlain impotent, or at least sexually dysfunctional, from age thirty-six on. For whatever reason, his marriage—already strained by his long absences during the war—began to fall apart during his four years as governor, Fannie Chamberlain choosing to spend most of her time at the Brunswick house rather than in Augusta. At one point, they were close to divorce. *In the Hands of Providence: Joshua L. Chamberlain and the American Civil War* (Chapel Hill, 1992), pp. 340-341.

5. Trulock, p. 342. Chamberlain, who was professor of rhetoric and oratory and lecturer in comparative philology, had served briefly in 1866 as acting president of the College upon Woods's resignation. His career as governor had been successful, though controversial. Although elected in the Republican sweep of the North in 1866, he proved independent-minded, opposing his party on the Fifteenth Amendment (he did not think newly freed slaves should have the right to vote) and siding with Senator Fessenden in opposing President Andrew Johnson's removal from office. The other two measures that brought him much criticism were his opposition to a special constabulary to enforce the state's prohibition laws and his refusal to commute the sentence of a former slave condemned to be hanged for rape and murder. He was an unconventional politician, but the voters of Maine elected him to four one-year terms. Trulock, pp. 338-339.

6. William Pitt Morgan [Class of 1869] to J. L. Chamberlain, Minneapolis, 29 June 1874. Chamberlain Papers, Maine Historical Society, Portland.

7. Harris deserves credit for taking the first steps to modernize the teaching of science at Bowdoin. In 1867-1868, the curriculum was expanded to include senior-year courses in botany, zoology, physiology, and geology, and two new faculty members were hired in the sciences. Surviving as a memorial of this local "renaissance" are the two volumes of the fortnightly *Bowdoin Scientific Review* (15 February 1870-17 September 1872), edited by professors Cyrus Fogg Brackett 1859 and George Lincoln Goodale m 1863.

8. J. L. Chamberlain, "The New Education," typescript copy, BCSC. Chamberlain's views on coeducation were in contrast to those of Harris, who, in his essay "The Complete Academic Education of Females," had argued that while women ought to study the same curriculum as men, amid similar collegiate facilities, this education should take place in exclusively female "institutes." Endorsing the notion of separate spheres, Harris saw well-educated women as providing "a more genial and liberal culture" that would "ennoble and refine the whole character of society," the masculine part of which was too given over to business pursuits and "the meaner and more worldly passions." *The New Englander* 11 (May

1853), pp. 295-320. A writer in *The Orient* in the year of Chamberlain's inaugural took a stronger stand: women's "standard of morality must deteriorate" if they were exposed to the temptations which men face in college. "When these ladies will give evidence of being able to resist strong temptation, and will manifest a disapproval of the dissipation that already is, it will be time to talk of admitting them to our colleges." *Orient* 1, no. 4 (29 May 1871), pp. 50-51.

9. Edward Chase Kirkland, *Brunswick's Golden Age* (Lewiston, 1940), p. 27.

10. In a similar spirit, *The Orient* reported: "One impulsive youth, acting on a classical model, has engaged his 'end-woman' [a housekeeper in the residence halls] to polish his armor. This delapidated Venus, clad in calico 'long-short,' may daily be seen, vigorously applying whiting and chamois-skin, while the gentler Mars, seated in his easy chair, pipe in mouth, contemplates her jute switch through 'neutral tint' eye glasses." *Orient* 3, no. 2 (14 May 1873), p. 21.

11. *Orient* 2, no. 5 (17 June 1872), pp. 66-67.

12. *Orient* 3, no. 6 (9 July 1873), p. 63.

13. "The Petition before the Boards," *Orient* 3, no. 14 (11 February 1874), p. 159.

14. Henry Johnson to "Dear Father," Brunswick, May 1874. Henry Johnson Papers, BCSC.

15. J. L. Chamberlain to "Dear Sir," 28 May 1874, one-page printed letter, with space left to fill in the son's name, copy in BCSC.

16. This feeling was widely shared by most of the commentators in the press. The *Brunswick Telegraph*, for example, noted: "People in this vicinity who remember the splendid Maine regiments in the war are surprised at the pother made on account of the few hours' weekly drill under an officer of the United States Army." 29 May 1874.

17. J. L. Chamberlain to Hon. Samuel H. P. Lake, Brunswick, 29 February 1878[?], copy in Chamberlain Papers, BCSC.

18. Chamberlain had to face one more rebellion, and this time he acted with greater skill. In 1880 a dispute over state election results between Republicans and a "Fusionist" ticket of Democrats and the Greenback-Labor Party almost resulted in civil war as Augusta filled with armed partisans of both sides. As commander of the state militia, Chamberlain was called in, for a tense twelve days, to keep the peace. As Trulock writes, "he accomplished that seemingly impossible task without calling out his troops or shedding blood, using only his judgment, courage, and the force of his personality," p. 359. *The Orient* commented: "As virtual dictator of the State of Maine, the whole strain of government came upon him in a time when that strain was the greatest. . . . It is a high compliment to his integrity, and a certain proof of their confidence in him, that both sides felt that the State was safe in his hands, and submitted willingly to his authority." Vol. 9, no. 13 (4 February 1880), pp. 150-151.

19. *Orient* 8, no. 11 (18 December 1878), p. 109. At the Chapel some days later, he was welcomed on behalf of the faculty by the aged Professor Packard, who pointed out that "this was the second occasion in the history of the College when its President was welcomed home from Europe" (Leonard Woods, Jr., being the first). After leaving the presidency (though not the faculty), Chamberlain busied himself on Wall Street and in Florida (where he had first gone for his health) and served on several corporate boards. He kept his Brunswick house (now the Pejepscot Historical Society's Chamberlain Museum), which in 1867 he had moved from Potter Street to its present Maine Street site, and which he had elevated in order to add a large first floor beneath the original cape. When Longfellow returned for his fiftieth Reunion in 1875, he was shown the rooms, now on the second floor, in which he had lived as a newly-wed young professor. Trulock writes: "Longfellow wept and declared that the rooms looked the same as in his day; he then told Chamberlain that he had composed several poems while gazing into the fireplace in the sitting room," p. 349. In 1893, Congress awarded the general the Medal of Honor for his gallantry at Gettysburg. He ended his days in Portland, where he held the patronage job of surveyor of the port and where he was "a familiar and distinguished sight in the city—a straight, upright figure with white hair and flowing white moustache" (Trulock, p. 372). He spoke often in public about his Civil War experiences. He died on 24 February 1914, in his own bed in Portland, from the cumulative effects of the wound at Petersburg, nearly fifty years earlier.

20. For a thoughtful and well-reasoned account of the students' point of view, see "The Situation," *Orient* 4, no. 3 (3 June 1874), pp. 26-32.

21. Quoted in Kirkland, p. 27.

22. Kirkland, pp. 28-29.

23. Hopkins, the most famous small-college president of the mid-nineteenth century, taught at Bowdoin in 1873-1874 (after retiring at Williams) as "provisional professor of mental and moral philosophy."

24. Henry Hill Pierce to "My dear Mother," Bowdoin College, 22 January 1896, Pierce Family Papers, West Baldwin, Maine.

25. William De Witt Hyde, "The Policy of a Small College," *Educational Review* 2 November 1891, pp. 320-321.

26. Hyde generously gave credit to Chamberlain for advocating "the very reforms, using often the very phrases, that are now the commonplaces of progressive educational discussion. Modern languages, science, classics in translation, political and social science, research, individual instruction: all these were included in the program of the professor in 1859 and the President in 1872." All that Chamberlain lacked, Hyde said, was the funds with which to implement them. "President Hyde's Eulogy," *Orient* 43, no. 30 (3 March 1914), p. 239.

Robert E. Peary 1877 as an undergraduate, wearing his Delta Kappa
Epsilon fraternity pin. Peary carried the fraternity banner with him
to the North Pole in 1909.

Robert E. Peary 1877 in his admiral's uniform.
Although some scholars feel that the surviving evidence is inconclusive, Peary is generally recognized
as being the first explorer to reach the North Pole.
He was accompanied in the entire trek across the ice
by Matthew Henson, veteran black member of the
crew. On his return, although in poor health, Peary
worked for the U.S. Government in promoting military airpower.

Alfred C. Kinsey '16 as an undergraduate.
Perhaps the only twentieth-century Bowdoin
graduate whose name is a household word, Dr.
Kinsey made his reputation first as an expert
on the taxonomy of the gall wasp and then as
a pioneering researcher in human sexuality.

The Sigma Nu house held a smoker the night Franklin Delano
Roosevelt was elected to his third term as president, 1940.
Listening to the results coming in over the radio were: l to r,
Alfred D. Shea '42; Professor Noel C. Little, who taught physics
from 1921 to 1966; unidentified; Professor Edward S.
Hammond, who taught mathematics from 1921 to 1963; Mr.
Russell; Dr. Lusker; Professor Robert P. T. Coffin '15 (sitting);
and Professor Orren C. Hormell, who taught history from 1911
to 1951. The College gave an honorary degree the following year
to Wendell Willkie, who lost the election.

Peary shaking hands with President Theodore Roosevelt at Oyster
Bay, New York, on board the S.S. Roosevelt, 7 July 1908.
Thomas Hamlin Hubbard 1857, a New York lawyer and
Bowdoin Trustee, was a major backer of Peary's expeditions to
the North. Peary exemplified the strong, vigorous, and determined
"college man" championed by Roosevelt and President Hyde.

CHAPTER EIGHT

The College that had been rebuilt during the thirty-two years of William DeWitt Hyde's presidency survived remarkably intact for much of the twentieth century, thanks in large part to the thirty-five-year stewardship of Kenneth C. M. Sills. The First World War and the Great Depression left a mark, but a superficial one; the Second World War, however, brought in its wake a range of social and cultural changes that not even a small college in coastal Maine could avoid. Some of these changes were not evident until the late 1960s and 1970s, a period that called into question many of the verities that to Hyde and Sills had seemed eternal.

BOWDOIN BEATA

From the 1930s until his death in 1955, there was no more famous an American on the poetry lecture trail than Bowdoin's Robert Peter Tristram Coffin. A member of the Class of 1915 and Pierce Professor of English at the College for much of his career, a tireless producer of poems and essays, an idiosyncratic teacher and crowd-thrilling public performer, he was as well known in his day as Robert Frost, that other great student of things New England. But Coffin's reputation—much of it based on live performance—did not survive his passing, and today he is remembered, if at all, as a Maine regionalist, an artist who captured a vanishing (often already vanished) piece of rural America. Above all, he was a poet of the Depression years and World War II, offering to troubled people the kind of solace that grew out of reading his idyllic recollections of childhood on a saltwater farm.

In 1951, he published a small book of essays on the art of georgic poetry called *On the Green Carpet*. He saw the poet as "the man of metonymy," a person for whom "the part must represent the whole but in quick, short particulars." Coffin said his formula for writing a lyric poem was "a process of narrowing in." The more confined his setting, the stronger the poet. "He grows through the provincialization of his emotions." He offered as an example his chosen Maine. It was not the Maine of "woods and lakes and mountains" but the Maine that is "woods and mountains and sea." But there were 3,000 miles of coast, and scores of great bays, and he knew he must choose one—Casco Bay.

Yet Casco bay has over two hundred islands in it, and several scores of handsome smaller bays. I must draw in. I take Harpswell as part of my bay. But there are two Harpswells: the Neck and its open fields; and the other, eastern, island half with its forests of pointed cedars and laces of firs and spruces bearded with age.

Still there are too many islands in Harpswell; so he chooses Sebascodegan. But which of its many coves and harbors?

I will select its northwestern spire, the peninsula of my father, Lost Paradise Farm. Still, when I come to write of this farm I lived on, certain hills and harbors of it, Apple Tree Cove, Lower Oak Landing, and Dragonfly Spring, stand out above all the rest. So, finally, I have come to my one dedicated greenest glade, under the ledge. . . . Concentration is consecration. I have put metonymy into practice. I have gone inward, gone homeward, come into my own.[1]

However successful this might have been as a formula for writing poetry, it certainly caught the mood of many of the people Coffin lived among—and even more it charmed those who lived elsewhere and who looked to Maine for an escape from their anxieties. As Coffin went on to say, "the green carpet that is Maine has been least changed in the process called progress, least invaded and discolored by cities and the urban mind. Its people are still chiefly country people; and its people have 'stayed put,' as the colorful and exact colloquial phrase is; they, in their ancestors, have been here a long time."[2]

So had his college, by American standards.

The College's collection of paintings and drawings was exhibited in the Walker Art Building until 1937 in the multi-tiered fashion seen in this late nineteenth-century photograph of the Bowdoin Gallery (in the center rear is a plaster cast of the Hermes of Praxiteles, Hawthorne's Marble Faun). Upon his arrival in 1937, Philip C. Beam, now Henry Johnson Professor of Art and Architecture Emeritus, the first professionally trained director of the museum, redesigned the permanent installations, initiated temporary loan exhibitions, and started publishing well-designed catalogues to accompany exhibitions. The Rembrandt to the left of Professor Beam in the right photograph, ca. 1950s, was on loan from the widow of Sir Harry Oakes 1896 h '41, a gold-mining magnate whose mysterious murder in the Bahamas in 1943 is still unsolved.

The fiftieth annual dinner of the Bowdoin Alumni Association of New York City, Hotel Brevoort, 31 January 1919. President Sills is at the head table. Some of the younger alumni are still in World War I uniform.

A meeting of the Bowdoin College faculty, ca. 1943, in the faculty meeting room on the third floor of Massachusetts Hall, which was in the process of being converted from the old Cleaveland Cabinet. Provisional identifications are as follows: back row on left side of table, l to r: Thomas Auraldo Riley '28 (German, 1939-1973), Cecil T. Holmes (mathematics, 1925-1964), Philip W. Meserve '11 (chemistry, 1915-1940), Reinhard L. Korgen (mathematics, 1931-1965), Fritz C. A. Koelln (German, 1929-1971), Charles H. Livingston (Romance languages, 1921-1957), Thomas Means (Greek and Latin, 1921-1954); front row on left side of table, l to r: unidentified, unidentified, Morgan B. Cushing (economics, 1922-1956), Nathaniel C. Kendrick h '66 (history, 1926-1966, dean of the College, 1947-1966), Roscoe J. Ham h '44 (German, 1901-1945), Orren Chalmer Hormell h '51 (history, 1911-1951), Dean of the College Paul Nixon (classics and history, 1909-1952); President Sills at the head of the table; Kenneth J. Boyer (library, 1927-1961, college editor, 1961-1967) at the foot of the table; Herbert W. Hartman, Jr. (English 1928-1945), Edward S. Hammond (mathematics, 1921-63), Frederic E. T. Tillotson h '46 (music, 1936-1963), unidentified, Stanley Perkins Chase '05 (English, 1925-1951).

Pulitzer-Prize-winning poet Robert Peter Tristram Coffin '15 h '30, Pierce Professor of English from 1934 to 1955, was not only a very dramatic teacher, but was also a popularizer, on a national scale, of the pastoral image of life on the coast of Maine. In the tradition of Longfellow, he and Robert Frost were perhaps the last of the American poets whose public performances drew large crowds.

The note of looking inward, of filiopiety, of slightly longing for more glorious times one had heard about from one's father or grandfather, of taking pleasure in things local and familiar—this was very much the mood of Bowdoin College for at least half of the new century. The College's sense of its ideal self had changed. For Joseph McKeen, the model of the College had been that of a classical seminary producing virtuous—and, he hoped, pious—republicans; for Leonard Woods, Jr., a retreat from the tensions of the Jacksonian Age into an invented "medieval" past. Joshua Chamberlain's would-be military academy for scientists and engineers had given way to William DeWitt Hyde's earnest country college, turning out Christian gentlemen who were nonetheless prepared, body and spirit, for the world's fight. In the second, third, and fourth decades of the twentieth century, yet another model emerged: that of the College as a family, a nurturing home where the wounds of two World Wars and the Great Depression could be healed. As a 1933 issue of the Bowdoin Alumnus characteristically announced, "More than a third of our freshmen are bound to Bowdoin by relatives who have preceded them here"—twenty sons, five both sons and grandsons, thirteen brothers, among the 152 members of the Class of '37.[3] (Their names were usually listed; their photo, on the museum steps, would soon appear in the Portland and Bangor papers.) If you hadn't any blood relations in the matriculation book—the book that had been signed by every new freshman since 1802—you nevertheless had a kind of honorary standing in the long, and frequently invoked, line of statesmen and poets and generals and Arctic explorers who had walked the campus before you. Some of their luster would rub off on you simply by your being at Bowdoin beata, the blessed place.

Above all, you were the inheritor of the college of William DeWitt Hyde. It was a place where knowledge was valued, but not more so than character. Verbal skills, wit, acquaintance with the best thoughts of the ages—all these were appreciated, but no more so than scoring the winning touchdown against Colby or helping to take a hockey trophy away from the University

One of Kenneth Sills's jobs as dean of the College (1910-1918)
was to carry the diplomas to the First Parish Church on
Commencement Day.

Kenneth C. M. Sills '01, of Portland, as he
looked on graduating from Bowdoin.

President and Mrs. Sills with friends on a visit to the Acropolis, 20 March
1934. Both Casey and Edith Sills were fervent classicists; he held the
Winkley Professorship of the Latin Language and Literature from 1907 to
1946, and Mrs. Sills, a graduate of Wellesley, taught Greek to Brunswick
high school students.

President Kenneth Charles Morton Sills '01 h '34 and his
wife, Edith Koons Lansing Sills h '52, in the library in the
President's House at 85 Federal Street, ca. 1950. Upon arriving at the President's House for tea, many freshmen were surprised to find that Mrs. Sills already knew their names and
hometowns. One of the factors in the Sillses' popularity was
their ability to make students, returning alumni, and visiting
dignitaries feel at home at 85 Federal.

of Maine. Your teachers were Christian gentlemen who were kind and attentive but often had no great expectations of you in the classroom. Much of your real life would take place in your fraternity's chapter house, where you would learn the real lessons of college life and where you would make the friends you would see again, at the courthouse or Legislature or bank or country club or at least at Homecoming Weekend, for the rest of your days. Several times a year, masses of females would descend on the campus; the rest of the time *you* had to go find *them* on the weekends. You sang a lot, and occasionally drank too much. You fell asleep in Chapel, or at least did your last-minute homework there. You were not rich, but you weren't poor either, and there was always a French-speaking world of laborers down by the mill to remind you that you lived in a privileged enclave.

Such was Bowdoin, allowing for various anomalies, during the years between the two world wars—and beyond. One way of trying to make sense of this now (mostly) vanished College is to see how each of the presidents since Hyde tried to live with his legacy, especially at those moments when they—or, more often, some external force—tried to change the place.

THE SILLS ERA

In the summer of 1917 President Hyde died, probably of overwork. His last public appearance had been to give a speech in support of the war effort. To many, the choice of a successor was obvious, but the Boards once again took their time. During Hyde's final years much of the administrative work of the College had been done by his very able young dean, Kenneth C. M. Sills, of the Class of 1901. Whether it was his religious denomination (Episcopal), his politics (Democratic), or his temperament (a good deal less frenetic than Hyde's), he was not the Boards' immediate choice. In retrospect this reluctance seems improbable, for "Casey" Sills—as he was to be known to a generation of graduates—was to become the first Bowdoin president not simply to be respected and obeyed but genuinely loved by

many of the students who passed through the College in his thirty-four years in office.

There are so many people on the scene who knew him, or thought they knew him, so well, it is difficult to separate the man from the legend. One place to start is the amiable biography *Sills of Bowdoin* by Herbert Ross Brown h '63. Trying to capture the "anomaly" of the man, Brown in 1964 described him in these terms:

President Sills was an Episcopal layman without formal theological training, yet none of the seven ordained Congregational ministers who had preceded him in office was more devoted to the Church. Although he faced the difficult experience of following a "giant," and believed William DeWitt Hyde was "the greatest president Bowdoin ever had or is ever likely to have," he immediately proved his fitness by relying on the momentum generated by his predecessor while quietly initiating an educational program of his own. Perhaps few college presidents possessed less of the managerial temperament or had more impatience with modern gadgets to increase efficiency, yet even fewer achieved his detailed mastery of the operation of his institution. Never entirely happy as a fundraiser, he nevertheless recognized the truth of President Robert Hutchins' dictum that a college which is not short of money has run out of ideas. The fivefold increase in Bowdoin's endowment during his administration is evidence not only of Kenneth Sills's persuasive statements of the needs of the college but also of the generosity of donors when a president exemplifies as well as endorses the values of a liberal education.[4]

The first great crisis to be dealt with was simply getting the College through the war. Most of the undergraduates had been persuaded to stay in school, but at various times in 1917 and 1918 the campus seemed less a college and more an armed camp. In the summer a Maine artillery regiment took over the Delta, its officers using the fraternity houses as quarters, its Catholic members using the Chapel for mass. The Students' Army Training Corps absorbed the attention of 225 undergraduates; social and extracurricular life almost ceased, especially when the coal shortage and later the influenza epidemic of 1918 reached Brunswick. Some 1,100 Bowdoin men were to serve in the war, 233 of them students who left college. Twenty-four alumni and students died in service, though very few of them in battle.[5]

The clay-floored General Thomas Worcester Hyde Athletic Building, 1913, better known to students as Hyde Cage (shown here, ca. 1940s), was the scene of track and field competition and early spring baseball practice until 1986. In 1993, it is being renovated to serve as the David Saul Smith Union, a campus center designed by Hardy, Holzman, Pfeiffer Associates, New York. The Hyde name will be perpetuated in the adjoining plaza.

For all the extraordinary disruption of routines, the general mood, judging from student publications, was upbeat, even energized. A writer in *The Bowdoin Orient* in October of 1918 captured the campus scene quite well:

It seems indeed strange to see uniformed soldiers marching across the Campus to their meals, to hear them lustily singing war songs under the leadership of an officer as they pass by and to catch glimpses, through the trees, of them at drill. It is impressive to hear the notes of the bugle summoning them to the work of the day or sounding taps at its close. Perhaps the most inspiring sight of all is to witness retreat. Lined up in straight erect rows before their respective barracks, as the dormitories are now styled, these student-soldiers stand at attention while the colors are lowered from Memorial Hall. Is it not an arresting thought that in the future upon the west wall in the auditorium of this building there may be placed the names of some of these very men as a sign that they have given all for their country?[6]

The small college towns of early twentieth-century New England were fertile ground for producing eccentrics, particularly among that class of scholars who had sufficient independence of means and a firm enough local footing to say and do whatever they pleased. Yet surely few others of this genre could match, either for eccentricity or for sharpness of tongue, Brunswick's Marshall Perley Cram, of the Class of 1904. He taught chemistry at the College from 1908, the year he received his doctorate from Johns Hopkins, until his death in 1933. Although a legend in his own day, he is remembered now chiefly because he left the family home at 83 Federal Street—where he had lived (first with elderly relations, then with a select group of students) most of his life—to the College, which now uses it as an alumni house. Even there only the William Morris tiles around one fireplace and the stone Chinese camels in the garden remain as a fragment of the densely arrayed collection of curiosities—the bear trap over the piano in particular being much commented upon—that once made his bachelor dwelling one of the sights of the town.

Cram deserves more recognition than that, however, because in the years 1917-1919 he proved himself a diarist of striking talents. A long-lost Brunswick comes back to life in the pages of this lonely man's reflections on the course of the war in a small college town; we know he knew the story was worth telling, for he made three extra copies (with the less kind remarks excised) and put them in the college library.

Cram's love of gossip, his sharp eye for details, his penchant for being suspicious about anything out of the ordinary—any stranger in town with a German accent was at risk of being reported by him as a spy—all appear in the diary. So do his many dislikes; at age thirty-six, already a curmudgeon, Cram did not approve of women, Germans, Jews, Democrats, Catholics, Episcopalians, French Canadians, Bolsheviks, or many of his neighbors, with the exception of Kenneth Sills next door. (When many of his friends departed for officer training at Plattsburg, he observed, "Probably a good many married men are welcoming it as a heaven-sent opportunity to get away from their wives in an entirely respectable and commendable manner.") He was the only member of the Medical School faculty to vote repeatedly in favor of closing it down—he compared its moribund state to that of the Ottoman Empire.

As a teacher, he had a very low opinion of the intellectual powers of his chemistry students; he took delight in giving an exam in which the answer to the first two questions was found in the third, just to see how many students would fail to notice it. His friends found him a singular combination of kindliness and asperity. Since so many of these friends were called away in wartime, Cram had to look to the students for intellectual company. "Two sophomores called in the evening and staid three hours and one half. I regard it as a tribute to the conversational ability of the three of us that we were not reduced to discussing athletics at all."

Part of the appeal of the diary lies in its everydayness. Cram—who is said to have asked for a copy of *Emma* on his deathbed—remembered a remark "of old Miss McKeen's, who once said that when she felt that she ought to go out and make calls and did not want to, she took down a volume of Jane Austen, and was certain to find there just what she would get if she went out calling in Brunswick." Much of his talent lay in being able to capture the mild absurdities of daily life: "Had a call from a boy scout who was out canvassing for Liberty Bonds," he notes in April of 1918. "He said that Dr. Gross had started an Audubon Society for them, but only a few of the boys had joined it. I asked him why. . . and he said it was because the boys wanted to kill birds."

Cram missed very little. Passing by the Chamberlain House, then rented out to students, he noticed that someone from the Medical School had propped open his window with a human arm or leg bone. In September of 1917 he drily notes:

At noon an alarm was turned in for the old house at the corner of Market Lane, known to the neighbors as Chateau La Pointe in honor of the name of the owner. Professor and Mrs. Hutchins noticed the shingles on fire, but kept still in the hope that the flames would get a good start.

The diarist Marshall Perley Cram '04 (left) taught chemistry from 1904 to 1933 at Bowdoin and at the Medical School of Maine. His house at 83 Federal Street, which he left to the College, now houses the Office of Alumni Relations.

On the subject of fires, in the midst of Brunswick's wartime coal shortage he reports:

Mrs. Slocum told Mrs. Nixon that she had never known a year when the medical school had such odiferous material for dissection. You can ordinarily smell it across the street by the school house, but this year Mrs. S. thought that she could smell it over at her house on Federal Street. What she smelled tho was not from the medical school, but from Prof. Copeland's furnace. He has been out of coal for a fortnight and has been burning the Lord knows what. The smoke from his chimney smells like a garbage incinerator or a crematory.

This penchant for the slightly macabre runs throughout Cram's diary, perhaps because he worked as a forensic chemist for various legal agencies. Amid routine references to his effort to grow potatoes in his backyard or deal with frozen pipes in the fraternity houses, Cram will without warning note: "Dead baby's stomach

213

Miriam Look MacMillan h '80, wife of Admiral Donald Baxter MacMillan 1898 h 1918, and a group of North Greenland Inuit on the deck of the Schooner Bowdoin *at Siorapudoo making wire recordings. Mrs. MacMillan wrote several books about the expeditions she and her husband undertook, and she served as curator of the Peary-MacMillan Arctic Museum in the 1970s.*

A group of students, some from other colleges, on the quarter deck of the Schooner Bowdoin *on the 1949 Labrador expedition. Horace A. Hildreth, Jr. '54 is second from the left, Miriam MacMillan at center.*

Donald B. MacMillan at rest on the ice cap at the head of Bay Fiord, North Greenland, on the 1923-1925 expedition. As a young man, MacMillan had accompanied Peary on his final, and successful, expedition to the Pole.

Some members of the crew of the 1922 expedition in front of the bow of the Schooner Bowdoin, *l to r: unidentified, unidentified, Donald MacMillan, Ralph S. Robinson '05, Harold Whitehouse, Richard Goddard.*

Between 1930 and 1954, Admiral and Mrs. MacMillan took several crews of faculty and students from Bowdoin and other schools with them on their cruises. The 1934 Schooner Bowdoin *expedition, with these men aboard, went up to northern Labrador and the Button Islands. Front row: Luther G. Holbrook '34; Dr. David Potter; Commander Donald B. MacMillan 1898 h '10; Professor Alfred O. Gross h '52, Josiah Little Professor of Natural Science 1921-53; George Crosby; Howard Vogel; back row: Lawrence B. Flint '34, Robert B. Wait '34, William Brierly, Samuel Braley Gray, Jr. '34, Henry B. Hubbard '34, William R. Esson '35. This photo was probably taken in Gross's classroom on the second floor of Searles: note the stuffed bald eagle behind the group. The Peary-MacMillan Arctic Museum has artifacts from the expedition, including William Esson's photographs, films, and diary.*

arrived today" or "remains of poisoned dog cooling on the windowsill." His expertise ranged from testing for foul play to assaying the homemade red wine the sheriff had seized from "some Italians" in Portland. Cram had always been an inveterate worrier—from an early age he had carried a list of "things to do" in his waistcoat pocket, should he suddenly learn he had only twenty-four hours to live—and the uncertainties of wartime had doubled his anxiety. (And Sills's, too: Cram reports that the still-unmarried president had a nightmare that all the faculty had been drafted and the Boards had replaced them with women.)

With frequent scare reports of German U-boat activity in the Gulf of Maine, Cram was taking no chances. He calmly assessed the probability that Portland's waterfront would be bombarded and that fire would rage uncontrolled because saboteurs would have broken the water main from

Sebago Lake. "Brunswick would be burned flat in case any German force landed near here, or was able to send a landing party. As for the College, the securities would be taken, or Germans placed in control. All teachers would be replaced by Germans." Cram—who kept a map of France in his study with Allied positions indicated with pins—was fascinated by every scrap of wartime news. He noted with interest, for example, a report by a Bowdoin student returned from the ambulance corps that "three quarters of the aviators take cocaine before going up for a battle flight." Given the idealization of the war later at the College, it is interesting to read the postcard message Jack (John Richard) Edwards, Jr., Class of 1918, sends back from ambulance service in France:

At night it is a 4th of July, batteries, star shells, fusee mitraileuse, shouts of camion drivers, rumble of artillery going up to the front, braying of burrows

For a generation of Bowdoin people, Clara Hayes, secretary of the College from 1918 to 1952, was a familiar presence, seated outside the president's office in Massachusetts Hall. This photograph was taken in March of 1935.

Well-known in his day as a translator of the Latin poet Martial and playwright Plautus, Paul H. Nixon h '43, dean of the College and professor of Latin for nearly all of the Sills years (1918 to 1946), shared an office with Sills—and one long table– in what is now the McKeen Study. Both men were classicists; Nixon, who had come to the College in 1909, continued to teach as Winkley Professor until his retirement in 1952. Nixon's translations of Plautus helped to inspire the film and musical A Funny Thing Happened on the Way to the Forum.

The installation of the Polar Bear in front of Sargent Gymnasium in 1938 with the sculptor, F. G. R. Roth, on the right. The polar bear was informally adopted as the mascot of the College as a result of Peary's fame as an Arctic explorer. The statue was the twenty-fifth reunion gift of the Class of 1912.

Hubbard Grandstand, 1904, at Whittier Field, was the work of the same architect, Henry Vaughan, and the gift of the same donor, Thomas Hamlin Hubbard, as the library, Hubbard Hall, the previous year. The later addition of further seating has somewhat obscured the lines of Vaughan's freestanding pavilion.

The Commencement procession, with honorary degree recipients, 1904: l-r, President Hyde h 1886; Trustee Samuel Valentine Cole 1874 h 1898, president of Wheaton College; man behind unidentified; Trustee (and former president) Joshua Lawrence Chamberlain 1852 h 1869; man behind unidentified; Trustee Oliver Otis Howard 1850 h 1888, founding president of Howard University; Edward Little Professor of Rhetoric and Oratory Wilmot Brookings Mitchell 1890; and Trustee Thomas Hamlin Hubbard 1857 h 1894. Author Kate Douglas Wiggin Riggs, behind Hubbard in the white dress, was about to become the second woman to receive an honorary degree from the College (Sarah Orne Jewett received the first one in 1901).

(asses). I bet you can hear it all, if you can picture me, scared as hell, with a cart full of "couches" groaning. To-day is Easter. I went to a little hospital church and was impressed with the spirit of the singing; the poor devils were singing for their salvation, for in a few days they will be blown in half and that means work for me. I sure am getting sick of cheese and wine. I found a lot of "Bosche" souvenirs in a deserted trench filled with many rotted unburied Germans. Good night. Americans don't know what war means, filth, mud, sickness, ruins, and rain.

On the homefront, there are other battles to attend to. At Sills's inauguration in 1918, one of Cram's many duties is to make sure that Donald MacMillan's stuffed polar bear is carted from the train station to the alumni luncheon on time—a chore that leads him to grumble that he saw no point whatsoever in Arctic exploration. But it is Kate Douglas Wiggin Riggs—the author of *Rebecca of Sunnybrook Farm*—who really puts him in a fighting mood.

Ladies were admitted to the gallery for the first time, and as there were two delegates from the women's colleges we had to let Mrs. Riggs into the Commencement Dinner. We did keep her off the platform in the church, however, by placing her at the

end of the procession, which I consider a triumph. She got an honorary degree from the college fourteen years ago, and since then has appeared regularly at Commencement in cap and gown, and preempted the front corner seat in the trustees section of the platform, the only woman there, and she being merely the holder of an honorary degree of which there must be several score.

(Mrs. Riggs was to have the last laugh, though a posthumous one: since 1986, the front sitting room of Cram's house has been designated by the Society of Bowdoin Women as the Kate Douglas Wiggin Room; her portrait hangs over Cram's tiled fireplace.)

Amid his sputterings, Cram proved himself a thoughtful observer of the College, severely strained as it was by the wartime disruptions, the shortage of fuel and food, and in 1918 the influenza epidemic. He reflects, for example, on "what kind of a character we should be trying to develop in college":

The graduate with whom a college has a right to be satisfied, should be scrupulously honest, reliable, and punctual. He should pay his bills promptly, and be firmly resistant to any temptation to incur obligations

217

McKim, Mead & White's Moulton Union, 1928, provided a club-like set-ting for student activities and dining facilities for students who did not join fraternities.

Cover of the Bowdoin Alumnus, *vol. 1, no. 1 (1927). The College established the magazine in 1927 to keep the alumni informed of events and class news. The first editor was Austin H. MacCormick '15, alumni secretary from 1921-1928, who went on to become a well-known crim-inologist and prison reformer. The magazine con-tinues under the name of* Bowdoin.

The cast of Macbeth *on the steps of the Walker Art Building, probably in June of 1924. The early twentieth-century custom of producing a Shakespeare play outdoors at Commencement began with* The Taming of the Shrew *in 1912.*

In 1919, the College commissioned McKim, Mead & White to design a war memorial, but it took until 1930 to raise the necessary funds. The original plan called for placing the memorial flagpole in the center of the Quad. Students, however, regarded this space as their own, and one spring night expressed their resistance to the plan by placing the newly delivered pole as far as it would go into the Chapel. The College got the point and erected the flagpole instead between the Walker Art Building and Hubbard Hall. President Sills is seen here inspect-ing the damage.

which he cannot fulfill. He should be generous and willing to support organizations, but courageous enough to refuse to support any which he is convinced are without value. He should have good judgment and be quick witted; virile and not effeminate. He should be kindly, agreeable, and clean minded, and should keep his person clean. He should be industrious and courageous, both physically and morally. He should have self control and a good temper, and possess a sense of proportion. Without being a busybody, he should in time of need voluntarily assume disagreeable duties and unpopularity, and should be able to keep his own counsel. He should speak and write good English, and should have ideas, wit, and something to say for himself.

But the real purpose of the diary seems to have been to keep Cram's own spirits up. Waiting for the impending death of his old friend Professor Henry Johnson, Cram reflects:

There are two ways of getting courage to meet great personal losses. The first is to erect the hypothesis that there is a personal God, who is interested in the welfare of each individual. . . . This is satisfactory if a person wishes to give morphine to his soul to get pleasant dreams. The second way is to erect a bulwark of selfishness about one's self, and not get harrowed up by sympathy for the sorrow of others, but to remember that few events anticipated as coming evils in the past have turned out to be so really distressing after they have actually happened.

He never completely loses his sense of humor. Inspecting the new infirmary—in which several students were soon to die of flu-related pneumonia—he notes the lack of suitable books in the waiting room to soothe an anxious mind. "At present the waiting visitor must choose between two volumes. 'The First American'—a book of poems by Dean Sills—and Dr. Gerrish's book for freshmen on 'Sex Hygiene.'"

He knows for certain that wartime has ended a month after the Armistice when he notices that "the boys are beginning to appear in civilian clothes once more, as bonny a sight as the crocuses in spring." Cram returns to this vernal theme the following March, when he launches into a long quotation from Swinburne on spring after witnessing a stranger's arrival home:

Have seen a rather moving incident in the street car from Portland recently. I was in the car coming from Yarmouth, to Freeport one morning about eleven o'clock. Sitting in the corner seat of the car was a young man in a private's uniform, with the gold

Four of Bowdoin College's most famous coaches, taken in 1937. Adam J. Walsh, captain of the 1924 Notre Dame team known as the Four Horsemen and the Seven Mules, coached by Knute Rockne, was one of college football's greatest centers. He was head coach of Bowdoin football from 1935 until World War II forced suspension of athletics in 1943. Rejected for Navy duty because skull fractures had disrupted his hearing, he coached the NFL Rams for one year before returning to Bowdoin 1947-1958. John J. Magee, coach of track and field from 1913 to 1955, after whom the Magee Track at Whittier Field is named; Malcolm E. Morrell '24, director of athletics 1925-1967, after whom Morrell Gymnasium is named; and George D. Shay, hired to coach football when Walsh was coaching in the NFL in 1946, who stayed on until 1950 as Walsh's assistant and as coach of tennis and basketball.

stripes on the arm to indicate service overseas. I had not noticed him especially until I saw that he was getting off the car in front of the waiting-room in Freeport, when it was apparent that he was walking lame. On the sidewalk about 50 feet away there were standing three or four girls, bare headed, who looked as tho they had suddenly come out from working in the shoe factory, who were watching the people get off the car. Suddenly one of the girls saw the man, and in one leap she had started towards him. She had no thought for time, place, crowd, or anything else; her man had come home. [7]

It was a tribute to Sills's administrative talents that the College returned so quickly to normal when the Armistice came. Bowdoin seemed less rattled by the Jazz Age than some other colleges, perhaps due to New England sobriety, perhaps

The Bowdoin College state championship hockey team, 1937-1938. Front, l to r, Charles Nelson Corey '39, later a coach at Bowdoin, 1955–1965; Daniel Hanley, later college physician (1943-1980) and longtime physician to U. S. Olympic teams; L. Frederick Jealous, Jr. '39; Leonard E. Buck '38, captain; C. Ingersoll Arnold '39; and Oakley A. Melendy '39. Back row, l to r, Manager Edwin L. Vergason '39, David G. Doughty '40, Robert N. Bass '40, William B. Allen '39, Roger W. Tucker '40, and Coach Linn S. Wells.

Until the 1970s, Bowdoin had only a handful of students of color. Masque and Gown took advantage of the presence of Richard K. Barksdale '37 h '72 (kneeling, center), to cast him in the lead of Eugene O'Neill's The Emperor Jones, 1937, along with various white actors in blackface. The cast included Stanley Perkins Chase '05, Henry Leland Chapman Professor of English from 1926-1951, thirteen other faculty members and faculty wives, and one other student, Matthew W. Bullock '40. Barksdale, now an Overseer Emeritus, went on to a career as a professor of English and administrator at Morehouse College, Atlanta University, and the University of Illinois.

The second floor auditorium of Memorial Hall was the scene of many public events before Pickard Theater was installed in its place in 1955.

220

World War II had an even more dramatic impact on the life of the College than had World War I. By the academic year 1943-1944, the number of civilian students on campus had fallen to 152, but there were many hundreds of new faces in uniform. The College played host to an Army-Air Force meteorology unit and a Naval radar school.

due simply to the lack of diversion in a rather quiet town. Across the country, the 1920s were the great age of "Campus Life," as the extracurriculum threatened to take over the nation's colleges, and it is worth noting that, according to his recent biographer, even so gifted a student as the writer and editor Hodding Carter, Jr. '27, seems to have spent almost no time on his not very demanding studies but a great deal working on the *Quill* or helping run his fraternity or messing about in undergraduate politics.[8]

The one major incident of student "unrest" in the interwar years was the much-publicized Memorial Flagpole incident in the spring of 1930. The McKim, Mead & White structure was to be placed in the center of the Quad, despite student protests over that choice of a site. The enormous pole had arrived, but enough students gathered one Saturday night to move it— or as much of it as would fit—into the central aisle of the Chapel. It was removed the next day

only with great difficulty, and the students' point was taken; the flagpole, with the names of the war dead on the neoclassical base, was erected between the Walker Art Building and the corner of Hubbard Hall. Although some newspapers in the state saw a conspiracy of "pacifists" at work, it was only a prank, though one with a message. Chamberlain might have gone ahead; Sills was reasonable enough to listen to his students.[9]

The interesting details of Sills's long presidency—including his landmark battle with a group of alumni over control of the College's increasing popular athletic program in 1934—can be found in the courtly pages of Brown's biography. But the essence of his approach can be summarized rather briefly: Sills intended to preserve the College as Hyde had left it to him. The results were mixed. Had he returned in 1952, there is much Hyde would have recognized, in the tone of the place, the easy manner in which the College blended into the community (at

An avid amateur photographer, Edward T. Richardson, Jr. '43 captured the flavor of student life at Bowdoin on the eve of World War II in the album of photographs that he took as official photographer for the Sigma Nu fraternity. His album is now in Special Collections.

"My corner, 1940." Edward Richardson's room in the Sigma Nu house.

Christmas Houseparty at Sigma Nu, 1941.

Frank P. Jones, George L. Hildebrand, and Edward E. Hawks, all Class of '46, in the Sigma Nu House about 1942.

"Shippie Leaves for the Army." Robert O. Shipman '43 served up to the rank of captain in the U. S. Army, 1941-1946.

"Freshman Tennis for the Class of '45."

Professor Copeland's zoology class at Coffin Pond, 1939. Bob Waite, teaching assistant, and Professor Manton Copeland, who taught biology at Bowdoin from 1908 to 1947 and taught embryology and histology in the Medical School of Maine from 1912 to 1921.

Professor Copeland's zoology class at Coffin Pond, 1939.

Christmas Houseparty, 1940. Burton E. Robinson '42, Doris Hellman, Milton C. Paige, Jr. '44.

The first Maine collegian to win an Olympic gold medal, Frederic D. Tootell '23 won the hammer throw in Paris in 1924 with a throw of 174 feet, 10 1/8 inches, beating his nearest rival by two feet. The only other Bowdoin Olympic gold medalist before Joan Benoit '79 was Geoffrey T. Mason '23, who won the gold medal in the bobsled event in the winter Olympics at St. Moritz in 1928.

Bowdoin had long been known as "a singing college," thanks to its fraternities and glee clubs, but it was not until the arrival of Frederic E. T. Tillotson h '46 in 1936 that music was firmly established as an academic subject. Professor Tillotson retired in 1963.

Hubbard Hall, designed in an Oxbridge style, closed the south end of the quad when it was erected in 1903. It served as the College's library until 1965, when the space in this photograph was converted to the use of the Peary-MacMillan Arctic Museum. Today Hubbard Hall houses the Departments of History, Government and Legal Studies, Economics, and Geology, and the Computing Center. Two parts of the building are administered by the Library: the glass-floored stacks in the south wing and the Susan Dwight Bliss Room, which houses a collection of rare books and fine bindings.

least the English-speaking part of the community), and the general happiness of the alumni with "Bowdoin Beata" and its many blessings. The price seemed rather high, though: a certain lack of curiosity about the world and its people beyond New England, and a gradual loss of the equal standing that Bowdoin had once enjoyed with some other distinguished country colleges, such as Williams and Amherst. Through it all, the ties with the landscape of Maine were constantly reinforced—in part, through the endearing symbols of pine trees, adventurous sea captains and explorers, quaint little Massachusetts Hall—though in reality the College's relations with the people of the state were becoming more ambivalent as Bowdoin found itself returning, by the whims of demography, to its Massachusetts roots. More and more of its students were coming from there.[10]

The charm of Sills's Bowdoin is elusive for those who did not experience it at first hand. William DeWitt Hyde was what you would have got had you mixed Mark Hopkins of Williams—the inspirer of boys—and Charles W. Eliot of Harvard—the educational reformer and foe of all things antiquated. Kenneth Sills is what you would have got had you turned Brunswick into a little cathedral town in a novel by Anthony Trollope—the last of the nineteenth-century college presidents, as his successor, not unfondly, was to describe him. Some of the atmosphere of the Sills era comes through in reminiscences of the time, notably this passage by one of those Massachusetts students, the historian Francis Russell '33:

The Bowdoin I entered was in transition, for I arrived in the worst Depression year. Undergraduates, however, were insulated from the more immediate effects merely by managing to be at college. My first surprise was at Bowdoin's pervading friendliness. Everyone spoke to everyone else on the campus, and unknowns on fraternity porches would nod amiably to me as I passed. Each freshman or newcomer entering Bowdoin was invited to an evening at President K. C. M. Sills's, whom we called, if not to his face, Casey. To my astonishment I found that Mrs. Sills not only knew who I was but where I came from. She was by any count the most gracious lady in the state of Maine, in all New England for that matter. She recognized the face and knew the name of, as well as something about, each of the four hundred or so undergraduates. . . .[11]

At the time of the First World War, Sills had resisted the wave of anti-German sentiment that had swept the country, although he warned that "German ought not to be taught in our American colleges by men who have the slightest sympathy with the hideous philosophy of the present Germany." By chance, the day after the attack on Pearl Harbor, when the students crowded into the Chapel seeking the counsel of their president in the face of war with both Germany and Japan, the normally scheduled speaker—in the rotation of faculty—was a German, Fritz Koelln. Would he be allowed to speak on such an occasion? As the writer Vance Bourjaily '44 recalled, Sills sat quietly at the back of the Chapel as Koelln proceeded with his planned talk. His text was "Blessed are the peacemakers . . . ."[12]

Perhaps because the precedent had been set, the Second World War seemed at first less of an obvious disruption. The transformation of Brunswick's municipal air field—in the blueberry fields stretching towards Harpswell where Hawthorne and so many others had rambled—into a naval air station meant that much of the direct military activity was off campus, although various radar and meteorological schools used Bowdoin's facilities. In 1942, Sills reported that he had seen a college of nearly 600 students change into one devoted to training men in the armed forces, with only half the usual number of civilian students and 375 men in the uniform of the Army or Navy on campus. (And one woman, as early as 1940—a student flier in a summer course.) Sills reflected on the earlier war:

To one who saw the undergraduate body through the First World War there are some inevitable contrasts to record. There is far less flag waving, less emotionalism, less talk, than there was in 1917. The students are well aware that the war is closing in on them, as on us. There is very little pacifism in our group; a few boys who are religious conscientious objectors, comprise not more than one per cent of the student body; there is no enthusiasm for war; service is accepted as a necessary duty, and most students want to have opportunity for commissions if they think themselves really capable of leadership. The College has been admir-

The Commencement crowd leaves the Quad in 1951 on its way to Hyde Cage.

Eleanor Roosevelt at the Delta Upsilon House (now the Delta Sigma Society) on her visit to campus on 12 December 1942. Mrs. Roosevelt had recently returned from England and spoke about the British war effort. She was invited by students as part of the Delta Upsilon lecture series that brought many public figures to the campus.

ably organized for blackouts and air raids. Practically everyone on the faculty has some duties in civilian defense.[13]

The real impact of the war was less in air raid drills or unfamiliar faces on campus, than in the tremendous social changes the 1940s brought to American society, including American higher education. What had seemed a privilege—a leisurely four years in which to read and write, socialize with one's peers, and discover one's vocation—suddenly emerged as a right, though perhaps one to be reduced to quick and highly concentrated technical or professional schooling. And it was a right to be enjoyed by all of American society—including those groups, such as Catholics, Jews, blacks, and women—who had been either excluded from or barely tolerated at many of the country's older colleges and universities. The full repercussions of this sea change

would not be obvious at Bowdoin for another twenty years—a reflection not only of the College's geographic location but of its innate conservatism—but if one had to choose a small hint that change was on the horizon, it might very well be the appearance in Brunswick amid the College's huge enrollments immediately after the war (1,086 in the fall of 1947, for example) of a sizeable group of student wives.[14]

Sills could have resigned once the College had resumed its prewar enrollment of about 750 students, but he stayed on until 1952, in a world in which he was beginning to seem somewhat out of place. The Sillses moved to Portland upon his retirement, and one of his last messages to all Bowdoin alumni was to give them his address at 134 Vaughan Street and his yet-to-be-listed phone number, so that anyone who wished to could drop by.

James Stacy Coles, Bowdoin's ninth president (1952-1967), was a chemist who brought to the office a very different style from that of his predecessors. Among his achievements in office were the modernization of the teaching of science, the increased professionalization of the faculty, and a major building program.

The presence of a young family brought a new pace of life to 85 Federal Street. Martha Coles not only fulfilled the traditional expectations of a president's wife as hostess, but also involved herself energetically in the Bowdoin community and traveled with her husband on fundraising trips.

President Coles congratulates Judy Luke, of Arlington, Virginia, after crowning her Queen of Bowdoin's 1962 Ivy Weekend.

Upon assuming the presidency in 1952—the 150th anniversary of the College's opening—James Stacy Coles had an even greater psychological barrier to cross than had faced Sills in 1918. Who could replace Casey—or Edith—Sills? Moreover, Coles was a chemist rather than an old-style humanist, a non-alumnus (he had three degrees from Columbia), and a man decidedly more austere in manner than the avuncular Sills. Moving very cautiously in his first four years, he paid homage to the Bowdoin of recent memory by commissioning a study in 1955 entitled "The Conservative Tradition in Education at Bowdoin College," an affirmation by several of the most distinguished (and by no means illiberal) members of the faculty that the College should keep largely to the path laid out by Hyde and Sills.[15]

Coles had little intention of doing any such thing. A thorough modernist and something of a social engineer, he showed consummate skill in persuading the Boards, the alumni, and the students to remake much of the intellectual structure of the College, while leaving most of its social structure as he found it (one exception being the innovative Senior Center, which drew students in their final year out of their fraternities and back into their class community, and also allowed faculty a degree of experimentation with the curriculum impossible under the *ancien régime*). In some respects much of the story of Bowdoin in the 1970s and 1980s was to be the College's efforts to work out the specifics of the new directions in which Coles had turned the institution. If presidents can be ranked, he is surpassed only by Hyde as the central shaping figure in the College's history.

Summing up the more obvious of these changes, Manton Copeland, Josiah Little Professor of Biology Emeritus, wrote that:

the decade from 1952 to 1962 has been highlighted by the construction of several new buildings, the beautifying of the campus, the raising of faculty salaries, the provision of large sums for student aid to offset increases in tuition rates, the Self-Study Report. . . the encouragement of faculty research, the introduction

President Sills's retirement in 1953 was a landmark event in the history of the College because it ended the sixty-six-year span in which he and President Hyde had dominated the institution. In order to give his successor some breathing room, Sills—with typical thoughtfulness—embarked on a year of travel abroad.

of the undergraduate research fellowship program, the inauguration of the Summer and Academic Year Institutes, the new joint television venture, the renovation of the Library and the formulation of plans for new library accommodations, the development of plans for handling an increase in student enrollment, and the conceiving of the Senior Center project.[16]

By 1967, when Coles left for another post, it was a very different looking College, to be sure. If the architectural symbol of the Sills era had been the President's House at 85 Federal Street—an old sea captain's dwelling with cupola and ornate woodwork, the interior half elegant, half frumpy—the symbol of the Coles presidency was the residential tower that now bears his name. Its vertical faces slightly splayed at the base, making it look as if it had sprung from the ground, the tower rises sixteen stories over the Brunswick plain, each "pod" carefully engineered to hold its passenger load of students. There was no really compelling reason to build up rather than over the ground; it was perhaps just a statement about the institution's willingness to look in a different direction for a change.[17]

Bowdoin's tenth president, Roger Howell, Jr. '58, was inaugurated in 1969 and resigned in 1978 to return to full-time teaching and research. A former Rhodes Scholar, Howell was the author of numerous books and articles on sixteenth- and seventeenth-century British history. Under his leadership, the College began to admit women, chartered the Afro-American Society and the Afro-American Studies Program, began offering a major in biochemistry and courses in environmental studies, established the Computing Center, increased enrollment from 950 to 1,350, initiated student representation in the governance of the College, and began a major capital campaign.

Alice C. Early (assistant dean of students 1972–1974, dean of students 1974–1977), the Polar Bear, President Howell, and his son, Christopher Howell, at a hockey game during Howell's presidency. President Howell was an avid hockey fan who rarely missed a home game and often led the Bowdoin fans in cheers.

Professor Nathan Dane II '37, who came to Bowdoin in 1946, taught classics until his death in 1979. This photograph shows him teaching in the Woodruff Room of Sills Hall in front of the Sewall Latin Prize plaque that bears his name. Amid all the curricular changes of the post-Sills era, undergraduates continued to show interest in the classics.

Matilda White Riley h '72, Daniel B. Fayerweather Professor of Political Economy and Sociology Emerita and the first woman to be named a full professor at Bowdoin, had an established reputation in the sociology of aging when she joined the Bowdoin faculty in 1973. She is now senior social scientist at the National Institute on Aging, National Institutes of Health, in Washington, D. C.

Coles was succeeded by Roger Howell, Jr. '58, a president who had the advantage, like Hyde, of youth—he was thirty-three—and who offered the reassurance, as in the case of Sills, of a deep love for the humanities. He was a specialist in the field of seventeenth-century British history, well-respected here and at his other alma mater, Oxford, and in this country one of the last of a species—the scholar-president, the administrator who could still find time to write books. With his St. John's College scarf draped over his shoulders, his pipe clenched in his teeth, his (somewhat exaggerated) reputation as a rugby player, Roger—as almost everyone called him—seemed the embodiment of an Anglo-American style that was dignified without being pompous.[18] He was also probably the most popular of all Bowdoin presidents with students—perhaps because of his age, perhaps because he seemed the *beau idéal* of Bowdoin alumni of his generation. (He was a familiar sight at hockey games as well as public lectures; he was surely the only Bowdoin president whose house students would call at, late at night, to ask if he wanted to join them for a beer at Harriet's Place, a pub down Federal Street in the Stowe House.)

This popularity and, one might guess, his familiarity with the ideological struggles of the English Civil War were to be drawn upon in his great moment of testing, the student strike of May of 1970. No other Bowdoin president since Chamberlain at Augusta in 1880 had faced so volatile, even so personally dangerous a crisis. Howell managed to keep the College open—in large part by siding with the students in their protest against the prolongation of the Vietnam War—but at the cost of losing the support of some conservative alumni and townspeople, unaccustomed to seeing Bowdoin men acting out in the streets the political drama of the day.

Although television had brought the news of Vietnam and civil rights, draft protests and the riots at the 1968 Democratic Convention into fraternity houses and the Union, few people at Bowdoin were prepared for the events of May of 1970. For several years *The Orient* and the *Alumnus* had published thoughtful comments from both sides on the war and its draft-related issues. There had been a lively but civil debate over the presence of Army R.O.T.C. on campus—most of the faculty opposed granting students credit for it, while the Boards continued to support the program until 1975—but Bowdoin was not a college that gave observers the impression of being an ideological battlefield. There were perhaps a dozen active members of the radical Students for a Democratic Society (SDS); they were balanced by about the same number of Young Americans for Freedom. In 1960, the entering class had voted 67 percent for Nixon, 28 percent for Kennedy in a presidential preference poll. Yet the day after the shooting of four students at Kent State University (which followed the sudden American invasion of Cambodia), some 300 Bowdoin students met in the Main Lounge of the Union. The "strike" had begun.

The name, it turned out, was unnecessarily provocative; there was more intense discussion and community outreach than public agitation. Yet by the time the spring term was over—marked by an outdoor Commencement (a first in modern times) and a refusal of caps and gowns—a mass meeting of 1,500 people had been held in the gymnasium (5 May), the normal academic routine had been disrupted (though much instruction went on), the Brunswick Town Council had condemned the College (fearing, among other things, that trouble would spread into the high school), and students at a small college in Maine had participated in the great generational upheaval that had swept the country. But no one was seriously hurt, and no one called out the National Guard. Overall, the College community handled the crisis in a civil fashion, thanks to the moral authority of Roger Howell—who had been told in an emergency meeting with Boards members in Portland that they would leave it to his good judgment how to act—and to a student strike leader, Everett B. Carson '69, who knew the war firsthand. Carson was a former Marine officer who had been wounded in Laos and awarded the Silver Star. In some ways, the impact of May of 1970 was more controversial off campus than on:

some conservative alumni, especially after they read of the student protest under the headline "Nixon's Bums at Bowdoin" in the spring *Alumnus*, reacted with as much anger as the anti-war activists had shown. The president's office received 168 letters, the majority critical of Bowdoin's handling of the unrest. [19]

The donnish Howell, who had not been very strong as an administrator and who for all his public success was painfully shy, was followed in 1978 by Willard F. Enteman, an exuberant philosopher who also happened to have an M.B.A. from Harvard. Within two years, however, Enteman found himself in such conflict with the Governing Boards—partly a matter of personalities, partly a question of the College's direction—that his term came to an end in 1980. Stepping into a very delicate situation, A. LeRoy Greason, a professor of eighteenth-century English literature and long-time dean, played the role of peacemaker, leading the College through the relatively lush days of the 1980s, as evidenced by a successful $56 million capital fund drive and an expansion of academic programs, especially in the sciences and computing. Robert H. Edwards followed as president in 1990, amid the prospect of leaner times and amid sharper conflicts nationally over the nature of liberal arts education.

Looked at from another perspective, by the late 1960s, Bowdoin was a conservative, all-male, sports-minded college of about 950 students, one in which an able youth could get a solid grounding in the liberal arts and sciences from a talented faculty. The turmoil of the Vietnam era, however, coincided with—some would say accelerated—a myriad of other social changes, and even the fraternity system began to be challenged. Unlike other institutions in which fraternities had always played something of an adversarial role vis-à-vis the faculty, at Bowdoin, as we have seen, the College and its social clubs had reached a rapprochement as far back as the 1890s: we provide the classroom education, the College said in effect, and you provide most of the dining, housing, entertainment, and socialization of new students. It was a system that worked well, in most people's minds at Bowdoin, until the 1970s brought a new type of student and the surviving fraternities became, in some instances, a kind of refuge from the social and ethical values the College itself was trying to teach.

The most radical change of all, particularly for a College that had always valued "manliness" (though its definition was reconstructed with each generation of students), was the arrival of coeducation in 1971 and an eventual increase in size to 1,400 students. Maine began to be "rediscovered" in that decade, and the College found its national profile rising, in large part due to its decision not to require SAT scores for admission (on the grounds that the tests were not a reliable index of intellectual or creative ability). In the 1980s the College undertook to reform the curriculum, expand the arts program, deal with environmental concerns, attract more minority students and faculty, and make the College coeducational in fact as well as in name.

By 1990, the College was, by national standards, a very small and highly selective liberal arts college, whose chief drawing points included a strong teaching faculty willing to give close personal attention to undergraduates, a particularly vigorous program in the sciences, and an enviable location in coastal Maine. For a place so steeped in tradition, the College continued to prove that it could innovate—for example, through programs using computers to teach classical archaeology and calculus, through access to live foreign television to teach languages, through student-constructed independent study projects and "years abroad," and, most notably, through the microscale organic chemistry teaching technique. As the College entered the final decade of the century, there was much to celebrate—and many questions still to be answered. Did the small four-year liberal arts college have a specific character of its own that deserved protection? Or did a college as ambitious as Bowdoin have to become a mini-university? Or would there be some middle way?

It was still a College that took considerable pride in its roster of alumni and, now, alumnae.

Among the twentieth-century names of note are those of Harold H. Burton '09, associate justice of the U.S. Supreme Court; Paul H. Douglas '13, economist and U.S. senator from Illinois; Alfred C. Kinsey '16, biologist and pioneer in the field of studying human sexuality; Hodding Carter, Jr. '27, Mississippi newspaper editor and writer; George J. Mitchell, Jr. '54 and William S. Cohen '62, U. S. senators from Maine; Thomas R. Pickering '53, diplomat; and Joan Benoit Samuelson '79, Olympic athlete.

Among the faculty the College's literary tradition was maintained by Lawrence S. Hall '36, whose story "The Ledge" (based on a local tragedy) was one of the most frequently anthologized short stories of the century, and by the poet Louis Coxe, perhaps best known to the general public for his dramatization of Melville's *Billy Budd.*

Among other Bowdoin faculty of the Sills and Coles years who had large reputations beyond campus were the economist Albert Abrahamson '26 (who during the New Deal was the first Bowdoin academic to travel back and forth frequently to Washington), the French medieval literature specialist Charles H. Livingston, the historians Ernst C. Helmreich, Edward Chase Kirkland, and Thomas Van Cleve, the philosopher Phillips Mason, the political scientist Orren Hormell, the psychologist Norman L. Munn, the ornithologist Alfred O. Gross, the literary historian Herbert Ross Brown (who edited the *New England Quarterly* for 35 years), and the Civil War bibliophile (and college librarian) Richard Harwell (the list is not intended to be definitive). U. S. Senator Paul H. Douglas '13 h '53 of Illinois gave much credit for his success as an economist to the encouragement he had received at Bowdoin from his teacher and friend of sixty years, Warren Catlin.[20]

Was it in 1990 a college that Hyde would still have recognized? Yes and no. Unless you stood at the base of Coles Tower and looked up, the general appearance of the central campus had not been altered too greatly (if you ignored the Visual Arts Center, straddling the walkway from Maine Street to the Chapel); if anything, the grounds were much better groomed. Most of the fraternity houses were still flourishing, though amid decor less clublike than utilitarian, and with no immediate answer to an obvious question: why were they still called "fraternities" when they had so many female "brothers"? The town had changed far more, crowding in on the campus, and adding the groan of rush-hour traffic on the Bath Road and of P3-Orions revving their engines at the Naval Air Station just through the pines.

The Chapel had become for much of the College of purely antiquarian interest, but a student could privately choose among a greater variety of faiths than would have been welcome at Hyde's Bowdoin. The signature building of the 1980s—the sleek William Farley Field House and Swimming Pool—would have assured Hyde that the students were still muscular, if not particularly Christian, and Dudley Sargent would have been absolutely fascinated by what the Nautilus exercise machines were doing to reshape the ideal student body. That the arts were quietly flourishing would not have impressed Hyde, who was something of a philistine, but that the Outing Club was a roaring success would have delighted him, and his friend Teddy Roosevelt (Harvard '80).

And the faculty? They were rushing off to conferences in the Sunbelt, upgrading their computer software, picking up their children at day care, looking for parking spaces, and spending much of their lives in committee. A few of them published voluminously, but for many—possibly most—the greatest of professional satisfactions was simply to stand in front of a room of intelligent young people and talk with them about things they ought to know.

NOTES

BCSC is Special Collections, Hawthorne-Longfellow Library, Bowdoin College.

1. Robert P. Tristram Coffin, *On the Green Carpet* (Indianapolis, 1951), pp. 165-166. On Coffin as a "georgic" poet and essayist, see, for example, Mark W. Anderson '74, "Images of Nineteenth Century Maine Farming in the Prose and Poetry of R. P. T. Coffin and C. A. Stephens," *Agricultural History* 63, no. 2 (Spring 1989), pp. 120-129. For his bibliography by Richard Cary, see the *Colby Library Quarterly,* series VII, no. 4, 6, 8 (December 1965, June 1966, December 1966). Another Bowdoin poet, Wilbert Snow '07, covered some of the landscape, though in a more realist vein; an account of Snow's working his way through Bowdoin appears in his memoir, *Codline's Child* (Middletown, Conn., 1968), pp. 85-104.

2. Coffin, p. 167.

3. *Bowdoin Alumnus* 8, no. 1 (November 1933), p. 13.

4. Herbert Ross Brown, *Sills of Bowdoin* (New York, 1964), p. viii. Actually, there had been only six ordained ministers chosen president; Chamberlain had graduated from Bangor Theological Seminary but was never ordained.

5. Edgar O. Achorn, ed., *Bowdoin in the World War: The Story of the Cooperation of the College with the Government and the Record of Bowdoin Men Who Served With the Colors* (Brunswick, 1929).

6. "Bowdoin a War-Time College," *Bowdoin Orient* 48, no. 10 (15 October 1918), p. 98.

7. Diary of Marshall P. Cram 1917-1918, original typescript with revisions, BCSC. Comments about Cram's character come from an undated speech in typescript prepared for the Town and College Club, Herbert Ross Brown Papers, BCSC. When Cram died in 1933, he left the use of his home to the three students living there, after which the property went to the College, which continued to house students there until the interior of the building was drastically remodeled as an alumni house in 1962. He also left $5,000 each to his neighbors, Kenneth Sills and Philip Meserve, and $20,000 to the Alpha Delta Phi fraternity to clear its mortgage. Cram had lodged carefully selected students since 1924 and each year took one of them traveling with him, often to Europe. The house was much publicized for its eclectic collections of antiques and curiosities, the camels being a souvenir of his 1931 trip to Peking. *Boston Globe,* 17 October 1933, and *Maine Sunday Telegram* (Portland), 12 March 1932.

8. Ann Waldron, "Hodding Carter," *Bowdoin* 64, no. 4 (Summer 1992), pp. 19-23. This is a chapter from her biography *Hodding Carter: The Reconstruction of a Racist* (Chapel Hill, 1993).

9. Brown, *Sills of Bowdoin*, does not mention the incident. For details, see Ernst C. Helmreich, *Religion at Bowdoin College* (Brunswick, 1981), pp. 140-142.

10. The number of entering students from Massachusetts (60, or 37 percent) exceeded the number from Maine (55, or 36 percent) for the first time in the fall of 1928, in part because the College's new entrance requirements had meant fewer eligible students from Maine high schools. Of that year's 152 freshmen, 83 percent were from New England (compared to 47 percent in the Class of 1996). Of the 152 freshmen, 129 (85 percent) pledged fraternities. The student body, which included three grandsons of Hawthorne, preferred Herbert Hoover for president by 3 to 1, although the faculty was more Democratic. See *Bowdoin Alumnus* 3, no. 1 (November 1928), p. 8.

11. Francis B. Russell '33, "Bowdoin Beata," *Bowdoin Alumnus* 53, no. 3 (Winter 1980), pp. 7-13. For a young teacher's view of Bowdoin just after World War II, see Norman L. Munn, *Being and Becoming, An Autobiography* (Adelaide, South Australia, 1980), pp. 118-149. Munn's introductory textbook, *Psychology* (1946), was one of the most widely used books of its type in U.S. colleges and universities.

12. Conversation with author, Brunswick, 28 May 1989. Fritz C. A. Koelln came to Bowdoin to teach German in 1929 and retired as George Taylor Files Professor in 1971.

13. *Report of the President of Bowdoin College*, 1942.

14. For the context of these changes, see, for example, David O. Levine, *The American College and the Culture of Aspiration 1915-1940* (Ithaca, 1986). On the impact on campus of the post-war student marriages, see the Bowdoin Wives' Association File, BCSC.

15. The study was published a year later as *The Conservative Tradition of Education at Bowdoin College* (Brunswick, 1956).The following paragraphs are based in part on an interview by the author with James Stacy Coles h '68 in New York City on 18 December 1990.

16. [Manton Copeland], "The Coles Years," *Bowdoin Alumnus* 42, no. 1 (Fall 1967), pp. 2-3.

17. For an assessment of the Senior Center by its director, see William B. Whiteside, "Innovation in the Small College: The Senior Center at Bowdoin," typescript, Senior Center Papers, BCSC; also, David F. Huntington '67, "Seven Years in Sixteen Stories," *Bowdoin Alumnus* 45, no. 4 (November 1971), pp. 8-10.

18. I am grateful to Paul C. Nyhus, Frank Munsey Professor of History, for his long conversations with me in 1989 and 1990 about the Howell presidency. For tributes to Howell from colleagues and former students, including Frances L. Kellner '82, see the introduction to R. C. Richardson, ed., *Images of Roger Cromwell: Essays for and by Roger Howell, Jr.* (Manchester, U.K., 1993).

19. For details of the protest, see the Student Strike 1970 File, BCSC, especially the detailed "Notes from a Reporter's Notebook" kept by Joseph D. Kamin, director of news services (1961–1982). For a very different point of view, see the box marked Bowdoin College in the Horace A. Hildreth '25 Papers, Maine Historical Society. An effort should be made to prepare a comprehensive oral history documenting these events.

20. Paul H. Douglas, *In the Fullness of Time: The Memoirs of Paul H. Douglas* (New York, 1972), p. 24.

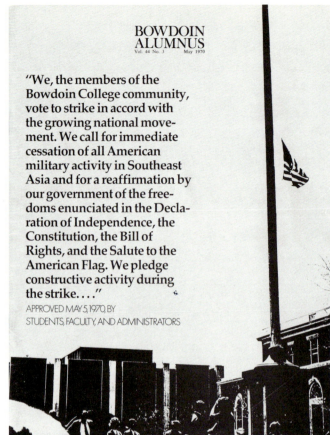

Founded by Kate Douglas Wiggin Riggs h 1904 and her daughter for the entertainment of the spouses of Governing Boards members at Commencement, the Society of Bowdoin Women is now a social and fundraising organization for the College. The officers in 1972 included (l to r) Mrs. Roger Howell, Jr., Mrs. John D. Clifford III, Mrs. Douglas L. Morton, Mrs. Leonard C. Mulligan, Mrs. Alden H. Sawyer, Jr., Mrs. Philip G. Clifford II, Mrs. Robert A. LeMieux, Mrs. Robert S. Stuart, and Mrs. Merton G. Henry.

BOWDOIN ALUMNUS
Vol. 44 No. 3   May 1970

"We, the members of the Bowdoin College community, vote to strike in accord with the growing national movement. We call for immediate cessation of all American military activity in Southeast Asia and for a reaffirmation by our government of the freedoms enunciated in the Declaration of Independence, the Constitution, the Bill of Rights, and the Salute to the American Flag. We pledge constructive activity during the strike...."

APPROVED MAY 5, 1970, BY
STUDENTS, FACULTY, AND ADMINISTRATORS

Thanks largely to President Howell's efforts, the College remained open during the student-faculty strike in the spring of 1970, in protest of the Vietnam War and the killings of four students at Kent State University. The cover of the May 1970 Bowdoin Alumnus angered many alumni who supported the war and whose letters of protest filled the next issue.

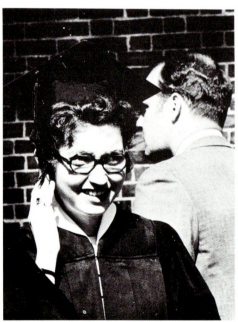

Susan D. Jacobson '71, the first woman to earn an A.B. from Bowdoin, was also the first woman Commencement speaker, winning the Class of 1868 Prize. Jacobson was a transfer from Connecticut College who came to Bowdoin on the Twelve College Exchange Program and applied for admission on 26 September 1970, the day after the Governing Boards voted in favor of coeducation. The first women degree candidates entered Bowdoin in the fall of 1971.

Perhaps the first woman in the country to be elected president of an undergraduate fraternity, Patricia A. (Barney) Geller '75 was elected to the post at Psi Upsilon in 1972, confusing the national organization, which had evidently assumed that "Barney" was male.

236

CHAPTER NINE

The ideology of the intimate Bowdoin of William DeWitt Hyde—white, male, athletic, fraternal, Christian, and inward-looking—had to be reshaped in many ways to meet the needs and expectations of late-twentieth-century higher education. The arrival of coeducation in the early 1970s caught the traditional College slightly unaware of what its full implications might be. While Bowdoin had enrolled a few black students in earlier decades, the 1970s also brought to Bowdoin, as to many colleges and universities across the country, new demands for a community that would better reflect the racial and ethnic diversity of the country. One enduring legacy of "Old Bowdoin" was a set of symbols—the pine tree, the polar bear, the Arctic explorers, and the Maine coast itself—that proved of great value in the image-conscious admissions "market" of the 1980s.

A QUESTION OF IMAGE

In the summer of 1989, after almost all of the students and much of the faculty had left town, visitors to Bowdoin were surprised to hear the roar of logging saws in the wooded strip of campus between Cleaveland Hall and Sills Drive, leading to the Harpswell Road. Some students and alumni were more than surprised: several undergraduate environmental activists, aware of plans to cut some ninety white pines for a parking lot, had intended to chain themselves to trees, but they had expected the cutting to take place later; alumni as far away as New York, alerted by classmates on their FAX machines, sent angry letters over what they feared was a wholesale destruction of the legendary Bowdoin Pines. Photos of the felled timber and student protesters appeared in the local papers. "How could Bowdoin, steeped in tradition back to 1794, chop down the pines that are its living, breathing symbol?" asked Phyllis Austin, the *Maine Times* reporter who was the state's leading journalistic advocate for reforms in Maine forestry practices.[1] Adding insult to injury, as some indignant students pointed out, was the fact that the additional parking spaces were required by Brunswick's zoning ordinance because of the square footage of a proposed new science complex—where students would be taught, among other things, about protecting the environment.

As it turned out, the well-landscaped parking lot did not look all that bad, as far as parking lots go, but the furor (which was briefly renewed when students returned in the fall) served as a reminder of how powerful visual images can be when associated with an institution's sense of its own place in the world. Ironically, to the men who established Bowdoin, pines were an exploitable resource, a quick source of cash while the more significant act of turning wilderness into farmland took place. But very early in the College's history, that particular grove of pines (partly owned by the institution, partly by the McKeen family) had acquired symbolic value—perhaps because of the forest worship associated with the incipient Romantic movement, perhaps simply as a link with the more heroic days of the Revolutionary generation. The Peucinian Society's name-taking in 1805 was only the most obvious tribute to an appreciation of the "academic grove" that filled many a student's letters and reminiscences of Bowdoin.[2]

And, like most such associations, legend soon was mixed with fact. The notion that the Bowdoin Pines were "remnants of the great virgin white pines" of early Maine added to their allure, and to the anger of the tree-loving section of the public whenever one was cut. In truth, the origin of the Pines is not clearly documented. They certainly were part of the landscape (and in far greater abundance) when the College was founded, and very early on were rec-

The Bowdoin Bachelors, an octet, performed in concerts on campus and throughout the Northeast and recorded several albums. They are seen here against the backdrop of Hubbard Hall in 1963 with the modified, classic Cadillac hearse that they drove to nearby concerts. On top of car: Robert B. Jarrett III '64; middle row: Edward R. Leydon '66, Richard B. Fontaine '65, Wayne W. Hulbert '64, Thomas E. Pierpan '66, James B. Weidner '64; sitting: William C. Thwing '64 (with dog), Harry K. Tressel '65.

Even better known are the Meddiebempsters, a male augmented double quartet formed in 1937 by Geoffrey R. Stanwood '38, assistant to the president emeritus, which, unlike the Bachelors, is still in existence. The Meddies—named for a town in northern Maine—often perform in concerts with Bowdoin's female augmented double quartet, Miscellania.

ognized as a special feature of the otherwise somewhat featureless Brunswick plain. As Cleaveland and Packard wrote, at a time when most of Brunswick's tree cover had long been cleared and before the late nineteenth-century elms had canopied the town's streets, "but for the protecting arm of the College, and the conservative care of the McKeens, which have preserved two invaluable remnants of the forest once so broad, scarcely a pine would have been left to remind us of old times."[3]

But the original forestation, according to the Wheelers' history of Brunswick, had been oak and beech.[4] Public confusion in our day between "virgin" forest—uncut, unburned, ungrazed, and otherwise unaltered by humans or livestock—and "old growth" forest—stands of trees of a certain age (say, 100 years)—has made Bowdoin's surviving grove seem more primeval than is actually the case. As a 1978 study by Philip Conkling of old-growth white pine (*Pinus strobus*) points out, white pine is "a successional species" which, in

the normal course of events, is replaced by hardwoods. Examination of the Bowdoin Pines in Conkling's survey found a twenty-nine-acre site with pines an average of ninety feet tall and 105 to 125 years old, "particularly impressive as they arch over the roadway." The College had managed the stand "to perpetuate the old-growth white pine"—i.e., by pruning hardwood competition from the understory.[5] The Bowdoin Pines, in other words, are as much an artifact as Massachusetts Hall and equally the beneficiary of a kind of self-conscious historical preservation.

From an early date, people nibbled at the edges of the stand. The present Pine Grove Cemetery, in which so many of the College's worthies rest in such peace as the heavy traffic on the Bath Road will allow, was deeded by the Governing Boards to its proprietors in 1821 and required some clearing of the grove. (How much was the subject of debate: by remaining nicely forested, the local burial ground had anticipated Mount Auburn and the "cemetery beautiful" movement, claimed one correspondent to the Brunswick *Telegraph* in the 1860s; too much shade kept the ground damp and a hazard to the public's health, argued another.) When the College's "nine" found that its left field in the "Delta" was blocked by a large pine in 1869, the friends of Bowdoin baseball took matters into their own hands one night ("a crash, followed by cheers was heard"). When a careless logger in 1863 damaged pines on the College's land near the cemetery, the ever watchful *Telegraph* called the public's attention to what was going on. Amid bulletins from the Civil War battlefronts, a letter a few weeks later over the signature "A Lover of Trees" reported, "I was grieved and indignant beyond measure at seeing hundreds of stumps of those noble old pines, which a century cannot replace . . . . Such vandalism I never expected or looked for in these classic shades." It turned out that a woodman hired by the McKeens had trespassed on the College's land. As "A Looker On" wrote a week later, public outrage had not abated. Furthermore, "I met to-day a gentleman of culture and taste from abroad, one of the Alumni of the College, who had just visited the scene of devastation and he was expressing in no measured terms, to one of the Professors, his indignation at the transaction."[6]

The turning point in the College's stewardship of its pines came in the 1890s, thanks to the efforts of Austin Cary 1887 h '22, who was to become a pioneer, in Maine and Florida, in the modern science of forestry and a landmark figure in the history of the paper-pulp industry. When the old stock of pines in the area behind the Chapel began to die out—hastened by disease and the College's annual burning of brush—Cary set out 5,000 young white pines over two or three acres in 1896, and followed up on this replanting in the years following. In a letter to *The Orient* in 1904, Cary reminded the community that "Bowdoin's pines are doubtless part of what attaches every alumnus to the college." He grew lyrical in describing the area between the Delta and Whittier Field: "Here in a small space is to be seen a wonderful variety of forest pictures, 'Waldbilder' if we may be

Bowdoin's team appeared five times on the television quiz show College Bowl *in December of 1963 and January of 1964, became undefeated champions, and established a new scoring record. Pictured are Charles P. Mills III, Kenneth C. Smith '64, Jotham D. Pierce, Jr. '65, and Michael W. Bennett '67. William C. Rounds '64 was the alternate, and Instructor Daniel G. Calder the coach.*

allowed the use of the original word for the idea meant to be conveyed." More professionally, from the forester's standpoint, here were pines in every stage of growth, many of them needing to be thinned out to produce the tall, straight trunks that were so admired. Cary urged judicious cutting and sale of mature pines, rather than letting trees stand until they were dead.[7]

It was part of this same section of the Pines that was "lost" for the parking lot, but earlier in the century much more of it had disappeared when the new Sills Drive was laid out in 1948 and when the athletic field, Sargent Gymnasium, Dudley Coe Infirmary, Moore Hall, Dayton Arena, and Morrell Gymnasium were built. To cite yet another irony to be found in the 1989 protest, the environmentalists were defending as "natural" and inviolate an area of woods that had been replanted less than a century earlier by one of the great champions of industrial forestry.

Whatever the merits of the College's decision—the parking lot, it turned out, could have been delayed, possibly avoided, since for financial reasons the science center was not to be built on the scale originally planned—the fierce reaction by both traditionalists and radical envi-

The Peary-MacMillan Arctic Museum was established in June of 1967 as a permanent home for the artifacts donated by the Pearys, the MacMillans, and students and professors who accompanied the MacMillans on their voyages. The museum was administered by the Museum of Art for many years, until a grant from the Russell and Janet Doubleday Fund in 1985 made possible the establishment of an Arctic Studies Center and the hiring of Susan A. Kaplan as director (she is now also associate professor of anthropology). This photograph, taken in 1987, shows the entrance to the museum in Hubbard Hall.

The groundbreaking exhibition The Portrayal of the Negro in American Painting, *organized by the Bowdoin College Museum of Art in 1964, occasioned the visit to campus of Dr. Martin Luther King, Jr. Curator Marvin Sadik, pictured here with King, collaborated with artist and printmaker Leonard Baskin on this and many other distinguished catalogues of that era.*

ronmentalists to any "attack" on the Pines demonstrated the power of symbols not only in the way the College presented itself to the world but in the way it thought about itself. There were to be many other adjustments in this self-image, some of them far from complete today, made necessary by various shifts of informed popular opinion. For example, the feisty notion—popular with colonial revivalists trying to reinvigorate "old" New England—of a hardy stock of Yankee individualists defying the elements in order to establish a foothold on the craggy coast of Maine was neither particularly accurate for much of the early population nor particularly welcomed, after about 1980, by those whose sense of ecology was based on a search for harmony with the land, for an acceptance of the moral claims of nature. But by far the most interesting attempt to "reinvent" the College, to create a new system of empowering symbols, came about in the late 1960s.

In retrospect, it was clear to many people on campus by the mid-1960s that President Coles's reforms had largely succeeded, thanks to his patience, the Boards' willingness to allow certain changes, and the general tenor of the times. The faculty had been strengthened and professionalized, the physical plant had been dramatically improved, and the curriculum had found new energy through the Senior Center's innovative seminars. All that remained was to do something about the students. In a 1968 report, the faculty's Committee on Preparatory Schools and Admissions, for example, had issued a trenchant critique of the College's recent entering classes. "The secondary school academic record of entering freshmen at Bowdoin is inferior to that of freshmen at the other good men's colleges in New England, with the College losing too many 'A' students and matriculating too many 'B's." Moreover, "there is some tendency for sports to predominate and for artistic and creative activities to be less important here than elsewhere."

The report added that Bowdoin students tended to be heavily pre-professional ("Bowdoin has more premedical students than all of its arts and humanities majors combined.") An over-reliance on "well rounded" as opposed to intellectual or

The Senior Center Council in its first year, 1964-1965, seen in the faculty dining room in the Moulton Union: 1 to r, Edward Pols, now research professor of philosophy and the humanities emeritus; William D. Shipman, now research professor of economics; A. LeRoy Greason, now president emeritus, then associate professor of English and dean of students; William B. Whiteside, now Frank Munsey Professor of History Emeritus and then chair of the Senior Center Council; Athern P. Daggett '25, then William Nelson Cromwell Professor of Constitutional and International Law and Government and acting president of the College between the Coles and Howell presidencies; and Gordon L. Hiebert, then assistant professor of chemistry. In the background are the original leaves from A Coastal Calendar, a series of poems on Maine themes written and illustrated by Robert Peter Tristram Coffin '15.

creative applicants had led to a "less interesting" student body than other good small colleges seemed able to attract. Bowdoin, in short, was in serious danger of slipping into second-class status; a college that liked to think of itself as belonging to the "little four" had to come to terms with the fact that Amherst, Williams, and Wesleyan thought simply of a "little three." The committee's recommendations were somewhat utopian—possibly eliminating football, for example, to spend the money elsewhere—but several of them—such as full coeducation and more concentrated efforts to recruit black students—were to become realities over the next decade.[8]

What the report demonstrates is that there was a growing consensus at least among the faculty that the institution had to change not only its

AS MAINE GOES

THE MAINE COAST & ITS DESPOILMENT
PHOTOGRAPHS BY JOHN McKEE

Poster made for the As Maine Goes *photography exhibition at the Museum of Art in 1964. The exhibition, widely commented upon, was a landmark in the development of an environmental consciousness for people in Maine. John McKee's photographs showed how rapidly a once-pristine coast was being despoiled. Associate Professor McKee came to Bowdoin as an instructor in French in 1962 and moved to the Department of Art in 1969.*

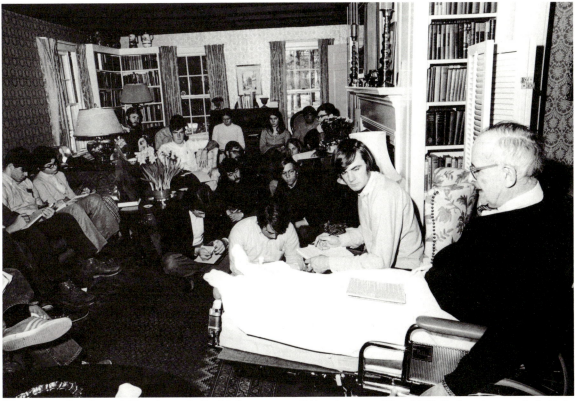

When Herbert Ross Brown h '63, who taught English from 1925 until his retirement as Edward Little Professor in 1972, broke his leg in the spring of 1971, he made sure the show went on: he taught Shakespeare at home. This photo of his parlor at 32 College Street was carried by the AP wire service across the country. Brown was known for grading student papers with the same meticulous care that he used in editing the New England Quarterly, *and his wit made him much in demand as an after-dinner speaker.*

admissions policies but its undergraduate culture. The substitution of "honors" grades for letter grades, the increasing questioning of the U. S. Army Reserve Officer Training Corps's presence on campus, the critique of the fraternity system by some of its most respected student leaders—all of these phenomena indicated that major change was on the horizon. But the immediate catalyst was the new director of admissions, Richard Moll.[9]

While Coles, operating in the shadow of Sills's reputation, had necessarily moved slowly, concentrating on converting the natives, Moll was a more impatient—and outward-looking—man. He quickly "fell in love with Maine," he recalled later, but found Bowdoin "painfully conservative and tired" and in need of "a publicly noticed shock that would persuade the world that Bowdoin was in fact trendy and ahead of its time."[10] He found his opening in the standardized College Board tests required of applicants

at every private American college and university of any academic respectability. While there had been many complaints about the tests—for example, that they measured certain types of verbal and mathematical "raw" intelligence, but revealed nothing about creativity, and that they were culturally biased against minorities—they were a well-established institution that suited the American love of quantification and made the job of admissions committees more "scientific."

Bowdoin's implementation in 1970 of Moll's proposal to make the College Board's Scholastic Aptitude Tests optional jolted the academic establishment. While it was not entirely a surprise—studies at Bowdoin in 1968-1969 had revealed that there was no necessary correlation between high scores and superior classroom performance—it was a revolutionary innovation for a college whose self-image since Chamberlain's short-lived reforms had been one of continuity and suspicion of "gimmicks." This, of course, was

Dining in Wentworth Hall, part of the 1964 Coles Tower complex. One aspect of the Senior Center Program was to bring the seniors together each evening to dine as a class.

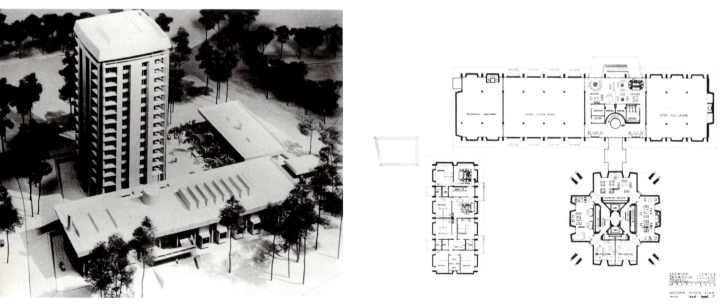

Hugh Stubbins's sixteen-story Coles Tower was quickly dubbed "Spike's Peak" (a play on President Coles's nickname) and was hailed at the time of its construction in 1964 as the tallest building north of Boston. The director of the Senior Center and his family and visiting scholars had quarters in adjacent Chamberlain Hall (today the offices of admissions and student aid); everyone met for dinner in Wentworth and attended lectures and social events in Daggett Lounge. For the seniors living in Coles Tower, the intent of the Senior Center was to reemphasize the residential element of traditional collegiate education.

no gimmick: the *New York Times* called Bowdoin's policy "a symbolic setback that could forecast a crumbling of the testing dike," and the *Saturday Review* saw it as further evidence of national dissatisfaction with the "numbers game" in admissions.[11] Two years later, *Time* ran Moll's photo with the "offbeat" material—paintings, poems, music—that would-be Bowdoin students sent the College as part of their applications in place of the traditional SAT scores.[12]

That very few other colleges followed Bowdoin's example was no condemnation of the basic idea; larger institutions, for example, still needed a quick screening device for their huge applicant pools. Moll's timing had been perfect, for the late 1960s and early 1970s witnessed a generational change, particularly among upper-middle-class Eastern college aspirants, related to Vietnam Era confrontational politics, widespread recreational use of drugs, a vibrant youth music culture, the further weakening of whatever sexual taboos were left, and a general disdain among the young for authority and tradition. Bowdoin would have seemed an unlikely venue for this new wave of shaggy-haired students, but the national publicity brought by the optional SAT policy and a widespread urge to escape the city for the country, especially if the country was as scenic and "unspoiled" as Maine, was in its own way a powerful stimulant. The applications flowed in, and Bowdoin captured much of the nation's student-age imagination in a way that gave it the sort of visibility that many other small colleges lacked.

In portraying Bowdoin as a countercultural phenomenon, Moll almost succeeded in making it one: enough non-traditional students showed up to alter perceptibly the institution's undergraduate culture. This did not change the College overnight; Moll himself said that he was too politic not to know a good hockey player when one was spotted by a scout, and many of the alternative students proved themselves creative in very focused, purposeful ways. It was, in retrospect, a small-scale golden age for Bowdoin, thanks to the teaching of Elliott S. Schwartz and Robert Beckwith in music, Thomas B. Cornell in art, John McKee in photography, Barbara J. Kaster in film, and A. Raymond Rutan '51 in the-

ater.[13] Although fraternity membership dropped, many of the houses adapted themselves to the new varieties of hedonism and survived quite well. At least a few students felt the College's new image had misled them; some transferred, others made the best of small-town life.

After Moll left in 1975, the College's admissions ideal tended to shift back to the "well rounded" model; by the late 1980s, there was considerable statistical evidence that the optional SAT policy was being taken advantage of by candidates whose strong points were more athletic than artistic.[14] Nonetheless, Moll's 1970 program was a striking example of how—in a highly competitive admissions "market" where image was at least as valuable as substance—one innovative administrator could leave his mark on a decade of an institution's history. The epilogue is worth noting: many of the free spirits of the 1970s went on to well-grounded, often quite prosperous careers, and have supported the College's alumni fund as enthusiastically as some of their more traditional predecessors.

ONE BOWDOIN, OR MANY?

One of the more useful of the new concepts taught at Bowdoin in the 1980s, in history of science courses and elsewhere, was Thomas Kuhn's now famous notion of the paradigm shift. Changes in scientific conceptual systems do not occur in a slow, evolutionary fashion, he argued, but in fits and starts. Pieces of information that had been available for some time suddenly come together in a new and persuasive way, with the result that old models no longer seem adequate and a new paradigm emerges in their place. Social scientists and humanists were quick to borrow this notion—which Kuhn had used to explain, for example, the Copernican revolution—to describe social and cultural changes in their own world. While the transition may be a little rough—for one thing, "real" communities (as opposed to scientific ones) rarely think alike, but rather act upon layers of belief of varying age and origin—the concept of a paradigm shift has proved a workable fiction to describe certain non-scientific types of change.

President Willard F. Enteman, Bowdoin's eleventh president, with his wife, Katie Enteman.

Richard W. Moll, director of admissions from 1967 to 1975, was largely responsible for Bowdoin's decision to stop requiring SAT scores of candidates for admission. The decision brought Bowdoin considerable national publicity and increased its applicant pool, especially among "non-traditional" candidates with strong interest in the arts.

Robert C. Johnson, Jr. '71, president of the Afro-American Society, received the Franklin Delano Roosevelt Cup from Craig W. Williamson '71 of the Alpha Delta Phi fraternity in 1970. The Afro-American Society was formed in 1968 and moved into its headquarters in the Little-Mitchell House at 6-8 College Street in 1969. The building was renamed the John Brown Russwurm Afro-American Center in 1979, in honor of the College's first black graduate. Now an attorney, Johnson is currently at work on a play about Russwurm, which is to be performed as part of the activities of the College's Bicentennial.

Representing a total of twenty-eight years at 85 Federal Street, Presidents Enteman, Coles, and Howell posed together for a photo on 1 June 1978, at Cram Alumni House.

When Joan Benoit '79 received the Lucy Shulman Trophy in 1979 from President Enteman as Bowdoin's outstanding woman athlete, she had already set Bowdoin, New England, American, and world records in distance running and had won the Boston Marathon and been a guest of President and Mrs. Jimmy Carter at a state dinner at the White House.

Take Bowdoin College, for example. Beginning in the 1960s, and in some respects unrelated to the more obvious lifestyle changes of the 1970s, an unmistakable shift took place in what might be called the dominant ideology of the College. The clearest evidence of this change was seen in the altered notion of who deserved to be included in the community—a change that had many other implications as well. The agent of change was often the faculty, many of whom reflected the values of the Coles years even when their appointments went back to the late Sills era.

This in itself was a significant new development, for the College since the Civil War had been largely the creation of its presidents, its Boards, and—from the 1880s on—its more active alumni. The antebellum College had been very much shaped by professors like Cleaveland, Newman, and Upham, but few such dominant figures had emerged after the war to challenge the governing authority of the institution's leadership. What happened in the 1960s, then, was not a "takeover"—fiscal policy, growth issues, and public relations remained very much the business of the president and the Boards—so much as a redefinition of how the College perceived itself. While major decisions—such as full-scale coeducation in 1971—were clearly the action of the Boards (after a good deal of nudging from the faculty), a surprising number of other developments between 1965 and 1990—including African American studies, environmental studies, the rapid growth of computerization, women's studies, Asian studies, film and photography courses, a dance program, and a yet-to-be-defined gay and lesbian studies—originated within and were largely carried out by the teaching faculty, who saw the administration's role largely as one of channeling foundation grants to broaden the curriculum. And while many of these new developments seemed strictly curricular, they had enormous implications for admissions, student life, fundraising, and institutional self-image.

The Bowdoin of Hyde and Sills had never been quite as homogeneous a place as it might have appeared. For one thing, the College's commitment to educate young men from Maine meant, given the state's economic decline after the Civil War, that a good number of students would be from modest financial backgrounds. Although its critics throughout the nineteenth century (and beyond) portrayed Bowdoin as an "aristocratic" institution, holding itself aloof from the majority of the state's population, and while the College maintained its historic ties with the Portland and Bangor business and professional elite, it was never a rich man's college in the sense that, say, Harvard was before World War II. There were always rich students on campus, to a degree not seen at Bates and Colby and the University of Maine, but they did not set the social tone for what—within its own walls at least—was a reasonably democratic institution. The nineteenth-century College reflected the English and Scotch-Irish origins of the state's early population but by the end of the century had begun to assimilate Catholic students of Irish or French-Canadian parentage as well; even a few Jewish students were admitted, most of whom came from the small, familiar Jewish communities of Portland and Bangor.

It was still a Christian college, as Coles assured alumni in 1952, but since 1908 it had had no formal connection of any kind with the Congregational Church (a requirement of the Carnegie Foundation's faculty retirement program). Socially, however, non-Christian students were still made to feel apart for much of the modern period. As the sociologist Milton M. Gordon '39 recalled:

College life at Bowdoin was very stimulating intellectually, and I took to it like a duck to water. But I was dismayed to find that social life there. . . was dominated by a pervasive fraternity system which generally excluded Jews and those few blacks who were then present in the student body. To my knowledge, only two boys of Jewish origin were ever invited to join a fraternity during my time on the Bowdoin campus. One was an all-New England guard on the football team and the other was a very wealthy Midwesterner, probably of German rather than Eastern European origin. . . . [M]y companions in college were other Jewish boys of modest New England origins like myself who made up a portion of the amorphous group characterized, with a barely hidden element of stigma, as "non-fraternity," the other segments of which were

Professor A. LeRoy Greason, who had been dean of the College from 1966 to 1975, was named acting president on 1 January 1981 and inaugurated the following October as Bowdoin's twelfth president. A scholar of eighteenth-century English literature, he served until 1990. His presidency saw the reestablishment of distribution requirements, the establishment of the Department of Computer Science, the Asian Studies Program and the Women's Studies Program, the building of the William Farley Field House and Swimming Pool and the Hatch Science Library, divestment of the College's South African stocks, and revision of the curriculum to emphasize writing for first-year students.

President Greason (second from left) walks with Maine Governor Joseph Brennan h '85 during the march to his inauguration in 1981. Ahead of them are Colin G. Campbell, president of Greason's alma mater, Wesleyan University, and Merton G. Henry '50 h '84, an Overseer from 1963 to 1974 and Trustee from 1974 until his retirement in 1987. The 1988 report of the Committee to Review Fraternities, chaired by Henry, established the College's policy of requiring fraternities to allow equal membership status to men and women.

Former President Coles (with curved cane) greets Dean of the Faculty Alfred H. Fuchs, who has taught psychology from 1962 to the present and was dean of the faculty from 1975 to 1991, at the beginning of President Greason's inaugural parade.

248

white Gentile boys probably too poor to pay the fraternity fees, the aforementioned blacks, and a few mavericks with idiosyncratic reasons for remaining outside the fraternity system. Needless to say, I felt the exclusion keenly, was deeply hurt by it, and probably subconsciously selected sociology as a major in order to try and understand what prompted racial and ethnic prejudice. . . .[15]

Unlike some larger New England institutions, Bowdoin never had Jewish quotas—they weren't necessary, so few Jewish students applied—but it was not until the 1970s that the College was able to escape its only-Gentiles-are-welcome reputation.

The question of racial integration was surrounded by more public spiritedness, at least after World War II, but the College, for all its good intentions, had to overcome its geographic distance from most black population centers, its rather high price tag, and a social atmosphere that until the 1970s seemed to discourage most forms of "otherness." Although much was made of John Brown Russwurm, whose degree from Bowdoin in 1826 made him the third black student to graduate from an American college, the undergraduate College did not have another black student until Samuel Herman Dreer in the Class of 1910. (There had been five black medical graduates.)

Before the twentieth century, a more typical view of blacks on the part of many Bowdoin students had been either as people easy to patronize—minstrel shows had been a popular student entertainment in the 1880s—or, as with the pious Phebe Jacobs before the Civil War, to be regarded as an anomaly. Hyde had spoken out against giving the vote to uneducated Southern blacks; Sills had told a correspondent who complained about the president's dialect joke at the 1947 Commencement that "while I have much sympathy with minority groups, . . . I think sometimes they are altogether too sensitive for their own good."[16] Those blacks who were strong enough to endure the social isolation and indifference of most of their fellow students often proved to be among the College's best scholars. As Kenneth I. Chenault '73, today an Overseer Emeritus, pointed out in his undergraduate study of "The Blackman at Bowdoin,"

President Greason and his wife, Polly Greason, with artist Samuel Ames, at the unveiling on 11 October 1986 of the latest in a series of presidential portraits, going back to Joseph McKeen, which are displayed on the second floor of Hubbard Hall. There is a reading room in Special Collections, Hawthorne-Longfellow Library, dedicated to Mrs. Greason, in gratitude for her volunteer work in Special Collections. Trained as a librarian, Mrs. Greason added considerable research in local and college history to her role as the wife of the president.

of the seventeen blacks who were graduated between 1910 and 1949, eight were elected to Phi Beta Kappa.[17]

Among distinguished alumni from this first half-century of blacks at modern Bowdoin were E. Frederic Morrow '30 h '72, who worked on the Eisenhower White House executive staff (the first black to hold such a post), the English professor and dean (and Bowdoin Overseer) Richard K. Barksdale '37, and the four Dickson brothers of Portland—Dr. Leon A. Dickson '35 and Dr. Frederick S. Dickson '45, both physicians, David W. D. Dickson '41, the president of Montclair State College and a Bowdoin Trustee Emeritus, and Audley D. Dickson '38, an optometrist.

The College's efforts to recruit black students after World War II were modest—three graduated in the 1950s, twelve from 1960 to 1965—but reflected a national trend, at least outside the South, to lower some of the barriers. However strong his belief in gradualism, Sills had been quietly putting pressure on the fraternities after World War II to drop all their restrictive prac-

The establishment of the Women's Center at 24 College Street in 1980 provided a place for a library (now above 5,000 volumes) and the offices of the Women's Studies Program. Shown at a meeting in the living room at the Women's Center is Marya Hunsinger (farthest left on couch), who came to the College in 1983 as an instructor in Spanish and was the first coordinator of the Women's Resource Center and the first instructor in women's studies.

Joan Benoit Samuelson '79 at the celebration in Portland's Monument Square in 1984 after she became the gold medalist in the first Olympic women's marathon. Behind her are Maine Senators William S. Cohen '62 and George J. Mitchell '54.

Dana W. Mayo (on left), Charles Weston Pickard Professor of Chemistry, and Samuel S. Butcher, professor of chemistry, in collaboration with their colleague at Merrimack College, Ronald M. Pike, made a major advance in the pedagogy of science with the publication of Microscale Organic Laboratory *(second edition, 1989). Butcher specializes in air pollution chemistry and the applications of computers to chemical measurements; Mayo, in the chemistry of natural products and the structural interpretation of infrared spectra. The two men were awarded the Bowdoin Prize in March of 1990. A new microscale laboratory was dedicated in Cleaveland Hall in October of 1992.*

tices. At least two of Bowdoin's fraternities were willing to sacrifice their national affiliations (Delta Upsilon as early as 1950 and Kappa Sigma in 1965) in protest of discrimination clauses.

An institutional turning point came in 1964, when the College launched its "Project '65" black student recruitment drive. Some 60 students representing most of the twelve fraternities had formed a group to attract more minority applicants both to help solve "the present crisis of Negro higher education" and to expose white students "to the numerous beliefs and backgrounds of people [they] will be living with after college."[18] Eight students and an alumnus visited black families during spring break in 1964. Meanwhile, in a different program another six students had exchanged places for the spring semester with students at Morehouse College, a black institution in Atlanta, Georgia. From these modest beginnings evolved the College's full-scale minority recruitment efforts of the 1970s and beyond.

Between 1966 and 1972, thirty-seven blacks graduated, many of whom formed the nucleus—along with white students—of the Bowdoin Undergraduate Civil Rights Organization (BUCRO). Everyone involved quickly realized that while recruiting minority students involved one set of challenges, making people of color feel a part of a rather tightly-knit New England academic community was another. Among the landmarks in this process of diversifying what had been a virtually all-white undergraduate culture were the Museum of Art's pioneering exhibition *The Portrayal of the Negro in American Art*, an Institute on Africa in 1968, the first Black Arts Festival in 1969, the opening of the Afro-American Center in 1970 (appropriately, in Professor William Smyth's old house), and its being named for Russwurm in 1978. In 1993, students of color and international students represented 15 percent of the College's enrollment.

Reflecting the pattern of the civil rights movement, other minority groups began in the 1970s to claim greater visibility on the nation's campuses and a sympathetic forum for their grievances. At a college that had put such a pre-

Sidney J. Watson played football for the Pittsburgh Steelers and the Washington Redskins before coming to Bowdoin in 1958 to coach hockey, lacrosse, and golf. Now Ashmead White Director of Athletics, he is shown here after a hockey game against Merrimack in 1976.

mium on "manliness," gay and lesbian activism proved a particularly difficult subject from 1978 on.

While the AIDS epidemic made sexual behavior, both gay and heterosexual, a matter of much more public discussion from about 1985 on—symbolized by the distribution of free or inexpensive condoms in the Infirmary—any attempt to reconstruct a gay and lesbian history for pre-1978 Bowdoin is going to be a difficult task. The documentation barely exists; the oral history that could exist has not been collected. However speculative such inquiries end up, they are being made today in academe, often in connection with broader gender identity questions about, for example, romantic male friendships in nineteenth-century colleges or the undergraduate fascination

Laurent C. Pinette, who came to Bowdoin as a fraternity chef in 1955 and went on to become director of dining services in 1986, put Bowdoin on the gastronomic map among American colleges. The quality of Pinette's food was widely publicized in the late 1980s. His high visibility on campus, until his retirement in 1989, also underlined the increasingly strong ties between the College and Brunswick's Franco-American community.

with cross-dressing in early twentieth-century drama productions.

Throughout the twentieth century at least, there had been a significant number of gay and bisexual (and later lesbian) people teaching or working at the College, but, while the post-war college community was far more tolerant and supportive than the country at large, the unwritten rule was that the less said about such things, the better. Student activism from the late 1970s on challenged that policy of silence—sometimes in the face of considerable hostility—and by 1993, the College had listed in its *Catalogue* courses in several disciplines in gay and lesbian studies. During the Greason administration, the College also added "sexual orientation" to its anti-discrimination clause.[19]

Blacks, Jews, gay people, and students of diverse ethnic and cultural backgrounds—all made their sometimes difficult accommodations with

the post-Sills-era College, but their numbers never challenged the existence of a white heterosexual male "Christian" majority. It took coeducation to do that, and the results are still not completely ascertainable. By the end of World War II, the old arguments against coeducation—that it muddled the boundaries between the separate spheres, that it ruined women's health, that it distracted males from their studies—seemed rather lame. But Bowdoin took another quarter-century to make the leap, amid considerable alumni opposition, and the cause may have been not so much dedication to equality of opportunity as a fear that the College would lose ground to its competitors, many of which at about the same time were going coed.

Feminists later maintained that the arguments in the Pierce Report of 1969 recommending coeducation were largely based on the benefits that the presence of women would bring to the College (e.g., an improved cultural atmosphere), not what the College could do for women. This was perhaps the best way to "sell" the recommendation to the Governing Boards at the time, but it foreshadowed some of the difficulties ahead as women tried to create a new role for themselves in campus life.[20]

From the fall of 1971, when sixty-six women arrived as the first A.B. degree candidates, through the late 1980s, when the male:female ratio almost reached parity, the College had to struggle with the fact that it was still, in some important respects, a male institution that nonetheless had large numbers of female students and a growing number of female faculty and staff members. Some of the adjustments were relatively minor (even if they did not seem so at the time)—equal sports facilities for men and women, and competent gynecological services at the Infirmary—but others could not be so quickly solved with a little money or sympathetic administrative attention.

What did it mean, for example, when departments like Romance languages and art history had an overbalance of female majors, while economics and government were overwhelmingly male? Was the whole system of education at Bowdoin so gender-determined that it would never change? Why was there evidence of so few female role models on campus? And why did fraternities, with their varying degrees of acceptance or rejection of women, still exercise such an influence on the life of the College? These were some of the questions being asked throughout the first twenty years of coeducation.[21]

It was in the fraternities in particular that the gender battle line was drawn in the late 1980s. One feature that set Bowdoin apart from many of its peer liberal arts colleges over the past twenty years was the survival of its Greek system. Although many observers had expected the houses to fold in the late 1970s, nine of a previous twelve fraternities survived into the 1980s, often in substandard physical condition but with enough alumni support to continue in operation. Although student membership rarely rose above 30 to 40 percent, the student culture of the 1980s found the fraternities useful as a social outlet—and, to some degree, so did the College, for there was still not room enough on campus to feed and house a student body that had grown, with coeducation, close to the 1,400 level. By the 1980s, the majority of the faculty had either lost interest in fraternity relations or actively opposed the system. The 1988 Henry Report was a generally successful attempt to bring the system back into order—thus allowing the College, in the face of highly vocal alumni pressure, to delay a final reckoning—and to assure their compliance with the College's principle of sexual equality (even if it meant breaking with male-only nationals). The "loophole" left by the Henry Report was closed in 1992 by declaring illegal any unrecognized single-sex social organizations.[22]

The only difficulty in the paradigm approach, as mentioned above, is that human behavior does not fall so neatly into patterns. While much had changed by 1990, there were pockets of resistance—among some alumni, for example, whose reaction to such issues as prayer at Commencement and sexual exclusivity in social organizations suggested that they were symbols of a valued and threatened collegiate way of life. And, at the other extreme, there were many clusters of dissent—feminists, gay activists, some students of color, for example, who accused the College of a

Barbara J. Kaster, one of Bowdoin's first women faculty members, came to Bowdoin in 1973 to teach speech and filmmaking, and retired as Harrison King McCann Professor of Communication in the Department of English in the fall of 1992. Several of her own films, including Green Seas, White Ice and To Serve the Common Good, document the history of the College.

degree of complacency and resistance to change that would prevent its ever becoming an institution that would attract the best minds of their generation. Where the truth fell between those viewpoints is not to be determined here; the conclusion is simply that between 1965 and the present, the terms of the debate radically changed, even if the College in some respects did not.

AS MAINE GOES

Amid the so-called "cultural wars" in higher education in the 1980s—the arguments over what should be taught and who was, professionally and ethically, competent to teach it—the science faculty at Bowdoin seemed, at least to non-scientists, to enjoy an enviable harmony. The body of knowledge was well defined, the teaching methods were innovative and widely admired, and the collaborative research projects broke down the old schoolroom barrier between teacher and student. The investment of the Coles presidency had paid off: if Bowdoin did anything well, it was the teaching of science. It is one aspect of this teaching that provides a final example of the post-1965 paradigm shift: environmental studies.

Robert Hazard Edwards, Bowdoin's thirteenth president, and his wife, Blythe Bickel Edwards, on Inauguration Day, 26 October 1990, in the William Farley Field House.

Again, this was a local manifestation of an international trend. But the College's Maine setting and its history of drawing its subsistence—at one early stage, quite literally—from the land and sea gave this new concern a special resonance. Already, the heroic urge to fulfill one's destiny by taking on Nature and defeating "her"—the motif of Peary's travels—had given way to the gentler explorations of MacMillan and the Schooner *Bowdoin* and, more recently, to an Arctic Studies Program that saw the Far North as a fragile environment to be protected, rather than conquered. Environmentalism was another variation on this process of the change from a culture of exploitation and consumption to one of appreciation, cooperation, even awe. Just as the feminist and racial and sexual diversity causes of the modern era embodied some of the same language and tactics of, say, the abolitionists of Smyth's day, the new scientist/humanists expressed, sometimes unwittingly, the religious fervor of the Bowdoin of 150 years earlier.

To appreciate how much had changed, consider the first organized scientific expedition in which Bowdoin students participated—Professor of Chemistry and Natural History Paul A. Chadbourne's trip to Greenland, which left Thomaston on 27 June 1860 in the schooner *Nautilus*. Off the coast of Labrador, Simeon

Adams Evans 1860 noted in his journal how thickly an island they visited was covered with nesting eider ducks: "As we climbed up the island and the frightened birds rose in the air, the noise of their wings and the screaming and chattering of the gulls was absolutely deafening . . . . No one, who has not seen the vast clouds of bird-life about some of these northern islands can have any conception of the vast multitudes." Like many explorers upon first encountering the Arctic, Evans was enraptured by much of what he saw—by the savagery of the dogs, the splendor of the *aurora borealis*, the castle-like mirages at sea ("Wonderful! Wonderful!!"). Then he finds the island where the puffins live.

For a long distance around the island, the water was covered with birds. The air was full of them and the noise of their wings was like continuous thunder. The rocks were covered by armies of them sitting in rows, like soldiers, and, when we landed, we found the whole island honey-combed with their burrows and a bird in every hole . . . . The water [for a mile] was covered with the fishing birds, the air above was darkened by the myriads going and coming in never ending swarms, each bird bringing and leaving one or more fish in his (or her) beak . . . . I pushed my protected hand into the burrows, which the bird would seize with a grasp so vigorous that they hung to my mitten until I could catch them by the throat and choke them to death with the other hand. In this way I took thirty birds. [23]

We are a long way in Evans's journal from the ecological sensibility that began to reveal itself in the 1960s. In Maine alone, we could trace a genealogy of this new spirit—for example, through the formation of Acadia National Park, Governor Percival Baxter's gift of Mount Katahdin and its surrounding forests, and Rachel Carson's writings. But there is a very interesting figure much closer to Bowdoin, standing quietly to the side, also pointing the way. In the years when a schoolboy-scientist like Evans was gleefully killing and mounting specimens, and when other young men from the cities were proving themselves in the Maine woods, a young woman in Brunswick was learning to draw and paint. She was also teaching herself, in her walks in the neighboring fields, how to tell one native plant from another. Kate Furbish would be forgotten today, other than as a talented amateur botanist who left her portfolios depicting the *Flora of Maine* to the Bowdoin College Library, had it not been for a happy accident. One of her discoveries in the St. John River valley of far northern Maine was of the lousewort which now bears her name, *Pedicularis furbishiae*. Her description of it led to its rediscovery as an endangered species in 1976, just in time to stop a hydroelectric project that would have flooded the Allagash waterway, perhaps the only truly unspoiled river in the East. What the new ecological movement sought to do was to combine the awe that Evans felt in the face of the fecundity of nature with the respect for the complexity of life that Furbish depicted.[24]

In tracing the ancestry of this movement, one could go back to Professor Leslie Alexander Lee and his "Bowdoin Boys" in Labrador in 1891 or, more directly, to the Bowdoin ornithologist Alfred O. Gross h '52 at the College's Kent Island scientific station in the Bay of Fundy.[25] But an important feature of late twentieth-century environmental activism is that it goes beyond the scientific profession to embrace a "civilian" population (indeed, sometimes the more radical environmentalists see the scientists as the enemy).

Here the turning point for Bowdoin may very well have been the 1966 photography show *As Maine Goes*, with its introductory text by Supreme Court Justice William O. Douglas and its succession of startling images by then-Instructor John McKee. Traveling around the state to what within memory had been pristine landscapes, McKee captured on film the environmental degradation of "Vacationland"—the half-buried junked car at Popham Beach, the roads littered with billboards, the rusting sewer pipes on the shore. There were many forces at work in creating the environmental movement of the 1970s in Maine, but McKee's photographs were one of the great energizing stimuli, at Bowdoin and elsewhere in the state.[26]

In 1970—the year of the first Earth Day, celebrated on campus among hundreds of other locales—an informal faculty group took the first steps toward establishing the College's interdisciplinary Environmental Studies Program, which was formally begun the next year.[27] It was appropriately—for the time and the place—a grass-

James Y. Cho '90 rock-climbing at Acadia National Park in 1988. The College's popular Outing Club brought together Bowdoin's traditional emphasis on vigorous outdoor activity and a late-twentieth-century awareness of Maine's ecology. For many new students, a pre-Orientation trip with the club by canoe, bicycle, or on foot marks the beginning of their Bowdoin experience.

roots effort, one which expressed a new vision for an old institution. Here again, the full implications are still being worked out—for example, is environmentalism just another specialized discipline, or is it an attitude toward life that should pervade every aspect of the College? But if one had to make an educated guess as to where Bowdoin would find one of its great strengths in the decades ahead, this tie to preserving the land and sea—particularly the land and sea of Maine—would be a likely venue.

Ecologists may invoke a global sensitivity, but their real work begins at home. Bowdoin, for

Professor Franklin G. Burroughs, Jr., has taught English at Bowdoin since 1968 and is the author of two books of essays, Billy Watson's Croker Sack *and* Horry and the Waccamaw. *In a 1991 interview with* Bowdoin *magazine, he discussed some aspects of Bowdoin's placement in the Maine landscape: ". . . being able to live in the country, in a town that still has a number of vestiges of being an agricultural community, . . . where you can see an eagle when you're walking the dog in the morning—yes, that's salutary."*

example, had begun on the banks of the Andro-scoggin. The mills and shipyards existing there in 1794 were what defined Brunswick and Topsham as promising towns; the river, like the forest, caught the imagination of the first generation of students and linked them with the great world beyond the Kennebec and over the sea. Bowdoin crews could row on the river into the 1890s, but the early twentieth century saw the Androscoggin turn into a sewer, threatening the rich ecosystem of landlocked Merrymeeting Bay. Yet by the spring of 1990, when a conference was held at the College under the title "Six Rivers, Twelve Towns, One Bay," Bowdoin students had an example within a mile of campus that some environmental battles can be won. The river was alive again. As the essayist Franklin Burroughs, professor of English, told the participants:

Old-timers around the bay still know the lore of a place that was far richer in game and fish. More recent memories recall a place that was poorer, particularly in aquatic life, than what we now have. Industrial and municipal waste made Merrymeeting Bay into as viscid and lifeless a body of water as anything you would find in the center of a city. When the cleanup began, only 30 years ago, it was not clear that there was anything left to save. No one predicted how quickly the bay would begin to cleanse and heal itself.[28]

On that quiet but encouraging note, spoken by a Bowdoin professor on the Bowdoin campus to an audience representing much of the state, this narrative of Bowdoin College's two-hundred-year relationship with the land and people of Maine can end.

BCSC is Special Collections, Hawthorne-Longfellow Library, Bowdoin College.

1. Phyllis Austin, "The sacrificial pines," Maine Times, 21 July 1989; see also the *Bowdoin Orient* 119, no. 1 (8 September 1989), p. 1.

2. The name Peucinian was adopted from the Greek *peukinos*, "piney" or "pine-covered." Initiates swore their oath holding a pine bough.

3. Nehemiah Cleaveland and Alpheus Spring Packard, *History of Bowdoin College* (Boston: James Ripley Osgood & Co., 1882), p. 2.

4. George A. Wheeler, M.D., and Henry W. Wheeler, *History of Brunswick, Topsham, and Harpswell, Maine*, vol. 1 (Boston, 1878; repr. 1989), p. 99.

5. Philip W. Conkling, *Old-Growth White Pine Stands in Maine*, Maine State Planning Office Report No. 61 (Augusta, 1978).

6. *Brunswick Telegraph*, 25 June 1869, 3 April 1863, 15 May 1863, 29 May 1863, 5 June 1863.

7. Austin Cary, *Bowdoin Orient* 33, no. 22 (28 January 1904), pp. 191–192.

8. "Report of the Committee on Preparatory Schools and Admissions," April 1968, copy in BCSC.

9. John P. Ranahan '67, Douglas P. Biklen '67, and Thomas H. Allen '67, "Fraternities Must Go," *Bowdoin Alumnus* 41, no. 4 (May 1967), pp. 9-11. This attack on the system by three prominent students brought a response, "A Report from the Fraternity Presidents," *Bowdoin Alumnus* 42, no. 2 (Winter 1968), pp. 14-17.

10. Interview with author, New York City, 18 December 1991.

11. *New York Times*, 23 January 1970, p. 11; *Saturday Review*, 21 February 1970, p. 57.

12. Reprinted in *Bowdoin Alumnus* 46, no. 3 (May 1972), pp. 4–5.

13. Schwartz joined the faculty in 1964; Beckwith taught from 1953 to 1987; Cornell and McKee came to Bowdoin in 1962; Kaster taught from 1973 until 1992; and Rutan directed the theater from 1955 to 1957 and from 1971 to his retirement in 1993.

14. The debate on athletics and admission standards is summarized in "Brains and Brawn," *Bowdoin* 61, no. 1 (September 1987), pp. 42-44.

15. Milton Gordon, *The Making of a Sociologist* (Cambridge, 1990), p. 6.
At a meeting of the Association of New England Deans in 1918, then-Dean Kenneth Sills told his colleagues: "We do not like to have boys of Jewish parentage [at Bowdoin]." Quoted in Marcia G. Synnott, "The Admission and Assimilation of Minority Students at Harvard, Yale, and Princeton, 1900-1970," in B. Edward McClellan and William J. Reese, eds., *The Social History of American Education* (Urbana, Illinois, 1988), p. 317. On the other hand, as president, Sills defended the appointment of the College's first Jewish professor, the economist Albert Abrahamson '26, in 1928. See William D. Shipman, "Jim Abrahamson Remembered," *Bowdoin* 62, no. 1 (Winter 1988), pp. 16-20. The College's first Jewish student is likely to have been Frank Mikelsky '04 of Bath.

Data on students' religious preferences was published in the annual *Reports of the President* from 1920-1921 through 1968-1969. In 1920-1921, for example, there were thirteen Jewish students (4 percent) out of 321; in 1968-1969, eighty-one (10 percent) out of 790. The art collector and Wall Street wizard Walter Gutman '24 was among those who never forgot that his Jewishness kept him out of Bowdoin's fraternities, most of which had Christians-only clauses through World War II. See "The Very Rich Hours of Walter Gutman," *Bowdoin* 60, no. 1 (Summer 1986), p. 7. On the Thorndike Club as an alternative social organization for Jewish students and others, see Ernst C. Helmreich, *Religion at Bowdoin College: A History* (Brunswick, Me., 1981), pp. 147–149. It evolved into the fraternity Alpha Rho Upsilon ("All Races United"), which welcomed a variety of students disaffected with traditional Greek organizations.
On the College's relations with Brunswick's large Franco-American population (descendants of French-speaking Canadians who had migrated south to work in the town's textile mills), see Katharine B. Hudson, "Brunswick's French Connection," *Bowdoin* 62, no. 1 (Winter 1988), pp. 21-25.
In 1966–1967, the number of Catholic students (176) surpassed the number of Congregationalists (170) for the first time (both groups representing about 19 percent of the total); by 1968–1969, there were 226 Catholics, 151 Congregationalists, 137 Episcopalians, and various other Christian denominations listed. Since 1974, the College no longer tabulates such data.

16. K. C. M. Sills to John Wilson, Brunswick, 23 June 1947, Sills Papers, BCSC.

17. Kenneth I. Chenault, "The Blackman at Bowdoin: An honors paper for the Department of History," Bowdoin College, 1973, p. 62. Copy in BCSC.

18. *Bowdoin Alumnus* 38, no. 3 (March 1964), p. 1.

19. For the experience in the late 1960s of a gay undergraduate, see "David P. Becker '70," *Bowdoin* 64, no. 3 (Winter 1992), pp. 13–15; for the experience in the early 1980s of a lesbian undergraduate, see "Linda Nelson '83" in the same issue, pp. 14–15.
Before the late 1960s the only person connected with the College to express any public sympathy with homosexuality was the expatriate art collector Edward Perry Warren h '26. Heir to a Maine paper company fortune, Warren gave the Bowdoin College Museum of Art more than 600 classical antiquities, among his many other benefactions to museums and universities. He also championed, albeit discreetly, an idealized Edwardian version of "Greek love." On his Bowdoin connection, see [Charles C. Calhoun], "An Acorn in the Forest," *Bowdoin* 61, no. 1 (September 1987), pp. 2–21. For a survey of recent scholarship on nineteenth-century male friendship, see E. Anthony Rotundo, *American Manhood: Transformations in Masculinity from the Revolution to the Modern Era* (New York, 1993), pp. 75-91.

20. "Report of the Study Committee on Underclass Campus Environment" ("the Pierce Report"), *Bowdoin Alumnus* 43, no. 3 (Spring 1969), pp. 1–19. Two options were kept open: full coeducation or a coordinate college "within walking distance," p. 4.

21. The first woman student officially on campus

(except for those allowed to sit in on lectures from time to time from Chamberlain's day on) was probably Ann Wood, an aviation student in 1940. See *Documentary History 1939-40*, p. 136, BCSC. The first woman to be granted an earned Bowdoin degree was Bernice Engler, who in 1962 was awarded an A. M. after attending four National Science Foundation summer institutes in mathematics (she was one of sixty women among 274 high school teachers to receive master's degrees in the program, which lasted from 1959 to 1974).

For a sample of views on the first twenty years of coeducation, see the special anniversary issue, *Bowdoin* 64, no. 3 (Winter 1992). See also the collection of papers for Education 105 (1992) on various aspects of the acceptance of women by the College, deposited in BCSC. I am grateful to Polly W. Kaufman for providing me copies of this study, the most thorough to date of the impact of coeducation. Assistant Professor of Education T. Penny Martin has written an unpublished paper on the history of the Society of Bowdoin Women.

22. The most comprehensive study of Bowdoin's fraternity system is Kimberly A. Hokanson, "The Changing Status of Fraternities at Northeastern Liberal Arts Colleges: Case Studies of Bowdoin and Colby Colleges," Ed. D. thesis, Harvard University, 1992; copy in BCSC.

23. Reminiscences of Simeon Adams Evans, A.B., M.D., based on his Journals, 1850–c.1870, unpublished MS, 1889, pp. 68, 83-86, BCSC. Michael Robbins '92 has edited the Civil War portion of this journal; copy in BCSC.

24. On her career, see Sara Wasinger '92, "Kate Furbish and the Flora of Maine," *Bowdoin* 64, no. 3 (Summer 1992), pp. 8–14.

25. On the history of the Arctic Museum, see its American Association of Museums 1993 Reaccreditation Report, Arctic Studies Center, pp. 6a–6h, copy in BCSC; on Lee's expedition, see Jonathan Prince Cilley, Jr., *Bowdoin Boys in Labrador* (Rockland, Me., n.d.); on the Bowdoin Scientific Station, in the Bay of Fundy, see Madeline Butcher, "Kent Island," *Bowdoin* 61, no. 2 (December 1987), pp. 2–6.

26. *As Maine Goes: Photographs by John McKee, Introduction by William O. Douglas*, Bowdoin College Museum of Art, 1966; see also *The Maine Coast: Time of Decision* and *The Maine Coast: Prospects and Perspectives, A Symposium 20–22 October 1966*, both published in 1966 by the Center for Resource Studies, Bowdoin College.

27. For a summary of the steps leading to this action, see "Environmental Studies at Bowdoin College: A Grassroots Creation," an unsigned paper written for Education 102, 28 November 1989. Copy in BCSC.

28. Franklin G. Burroughs, Introduction to "Six Rivers, Twelve Towns, One Bay," *Bowdoin* 63, No. 2 (Summer 1990), p. 3.

CODA

One fine fall afternoon, in the parking lot of L. L. Bean, the world-famous purveyor of outdoor goods in Freeport, Maine, I saw a well-weathered Ford pickup truck, with gun rack and National Rifle Association sticker, parked amid the Volvos and Toyotas and Saabs. The driver and his buddy were walking toward the store, perhaps for a pair of the famous hunting boots, perhaps just for the free cup of coffee sometimes offered there. In the bed of the pickup—head drooped over the open tailgate, damp hair stiff, blood slowly oozing out of its mouth—rested a dead buck. Now this was a scene common enough in any Maine town in deer season, but what gave it special shape that day in Freeport was the troubled glance—half anxious, half disapproving—of the prosperous-looking shoppers who passed by on their way, well, perhaps to the hunting boot department.

It is easy enough, any time of the year in coastal Maine, to find juxtaposed two ways of life: one rural, seemingly timeless, defiantly individualistic; the other suburban, nostalgic for a certain kind of reconstructed past, yet committed to modernity's obsession with change. The division is not always between old and young, or native and newcomer. Many people—including a good number of Bowdoin's current faculty and staff members—moved to the state in the 1960s and 1970s in pursuit of a life that was self-consciously archaic, devoted to natural fibers and pumpkin-pine floors; many descendants of the people who had come to the District of Maine in the Reverend Samuel Deane's day, on the other hand, looked with satisfaction at the building lots the developers had just sliced out of grandfather's farm. The coexistence of both styles of life, in their infinite variations, is what gives the place its interest to the cultural geographer, however short much of it falls of the idealized world of Down East postcards and country-life calendars.

It occurred to me, that day in Freeport, that acceptance of these composite scenes is one way to understand the history of Bowdoin College. Much of the hold that Bowdoin has had on its alumni and friends arises from an act of the imagination. They have persuaded themselves that a collection of bricks and mortar, classrooms and labs, pine trees and depictions of polar bears is something that rises beyond mere pedagogy to a light-filled realm of sea air and the smell of balsam sap on your hands. There is nothing false about this. We create the mental landscapes we most wish to inhabit, and feel vaguely pleased with ourselves when, by chance or calculation, we find the sublunary locale that meets our expectations. But the price is having to accept the sometimes ungainly ways past and present bump into each other.

It occurred to me, too, that the splendid store in Freeport had more in common with the College than merely being, so to speak, in the same neck of the imaginary woods. The virtues the store embodied—friendliness, personal attention, good health, purposeful leisure, a feeling that somewhere in its 90,000 square feet of retail space was the little country store where it had all begun, where maybe even old L. L. Bean himself would be waiting to help you pick out a trout fly—were these not the same virtues, transmuted into a different sphere, that the College offered its 1,400 students? I would not want to push the point too far; for one thing, more people around the world have heard of L. L. Bean than of Bowdoin. Yet there was something similar in their sense of mission—they conveyed Maineness to people, and in 1993 Maineness was something an awful lot of people seemed to want.

I think Talleyrand would have approved of Bean's. A sort of M.B.A. *avant la lettre*, he would have admired its marketing skills, its managers' financial acumen, its global reach. What he would have made of Bowdoin I am not so sure. But, cynic that he was, he would have warned both institutions not to push it too far. The store, I am certain, has expertly calibrated the proper ratio of Maineness and size. The College, however, has seemed at times not quite sure how modern it wanted to be.

Its very Maineness was part of the problem. As the Harvard cultural geographer John Stilgoe pointed out to a conference of historic preservationists in 1987, New England's touristic identity has long depended, perhaps excessively, on the notion that it is "a place apart," "the land of the time before." Nowhere is this more true than in Maine, whose economic fate as Vacationland depends on satisfying the expectations of visitors seeking a place that is "quaint" and non-urban yet easily accessible by car. People come to Maine, Stilgoe said, in search of "the landscape of the Early Republic, of the time before the Gilded Age"; they are "people looking for a life they never had."[1] This is not a particularly new phenomenon: there are traces of it as early as the 1850s, when Fitzhugh Lane painted his luminist seascapes of Camden Harbor and Mount Desert; and the slow decline of rural and coastal life in Maine after the Civil War had the effect of "freezing" a landscape that in more prosperous parts of the country was rapidly disappearing.

Until the mid-1960s, much of the College's self-identity rested on just such a sense of its apartness, its rejection of the more intrusive demands of modern life (and modern mass-market education), its allegiance to the world of one's father. When the faculty in 1955 expressed their faith in "the conservative tradition in education," they were not simply endorsing the curricular status quo; they were invoking the gentlemanly ideals and anti-urban values of the Bowdoin of William DeWitt Hyde. Even in more recent days, the College has worked hard at presenting itself as a sort of fresh-air experience, taking place in a pastoral world in which little of the ungainly, the industrial, or even the suburban is allowed to intrude. A glance through any recent Admissions Office "viewbook"—the richly illustrated pamphlet sent to prospective students—will confirm this general impression of leafiness.[2] Once it was a pastoral of place; now it

is also a pastoral of race and ethnicity, for the photos are designed to convey a sense of multiculturalism that would have astonished the collegians of Sills's day. Yet in reality Maine is one of the least multicultural states in the union, save for a now elderly population of Franco-Americans who, unlike their children, have not allowed themselves to become completely assimilated into the majority culture. Can a college that aims to replicate the diversity of the nation still feel strongly that it should be a "Maine" cultural artifact?

As we have seen, for much of the twentieth century, Bowdoin has been in terms of numbers of students more a Massachusetts college than a Maine one. One thing that has kept the institution tied to its roots, ideologically speaking, has been that much vaunted, at times almost mystical "Maine commitment." At one level, this has been embodied in the admissions policy of seeking out promising youths from small Maine towns and helping those among them in need to find the financial aid necessary to see them through Bowdoin. (This policy suggests both a Jeffersonian faith in the purity of small-town and rural life and a late nineteenth-century suspicion of urban corruption.) In less direct fashion, the "commitment" has taken the form of the College's federally-funded Upward Bound program, which in the summers has given a taste of academic life to bright high school students from low-income families in Aroostook, Washington, and southern Maine counties (some of whom later matriculate at Bowdoin). The "commitment" is also evident in the fact that, despite comparatively modest salaries, so many Bowdoin graduates continue to go into public school teaching in the state.[3] Moreover, part of the ethos of teaching at Bowdoin for much of its faculty has been the conviction that these Maine students are among the most earnest, the most intellectually curious, and the most fulfilling to have in class.

For the moment, then, Bowdoin remains closely connected with the land and people of Maine—partly because of history and tradition, partly because of conscious decisions to maintain ties that could have been allowed, if not quite to dissolve, then at least to become weakened. As the twenty-first century approaches, however, three long-term complications remain.

The first is the discrepancy between the high cost of private liberal arts education—at the time of writing, close to $25,000 a year—and the rather modest resources of many Maine families. This is hardly a problem unique to Bowdoin and its equally expensive Maine neighbors, Bates and Colby. It afflicts every private college and university that still has some sense of public responsibility. It is a problem that not even better endowed scholarship funds would fully solve, for the reality of small-college financial life is that a certain number of students have to be accepted whose parents can afford to subsidize at least a part of the education of their less fortunate classmates. (Thanks to endowment income, though, nobody actually pays the full cost of being educated.) Whatever Bowdoin's shortcomings, in the past it could claim with some accuracy that, for its time and place, it was a reasonably egalitarian institution. Since the 1980s, this has been—on the surface at least—less the case, given the opulence of about a third of its student population. There is no immediate answer to this problem—which is psychological as much as it is material—but a college that does not show that it is aware of the alienating effects of its price tag and at least try to lessen the damage will rapidly lose the confidence, the sense of shared destiny, of many of the people of the state.

The second complication is almost as intractable, and similarly tied to Bowdoin's desire to perpetuate its identity as a quintessentially Maine college. It can be summed up in a statement by the essayist Wallace Stegner: "If you don't know where you are, you don't know who you are." He was writing about the American West, but the thought is especially apposite here, for part of Maineness has been an intense sense of the local. Yet each year seems to make Maine a little less itself, a little more like the rest of America.

In an ironic way, the ideal "middle landscape" of Samuel Deane and Timothy Dwight—a humanized, peaceful, productive world between the chaos of the forest and the dreadfulness of the city—has been realized all along the interstates of America, in a strip of industrial "parks" and shopping "malls" and "garden" suburbs. At times Brunswick already seems at the edge of the mid-Atlantic housing sprawl that starts somewhere in Virginia and creeps northward. Today it is still possible in any Maine town to escape quickly into what feels like a nineteenth-century landscape, but the drive to reach that place will grow longer and longer. For a college that is identified so strongly with the pastoral, pre-modern side of Maine life, these changes are both a blessing and a curse. Too often in the past, the College took refuge in its geographic isolation; too many times, a provinciality of spirit prevailed. (On some gate at Bowdoin should be inscribed the words, "Kant wrote in Königsberg, in Weimar Goethe thrived"—small towns, too.) On the other hand, the College's psychic capital is very much invested in a relatively unspoiled version of coastal Maine.

Fortunately, in recent years the sentiment has spread that certain landscapes can—and should—be preserved. As Tony Hiss has written, we are beginning to understand better the notion of "perceptive reach" in our everyday environment—the fact that "particular places around us, if we're wide open to receive them, can sometimes give us a mental lift."[4] He was writing specifically of how he felt upon walking into Grand Central Station, but the experience can be verified in the countryside as well. The point is that the experience needs to be *every day*, not just part of the pilgrimage to Acadia National Park.[5]

The third great complication reaches beyond geography, yet how it is dealt with over the next few decades will very much shape the human environment of places like Bowdoin. Just what *is* a liberal arts college? What does a student go there to do? Is it just another version of a university, but with fewer people about? Or at its best can such a place offer an intensity of experience, a shaping of one's inner life, that is increasingly less possible to achieve in the modern multiversity? As of 1993, there was certainly no agreement on these matters. The older paradigms—the early nineteenth-century notion of pursuing republican virtue, the Victorian belief in ethical training at the hands of clergyman-presidents, the "liberating" impulses of the twentieth-century reformers—have never totally disappeared, but they no longer present a completely persuasive rationale for the small residential liberal arts college. No consensus on what a college should teach, no theory of what it takes to be an educated citizen is widely enough accepted today to enjoy the prestige of the earlier models.

Despite their popularity, despite their probable ability to survive the financial difficulties that the 1980s bequeathed to them, despite the prestige and market value of their degrees, these colleges seem to have lost some of their sense of mission. For the moment this can be disguised—sometimes in New Age language about community and caring, sometimes by echoing the brisker rhetoric of William DeWitt Hyde—but the problem remains. The brighter students, the more alert teachers seem aware of it. One reason may be that, despite the extraordinary changes in American society since World War I, the basic organizational principles of the liberal arts colleges have not changed in a century or more. Another explanation is simply the devaluation throughout American society of some learned skills—writing and speaking, for example—which the traditional college was designed to teach, and there is no longer any consensus as to what a student needs to know to be liberally educated.

Whether Bowdoin College, whether any college, overcomes those difficulties is a subject for someone else's book. It is an encouraging sign that people do want to talk about these issues: the final event in Bowdoin's bicentennial year, for example, is to be a colloquium on the future of the liberal arts in undergraduate education. And however shrill the debate over the liberal arts curriculum has been of late, it helps to remember that now, as before, students go about their business, often happily unaware of the institutional quarrels raging in the next room.

In looking back on the writing of this book, I am struck again and again by the intimacy of Bowdoin's history. Not just by the smallness of numbers (some 14,000 living alumni, fewer peo-ple than are currently enrolled at many American universities), but the nearness of things past. When I sat in Special Collections reading Professor Smyth's writings against slavery, I could look out the window at the house in which he had written them. When I walked home in the evening, I passed the room where James Hanscom 1846 kept his diary, where he listened to the stonemason's chisel on the gray granite of the Chapel. One day the Portland bookman Francis O'Brien h '90 told me he remembered seeing the elderly Chamberlain walking stiffly around Portland. Another day William Curtis Pierce '28, a Wall Street lawyer and Trustee Emeritus and a central figure over several decades in the life of the College (as his father had been before him), handed me a briefcase. It was full of letters, from his Pierce ancestors in the Classes of 1818, 1846, and 1896, written from Bowdoin back home to the farm in West Baldwin. Keep them as long as you like, he told me.

If there is some danger in this intimacy, it is in ignoring how quickly history can transform itself into myth. New England, with its love of commemoration, its urge to find historical anniversaries to celebrate, is particularly fertile ground for this kind of transformation. On a more national scale, we have recently seen how the filmmaker Ken Burns h '91—to the discomfort of many professional historians—re-created the Civil War as a kind of Homeric epic. It became pure spectacle: emotionally wrenching, cathartic, unforgettable. But it was a war that had almost no connection with the political economy or the religious ferment or the free soil debates of America in 1860.[6]

In the case of educational institutions, with their continually renewed student populations and their unquenchable need for the kindness of both friends and strangers, a certain amount of myth-making is probably the glue that holds it all together. Sometimes, this is an innocent rewriting of the truth. For example, at some point in the last century the story developed that the sun was chosen for Bowdoin's seal because it was (at the time) the easternmost college in the country—the first college the sun touched each morning. In fact, the sun is an ancient symbol of divine wisdom, with a rich iconography from the Renaissance into the eighteenth century, and the men who established Bowdoin were trying to bring the District of Maine into the metropolitan culture of Boston, not to call attention to the region's remoteness. It was a century later, when the rusticators discovered coastal Maine and its rural virtues, that "easternness" would be a quality to turn to promotional effect.[7]

While history describes, compares, pulls apart, myth aims at an ideal truth. It does not seek to inform so much as sustain. One of the sustaining myths of Bowdoin College, for example, is that it has always been a place to which poor but able Maine youths could come and improve themselves. From the earliest classes on, there is much evidence to suggest that this often happened. But, as we have seen, there were other aspects of Bowdoin that served to distance it from the lives of the people of Maine. Perhaps both a sustaining myth and its counter-myth can be at once true.

But there are more ways in which history can work, other than through myth. There is history as exemplum. In the eighteenth century, this meant reading Plutarch or Livy to learn how great men behaved. Today, why could it not mean learning about John Albion Andrew or Thomas Brackett Reed, Paul Douglas or Hod-

ding Carter, Alfred Kinsey or the physicist Edwin H. Hall, Matilda White Riley or Joan Benoit Samuelson? The rediscovery in recent years of Joshua L. Chamberlain—virtually forgotten outside of Maine until Ken Burns, among others, brought him back to the nation's attention as an exemplar of the citizen-soldier—is a case in point. A college like Bowdoin becomes then a place to practice a certain *pietas*—not worshipping those who were here before us, but simply thinking about them, taking them seriously. And there is history as a sense of place. Since 1802 students at Bowdoin have been able to discover how the physical presence of a small college in Maine can embody an educational ideal.

This can be seen most clearly in the late afternoon in winter after a fresh snowfall. The streets are quiet. Most people are indoors. As the darkness thickens, the white snow turns blue. The boundary between the settled world and the unpeopled one beyond your sight begins to blur. You can imagine the uncreased skin of snow stretching north, into the night. Crossing the Bowdoin Quad, you suddenly turn and see, down the alley of bare maples, the lights of Massachusetts Hall in the darkness. Knowledge survives, they say. Come in and find it.

— Charles C. Calhoun

NOTES

1. John Stilgoe, lecture at the conference "Historic Gardens and Landscapes: Preserving Maine's Legacy," sponsored by Maine Citizens for Historic Preservation, Bar Harbor, 20 June 1987.

2. Recent viewbooks, it is interesting to note, *also* show scenes of Portland, notably the picturesque, consumer-oriented Old Port; prospective students, after all, may want the best of both worlds. If it is objected that most American colleges and universities try to convey a pastoral campus image in luring their "customers," one could point out that Bowdoin has done a more persuasive job of it than most of them.

3. Approximately 15 percent of the graduating class in recent years has gone into teaching.

4. Tony Hiss, "Experiencing Places," *The New Yorker*, 22 June 1987, p. 56. See Tony Hiss, *The Experience of Place* (New York, 1990). Hiss argues that environment is not only of aesthetic importance but directly affects one's sense of well being and ability to function in the world. The late nineteenth-century argument for the country college may have had something to it, after all.

5. The local aspects of this international problem are outlined in Holly Dominie, "Maine's Changing Landscape," Richard Barringer, ed., *Changing Maine* (Portland, 1990), pp. 89-106. Dominie's work on "viewscapes" has had much influence on Maine's comprehensive land use planning movement.

6. The issues raised by Ken Burns's much praised series *The Civil War* (1989) were debated, for example, at the conference "Telling the Story: The Media, the Public, and American History," Boston, 23–24 April 1993, sponsored by the New England Foundation for the Humanities—not just specific criticisms (e. g., did the series glorify mass slaughter? Did the narrative have a Southern bias?) but the broader question of how much history has to be simplified and dramatized to hold a popular audience. Burns candidly admitted at one session that it was "his" Civil War—i.e., that elements of the story were chosen for their visual impact, or because of their emotional impact on his own sensibility. For a discussion of these matters, see Jane Turner Censer, "Videobites: Ken Burns's 'The Civil War' in the Classroom," *American Quarterly* 44, no. 2 (June 1992), pp. 244–254, and, more generally, Robert Brent Toplin, "The Filmmaker as Historian," *American Historical Review* 93, no. 5 (December 1988), pp. 1210–1227. In Burns's defense is the fact that millions of viewers learned more about the Civil War from his film than they had learned in school—and, in many instances, were inspired by him to read further.

7. The alacrity with which nineteenth-century Americans invented traditions in this fashion has been chronicled in Michael Kammen, *Mystic Chords of Memory: The Transformation of Tradition in American Culture* (New York, 1991), and, closer to home, Sarah L. Giffen and Kevin D. Murphy, eds., *"A Noble and Dignified Stream": The Piscataqua Region in the Colonial Revival, 1860–1930* (York, Me., 1992). On the Bowdoin sun, see Gerard J. Brault, "The Sun on the Seal: A New Interpretation," *Bowdoin Alumnus* 33, no. 2 (December 1958), pp. 4–5.

APPENDIX I

THE CHARTER OF BOWDOIN COLLEGE

The Charter of Bowdoin College was adopted by an Act of the General Court of the Commonwealth of Massachusetts passed on June 24, 1794.

The Charter has been amended three times since it was granted, in 1891, 1973, and 1978. In 1891, limitations on the amount of property that could be taken and held by the College and on the amount of income that could be received were eliminated. In 1973, changes were made (1) to enable the Trustees and the Overseers to establish terms of office for their members in lieu of life tenure and (2) to permit officers of the College other than the Treasurer to execute deeds. The most recent amendment, in 1978, removed the position of Treasurer as an *ex officio* member of the Board of Trustees although the number of Trustees continues to be from seven to thirteen. All three amendments have been incorporated in this copy of the Charter.

CHARTER OF BOWDOIN COLLEGE

An act to establish a College in the Town of Brunswick, in the District of Maine, within this Commonwealth.

Sect 1. Be it enacted by the Senate and House of Representatives, in General Court assembled, and by the authority of the same, That there be erected and established in the Town of Brunswick, in the District of Maine, a College for the purpose of educating youth, to be called and known by the name of Bowdoin College, to be under the government and regulation of two certain bodies politick and corporate, as hereafter in this Act is provided.

Sect 2. And be it further enacted by the authority aforesaid, That the Rev. Thomas Brown, Rev. Samuel Dean, D.D., John Frothingham, Esq., Rev. Daniel Little, Rev. Thomas Lancaster, Hon. Josiah Thacher, and David Mitchell, Esquires, Rev. Tristram Gilman, Rev. Alden Bradford, Thomas Rice, Esq., and Mr. William Martin, together with the President and Treasurer of the said College, for the time being, to be chosen as in this Act is hereafter directed, be and hereby are created a body politick and corporate, by the name of The President and Trustees of Bowdoin College, and that they and their successors, and such others as shall be duly elected members of the said Corporation, shall be and remain a body politick and corporate, by that name forever.

Sect. 3. And be it further enacted by the authority aforesaid, That for the more orderly conducting the business of the said corporation, the president and trustees shall have full power and authority, from time to time, to elect a vice president and secretary of the said corporation, and to declare the tenures and duties of their respective offices; and to elect trustees of said corporation, for such terms and upon such conditions as they may from time to time determine, and also to remove any trustee from the same corporation, when, in their judgment, he shall be incapable or shall neglect or refuse to perform the duties of his office. Provided nevertheless, that the number of the said trustees, including the president of the said college, for the time being, shall never be greater than 13, nor less than 7.

Sect. 4. And be it further enacted, That the said corporation may have one common seal, which they may change, break or renew at their pleasure; and that all deeds signed and delivered by the treasurer, or by such other officer as the trustees may from time to time appoint, and sealed with their seal, by order of the president and trustees, shall when made in their corporate name, be considered in law as the deeds of the said corporation; and that the said corporation may sue and be sued in all actions, real, personal or mixed; and may prosecute and defend the same to final judgment and execution, by the name of the president and trustees of Bowdoin College; and that the said corporation shall be capable of having, holding and taking, in fee simple or any less estate, by gift, grant, devise, or otherwise any lands, tenements, or other estate, real or personal.

Sect. 5. And be it further enacted by the authority aforesaid, That the said Corporation shall have full power and authority to determine at what times and places their meetings shall be holden, and on the manner of notifying the Trustees to convene at such meetings, and also, from time to time, to elect a President and Treasurer of the said College, and such Professors, Tutors, Instructors, and other Officers of the said College as they shall judge most for the interest thereof, and to determine the duties, salaries, emoluments and tenures of their several offices aforesaid: (The said President for the time being, when elected and inducted into his office, to be, ex officio, President of the said Corporation) and also to purchase, or erect and keep in repair such houses and other buildings as they shall judge necessary for the said College; and also to make and ordain, as occasion may require, reasonable rules, orders and by-laws, not repugnant to the laws of this Commonwealth, with reasonable penalties, for the good government of the said College; and also to determine and prescribe the mode of ascertaining the qualifications of the students requisite to their admission; and also to confer such degrees as are usually conferred by Universities established for the education of youth; and a majority of the members of said Corporation, present at any legal meeting, shall decide all questions which may properly come before the said Trustees: Provided nevertheless, That no corporate business shall be transacted at any meeting, unless seven, at least, of the trustees are present: And provided further, That the said Corporation shall confer no degrees other than those of Bachelor of Arts and Master of Arts, until after the first day of January, which will be in the year of our Lord one thousand eight hundred ten.

Sect. 6. And be it further enacted by the authority aforesaid, That the clear rents, issues and profits of all the estate, real and personal, of which the said Corporation shall be seized or possessed, shall be appropriated to the endowment of the said College, in such manner as shall most effectually promote Virtue and Piety, and the knowledge of such of the Languages, and of the useful and liberal Arts and Sciences, as shall hereafter be directed, from time to time, by the said Corporation.

And more effectually to provide for the wise regular government of the said College, and for the prudent administration of the funds belonging to it, by establishing a supervising body with proper powers;

Sect. 7. Be it further enacted by the authority aforesaid, That no election made by the said Corporation, either of Trustees to fill up vacancies, or of President or Treasurer of the said College, for any vote or order of the said Corporation to remove any Trustee, or any officer of the said College or to purchase or erect any house or other building for the said College, or to determine what officers shall be established for the said College, or the duties, salaries, emoluments or tenures of such officers, or for the appropriation of any of their funds or monies, or for the acceptance of any estate, when the donation thereof was made upon condition, or for determining qualifications for conferring of any degrees, or for the making, altering, amending or repealing any rules, orders or by-laws for the government of the said College, shall have any force, effect or validity, until the same shall have been agreed to by the Overseers of the said Bowdoin College hereafter in this Act created.

Sect. 8. And be it further enacted by the authority aforesaid, That the Hon. Josiah Thacher, Esq., be and he is hereby authorized and empowered to fix the time and place for holding the first meeting of the said Trustees, and to notify each of said Trustees thereof in writing.

And for the establishing of the supervising body with proper powers above mentioned;

Sect. 9. Be it further enacted by the authority aforesaid, That Edward Cutts, Thomas Cutts, Symon Frye, David Sewall, and Nathaniel Wells, Esquires, Rev. Moses Hemmenway, D.D., Rev. Silas Moody, Rev. John Thompson, Rev. Nathaniel Webster, Rev. Paul Coffin, Rev. Benjamin Chadwick, Rev. Samuel Eaton, Rev. Samuel Foxcroft, Rev. Caleb Jewett, Rev. Alfred Johnson, Rev. Elijah Kellogg, Rev. Ebenezer Williams, Rev. Charles Turner, Daniel Davis, Samuel Freeman, Joshua Fabyan, William Gorham, Stephen Longfellow, Joseph Noyes, Issac Parsons, Robert Southgate, John Wait, Peleg Wadsworth, and William Widgery, Esquires, Rev. Ezekiel Emerson, Jonathan Ellis, Jonathan Bowman, Edmund Bridge, Daniel Cony, Henry Dearborn, Dummer Sewall, Samuel Thompson, John Dunlap, Francis Winter, Nathaniel Thwing, Alexander Campbell, and Paul Dudley Sargeant, Esquires together with the President of the College, and the Secretary of the Corporation, first created in this Act, for the time being, be and they are hereby created a body politick and corporate, by that name forever.

Sect. 10. And be it further enacted by the authority aforesaid, That the Members of the said Corporation of Overseers may have one common seal, which they may change, break and renew at their pleasure, and that they may sue or be sued, prosecute and defend unto final judgment and execution, by the name of The Overseers of Bowdoin College.

Sect. 11. And be it further enacted by the authority aforesaid, that for the orderly conducting the business of the said last mentioned corporation, the members thereof shall have full power, from time to time, as they shall determine, to elect a president, vice president and secretary, and to fix the tenures and duties of their respective offices; and also, to determine at what times and places their meetings shall be holden, and upon the manner of notifying the Overseers to convene at such meetings; and to provide for the election of persons for Trustees, from time to time, shall determine; and to remove any Overseer from the said Corporation when, in the judgment of the Overseers, he shall be rendered incapable, or shall neglect or refuse to perform the duties of his office; and a majority of the members present, at any legal meeting, shall decide all questions which may properly come before the said Overseers: Provided nevertheless, that the number of the said Overseers, including the President of the College, and the Secretary of The President and Trustees of Bowdoin College, shall never be greater than forty-five, nor less than twenty-five.

Sect. 12. And be it further enacted by the authority aforesaid, That the Overseers of said Bowdoin College shall have power to agree or disagree to any election, vote, order or act of the President and Trustees of said College, where the agreement of the said Overseers is made necessary by this Act to give force, effect and validity to such election, vote, order, or act; and they are hereby directed to notify the said President and Trustees of such agreement or disagreement, in convenient time thereafter; and the said Overseers are also empowered to call upon any Treasurer of the said College, his Executors and Administrators, to render to them a just and true account of all the doings of such Treasurer, in his said office, as often as the said Overseers shall direct. Provided nevertheless, That no corporate business shall be transacted at any meeting of the Overseers aforesaid, unless fifteen of them, at the least, are present.

Sect. 13. And be it further enacted by the authority aforesaid, that the Treasurer of the said College, shall before he enter upon the execution of the duties of his office, give bond to the said Overseers, in such penalty, and with such sureties, as they shall approve of, conditioned for the faithful discharge of the duties of the said office, and for rendering a just and true account of his doings therein, when required, and that all the monies, securities, and other property of the President and Trustees of Bowdoin College, together with all the books in which his accounts and proceedings, as Treasurer, were entered and kept, that appertain to his office of Treasurer as aforesaid, shall, upon demand made upon him, his Executors or Administrators, be paid and delivered over to his successor in that Office; and all monies to be recovered by virtue of any suits at law, upon such bond, shall be paid over to the President and Trustees aforesaid, and subjected to the appropriations above directed in this Act.

Sect. 14. And be it further enacted by the authority aforesaid, that no Trustee of the said College, excepting the President and Secretary, first above mentioned, shall be an Overseer of the said College; and if any Trustee (excepting as aforesaid) shall be chosen an Overseer, he shall cease to be a Trustee immediately, upon his accepting the place of an Overseer; and if any Overseer of the said College (excepting as aforesaid) shall hereafter be elected a Trustee, he shall cease to be an Overseer, upon his accepting the place of a Trustee.

Sect. 15. And be it further enacted by the authority aforesaid, That the Hon. DAVID SEWALL, Esq., be and he hereby is authorized and empowered to fix the time and place of the first meeting of the Overseers of said Bowdoin College, and to notify the said Overseers thereof, by publishing the same three weeks successively in each of the Portland newspapers; the last publication to be made three weeks, at least, before the time fixed for the said meeting.

Sect. 16. And be it further enacted by the authority aforesaid, That the Legislature of this Commonwealth may grant any further powers to, or alter, limit, annul or restrain any of the powers by this Act vested in the said Corporation, as shall be judged necessary to promote the best interests of the said College.

Sect. 17. And be it further enacted by the authority aforesaid, that there be and hereby is granted five townships of land, of the contents of six miles square each, to be laid out and assigned from any of the unappropriated lands belonging to this Commonwealth, in the district of Maine, the same to be vested in the Trustees of Bowdoin College, and their successors forever, for the use, benefit and purpose of supporting the said College, to be by them holden in their corporate capacity, with full power and authority to settle, divide, and manage the same townships, or any part thereof, or to sell, convey, and dispose of the same in such way and manner as shall best promote the welfare of said College, the same to be laid out under the direction of the Committee for the sale of eastern lands, and a plan or plans thereof returned into the Secretary's office: Provided, The Trustees aforesaid, or their assigns, shall cause to be settled fifteen families in each of said townships within twelve years from the passing this Act: And provided also, There shall be reserved in each township three lots of three hundred and twenty acres each, for the following uses, viz. one lot for the first settled Minister—one lot for the use of the Ministry—and one lot for the use of schools in each of said townships.

APPENDIX II

CHAPTER I
Admission into College.

1. There shall be four Classes in the College, namely, the Freshman, Sophomore, Junior, and Senior Classes; and no person shall be admitted into either of them, unless he produces satisfactory testimonials of his good moral character.

2. No person shall be admitted into the Freshman class under fifteen years of age, nor unless, upon examination by the President and Instructers of the College, or a majority of them, he is found accurately acquainted with the Grammar of the Latin and Greek languages, including Prosody, with Sallust, Cicero's select Orations, the Bucolics, Georgics and Æneid of Virgil, the four Gospels of the Greek Testament, and Jacob's Greek Reader, and is able to write Latin correctly; and is also well versed in ancient and modern Geography, the fundamental rules of Arithmetic, vulgar and decimal fractions, proportion, fellowship, alligation, progression, and the doctrine of roots and powers.

3. No person shall be admitted into the Sophomore class under sixteen years of age, nor to an advanced standing, unless upon examination he is found acquainted with the studies, which have been pursued by the class, into which he seeks admission; and every person, thus admitted, unless he comes recommended from some other College, shall immediately pay to the Treasurer, for every full term's advancement, the sum charged for a term's tuition.

4. Every Student, when admitted, shall receive a copy of the Laws, with a certificate of his admission into College, signed by the President; and shall immediately deliver to the Treasurer a bond, with satisfactory surety or sureties, in the sum of two hundred dollars, for the payment of his Term bills, according to the laws and customs of the College, and also of such sum, as may be assessed to repair the damage done to his room, or other damage, for which he may be responsible, at the time of Commencement, when he shall take his degree.

5. Every Student, admitted into the Freshman or Sophomore class, unless he comes recommended from another College, shall be put upon probation for one term; and if, during that period, he shall not be diligent in study and correct in all his conduct, the Executive Government may dissolve his connexion with College.

CHAPTER II
Officers and Discipline of the College

6. The Executive authority of the College is vested in the President, Professors, Tutors, and librarian, who constitute the *Executive Government,* and have power to govern the Students, according to the laws and rules of the College.

7. The President, during the College Terms, shall reside at Brunswick, and shall pray in the Chapel morning and evening, and read or expound some portion of the Holy Scriptures, or deliver some religious discourse, or theological lecture. When he cannot attend, the other Officers shall successively pray in the Chapel, and read some portion of Scripture.

8. The President is to superintend the course of instruction, and the general concerns of the College; to call meetings of the Executive Government and to preside and vote in the same; to preside at Examination, Exhibitions, and Commencements; to cause to be kept a fair record of every case of punishment under these laws; and to address, as he may find occasion, public and private instruction and counsel to the Students.

9. In case of the death or resignation of the President, the duties of his office shall be performed by such person or persons, as may be designated by the Executive Government, until, another President shall be elected, and inducted into office. In case of vacancy in the office of Tutor, Librarian or Proctor, his duties shall be performed by such person, as may be designated by the Executive Government, until the next meeting of the Boards.

10. The Executive Government shall faithfully instruct the Students in the Languages, Arts, and Sciences in the manner prescribed, and shall faithfully execute the laws of the College, and maintain discipline and order, always taking special care to exercise, as far as possible, a parental government over the Students, and to give them the counsel of friendship; to visit them at their chambers, to superintend their deportment, to assist them always in their studies, to encourage them in the practice of virtue, and to endeavor to substitute a moral power over the heart, as a principle of order, in the place of the fear of punishment, so that the penalties of the law shall fall only on those, who yield not to higher and better motives, and are not influenced by a regard to character, by filial gratitude, by the love of excellence, and the sense of duty to God.

11. The Executive Government shall hold frequent meetings to deliberate on the concerns of the College, and to secure the most perfect co-operation and uniformity of discipline, to inquire into all violations of the laws, and to inflict by vote the necessary punishments.

When the Government shall have reason to believe, that any Students are wasting their time and are in the habit of being irregularly absent from their chambers, it shall be the duty of the Officer of the entry, in which such Students may live, to visit their rooms in study hours, especially in the evening, and make a record of such absence, the reasons of which shall be inquired into by the Government; and if, after repeated admonition, the offender does not reform, the Executive Government shall request his parent or guardian to remove him from College, or may dismiss him.

12. The punishments, which may be inflicted, are the exaction of special lessons, and of studies in vacations, private admonition, official notice of delinquency to the parent or guardian of a Student, dismission from College, suspension, degradation, rustication, and expul-

sion—The frequency and repetition of offences shall aggravate the punishment milder than the severest, which is authorized by the law, applicable to the particular case.

13. The term of suspension shall never exceed nine months. A time shall be assigned to every suspended person for leaving the College and the town of Brunswick, unaccompanied by any Student; and if he remain beyond that time, he shall be liable to an additional punishment. He shall pursue his studies, agreeably to the direction of the Government, under such person, as they may appoint, or as his parent, at their request, may provide; and on his return shall produce from the gentleman, under whom he was placed, testimonials of his good conduct, during his whole absence. If upon examination, he shall appear to have pursued with diligence the studies of his class, and other assigned studies, he shall be readmitted to his class; but, if he appears to have been indolent, or fails to bring the testimonial required, he may be degraded to the next lower class, or shall be further suspended for a term, not exceeding six months, at the end of which, if he be not found qualified for read-mission into his class, he shall be degraded.

14. Every rusticated person, shall, in like manner, leave the College and the town of Brunswick, and shall not return before the end of twelve months. If the testimonials of his good behavior and the evidence of diligence in study be perfectly satisfactory to the Government, he may be permitted to rejoin his class on probation, for as long a term as the Executive Government may appoint, during which period he may be dismissed at their discretion.

15. If any Student, having a public censure passed upon him, shall, on account of it, insult the Executive Government, or any member of it, his punishment shall be increased. If any Student shall offer an insult to the Government, or to any individual of the Government, or shall behave in a disorderly manner, in consequence of the infliction of a public censure on a fellow Student, he shall be punished by suspension, rustication, or expulsion, according to the degree and aggravation of the offence.

16. Whereas offences of various kinds may be committed by a number of the Students, and it may be thought unnecessary to punish all the offenders; in such cases, the Executive Government may punish so many of them as may be necessary to secure good order, due regard being had in the punishment to the previous conduct and general character.

CHAPTER III
Devotional Exercises, and the Observance of the Lord's Day.

17. All resident graduates and undergraduates shall seasonably attend morning and evening prayers in the Chapel, and such exercises on the Sabbath, as may be appointed, all Theological lectures, and the usual meetings for public Worship at the appointed place, on the Lord's day, and on public Fasts and Thanksgivings; and every Student for disorderly, irreverent, or indecent behavior at a religious exercise shall be admonished, sus-

pended, or rusticated, according to the aggravation of the offence. For frequent tardiness, or for any absence without permission or leaving the place of worship during the services, he shall be liable to admonition or suspension.

18. Whereas some Christians consider the evening of Saturday, and others the evening of the Lord's Day, as a part of the Sabbath, every Student shall on the evening of Saturday retire to his chamber, and not unnecessarily leave it, and on both those evenings shall abstain from diversions of every kind. It is enjoined upon all the Students carefully to apply themselves to the duties of religion on the Lord's Day. They, who profane the same by unnecessary business, visiting, or receiving visits, or by walking abroad, or by any amusement, or in other ways, may be admonished or suspended.

19. The Students are required to attend public worship at the appointed place. But, in order to secure the rights of conscience, it is provided, that, if any one shall desire to attend the services of any other regular Christian society in the town of Brunswick, he may, at his own request, if he is twenty one years old, or, if a minor, at the written request of his parent or guardian, be allowed to attend the meeting of that society, but not on any other. Any Student, an inhabitant of Topsham, and boarding at home, may also be allowed to attend public worship in that town. In these cases, such evidence of punctual attendance shall be given, as the Executive Government may require.

CHAPTER IV
Studies and Literary Exercises.

20. The hours of study, in the forenoon, from Commencement to the first of April, shall be from nine to twelve o'clock, and thence to Commencement from half an hour after eight to twelve; and during the year from two o'clock to evening prayers. They shall begin in the evening, in October and April, at eight o'clock, in November and March, at half an hour after seven, in December and February, at seven, and in the other months at nine o'clock; subject to variations by the Executive Government.

During the hours of study, the Students shall remain in their respective chambers, and diligently pursue their studies. For unnecessary absence, and for interrupting the studies of others by resorting to their rooms, by singing, playing on any instrument, calling from a window, or by any tumult, outcry or noise, they shall be liable to admonition or suspension.

21. The Course of Studies shall comprehend the Languages, Rhetoric, the various branches of the Mathematics, the Philosophy of the Human Mind, the different departments of Natural, Moral, and Political Science, the evidences of Natural and Revealed Religion, together with such other branches of learning, as the Executive Government may require to be studied. With these pursuits shall be intermixed frequent essays in Elocution, English Composition, and Forensic Disputation.

The several classes shall recite in such books, and in such manner, and attend and perform such other exercises, as the Executive Government may appoint and direct.

22. The times of recitation shall be immediately after morning prayers, at eleven o'clock, and one hour before evening prayers; subject however to such variations, as the Instructers may find convenient. The classes shall attend recitations three times a day, excepting the Seniors, who may be excused from three recitations in each week; but on the afternoon of Saturday no recitation shall be required. An unseasonable attendance without excuse may be marked as an absence. The recitation rooms are not to be entered by Students, except at the times of recitation.

If any Student shall be absent from a stated Exercise, or in the performance, give evidence of negligence, a record shall be made of such absence or neglect; and if his absence or neglect become frequent and obstinate, he shall be admonished, suspended, or rusticated. In punishment of idleness, an Instructer may require special lessons, either in study hours or play hours.

23. The Freshmen shall read or declaim statedly before one of their Instructers; and the members of the other classes, with the Freshmen in their last term, shall declaim alphabetically in public, as many each week as the Executive Government shall direct. The piece to be declaimed must be offered for the approbation of the presiding Officer, as early as Friday before the day of declaiming. Nothing shall be spoken, which shall not have been approved. No loud applauses, nor any disorderly expressions of approbation or disgust shall be permitted.

24. Every Student shall be decorous in his behavior at all lectures and exercises, public and private. Any conduct disrespectful to the Instructer, or tending to divert the attention from the object of the exercise, shall subject the offender to an adequate punishment.

25. Any exercises, which have been omitted by reason of absence not exceeding one week, or from other causes, shall be performed on the next attendance of the Student with his class, or as his Instructer shall direct, unless excused for sufficient reasons.

26. No Student, without the permission of the Executive Government, shall attend the instructions of any person, who may undertake to teach any language, science or art, in Brunswick or Topsham.

27. In order to correct the disposition to be idle and negligent, and to render exact justice to every Student, there shall be formed in each term a general *Scale of Merit* for every class. In forming it, each Instructer of a class shall make out a weekly list, exhibiting the merit or rank of every Student agreeably to one common method of notation. From these various lists a general list shall be formed; from the general weekly lists shall be made a Term list at the close of each Term; and from the three Term lists an annual list at the close of each year.

To this scale of merit reference shall be had in assigning parts for Exhibitions and Commencements, and also in judging at the annual examinations of the necessity of degradng a scholar to the next lower class. It shall be open to the examination of the Boards of Trustees and Overseers at their annual meetings. There shall also be kept a list of absences from College exercises and of pun-

ishments, and an account of moral deportment and application to study; and an abstract of these lists and accounts, with a copy of the Term bill, shall be sent every term to the parents or guardians of Students, and may be exhibited to the Boards.

28. There shall be in every term an Examination of each class in the studies of the term before the Executive Government and such other gentlemen as may attend. The time of examination shall be for the first and second terms on Tuesday and Wednesday preceding vacation. In the third term, the time of the examination of the Senior class shall be on the fifth Tuesday preceding Commencement, and that of the other classes on Tuesday and Wednesday of the week preceding Commencement.

The examinations for the third term shall include the studies of the whole year, and will be attended by a Committee of the Boards. If any one, in consequence of his past negligence, shall, on examination, be found grossly deficient, he shall be put on probation, if a member of the Senior class, till the week preceding Commencement, or be deprived of his degree, or degraded to the next lower class; if a member of one of the other classes, he shall study, as the Executive Government may direct, during the next vacation, or he may be degraded or dismissed. Should any Student be absent, he shall be examined, as soon as may be, after his return. And at any examination the Executive Government shall put on probation any Student, who appears to be grossly deficient in the studies of his class.

29. There shall be annually at least two Exhibitions, parts in which shall be assigned to select scholars of the two upper classes, reference being had in the selection to the Scale of Merit, and to the general conduct. One exhibition shall be on some day of the week, in which the vacation begins in the month of May, and the other in October. There shall be a rehearsal before the President or some other Officer.

A fair copy of each part, after it has been examined and approved, shall be lodged with the President at least one week before the Exhibition. Nothing shall be delivered in public varying from this copy. Students, who have been grossly negligent of Composition, or Declamation, or of any branch of Study, or who have been disorderly or irregular in their conduct, shall be considered as disqualified for receiving a part, unless there is decided evidence of reformation.

30. A premium of the value of ten dollars in books, to be denominated the *Sewall premium*, shall be annually given, at the pleasure of a Committee appointed by the Executive Government, to a member of the Junior class for excellence in Oratory, as evinced in a public trial at the time of Commencement.

31. No public exercise shall be performed by any Student in Brunswick, or in any neighboring town, unless it shall have been examined and approved by one of the Executive Government appointed for the purpose, nor shall any thing be spoken contrary to the directions of such Officer under pain of admonition or suspension.

32. The public Lectures on Natural and Experimental Philosophy, on Chemistry, on Mineralogy, on Metaphysics and Ethics, and on other subjects, such as Public

Law and Political Economy, Classical Literature, Rhetoric and Oratory, Natural History, and the Sciences as connected with the Arts, when they shall be established, may be attended by young gentlemen, not members of the College, by permission of the Executive Government, on condition of producing evidence of good moral character, and engaging to observe such of the College laws, as may be designated. The fee to be paid to the Treasurer shall be ten dollars for each course of Lectures, excepting the Medical.

CHAPTER V.
Misdemeanors and Criminal Offences.

33. If any Student shall be guilty of profaneness, intoxication, or dissoluteness; of lying or purloining, of challenging, assaulting, or fighting with any person; or shall sing indecent songs, or be indecent in conversation; or shall lead a dissipated life; or shall associate with any person of known dissolute morals; or shall violate in any other way the moral law of God; he shall be admonished, suspended, rusticated, or expelled.

34. No Student shall eat or drink in any tavern, unless in company with his parent or guardian, nor attend any theatrical entertainment or any idle show in Brunswick or Topsham, nor frequent any tavern, nor any house or shop after being forbidden by the President or other Instructer, nor be guilty of disorderly behavior, nor occasion disturbance to any citizen; nor play at cards, billiards, or any game of hazard, nor at any game whatever for money or other things of value; nor shall bring any spirituous liquors into College; nor make any bonfire, nor play off fire works, nor be in any way concerned in the same;—nor, without permission of the Executive Government, engage in any military parade, nor keep a gun or pistol or any gunpowder in College, nor discharge a gun or pistol near the College, nor go shooting or fishing under penalty of admonition, suspension, or rustication.

35. If any Student shall disobey the lawful command of any Officer of College, or treat with contempt the person or authority of anyone of the Executive Government, or shall willfully and maliciously insult any Officer of College, he shall be admonished, suspended, rusticated, or expelled; but the Officer so insulted shall not be present during the deliberations of the Government in relation to the offence committed, nor have any vote in determining the punishment to be inflicted.

36. No Class meeting nor assemblage of Students for consultation shall be held without permission of the President.

If any Students shall combine to absent themselves from any stated exercise, or to commit any disorder, or to disobey any lawful injunction, the Executive Government may punish so many, as they deem necessary, and particularly the mostly active in the affair, by admonition, suspension, or rustication.

37. Every Student may be required in case of high offences to give evidence under pain of suspension, and if he prevaricate in his testimony, or shall refuse to admit an Officer of College into his room, or to render suitable assistance for the preservation of good order, he shall be admonished, or suspended, or expelled; and no College censure beyond admonition shall be inflicted on any individual, until after the testimony against him has been stated to him by the Executive Government, and he has had an opportunity to adduce evidence in his defence.

38. No Student shall be concerned in loud and disorderly singing in College, in shouting, or clapping of hands, nor in any Bacchanalian conduct, disturbing the quietness and dishonorable to the character of a literary Institution, under penalty of admonition or suspension; —nor shall he furnish an entertainment on account of any part assigned him, under penalty of the loss of such part, suspension, or other punishment.

39. Whereas Students may be guilty of disorders or misdemeanors, against which no express provision is made in the laws; in such cases the Executive Government may punish according to the aggravation of the offence. And if any Student shall speedily evince his penitence for his fault, it shall be in the power of the Government, on his private or public confession, to pass over the offence without entering the case on their Records.

And whenever any Club or Society exists in College, which, in the opinion of the Executive Government, has a tendency unfavorable to Science or Morality, it shall be their duty to prohibit the meeting of such Club or Society; and if after such prohibition there shall be a meeting, all persons, concerned in it, shall be liable to suspension, rustication, or expulsion. If any Student shall be dismissed or expelled, he shall have a right to apply to the Boards at their next meeting for a reversal of his sentence.

CHAPTER VI.
Vacations and Absence.

40. There shall be three Vacations in the year;—the first of four weeks, from Commencement, on the first Wednesday of September; the second of six weeks, from the Friday after the first Wednesday of January; and the third of three weeks, from the Friday after the third Wednesday of May.

At the end of each term, the key of every room shall be left with the Officer of the entry, under penalty of the expense of a new lock upon the door, to be charged to the occupants.

41. Four weeks before Commencement the Seniors, on application to the President, may have leave of absence for twenty four days; those, who do not obtain leave of absence, will continue subject to the College laws.

42. No Student shall go out of town, except into Topsham, without permission, nor be absent a night in term time but by leave granted by the President for some urgent reason, expressed in writing by his parent or guardian; excepting, however, in extraordinary cases leave may be granted on the application of the Student for urgent reasons, stated in writing, which shall be recorded, and communicated to his parent or guardian.

If his absence exceed one week, he shall be examined in the studies of his class; if it exceed two months, he may be dismissed from College.—If any one shall go out of town, after leave has been denied, he shall be admonished or suspended.

It shall be in the power of the Executive Government to require a residence at Brunswick in vacation for a length of time, equal to the time of absence, and diligent attention to study. If on examination it appears, that such Student has been negligent, he may be suspended.

43. No Student shall reside in College, nor in Brunswick, excepting an inhabitant, during vacation, but by permission of the Executive Government, and under such regulations, as they may prescribe.—For disorderly or immoral conduct in vacation, every Student shall be responsible, as in term time.

Every Student, on his return to College after vacation or after absence of a night in term time, shall cause the time of his return to be recorded in the book, kept for that purpose by one of the Officers of College, with whom all excuses for absence must be left in writing on the return of the Student. A minor must bring an excuse from his parent or guardian. Specific excuses, assigning the reasons of absence, are required, and of the sufficiency of these reasons the Executive Government will judge.

CHAPTER VII.
The Library.

44. The Librarian shall attend in the Library from twelve to one o'clock of every Wednesday and Saturday, in term time, to deliver and receive books; and no book shall be borrowed or returned without his presence or that of his assistant.

45. The right to borrow books shall belong to the Executive Government, to resident Graduates, pursuing their studies at the College, and whose names are inserted in the term bills, and to Undergraduates.

No Student shall borrow books at the Library oftener than once in three weeks, unless by special permission, nor any Senior or Junior more than three volumes, nor any Sophomore more than two volumes, nor any Freshman more than one volume at a time.

Every book, when taken from the Library, shall have a paper cover, which shall be kept constantly upon it.

46. No person shall write in a book, borrowed from the Library, nor deface it, nor lend it to another, nor carry it out of town, under penalty of losing the privilege of borrowing for such period as the Government may determine. If a book be injured or lost, the borrower, or person doing the injury, shall replace it, or the set, of which it is a part; and the Executive Government may also assess him in a sum, not exceeding the value of the book or the set.

47. No Student, under penalty of being deprived of the use of the Library, shall keep a book longer than six weeks, nor neglect to return the books borrowed, on Wednesday before each vacation; but on this day the Students, who have permission to remain in Brunswick during vacation, may borrow books to be returned at the beginning of the term.

48. It shall be the duty of the Executive Government to designate, for the direction of the Librarian, such books, as will be most useful to the Freshmen, and also such books, as they may deem it proper to prohibit any of the classes from taking out of the Library.

49. The President may draw annually from the Treasury the monies paid into it for the use of the Library. Of the expenditure of such money for the repairing or purchasing of books he shall render an account annually in September.

50. The Executive Government shall have power to examine, at their discretion, all the Libraries of Societies in College and to remove from them all such books, as they may deem worthless or injurious to morals; they may also impose suitable restraints upon such Societies and Libraries in order to prevent unreasonable and burdensome expenses.

CHAPTER VIII.
Chambers, Bills, Boarding, Expenses.

51. No Student shall reside in any room but by permission of the Executive Government who shall first assign all the College chambers before they assign rooms out of the College Halls. Petitions for rooms must be offered one week before Commencement.

52. In each term every room shall be inspected by the Executive Government; and a record shall be kept of all damages to be assessed upon the residents, or persons committing the injury.

All damages by persons unknown, done to the College buildings, or other property of the College, shall be assessed equally on all the Undergraduates, unless there is reason to believe, that the injury was done by other persons.

53. The wood, necessary for the Students in their chambers, shall be provided at the expense of College, and kept on hand for their supply to be charged in their Term bills at its cost. And it shall be the duty of the Treasurer to purchase the wood, and cause it to be delivered at convenient periods to the Students, who request to be supplied, and to keep all necessary accounts respecting it. Each Student shall furnish his equal proportion of the wood, used in his room.

54. In each term the Executive Government shall make out a Bill, and, retaining a copy, shall deliver it for collection to the Treasurer, who shall give his receipt for it. In this Bill, every Student, whether present or absent, unless application is made for dismission, shall be charged eight dollars for tuition; three dollars and thirty four cents for room rent; fifty cents for the use of the Library; twenty five cents to defray the expense of Chemical Lectures; his just proportion of expense for repairing damages and for sweeper and bed maker; his proportion of expense for the employment of monitor, bell ringer, and keepers of the recitation rooms, and for printing the triennial Catalogue; and his proportion of other reasonable assessments. A proper sum shall be charged for the instruction, which may be provided for any Student, required to study in vacations.

55. If any bill is not paid within one month after the commencement of the next term, interest shall be charged; and if not paid within six months from the date

of the bill, there shall be an assessment of twenty cents for every day's neglect, and the Student against whom the bill is made may be dismissed from College.

56. No Student shall board at any house, disapproved by the Executive Government, and in order to prevent an increase in the expense of boarding and to promote a necessary economy, it shall be in the power of a prudential Committee, if appointed for the purpose by the Trustees and Overseers, to prescribe or limit the ordinary bill of fare, and to require Students to board in certain numbers, only at certain designated houses, in which the boarding is agreed to be provided, agreeably to the prescribed bill of fare, for a definite sum, or to establish commons.

57. The Executive Government may request all traders and other persons to keep and exhibit to them at all times a faithful account of all credits, given to Students, and on a neglect to comply with this request, may interdict the Students from obtaining further credit or making any purchase of the person, who thus withholds the desired information.

The Executive Government may limit the expense incurred voluntarily by the Students in procuring music for Commencement, or may themselves contract for the music, and have all or any part of the amount charged in the last Term bill of the Senior Class.

A reasonable sum may be charged for any book, employed in the course of study, and furnished at the expense of College.

58. No Undergraduate of the College shall obtain credit of any innholder, tavern keeper, retailer, confectioner, or keeper of any shop or boarding house for drink or food, or of any livery stable keeper without the consent of the President, who is hereby authorized, as an Officer of the College, to act in such cases, according to the Statute making provision "in furtherance of good Discipline in the Colleges of this State."

CHAPTER IX.
Commencement and Degrees

59. The Commencement shall be held on the first Wednesday of September annually. None but regular members of the Senior Class, of good moral character, as certified by the Executive Government, shall be admitted to the Degree of Bachelor of Arts; nor any one who neglects to perform the part assigned him as a Commencement exercise. A fair copy of each part, after it has been approved by the President, shall be delivered to him as early as the day before the Seniors are by law allowed to leave Brunswick, under penalty of being denied a Degree. If any one shall neglect to rehearse at the appointed time, or shall presume to deliver in public what was not approved by the President, or what he was directed to omit, he shall be liable to the same penalty and shall not be allowed to proceed with his performance.

60. Every Bachelor, who, in the third year after the first degree given to his Class, having preserved a good moral character, shall attend at Commencement and perform the appointed public exercises, unless excused, may receive the Degree of Master of Arts. The part, to be performed by a Bachelor, shall be presented to the President for his examination as early, as the Monday before Commencement. The Candidates for a Medical Degree must also attend at Commencement, and possess a good moral character.

61. The Candidates for the first Degree shall pay five dollars each for the public dinner. Candidates for both degrees shall pay five dollars each to the Treasurer for the President.

A Diploma shall be prepared for the candidates for the first Degree, signed by the President and Secretary of the Trustees, for which three dollars shall be paid to the Treasurer, one of which is for the President. Candidates for the second Degree are not obliged to take a Diploma; but if they seasonably request it, may be furnished on the same terms.

62. Persons, who have received a Degree at another College, may, on paying the customary fee to the Treasurer for the President be admitted to the same Degree. But honorary Degrees, conferred by the Trustees and Overseers on account of distinguished merit, shall be free from all charge.

APPENDIX III

From the *Catalogue of Bowdoin College and the Medical School of Maine*,
Spring Term, 1849, from the Press of J. Griffin

TERMS OF ADMISSION

Candidates for admission into the Freshman Class are required to write Latin grammatically, and to be well versed in Geography, Arithmetic, six sections in Smyth's Algebra, Cicero's Select Orations, (Folsom's edit. preferred,) the Bucolics, Georgics and Aeneid of Virgil, (the *whole*,) Sallust, (Andrews' edit.) the Gospels of the Greek Testament, and Jacob's (or Felton's) Greek Reader; together with Latin and Greek Prosody. They must produce certificates of their good moral character. The time for examination is the Friday after Commencement, and the first Thursday in the Fall term. Candidates for admission into the other classes will be examined also in the books which have been studied by the class, into which admission is requested. Students from other Colleges, before they can be examined, must produce a certificate of their regular dismission. The Geography to be studied may be Morse's, Worcester's, or Woodbridge's. There will be a special examination in Ancient Geography.

N. B. Particular attention to *the writing of Latin* is urged as essential to a suitable preparation for the College Course. The examination *in the Grammar of the Greek and Latin Languages, including the Prosody of both*, and *in writing Latin* will be particular.

Andrews and Stoddard's Latin Grammar and the Greek Grammar of Sophocles are preferred.

COURSE OF STUDY

FRESHMAN CLASS

1. TERM. Memorabilia of Xenophon.
Greek Grammar.
Folsom's Livy.
Lacroix's Arithmetic, Smyth's Algebra.
Weekly Exercises in Latin Composition.

2. TERM. Memorabilia.
Greek Grammar.
Livy.—Smyth's Algebra.
Eschenburg's Manual; tr. by Fiske.
Weekly Exercises in Latin Composition.
Arnold's Greek Prose Composition.

3. TERM. Odyssey, (Owen's Edition, commenced.)
Greek Grammar.
Excerpta Latina, (Paterculus and Quintus Curtius.)
Eschenburg's Manual.
Smyth's Algebra.—Hedge's Logic.
Exercises in Elocution.
Weekly Exercises in Latin Composition.
Arnold's Greek Prose.
Review of the studies of the year.

SOPHOMORE CLASS.

1. TERM. Odyssey, continued.
Horace, (Odes.)
Legendre's Geometry.
French Language, (Guizot's History of European Civilization.)
Newman's Rhetoric.

2. TERM. Electra of Sophocles commenced.
Horace, (Satires and Epistles)—Terence, (Andria.)
Smyth's Trigonometry.
Cam. Math., (Heights and Distances, Surveying, and Navigation.)
French Language. (Guizot continued, and Moliere.)

3. TERM. Electra, finished.
Terence—(Adelphi.)
Cam. Math., (Projections, Leveling.)
Smyth's Application of Algebra to Geometry.
French Language, (Moliere.)
Review of the studies of the year.

JUNIOR CLASS.

1. TERM. Satires of Juvenal.
German, (Follen's German Reader,)—or Greek, (Demosthenes de Corona.)
Mechanics.

2. TERM. Calculus.
Electricity—Magnetism—Optics.
German, (Schiller's William Tell, or Fouque's Undine.)
Greek, (Demosthenes finished. The Antigone.)
Tacitus, (Germania and Agricola.)
Spanish Language.

3. TERM. Greek, (Gorgias.)
Calculus.—Mechanics.
German, (Goethe's Faust.)
Moral Philosophy.
Vattel's Law of Nations.—Spanish Language.
Review of the studies of the year.

SENIOR CLASS.

1. TERM. Astronomy and Mathematics.
Paley's Evidences.—Guizot's Hist. of Civilization.
Upham's Mental Philosophy.

2. TERM. Chemistry.
Butler's Analogy.—Guizot's Hist. of Civilization.
Mental Philosophy continued.
Hebrew and Italian Languages.

3. TERM. Natural History.—Cleaveland's Mineralogy.
Wayland's Moral Science.
Upham's Treatise on the Will.
Hebrew and Italian, continued.
Review of the studies of the year.

APPENDIX IV

MORITURI SALUTAMUS
Poem for the Fiftieth Anniversary of the Class of 1825 in Bowdoin College

"O CAESAR, we who are about to die
Salute you!" was the gladiators' cry
In the arena, standing face to face
With death and with the Roman populace.

O ye familiar scenes,—ye groves of pine,
That once were mine and are no longer mine,—
Thou river, widening through the meadows green
To the vast sea, so near and yet unseen,—
Ye halls, in whose seclusion and repose

Phantoms of fame, like exhalations, rose
And vanished,—we who are about to die,
Salute you; earth and air and sea and sky,
And the Imperial Sun that scatters down
His sovereign splendors upon grove and town.

Ye do not answer us! ye do not hear!
We are forgotten; and in your austere
And calm indifference, ye little care
Whether we come or go, or whence or where.
What passing generations fill these halls,
What passing voices echo from these walls,
Ye heed not; we are only as the blast,
A moment heard, and then forever past.

Not so the teachers who in earlier days
Led our bewildered feet through learning's maze;
They answer us—alas! what have I said?
What greetings come there from the voiceless dead?
What salutation, welcome, or reply?
What pressure from the hands that lifeless lie?
They are no longer here; they all are gone
Into the land of shadows,—all save one.
Honor and reverence, and the good repute
That follows faithful service as its fruit,
Be unto him, whom living we salute.

* * *

And ye who fill the places we once filled,
And follow in the furrows that we tilled,
Young men, whose generous hearts are beating high,
We who are old, and are about to die,
Salute you; hail you; take your hand in ours,
And crown you with our welcome as with flowers!

How beautiful is youth! how bright it gleams
With its illusions, aspirations, dreams!
Book of Beginnings, Story without End,
Each maid a heroine, and each man a friend!
Aladdin's Lamp, and Fortunatus' Purse,
That holds the treasures of the universe!
All possibilities are in its hands,
No danger daunts it, and no foe withstands;
In its sublime audacity of faith,

"Be thou removed!" it to the mountain saith,
And with ambitious feet, secure and proud,
Ascends the ladder leaning on the cloud!

As ancient Priam at the Scaean gate
Sat on the walls of Troy in regal state
With the old men, too old and weak to fight,
Chirping like grasshoppers in their delight
To see the embattled hosts, with spear and shield,
Of Trojans and Achaians in the field;
So from the snowy summits of our years
We see you in the plain, as each appears,
And question of you; asking, "Who is he
That towers above the others? Which may be
Atreides, Menelaus, Odysseus,
Ajax the great, or bold Idomeneus?"

Let him not boast who puts his armor on
As he who puts it off, the battle done.
Study yourselves; and most of all note well
Wherein kind Nature meant you to excel.
Not every blossom ripens into fruit;
Minerva, the inventress of the flute,
Flung it aside, when she her face surveyed
Distorted in a fountain as she played;
The unlucky Marsyas found it, and his fate
Was one to make the bravest hesitate.

Write on your doors the saying wise and old,
"Be bold! be bold!" and everywhere, "Be bold;
Be not too bold!" Yet better the excess
Than the defect; better the more than less;
Better like Hector in the field to die,
Than like a perfumed Paris turn and fly.

And now, my classmates; ye remaining few
That number not the half of those we knew,
Ye, against whose familiar names not yet
The fatal asterisk of death is set,
Ye I salute! The horologe of Time
Strikes the half-century with a solemn chime,
And summons us together once again,
The joy of meeting not unmixed with pain.

Where are the others? Voices from the deep
Caverns of darkness answer me: "They sleep!"
I name no names; instinctively I feel
Each at some well-remembered grave will kneel,
And from the inscription wipe the weeds and moss,
For every heart best knoweth its own loss.
I see their scattered gravestones gleaming white
Through the pale dusk of the impending night;
O'er all alike the impartial sunset throws
Its golden lilies mingled with the rose;
We give to each a tender thought, and pass
Out of the graveyards with their tangled grass,
Unto these scenes frequented by our feet
When we were young and life was fresh and sweet.

What shall I say to you? What can I say
Better than silence is? When I survey
This throng of faces turned to meet my own,
Friendly and fair, and yet to me unknown,
Transformed the very landscape seems to be;
It is the same, yet not the same to me.
So many memories crowd upon my brain,
So many ghosts are in the wooded plain,
I fain would steal away, with noiseless tread,
As from a house where some one lieth dead.
I cannot go;—I pause;—I hesitate;
My feet reluctant linger at the gate;
As one who struggles in a troubled dream
To speak and cannot, to myself I seem.

Vanish the dream! Vanish the idle fears!
Vanish the rolling mists of fifty years!
Whatever time or space may intervene,
I will not be a stranger in this scene.
Here every doubt, all indecision, ends;
Hail, my companions, comrades, classmates, friends!

Ah me! the fifty years since last we met
Seem to me fifty folios bound and set
By Time, the great transcriber, on his shelves,
Wherein are written the histories of ourselves.
What tragedies, what comedies, are there;
What joy and grief, what rapture and despair!
What chronicles of triumph and defeat,
Of struggle, and temptation, and retreat!
What records of regrets, and doubts, and fears!
What pages blotted, blistered by our tears!
What lovely landscapes on the margin shine,
What sweet, angelic faces, what divine
And holy images of love and trust,
Undimmed by age, unsoiled by damp or dust!

Whose hand shall dare to open and explore
These volumes, closed and clasped forevermore?
Not mine. With reverential feet I pass;
I hear a voice that cries, "Alas! alas!
Whatever hath been written shall remain,
Nor be erased nor written o'er again;
The unwritten only still belongs to thee:
Take heed, and ponder well what that shall be."

* * *

The scholar and the world! The endless strife,
The discord in the harmonies of life!
The love of learning, the sequestered nooks,
And all the sweet serenity of books;
The market-place, the eager love of gain,
Whose aim is vanity, and whose end is pain!

But why, you ask me, should this tale be told
To men grown old, or who are growing old?
It is too late! Ah, nothing is too late
Till the tired heart shall cease to palpitate.
Cato learned the Greek at eighty; Sophocles
Wrote his grand Oedipus, and Simonides
Bore off the prize of verse from his compeers,
When each had numbered more than fourscore years,
And Theophrastus, at fourscore and ten,
Had but begun his "Characters of Men."
Chaucer, at Woodstock with the nightingales,
At sixty wrote the Canterbury Tales;
Goethe at Weimar, toiling to the last,
Completed Faust when eighty years were past.
These are indeed exceptions; but they show
How far the gulf-stream of our youth may flow
Into the arctic regions of our lives,
Where little else than life itself survives.

As the barometer foretells the storm
While still the skies are clear, the weather warm
So something in us, as old age draws near,
Betrays the pressure of the atmosphere.
The nimble mercury, ere we are aware,
Descends the elastic ladder of the air;
The telltale blood in artery and vein
Sinks from its higher levels in the brain;
Whatever poet, orator, or sage
May say of it, old age is still old age.
It is the waning, not the crescent moon;
The dusk of evening, not the blaze of noon;
It is not strength but weakness; not desire,
But its surcease; not the fierce heat of fire,
The burning and consuming element,
But that of ashes and of embers spent,
In which some living sparks we still discern,
Enough to warm, but not enough to burn.

What then? Shall we sit idly down and say
The night hath come; it is no longer day?
The night hath not yet come; we are not quite
Cut off from labor by the failing light;
Something remains for us to do or dare;
Even the oldest tree some fruit may bear;
No Oedipus Coloneus, or Greek Ode,
Or tales of pilgrims that one morning rode
Out of the gateway of the Tabard Inn,
But other something, would we but begin;
For age is opportunity no less
Than youth itself, though in another dress,
And as the evening twilight fades away
The sky is filled with stars, invisible by day.

—Henry Wadsworth Longfellow 1825

RESEARCH ON BOWDOIN COLLEGE

This book will have served part of its purpose if it persuades others to pursue topics in Bowdoin history. The rather summary treatment of the subject required in this volume and the prospect of new archives opening up mean that there will be plenty of opportunities for further research.

Three invaluable sources to begin with are the series of biographical compilations that runs from Nehemiah Cleaveland and A. S. Packard's *History of Bowdoin College with Biographical Sketches of its Graduates from 1876 to 1879, Inclusive* (Boston, 1882) through the *General Catalogues* that cover 1794–1894, 1794–1950, and 1900–1975; Ernst C. Helmreich's *Religion at Bowdoin College: A History* (Brunswick, 1981), and Patricia McGraw Anderson's *The Architecture of Bowdoin College* (Brunswick, 1988). Older books such as Louis C. Hatch's *The History of Bowdoin College* (Portland, 1927), Herbert Ross Brown's *Sills of Bowdoin: The Life of Kenneth Charles Morton Sills, 1879–1954* (New York, 1964) and Charles T. Burnett's *Hyde of Bowdoin: A Biography of William DeWitt Hyde* (Boston, 1931) remain useful for their details, if not always for their interpretations.

To that list might be added Angela M. Leonard, ed., *Antislavery Materials at Bowdoin College* (Brunswick, 1992); two pamphlets published by the College, *Named Professorships at Bowdoin College 1986–1987* (n. d.), and Gerard J. Brault, "A Checklist of Portraits of the Campus of Bowdoin College Before the Civil War," typescript (1960), copy in Special Collections.

Student diaries are a useful supplement to the official records, but few exist after the 1860s (scrapbooks of ephemera tend to replace them for about a generation). According to a list compiled by Truax O. McFarland '93, the College owns diaries or account books for Isaac Chase 1848, Charles Peleg Chandler 1854, Peleg Chandler 1834, Moses Parker Cleaveland 1827, John Deering, Jr., 1864, James Hanscom 1846, Hiram Hobbs 1823, Theodore Jewett 1834, John Mitchell 1843, Galen Moses 1856, Joseph

O'Brien 1847, George Packard 1865, Edward Rand 1857, Charles Roberts 1845, George Talbot 1837, Joseph Weston 1843, and George Woods 1837. The most accessible Bowdoin diary is Charles H. Foster's edition of Benjamin Browne Foster, *Down East Diary* (Orono, 1975).

For a newcomer to the field, some essential background works include Lawrence A. Cremin, *American Education: The Colonial Experience 1607–1783* (New York, 1970), *American Education: The National Experience 1783–1876* (New York, 1980), and *American Education: The Metropolitan Experience 1876–1980* (New York, 1988), all of which have extensive bibliographies; Frederick Rudolph, *The American College and University* (New York, 1962) and *Curriculum: A History of the American Undergraduate Course of Study Since 1636* (San Francisco, 1978); and Colin B. Burke, *American Collegiate Populations: A Test of the Traditional View* (New York, 1982), which is a refutation of the disparagement that antebellum colleges suffered at the hands of Richard Hofstadter and Walter P. Metzger in *The Development of Academic Freedom in the United States* (New York, 1955). Students of New England colleges will also find much that is thought-provoking in Helen Lefkowitz Horowitz, *Campus Life: Undergraduate Cultures from the End of the Eighteenth Century to the Present* (New York, 1987).

Anyone setting out to write a comprehensive institutional history of a college has two admirable models: David Stameshkin, *The Town's College: Middlebury College, 1800–1915* (Middlebury, Vt., 1985) and David B. Potts, *Wesleyan University, 1831–1910: Collegiate Enterprise in New England* (New Haven, 1992).

The most urgent need in terms of Bowdoin research at this point is probably a full-scale attempt to determine who the people were—in terms of religion, politics, career motivation, and parental wealth—who attended the College in its first century. Much else depends on settling that question. Three other avenues of inquiry are a study of the relations between Bowdoin and the

Portland elite (along the lines of Ronald Story's work on Boston and Harvard), between the College and the town of Brunswick, and between the College and the rest of the state, especially in the time early in this century when Bowdoin was trying to keep the University of Maine from expanding beyond an agricultural and technical institution. And the archives of the Medical School of Maine (1820–1921) are an untapped source of great wealth, especially the insights that the students' theses could offer into nineteenth-century theory and practice.

Although Bowdoin's twentieth-century archives are still being assembled (for the purpose of this book, the papers of President Sills and some of those of President Coles were accessible), its nineteenth-century records are admirably diverse and reasonably complete. Dianne M. Gutsher, curator of Special Collections at Hawthorne-Longfellow Library, has kindly prepared the following checklist of the archive:

Those records located in Special Collections include original votes of the Governing Boards, 1794–1896; executive government and faculty minutes of meetings, 1805–1968; faculty committee reports, 1966–present; admissions and matriculation entries, 1802–present; library records, 1803–present, such as manuscript and printed catalogs of books, accession records, loan books, and library accounts; treasurer's reports, 1859–1895; Alumni Association minutes, 1857–1950, and Alumni Council records, 1914–1978; Senior Center program records, 1963–1979, including Council minutes and reports, and seminar and lecture series records; minutes, accounts, and catalogs of the two student literary societies, Peucinian, 1807–1877, and Athenaean, 1817–1875; records of fraternities; and records of other student societies, such as the Benevolent Society, 1814–1827, and Theological Society, 1836–1850; commencement parts, 1802–present; oratorical exhibition parts, 1810–1905; and honors theses, 1924–present.

Non-current alumni files (including honorary degree recipients), and files for faculty, Governing Boards members, and staff, are also kept in Special Collections. They include biographical material, correspondence, obituaries, and newsclippings, and are arranged alphabetically by name. An index is available for letters in alumni files written while attending Bowdoin. These letters and a collection of student diaries, spanning the decades from the 1830s to the 1870s, provide a detailed view of nineteenth-century college life. Scrapbooks kept by students during their years at Bowdoin continue this record from the 1870s through the 1920s with programs for Bowdoin and Brunswick events, ticket stubs, photographs, and a variety of other memorabilia. Autograph albums, circulated by seniors among their classmates, sometimes contain recollections of incidents occurring during their college years. The albums begin in 1834, and in 1856 photographs are added, but by the end of the 1860s the autograph sentiments have diminished to signatures accompanying the photographs. The albums often contain photos of faculty members, college buildings, and views of Brunswick, although those of the 1890s and early 1900s are primarily of the graduating class. Special Collections also contains nine thousand photographic prints of alumni, faculty, college buildings and fraternities, group pictures of societies and athletic teams, and college events.

Reading lists, syllabi, nineteenth-century class notes, and other curricular materials are part of the archival collection, too. Information on college buildings and plans for some buildings are on file in Special Collections, as well as records of the establishment of the Walker Art Building and the Peary-MacMillan Arctic Museum. Records of the Medical School of Maine, which was affiliated with Bowdoin College, are also housed with the archival material in Special Collections. The records include those of the medical faculty, 1820–1921, medical theses, 1820–1921, and accounts, 1818–1920. Files for individual Medical School graduates are also maintained. The papers of those Bowdoin presidents, faculty members, Overseers, and Trustees that are housed in Special Collections provide much information about the College, as well.

A series of scrapbooks called the Documentary History contains newsclippings, programs, form letters, and memorabilia concerning the College. The material is arranged chronologically, with the first volume covering the years 1806 through 1859 (rather sparsely), and the final volumes, ending with March 1962, containing primarily sports clippings.

Printed records are retained, as well. They include annual catalogues beginning in 1807; charter and laws, 1817 to date; president's reports, 1891 to date; treasurer's reports, 1896 to date; librarian's reports, 1885 to date; Museum of Art publications, 1894 to date, and early catalogues of the art collection, beginning in 1870; commencement programs, 1806 to date; programs of oratorical exercises, 1805–1969; music programs, 1822 to date; athletic programs, 1864 to date; student publications, such as the *Bugle*, 1858 to date, and the *Orient*, 1871 to date; and alumni publications, including *Bowdoin* magazine, 1927 to date.

Although records housed in Special Collections span Bowdoin's history, including not only historical documents, but also college publications and photographs, some nineteenth- and most twentieth-century records are located elsewhere. In a vault in college administration headquarters are kept bound copies of the complete minutes and votes of the Trustees and Overseers, 1794–present, and original Visiting Committee reports, beginning in 1826. The latter contain reports of the president, treasurer, librarian, and other faculty members, student petitions, and other documents appended to the annual committee report. The records of the administrations of President Kenneth C. M. Sills, 1918–1952, and of President James Stacy Coles, 1952–1967, were housed in the Massachusetts Hall vault, but those of President Sills have been moved to library storage space used by Special Collections. Those of Roger Howell, Willard Enteman, and A. LeRoy Greason are located in the Office of the President or in storage space assigned to that office. Non-current records of other college offices are similarly stored. Alumni records from the Class of 1911 to the present are maintained by the Office of Alumni Relations. A survey, conducted in July 1992, located an estimated 5,725 cubic feet of current and non-current records in campus offices and storage areas.

Until 1993, Bowdoin College did not have an officially designated Archives with a concomitant archival policy authorizing the collection of college records of permanent value. However, on 1 July 1993, an archivist, funded by a National Historical Publications and Records Commission grant, will begin inventorying records across campus and developing an archival policy for the College. Specified records will be transferred to the new Bowdoin College Archives, located near Special Collections, where they will be cataloged and permanently housed. President Edwards states, in his letter supporting the grant application, that Bowdoin's records reflect two hundred years of commitment to excellence in liberal education and the life of the mind, and that they are a resource that should be made available to today's scholarly community and preserved for future generations of scholars, as well. Now, on the eve of Bowdoin's bicentenary, that process will begin!

PHOTO CREDITS

Photographs not listed here were supplied by Special Collections, Hawthorne-Longfellow Library, Bowdoin College; copy photographs not listed here were taken by Dennis Griggs.

FRONT ENDPAPER
Collections of the Maine Historical Society, Portland, Maine

CHAPTER ONE
p. 5. City plan © 1993 by M. W. Cutler, based on Osgood Carleton's 1797 map of Boston
p. 6. Courtesy of the Bostonian Society, Old State House
pp. 7 and 12, top. Courtesy of the Bowdoin College Museum of Art
p. 8. Collections of the Maine Historical Society
p. 14, left. Office of Communications files
p. 14, right. Courtesy of the Collection of Historical Scientific Instruments, Harvard University. Photograph of Bowdoin figure by T. F. Hartley
p. 16. *Bowdoin* magazine files
pp. 19 and 20, top. Collections of the Maine Historical Society

CHAPTER TWO
p. 28, bottom. Courtesy of the Department of Art, Bowdoin College, from a glass slide
p. 28, upper right. Office of Communications files
pp. 32 and 35. Courtesy of the Bowdoin College Museum of Art
pp. 36 and 38. Map © 1993 by M. W. Cutler
p. 42. Reconstruction © 1993 by M. W. Cutler
p. 44. Reprinted from the collection of the Bowne House Historical Society, Inc., Flushing, New York
p. 45. Book from the collections of the Maine State Library
p. 46. Reproduced from a photocopy; present whereabouts of scrapbook unknown
p. 47. Courtesy of the Massachusetts Historical Society

CENTER PHOTO SECTION
p. 52, upper right and center. Courtesy of the Maine Historical Society, Wadsworth Longfellow House
p. 52, bottom. Courtesy of the Pejepscot Historical Society
pp. 53–62 and 64. Courtesy of the Bowdoin College Museum of Art
p. 63. Courtesy of the Avery Architectural Library, Columbia University

p. 65. Courtesy of the Peabody Essex Museum, Salem, Mass.
p. 67. Courtesy of the Department of Art, Bowdoin College, from a glass slide
p. 68. Courtesy of William W. Gilchrist
p. 69. *Scribner's* magazine, 1876

CHAPTER THREE
p. 70, lower right. Office of Communications files
p. 78. Courtesy of the Pejepscot Historical Society
p. 79. Portrait by Gilbert Stuart, from the Collections of the Maine State Museum, Augusta
p. 86. Courtesy of the Massachusetts Historical Society
p. 88. Courtesy of the Society for the Preservation of New England Antiquities, Boston

CHAPTER FOUR
pp. 100, lower left, and 104, upper left. Office of Communications files
pp. 102, 104, upper right, and 106. Courtesy of the Department of Art, Bowdoin College, from glass slides
p. 116. *Bowdoin* magazine files

CHAPTER FIVE
p. 120, bottom. Courtesy of the Bowdoin College Museum of Art
pp. 122, 128, 130, lower left and right, and 134, top. Courtesy of the Department of Art, Bowdoin College, from glass slides

CHAPTER SIX
p. 150, top. Photograph by Annalisa M. Ravin '92.
p. 152. Courtesy of the Stowe-Day Foundation, Hartford, Connecticut
p. 153. The Schlesinger Library, Radcliffe College
p. 154, top. Photograph by G. B. Webber, courtesy of the Pejepscot Historical Society
p. 158, lower right. Courtesy of the Massachusetts Historical Society
p. 162. Office of Communications files
p. 163. Courtesy of the Photographs and Prints Division, Schomburg Center for Research in Black Culture, the New York Public Library, Astor, Lenox, and Tilden Foundations

p. 165. Attributed to Montgomery Pike Simmons. Eleanor S. Brockenbrough Library. The Museum of the Confederacy. Richmond, Virginia. Copy photography by Katherine Wetzel
p. 168, bottom. Private collection of Carolyn Page, Troy, Maine. Copy photograph by Erik C. Jorgensen '87
p. 177. Copy photograph by Annalisa M. Ravin '92
p. 178. Courtesy of the Pejepscot Historical Society
p. 179. Courtesy of the Department of Art, Bowdoin College, from a glass slide

CHAPTER SEVEN
p. 192, upper right, and 194, lower right. Courtesy of the Department of Art, Bowdoin College, from glass slides
pp. 196 and 203, lower right. *Bowdoin* magazine files
p. 202, lower left. Courtesy of the Pejepscot Historical Society.

CHAPTER EIGHT
p. 206, lower left. From the photograph album of Edward T. Richardson, Jr. '43, Special Collections; lower right, courtesy of the Peary-MacMillan Arctic Museum, Bowdoin College
p. 208, bottom. Photo: Schlesinger, N.Y.
pp. 209, right, 215, 216, top, 220, top, 228, bottom, and 230. Office of Communications files
p. 214. Courtesy of the Peary-MacMillan Arctic Museum, Bowdoin College
p. 220, center. From Masque and Gown scrapbook, courtesy A. Raymond Rutan '51
pp. 222 and 223. From the photograph album of Edward T. Richardson, Jr. '43, Special Collections
p. 228, top. *Bowdoin* magazine files

CHAPTER NINE
pp. 236, top left, 238, 240, lower right and left, 241, 243, 246, all but lower left, 248, 249, 250, 253, photo by David T. Wilkinson '67, and 254. Office of Communications files
p. 236, top right and lower left. *Bowdoin Alumnus* magazine cover photos
p. 236, lower right, and 251. *Bowdoin* magazine files
p. 240, top. Courtesy of the Peary-MacMillan Arctic Museum, Bowdoin College
p. 242. Courtesy of Chaké Kevookjian Higgison '78
p. 244, top. © Ezra Stoller Associates
p. 252, 255, and 256. *Bowdoin* magazine cover photos

BACK ENDPAPER
Courtesy of the Pejepscot Historical Society, Brunswick, Maine

EDITOR'S ACKNOWLEDGMENTS

For help in furnishing and identifying the photographs in this book, I am grateful to Dianne M. Gutscher and Susan B. Ravdin '82 of Special Collections, who provided several hundred images, and to their student assistant, Truax O. McFarland '93; to the members of the Editorial Review Committee, especially Peter C. Barnard '50, Alfred H. Fuchs, and Elizabeth J. Miller; and to Richard W. Anderson, Martha J. Adams, Philip C. Beam, Suzanne K. Bergeron, Gerald F. Bigelow, Katharine B. Bunge, Mark W. Cutler, Pauline M. Farr, A. LeRoy Greason, Heather T. K. Hietala '83, Chaké Kevookjian Higgison '78, David H. Hirth '64, Erik C. Jorgensen '87, Mattie Kelley, Mary Jo Maguire, Elsa N. Martz, Clifton C. Olds, Carolyn Page, David S. Page, Edward Pols, Annalisa M. Ravin '92, Marilyn Reizbaum, Edward T. Richardson, Jr. '43, A. Raymond Rutan '51, Paul E. Schaffner, William D. and Alison Shipman, Geoffrey R. Stanwood '38, Alice Steinhardt, John R. Ward '82, Susan E. Wegner, James B. Weidner '64, Nathaniel T. Wheelwright, and many other members of the College's faculty and staff who have graciously taken time to answer my questions.

I am particularly indebted to the members of the staff of the Office of Communications at Getchell House. This book would have been infinitely more difficult to produce without the generous advice and labor of Craig C. Cheslog '93, Alison M. Dodson, Scott W. Hood, Marita H. Miller, Norma J. McLoughlin, Lucie G. Teegarden, and Joan D. Viles, and student assistants Sara A. Pekow '95, Kristin M. McKinlay '94, and Jennifer L. Ramirez '95.

Susan L. Ransom

INDEX

Page numbers in italics refer to illustrations. Listings like "49n. 4" refer to endnotes;
the first number is the page, the second the note.